Dead Was Everything

We went to see the dead people at Isandhlwana. We saw a single warrior dead, staring in our direction, with his war shield in his hand. We ran away. We came back again. We saw countless things dead. Dead was the horse, dead too, the mule, dead was the dog, dead was the monkey, dead were the wagons, dead were the tents, dead were the boxes, dead was everything, even to the very metals.

C. de B. Webb, 'A Zulu Boy's Recollections of the Zulu War',
Natalia, No. 8, December 1978, p. 13.

Also by Keith Smith

Local General Orders of the Anglo-Zulu War 1879, 2005.
Select Documents: A Zulu War Sourcebook, 2006.
Harry Smith's Last Throw: The Eighth Frontier War, 1850–1853, Frontline, 2011.
The Wedding Feast War: The Final Tragedy of the Xhosa People, Frontline, 2012.

Dead Was Everything

STUDIES IN THE ANGLO-ZULU WAR

Keith Smith

FRONTLINE BOOKS, LONDON

FRONTLINE BOOKS, LONDON

Dead Was Everything: Studies in the Anglo-Zulu War

This edition published in 2014 by Frontline Books, an imprint of
Pen & Sword Books Limited,
47 Church Street, Barnsley, S. Yorkshire, S70 2AS
www.frontline-books.com
Email info@frontline-books.com or write to us at the above address.

Publishing history
First edition published in 2008 by Keith Smith.
Second edition published in 2014 by Frontline Books Ltd.

ISBN 978-1-84832-731-3

Typeset in Caslon Pro by JCS Publishing Services Ltd,
www.jcs-publishing.co.uk

Printed and bound by CPI Group (UK) Ltd, Croydon, CR0 4YY

Contents

Maps

Illustrations

Plates

Abbreviations

BPP British Parliamentary Papers, Command Series
CO British Colonial Office
CSO Records of the KwaZulu-Natal Colonial Secretary's Office, in PAR below
GH Records of KwaZulu-Natal Government House, in PAR below
GRO Gloucester Record Office, UK
ILN *Illustrated London News*
JSA C. de B. Webb and J.B. Wright (eds), *The James Stuart Archive of Recorded Oral Evidence Relating to the History of the Zulu and Neighbouring Peoples*, in five volumes, Pietermaritzburg, 1976-2001
KCAL Campbell Collections, Durban, KwaZulu-Natal
NAM National Army Museum, Chelsea, UK
PAR Pietermaritzburg Archives Repository, KwaZulu-Natal
REM Royal Engineers Museum, Chatham, UK
RMRW Regimental Museum of the Royal Welsh, Brecon, UK
SNA Records of the KwaZulu-Natal Secretary of Native Affairs, in PAR above
TNA The National Archives, Kew, UK

Acknowledgements

I have been fortunate to be writing at a time when secondary accounts have begun to examine the war from a Zulu perspective. While the Zulu in 1879 did not have the ability to record their proceedings in the same way as did British and Colonial authorities and individuals, they nevertheless left oral accounts and many of these were carefully collected over a number of years by James Stuart; the ability to use these volumes in my research has been a great privilege.

I am indebted to those curators and staff of museums and libraries who have been so sympathetic to my enquiries. In particular, I must mention the staffs of the Campbell Collections in Durban, now a part of the University of KwaZulu-Natal; the library of the University of KwaZulu-Natal, Pietermaritzburg; the Pietermaritzburg Archive Repository; The National Archives, Kew; the National Army Museum, Chelsea; the Royal Engineers Museum, Chatham; the Regimental Museum of the Royal Welsh, Brecon; the State Library of New South Wales, Sydney.

During the last eight years I have visited all of the battlefields in Zululand, some of them a number of times; local guides who have assisted me with some of these visits include Jeremy Krone of Dundee, Sean Friend of Vryheid, the late Petros Sibisi of Rorke's Drift and Rex Duke of Melmoth. I was also privileged to meet Rex's father, the eminent guide and Zulu War authority Fred Duke. Sadly, Fred died shortly after our only meeting but his grand companionship at his home and later at the Vryheid 'Bomb Hole' will not be forgotten. Nor must I omit to thank Nicki van der Heyde of Gillitts, near Durban, with whom I shared a glorious day riding across Hlobane mountain. Whilst not among my travel companions, Ron Lock and Peter Quantrill have also been a source of inspiration and assistance.

The photographs reproduced in this work are, with a single exception, my own. I am greatly obliged to Bill Cainan for permission to use his photograph of the Ngwebeni ravine. Maps 2, 3, 4, 7 and 8 were specially commissioned by the writer from Demap Cartographic Design, Melbourne.

I must also mention here a fine Internet website. I refer to the contributors of the forum hosted by www.rorkesdriftvc.com, whose administrators, Peter and Alan Critchley, deserve the greatest praise for the sterling work they do in maintaining this excellent site, at no small cost to themselves. It is clearly a labour of love and this is shared by the contributors, a fact demonstrated by the quality of the postings. The arguments are often robust but rarely damaging and I must here acknowledge the great amount I have learned from those discussions.

A number of these papers have previously been published in the *Journal of the Anglo-Zulu War Historical Society* and the journal of the Victorian Military Society, *Soldiers of the Queen*. My thanks are due to the editors of these publications for permission to include some of those papers in the present work, although most of them have been modified, some of them substantially, since they were first published.

My own efforts stumbled when I considered the battle of Hlobane. Of course, I have some views about this engagement but any attempt on my part to write intelligently and comprehensively about it would have been greatly overshadowed by a paper first published in 1997 by the late Huw M. Jones, whom I valued as a very good friend and an engaging companion. Huw and the publishers of *Natalia* kindly gave me permission to reproduce his ground-breaking paper in this work and I am greatly in their debt for so doing.

Finally, and on a personal level, thanks are due to my good friends Julie and John Parker of Durban and their two daughters, who have given me shelter and put up with my documents, books and general nuisance during many visits.

A multitude of other people, both black and white, have helped me from time to time during my many solo travels across the length and breadth of KwaZulu-Natal. The hospitality which I invariably found there is perhaps my most cherished memory. Sadly they are too numerous to mention individually, but they will know who they are. If I have omitted thanks to any other helpful person or institution I trust they will forgive my lapse.

Preface to the Second Edition

This work was first published in 2008, in a very limited edition. It is most pleasing, therefore, that a second edition is to be published by Frontline Books, who have also kindly supported me in the publication of two of my more recent works.

As noted elsewhere, the papers written so long ago have been thoroughly revised. In particular, the papers on Isandlwana have been carefully reviewed and, in the case of that dealing with the discovery of the Zulu army, considerably updated. Nonetheless, new theories or findings are published frequently, and the Zulu War is no exception. As mentioned elsewhere, however, I have not found anything more recently published that invalidates my findings in this new issue of my papers.

I hope that my readers will indulge my use of Latin for the three chapter names dealing with the battle of Isandlwana. Their meanings are: *exordium* is a beginning or commencement, *proelium* is the battle itself and, of course, everyone knows what a postscript is. If I may share a secret, it was my brief encounter with that concise, precise language, and with ancient Greek too, that brought about my better understanding of, and deep love for, that idiosyncratic, imprecise, sometimes ambiguous and often illogical language that is English.

Keith Smith
Northern New South Wales,
Australia

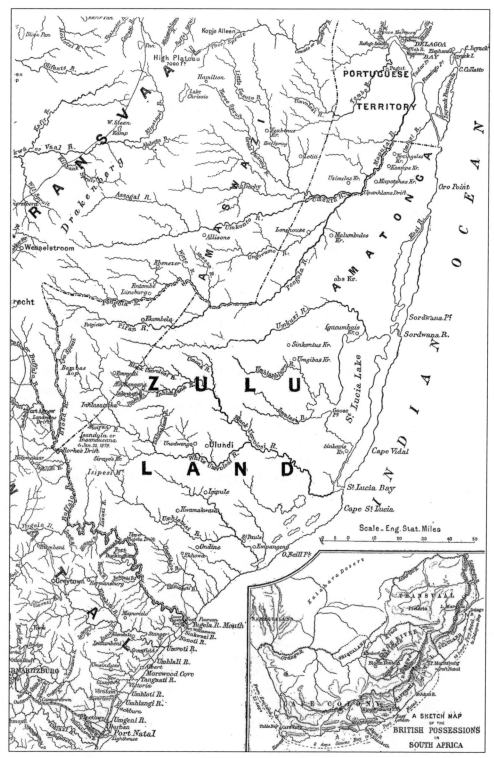

1 Map of Zululand

Introduction

The Anglo-Zulu War of 1879 still intrigues both scholar and casual reader alike more than 130 years after it was fought. Its story contains tragedy, high drama and the heavy loss of human life, not to mention the snuffing out of the direct Napoleonic line of France. All this within the space of less than one year, while the actual conflict lasted only from the invasion of Zululand on 11 January until the fall of Ulundi on 4 July 1879, a period of less than six months. King Cetshwayo kaMpande was captured in the Ngome forest on 28 August, following which he was sent into exile in Cape Town. There was sporadic fighting in the north-west of Zululand after 4 July but the conclusion of the war was signalled on 1 September 1879 when Sir Garnet Wolseley held an *Indaba* for the Zulu signing of the instrument creating the thirteen 'kinglets' into which the country was to be divided.

Professor John Laband, an eminent scholar and writer on the Zulu war, has suggested that there is little more to be written about the war, and has himself moved on to other areas. His words, however, seem to be contradicted by the plethora of new secondary works that continue to be published almost monthly, yet they are paradoxically confirmed by the fact that few of them have anything new to say. It is the same story told in different words; only occasionally is there something new to consider.

After reading, and thoroughly enjoying, Donald Morris' *The Washing of the Spears* soon after it was published in 1965, I put it to the back of my mind since that was a very busy time in my life: among other things, I was shortly to migrate from the UK to Australia. It was not until many years later, in the late 1990s, that I bought another copy of the book to read again. This time, having in the meantime undertaken tertiary history studies, I looked at the book through new eyes and realised that there was more to the story than I had thought. I was sufficiently stimulated to buy other books on the subject. In the year 2000, I visited Isandlwana for the first time. Gradually, what began as an interest developed into a passion and, as I read more, so a number of emerging puzzles began to worry me. I tried as best I could to resolve them by further reading and then began to research the primary sources in both South Africa and England. As some of these questions were answered to my own satisfaction, I began to seek publication of papers I had written as part of their resolution. In total, I wrote nearly forty papers, about half of which have been published; I have had two books published and completed postgraduate studies in the Anglo-Zulu War. A new difficulty now arose: my continuing research had modified, and often extended, the findings published in many of my papers. The essays reproduced here, therefore, are my attempt to update the earlier papers, and supplement them with a coherent range of material which completes my picture of the war.

There is always a thrill when handling documents handwritten so many years ago, often stained by the conditions prevailing when they were written. Some of them are written in pencil, and are written on varying qualities of paper, which was always in short supply. Too often, the documents themselves are in very poor condition. Some are written on 'onion-skin' paper which, after so many years, has absorbed the ink written on them so that they are now extremely difficult to read. The long hours of transcription work, however, were occasionally leavened by moments of exhilaration – something was found that I believed really did add to our store of knowledge, or confirmed what had previously been mere speculation. It is those rare instances of discovery that make all the tedium worthwhile because, at the moment of realising a document's value, the heart skips a beat and a broad smile will spread across one's face. This is when history comes alive and the 135-year gap separating us from the events of 1879 dissolves completely: we are there.

As one penetrates the shroud of mystery surrounding the events of that momentous year, matters emerge that often surprise, and give valuable insights into the minds of those in command. It has often been noted, for example, that Lord Chelmsford was a basically decent, kind and thoughtful man, and the documents demonstrate this fact over and over again. But there was also a ruthless streak in him that was well concealed, and it comes as something of a surprise when it is revealed. The documents also show him to have been a man who found it almost impossible to delegate, causing him to become bogged down in a myriad of detail which, in hindsight, would have been better left to others. The echelon of officers below him in the Zulu campaign are revealed to have, as one might expect, frailties of their own.

Many people expect a book on the Zulu War to deal in detail with each of the many engagements that took place in 1879. I have chosen not to follow this path and have deliberately omitted descriptions of battles for their own sake. Rorke's Drift, Nyezane, Ntombe Drift, Gingindlovu, and even Ulundi, are therefore mentioned only in passing: other writers have dealt with these matters quite adequately. What has intrigued me, and continues to do so, is the battle that poses the most difficult problems. In this work, three chapters are devoted to it.

Isandlwana is the most impenetrable engagement to comprehend because all of the major European participants lost their lives. Had Colonel Durnford, Lieutenant-Colonel Pulleine, or even Lieutenant and Adjutant Melvill survived, then the story of the events of that dreadful day would now be easier to tell. But they did not, and it is thus no accident that this battle engages us still.

For my own part, rather than tell the whole story once again, I have addressed only the key questions, which I believe may make a useful and sometimes novel contribution. New evidence and a re-examination of the old have thrown additional light on some of the problems of this battle, and selected topics have been isolated and discussed to illustrate some of our difficulties. Certainly, these papers were written some time ago, and then more recently updated, but I have seen no evidence that the orthodox positions of most Zulu War historians have changed since that time.

This work is not just about that battle, intriguing as it is. There are also a number of more pedestrian matters about which I have chosen to write and I hope that they add to our wider knowledge of this conflict. There is, for example, a day-by-day analysis of the route of the Second Invasion, a subject which has received little attention in the literature to date.

I believe that the papers presented here are all more or less illuminating and that at least some of them will begin to reveal the characters of the men who might hitherto have been simply names on a page. They are not: they lived and breathed, loved and procreated, fought and died. Some were heroes while others were less than that. Most of them were ordinary men who chose a military career and did their best as far as they were able. Let us not forget, either, the Zulu, who have sometimes been painted as the villains of the piece. They too were men who lived and died, and all of them fought with incredible courage for the continuation of the 'old Zulu order'. For the most part they were men who simply fought according to their own concept of honour. White or black, British or colonial, they were all exceptional men.

In two earlier works, I have shared with the interested reader many of the primary sources I have examined as part of my study of this war. These documents, together with many others, were the material that underpins the papers printed here. At the risk of inducing a severe attack of ennui, they are all cited in the end-notes.

Like my earlier works, this is not a book for those who want to learn the elementary facts of the Zulu War. Better, perhaps, to have read one or more of the general works which give an outline of the war before coming here. This is, rather, a book for those who have already read something about this fascinating conflict and who have then asked themselves some of the same questions that I have asked myself. Perhaps the papers that follow will answer just one or two of them.

Chapter 1

Some Preliminary Matters

There is properly no history; only biography.

Ralph Waldo Emerson, 1803–1882

The Hazards of Primary Sources

The writing of history can be a nebulous exercise. In the hands of a gifted author, the recounting of some historical event can be astonishingly real, bringing to life the look and feel of the past with which our own imaginations collude to feed the other senses. On the other hand, if poorly presented, written history can be pedestrian and, worse, if poorly researched it can be utterly misleading. A talent for written expression is desirable to achieve the first but nothing can replace the sheer effort required to avoid the second.

To put flesh on the bones of history, one needs to feel, to touch, to know the primary material. All the history we know is derived originally from primary oral or written sources and they take many forms. It is an odd fact, but we know more about the ancient Rome of the first century BC than we do about the five-hundred-year period after its fall. The reason is simple: the Romans left a rich inheritance of primary documents. In their efforts to achieve the immortality they craved, they left behind them books, letters, inscriptions, coins – all giving more or less information to enable those who followed them to reconstruct the past.

The problems for those wishing to examine periods closer to our own time are in some ways simpler. For the common man, literacy was more widespread in nineteenth-century Britain, surprisingly so in the period under consideration here.[1] Thus there are more documents to examine, and they were the product of a considerably wider range of people than the wealthy senatorial class of Rome. While the archives of Rome have, by and large, perished, we have access to most of the documents of more recent governments, while even the oral history of people who then lacked literacy has been preserved.

Of course, the difficulties associated with the evaluation of even recent primary materials are as prolific as ever. Memories dim with time; accounts of events are modified slightly to enhance or diminish reputations; time is distorted when violent events occur; the accounts of two observers of the same event often differ, sometimes markedly.

It is the historian's task to be aware of these difficulties, to take into account the partiality implicit in the words of those with an axe to grind, a matter to hide, a cause to defend. He or she must negotiate the minefield of misordered proceedings, events deliberately omitted, forgotten or even invented. Self-aggrandisement is much to blame when the writer is his own subject.

The documents of the period leading up to, and including, the Anglo-Zulu War of 1879 are no exception. Indeed, they could not be more suspect if they had been deliberately designed to mislead and, like those in every other period of history, the documents always seem to conspire to omit the very information one seeks.

This paper will demonstrate the errors to which a student might be prone when depending upon narratives of the Anglo-Zulu War. It uses as its major text the work written by George Hamilton-Browne *c.*1912. (No publication date is given, but it may be assigned to 1912 from his remark 'Isandlwana happened in January 1879 . . . since which date, 33 years have passed . . .'[2]) The work is quite light-hearted in a *Boy's Own* way and is full of amusing anecdotes, but it is also laden with self-promotion (in both senses) and self-indulgence. The method to be used here will be to quote briefly from his book, and to compare his version of events with observations from other participants of the same affairs.

We should begin with the crossing of the Mzinyathi (Buffalo) River at Rorke's Drift by the Centre Column, with Lord Chelmsford[3] and his staff in attendance, on 11 January 1879,[4] which Hamilton-Browne wrongly states took place on the 10th. At this time, he says: 'I had a few days before been appointed commandant of the 1st Battalion of the 3rd Regiment of the Natal Native Contingent . . .'[5] In fact, Hamilton-Browne was appointed a captain in the 1st Battalion, 3rd Regiment, Natal Native Contingent (NNC) on 3 December[6] and was not given command of the 1st Battalion until 12 January.[7] It is unlikely that he would have heard of his promotion until the 12th at the very earliest, and probably not until some time later.[8] The actual state of affairs was that Commandant Rupert la Trobe Lonsdale was in command of the 3rd Regiment, and also its 1st Battalion, a not unusual circumstance.[9] Indeed, Lonsdale was still reported as commanding both the 1st battalion and regiment as late as 20 January.[10] While Lonsdale nominally led the regiment, the commander on the ground was Major Wilsone Black, 2/24th Regiment, owing to Lonsdale's indisposition as a result of sunstroke, a fall from his horse or both.

The first engagement was at Sihayo's homestead on 12 January. Here Hamilton-Browne refers to Lonsdale and Black: 'There was in the second 24th a major (Wilson [sic] Black by name), and Commandant Lonsdale having been knocked over by sunstroke during the previous day [11th], Major Black had been placed, for the time being, in full command of the 3rd N.N.C.'[11]

Hamilton-Browne clearly has the wrong date for this. Compare his version with that of Captain (local rank) Henry Charles Harford, staff officer to Lonsdale. He does not mention sunstroke, but on 9 January, during hasty preparations for a general's inspection forgotten by Lonsdale, he reported: 'We had scarcely parted when Lonsdale's pony shied at something and threw him off. I saw the fall . . . I got off at once and ran to his assistance, only to find that he was unconscious and rigidly stiff . . . It was found afterwards that he had received concussion of the brain . . .'[12]

As a result of Lonsdale's incapacity, Major Black was given temporary command of the 3rd NNC.[13] It is also extremely likely that Lonsdale's ill-health was the principal reason for Hamilton-Browne's elevation to commandant. Lonsdale did not resume his duty as commandant of the 3rd Regiment until 20 January.

At dawn on 21 January, eight companies of each of the 1st and 2nd Battalions, 3rd Regiment, NNC, left the Isandlwana camp under the command of Lonsdale for a reconnaissance-in-force of the Malakatha range of hills forming the southern flank of the Isandlwana plain.[14] The 1st Battalion was led by now-Commandant Hamilton-Browne while the 2nd was under the command of Commandant Edward Russell Cooper.

Hamilton-Browne's 1st Battalion consisted of seven companies of amaBhele people (numbered 1 to 7) and three companies of iziGqoza (numbered 8, 9 and 10).[15] The iziGqoza were of Zulu origin and Hamilton-Browne was at pains to describe the difference in fighting qualities between these men and the remainder of his unit.[16] The identification of the tribal affiliations of each company will be seen as important shortly. Thus, since one of Hamilton-Browne's iziGqoza companies remained in the camp,[17] the 1st Battalion went on its expedition with the remaining two iziGqoza companies and six amaBhele companies.

We know very little of the commanders of the individual companies, but it is most unlikely that No. 8 Company was under both Captains Duncombe and Murray, as stated by Hamilton-Browne.[18] Indeed, Murray did not even belong to the 1st Battalion, but to the 2nd.[19] However, Hamilton-Browne later describes an action in which Captain 'Duncombe and his men' were involved and therefore we may be forgiven if we speculate that in fact Duncombe was in command of No. 8 Company.[20]

The route followed by each of the battalions after they separated is also rather difficult to unravel but it does have a tangential bearing on this discussion. Reading Hamilton-Browne's account, one might come to the conclusion that it was his battalion which went through the steep valleys to the east and north of Malakatha mountain and eventually climbed out to rejoin the 2nd, which had enjoyed an easier route by following round the rim:

> At the head of my men I crossed a donga to join up with Lonsdale who was with the 2nd Battalion, and on doing so he instructed me to make a detour of a hill and descend into some valleys, he working round the other side in such a manner so as to catch anything or any one who might be between us.[21]

Shortly afterwards, he continues: 'The day wore on. The valleys became as hot as furnaces. We captured more cattle. So towards evening we left the low country after the most trying day and made for the high land.'[22] He also indicates that they captured 'some hundreds of head of cattle' and only left the valley towards evening.[23] This is not quite the view of three other parties who were present and who wrote their accounts much closer in time to the events. Harford agrees that Lonsdale went with the 1st Battalion, while he went with the 2nd: 'As we worked our way along, the 1st Battalion managed to capture a considerable number of cattle, but we saw none.'[24]

Norris-Newman, who accompanied the 2nd Battalion, describes affairs as follows:

> . . . when both battalions were a few hundred yards off the waterfall, the first [Battalion] was ordered to right-turn, cross the stream, and ascend the steep height on the opposite side, and then proceed on the top of the mountains, right round the edges, keeping parallel with the 2-3rd, which was then wheeled back, and sent in skirmishing order round the base and sides to the right, through the great Thorn Valley of the Malakata . . .[25]

Finally, the account of John Maxwell, who was a lieutenant with the 2nd Battalion:

> On arriving at the base of the range, the name of which, as I recollect, is the Malagali [Malakatha], covered pretty well with thorns, and as we found out

afterwards rather difficult to get through owing to the thickness of the thorns and very broken country, we formed (at least our company and some others did) in skirmishing order, and scoured the western side of the range arriving at the southern end of it, not far from the Umzinyali [Mzinyathi] River, about noon.[26]

Harford and Norris-Newman agree with Maxwell that both battalions had a light meal about noon before carrying on with the reconnaissance and all concur that they finally came together on the top of the Malakatha about 4 p.m.

The regiment had collected a number of cattle from homesteads along the way and they sent them back to camp under the command of Captain Orlando Murray: '. . . as we were then seven miles from camp Captain O. Murray was immediately dispatched, with two companies, to drive the captured cattle there.'[27]

This again seems to infer that Murray was with the 1st Battalion, but we already know that he belonged to the 2nd; John Maxwell's account is more convincing: '[. . . about noon]. We were rewarded thus far by having seen some old men and women and having captured some thirty or forty head of cattle. Captain Orlando Murray with his company was ordered to return to camp with the cattle – this was the last we saw of Captain Murray or his subaltern Lieutenant [R.A.] Pritchard.'[28]

From this, it seems clear that Hamilton-Browne had it wrong again and that only one company was sent back, and that company was Murray's own, which has been identified as No. 1 Company, 2nd Battalion.[29]

Hamilton-Browne was a distant observer of the battle of Isandlwana on the following day, 22 January, having been sent back to the camp by Lord Chelmsford to assist with the intended movement of part of the camp to the Mangeni Falls area. His official report on these events is short and concise, and in it he describes sending five messages to Lord Chelmsford's force, with two other key times:[30]

Sent with Captain Pohl:	10.30?[31]
Sent with Sergeant Turner:	11.00?
Sent with unnamed messenger:	1.15?
Sent with Captain Develin:	1.45?
Sent with Captain Hayes:[32]	3.00.

In his memoir thirty-three years later, he can remember only four messages, but assigns times to others of them, instead of only one:[33]

Sent with well-mounted officer (Pohl?):	10.00
Sent with mounted officer (Turner?):	11.00
Sent with Captain Develin:	1.15?
Sent with Officer (Hayes?):	3.00?

It is easy to see the inconsistencies here, and how the passage of time can alter the detail of events long ago. From the foregoing, which show examples of muddled recollection and the need to impress his reader, one can readily discern the types of error into which one might fall without careful examination of other sources. The general outline of the subject matter remains true but the devil is in the detail.

Better, then, to look askance at the memoirs, or perhaps memories, of such worthies as George Mossop (1937), Sir Bindon Blood (1933), General Sir Henry Smith-Dorrien (1925) and even Sir Evelyn Wood (1906). A number of people also wrote articles for the fiftieth anniversary of Isandlwana in the *Natal Mercury* of 22 January 1929. Among these were: Sir William Beaumont, W.H. Stafford,[34] H.D. Davies,[35] Samuel Jones and Dugald Macphail, not to mention the accounts by Zulu combatants Gumpega Gwabe and Zimema. At such a distance in time, one must question their detailed recollections, allowing that the general framework may still be correct.

Another serious trap for the unwary is bogus documents, even though some of these have been written with formal intent such as education. The writer was once sent a letter purportedly written by Charlie Raw which describes his discovery of the Zulu army before Isandlwana, but unfortunately frequently using phrases appropriated directly from Donald Morris' *The Washing of the Spears*. In fact, the document was created for use in an educational project for gifted young high-school students. The document was written in 1984 by Julian Whybra and was clearly identified as such, but it had assumed the status of a genuine document.[36] Other creations seem to have been for the author's own mischievous satisfaction: the writer came across a document in an eminent South African museum entitled 'The Gaudy Cloth', edited by Oliver Ransford and purporting to relate the account of Isandlwana by the Zulu warrior Zabange.[37] The editor eventually admitted that the account was his own invention.[38] Whatever their original purpose, such documents can bring the researcher undone, should he rely solely on 'evidence' to be found in them.

Almost as serious a problem as reviewing too little of the primary sources is to read too much. There are very many accounts of the battle of Isandlwana, for example, by both European and African sources. Add to these the second-hand accounts, and then those at third hand and the numbers proliferate. In such cases it is, therefore, quite easy to fail to 'see the forest for the trees'.

The final duty of the historian is to advise his reader of the basis for his statements or hypotheses. Many years ago, when I read *The Washing of the Spears* for the first time, I was in awe of Morris' grasp of the minutiae of detail in an area of history which at that time was not widely known. Even more, however, I admired his self-effacing words in the section after the narrative in which he discusses his sources, and here I quote: 'After considerable deliberation, I have decided to dispense with detailed text notes, primarily because I do not wish to claim for this work an academic status to which it is not entitled.'[39]

I still admire his diligence but have cursed his modesty roundly almost every time I have referred to it since. But at least Morris goes on to identify his sources in his bibliography while hoping the sources for quoted material are self-evident, and has clearly labelled speculative passages. (This is not entirely true, and is the origin of some of my curses.) Would that some of those following him had done even as much.

The war of 1879 has become fertile ground for writers since Morris produced his groundbreaking work and some have fallen into the trap of ignoring, or worse, misusing, the primary sources. The sources inevitably leave gaps in our knowledge and where speculation is used to fill the gaps, such speculation must not only be well informed but acknowledged. Still worse is the refusal to acknowledge primary source material and its original location, instead quoting from some secondary narrative containing it, when the location of the former is well known.

From the foregoing, it will by now be apparent that the researcher must tread carefully through the minefield of primary sources. This is particularly true of so-called 'memoirs' which were written long after the events narrated. Some, it is true, were based on journals but even these might not be sufficiently comprehensive to fill the void facing the writer, who is thus compelled to fall back on his own frail memory for details of the events under discussion.

Just as important is the need to examine carefully the provenance of the document, to ensure that it is indeed genuine. It is also wise to have more than one source for an assertion, although this is not always possible. When there is any doubt, it is better to tell the reader what you know, and then identify any speculation which may follow.

A Question of Time

One of the most vexed questions concerning the Anglo-Zulu War in general, and the battle of Isandlwana in particular, is the unreliability of the times mentioned in military reports and accounts. Discrepancies of between thirty minutes and two hours in reported times for the same event are not uncommon. The problem, however, has not received the recognition that it should, because an understanding of time-measurement procedures could throw light on some of the reasons for the apparent discrepancies. This paper tries to address the issue and illuminate a quite fundamental problem.

Today, we take for granted the recording of reasonably accurate times for events, especially in official reports, because the accuracy of our timing devices, even down to a relatively inexpensive wrist watch, is so reliable. This is largely due to the establishment of international standards, about which more later, and advances in time-keeping devices, not the least of which is the replacement of the mechanical 'clockwork' movement by the oscillation of a quartz crystal. However, the capturing of time was as much taken for granted in 1879 as it is now, so there is rarely any mention of how this was regulated, even though the devices were so much more unreliable at that time.

A typical example of the difficulty is shown by the times of two events which occurred on 22 January 1879. They were reported in the same document by Major Cornelius Francis Clery, senior staff officer to Colonel Richard Thomas Glyn, and were subsequently corrected by two senior officers.[40] The first occurrence in Clery's report was 9.30 a.m., when Lord Chelmsford despatched an order to Colonel Pulleine at the Isandlwana camp that tentage, etc. should be sent on to the proposed next camp site at the Mangeni River. Lord Chelmsford himself subsequently noted against this paragraph that the event occurred 'an hour *later*, at least'.[41] The second occurred when Clery noted that he had followed the general onto a small hill (Mdutshana), from which to observe the camp, at 3.30 p.m. This was corrected in an annotation made by Assistant Military Secretary Lieutenant-Colonel John North Crealock to 2.30, or one hour *earlier*. This suggests that three senior officers, including the general commanding, each had watches recording different times on the same day!

Another example is the reported time of Colonel Anthony William Durnford's arrival at the Isandlwana camp after being summoned from Rorke's Drift. The most correct determination of the time of this event would allow a more precise timing for the principal events of the battle of Isandlwana, the opening of which was precipitated shortly after Durnford's arrival.

The official history of the war gives the time of his arrival as 'about 10 a.m.'.[42] However, no less than thirteen (and perhaps more) survivors recorded times, or ranges of times, for this important event:

Lieut. H.L. Smith-Dorrien	8.00[43]
Capt. W. Stafford, NNC,	8.30–9.00[44]
Capt. H. Hallam Parr	9.30[45]
Lieut. W. Higginson, NNC	10.00[46]
Lieut. H.T. Curling, RA	10.00[47]
Capt. E. Essex	10.00[48]
Pte J. Trainer, Rocket Battery	10.00[49]
Lieut. H.D. Davies, NNMC	10.00[50]
Lieut. W.F.B. Cochrane	10.00–10.30[51]
Pte D. Johnson, Rocket Battery	10.30–11.00[52]
Pte E. Wilson, bandsman	10.30–11.00[53]
Lieut. A.F. Henderson, NNMC	11.00[54]
Pte H. Grant, Rocket Battery	11.00.[55]

The time given by Captain Penn Symons, who was not present, is more precise, based upon discussions with survivors shortly afterwards: he gives the time as 10.45 a.m.[56]

It is particularly interesting to note the discrepancy of one hour between the times offered by Lieutenants Harry Davies and Alfred Henderson, both of whom arrived at Isandlwana together as part of Durnford's column. Note, too, that three of the survivors were members of the ill-fated rocket battery and one would expect that at least their times would be consistent but such is not the case.

How could such discrepancies occur? We know that there were problems in keeping accurate time when soldiers became isolated from the mainstream of civilisation. The difficulty is freely acknowledged in a letter from Captain Macgregor, RE, on the staff of the First Column under siege in Eshowe: 'I'm making a sundial now, as we often get out of our time reckoning.'[57] The Eshowe column had left Fort Tenedos on 18 January and it took only a little over two months for their timepieces to have become quite unreliable, assuming that they had been correct at the time of their departure. We know, however, that a 'time gun was instituted, to fire daily, at noon' at the Lower Thukela.[58]

To go from the specific to the general: timekeeping was, until quite recent times, a very local matter. In 1879 there was no such convention as international time zones. The prime meridian at Greenwich was not universally adopted until the International Meridian Conference in Washington in 1884.[59] It was only then that the globe was divided from east to west into twenty-four time zones, each covering fifteen degrees of longitude, treating the Greenwich, or prime, meridian as both zero and 360 degrees. Each zone was accorded a 'local' time which increased by one hour for each zone moving east from Greenwich, to be adopted by all places within seven and a half degrees on either side of each meridian.

Prior to that standard, every town and city in the world maintained its own version of local time, based on the concept that noon was declared to occur when the sun reached its zenith. This explains why, in a large number of places, a noon-day gun was fired (in Hong Kong, for example)[60] or a large ball was lowered on a tower visible from a wide area.[61] In the *Natal Almanac* for 1879, however, it is noted that in Pietermaritzburg, the gun was fired at 8 a.m.[62] When these signals occurred, people would check, and correct, their own clocks and watches and ships in port would do the same. This led to some difficulty in Pietermaritzburg in 1875:

> For many years the city of Pietermaritzburg, known as 'Sleepy Hollow' to its rivals of another and, in its own opinion, a busier town, had set all its clocks and watches, and regulated all its business hours by the sound of a gun, fired daily from Fort Napier at nine o'clock A.M., the signal for which came from the town itself.[63] The gun was frequently credited with being too fast or slow by a few seconds or even minutes, and on one occasion was known to have been wrong by half an hour; a mistake which was remedied in the most original fashion, by setting the gun back a minute and a half daily till it should have returned to the proper time; to the utter confusion of all the chronometers in the neighbourhood.[64]

There could exist, therefore, many versions of the 'right' time: Cape Town was one hour and fourteen minutes ahead of Greenwich, and Pietermaritzburg was ahead by two hours and fourteen minutes.[65] It is most likely that Durban would have differed slightly from Pietermaritzburg, if only by a minute or two. It is easy to see that with differing standards, the common concept of 'time' was not so common after all.

This was a problem apparent in other theatres of war. In a fight with some parallels with Isandlwana, time was also elusive at the battle of the Little Bighorn in 1876: 'As to the time of day, there are discrepancies. In Montana it could not have been much later than noon, although watches carried by soldiers registered mid-afternoon. Until 1894 [sic] there were no times zones; each settlement or village or fort correlated its clocks with a metropolis. Fort Lincoln operated on Chicago time.'[66]

In 1879 the ownership of a 'fob' or pocket watch was beyond the means of most soldiers, other than officers and other 'gentlemen' volunteers.[67] As with many things, quality came at a price and the more reliable the watch, the more expensive it was, to be afforded only by the wealthy. Many officers came into this category, of course, although not every officer was affluent.[68] But even the best pocket watches of the day might have gained or lost a minute a day and watches of lesser quality would have lost or gained an hour in a month or less.[69] This daily loss or gain is, of course, cumulative and the frequency of adjustment of watches to compensate for error when in the field, and the accuracy of the adjustment, is quite unknown.

We do know that the British army issued watches to its men. The first of these was approved for issue in November, 1870: 'Watch in German silver case with strap and key, for telegraphers and signallers of the Royal Engineers'.[70]

Whether these issues were later extended to include the staff of officers such as Lord Chelmsford is difficult to say with any certainty, but it seems unlikely, because Taylerson goes on to state that the next watch was to be issued only for 'signalling and telegraph services', occurring in August 1883.[71]

A still-worse scenario is that of men trying to establish a time without the benefit of a watch at all. This is especially true when events are moving quickly, such as during a battle. Theoretically, given that everyone had a standard time for the start of such an event, the variation in estimated times after, say, thirty minutes, would be quite revealing.

Divorced from the convenience of being stationed in a large town or city, and thus having a daily signal, how then did the army in the field keep time? There is one clue based on a statement of Captain Molyneux, one of Lord Chelmsford's aides-de-camp (ADC): 'Then I had to find the variation of my compass, rate my watch, fix the latitude, and draw maps.'[72]

One might surmise here that Molyneux rated his watch to local time by observation of the sun's zenith above the horizon, thus indicating noon. By using a sextant, this can readily be done, and at the same time the angle between the sun's height and the horizon can be used to determine one's latitude. In naval parlance this is called 'shooting the sun'. It is rather interesting that this duty, if such it was, fell to an army officer when Lieutenant Milne, RN was also an ADC to Lord Chelmsford, for who better than a naval officer to determine these things? Another alternative was to ignore minor differences between localities and determine the time from that of sunrise and/or sunset as published in the *Natal Almanac* to which reference has already been made. This method, however, is also prone to error, though not more than a few minutes.

With the above factors in mind, it becomes easier to understand the difficulty of men trying to establish a time, but it does not change the basic fact that such times may be wildly inaccurate. Given a range of times for the same event, therefore, it is often easiest to use a 'mean' time; for example, 10.30 a.m. in the case of Durnford's arrival.[73]

We may take some comfort from the observation that a more reliable yardstick than a single or a range of times is the elapsed time reported between events. Even watches which lose two minutes a day will still record time intervals between two events on the same day with reasonable accuracy, provided they come from the same timepiece and this is one way in which our difficulty may be circumvented.

A good example is the time taken to travel from Rorke's Drift to Isandlwana, a journey made by a number of people. Durnford is reported as having left his camp about 800 metres north of the Mzinyathi (Buffalo) river between 7.30[74] and 8.00[75] a.m. and arrived between 10.00 and 10.30. It would thus be fair to say that the journey of about sixteen kilometres (ten miles) took about two and a half hours.[76] Since this same trip, or the reverse, was made by a number of other people on that same day (Chard, Smith-Dorrien, Adendorff, Hamer, etc.) then one can assign a similar duration for their trips and so gain a better idea of times for either arrival or departure.

There is one additional advantage to this sort of estimate: it gives the researcher another tool for estimating time by rate of travel. The ride from Rorke's Drift to Isandlwana is mostly uphill and would therefore be covered by a horse at a fast walk. Since the distance is about sixteen kilometres, then the rate of travel was about 6.4 kilometres (four miles) an hour, a not unreasonable figure.[77] Sir Garnet Wolseley wrote that a horse could walk a mile in 16 minutes (3.75 miles per hour) and would therefore cover the same distance in a little under three hours.[78] One might use the same method for the rocket battery, which was mounted mostly on mules and therefore took rather longer,[79] and for the baggage train and a company of NNC, which took longer still, arriving about noon.[80]

To sum up, it is important that the researcher into these events looks carefully at any times presented, because there could be a number of reasons why they might be incorrect (and much fewer for them being right). By using the methods I have proposed – that is, estimating the time between two events on the same day, and using rates of travel, be they for infantry marching, mounted men riding or even Zulus jogging – such times as are presented may be much more closely examined and either confirmed or adjusted.

Sir Bartle Frere's Ultimatum

The new governor and high commissioner to South Africa, Sir Henry Bartle Edward Frere, arrived in Cape Town in April 1877. He was born in 1815 and joined the Bombay civil service in 1834. After considerable administrative experience he became governor of Scinde in 1842 and was appointed governor of Bombay in 1862, a post he held for four years. In 1867 he returned to Britain to join the India Council, and in 1872 he visited Zanzibar to negotiate an anti-slavery treaty with the sultan. During his career he had earned the distinction of being a Grand Commander of the Order of the Bath, was rewarded with a baronetcy and was appointed to the Privy Council. By the time he was sent to South Africa he was sixty-three years old, of modest means and had been anxious to retire, but was persuaded to accept this last post with a veiled promise of a peerage, and the monetary rewards were not to be passed by.

Frere was a very talented man. Donald Morris reported that in one month in Malta, he learned enough Arabic to 'scold his way through Egypt'.[81] Within a year of landing in India, he could speak Hindustani, Marathi and Gujarti. His was a remarkable intellect and he had exceptional administrative ability, both of which he brought to bear on the posts to which he was appointed. Frere has also been described as having 'a certain recklessness, strange perhaps in so experienced an administrator, and yet the natural defect of his strongest qualities'.[82] It was a characteristic which was to impel him to draw both the British and Natal governments into a violent conflict with the Zulu king and his people.

He had been given a remit to create a confederation from the several colonies and Boer republics in South Africa, following the model which had earlier proved successful in Canada. He had two major problems in so doing. The first was the issue of land claims on the western border lands of the Zulu land which the Boers had pursued since the accession to the throne of King Mpande in 1842, claims which they justified by the assistance they had rendered to that monarch in winning his throne.[83] The British had opposed these land claims, siding with both Mpande and later with his son and successor, Cetshwayo. The matter was seemingly resolved soon after Frere's arrival in Cape Town: the Crown annexed the South African Republic of the Transvaal only days later. But this only brought with it a further difficulty: having assumed control of the Transvaal, its administrator, Sir Theophilus Shepstone, was compelled to reverse British policy and support the Boer cause in the land dispute, as was Sir Bartle himself.

The second problem was Frere's perception of the military power of the Zulu people and the potential threat it posed to Natal. It really was a baseless motive: the Zulu had only once seriously infringed the river borders of Natal since colonisation in 1824, an argument which the lieutenant-governor of Natal was to use. (Mpande's brother Dingane had invaded Port Natal, the name by which Durban was originally known, in 1831, and then only to take retribution for the perfidy of one of the colonists, John Cane.) Other than that, and a few minor issues, relations under all of the Zulu kings had been very sound and there was considerable commerce between the two territories. Certainly, there had been recent examples of Zulu hostility in the disputed region, but these were largely because the ownership of the land was in question.

In a belated attempt to finally resolve the impasse, Sir Henry Bulwer, lieutenant-governor of Natal, established a Boundary Commission which assembled for the first time on 7 March 1879 at Rorke's Drift. When the commission made its report on 20 June, it proved a bombshell to Frere, finding entirely for the Zulu and dismissing the Boer claims as spurious, stating that they were based either on forgery or fraud.[84] Had the finding been in favour of the Boers, Frere had hoped to use a violent Zulu reaction as his *casus belli* for an invasion of Zululand; now he had to seek other justification. The commission's findings were sent off to London while Frere delayed announcement of the report in Natal, lest news leak out to the Zulu king. (It has been argued that Frere was not personally responsible for the subsequent delay in announcing the commission findings, but rather that it was the result of delays inherent in the Natal bureaucracy.[85] By this, it is assumed that the writer was referring, in part at least, to the length of time for the findings to be studied and reported upon by other government officials.[86])

Frere had requested military reinforcements in anticipation of a confrontation, at the same time sounding out the London government view of the annexation of Zululand. His descriptions of a belligerent Zulu king grew more lurid by the week.[87] Some additional troops were sent out, but nothing like the numbers requested and, what was worse, the high commissioner was given specific instructions not to make war on the Zulu.[88]

Three separate incidents occurred in late July, August and September which Frere seized upon as his *causes célèbres*. The first two incidents related to the flight into Natal of two wives of Sihayo kaXongo, and their subsequent seizure and execution by his brother and sons, and were described thus:

> A wife of the chief Sihayo had left him and escaped into Natal. She was followed [on 28 July 1878] by a party of Zulus, under Mehlokazulu, the chief son of Sihayo, and his brother, seized at the kraal where she had taken refuge, and carried back to Zululand, where she was put to death, in accordance with Zulu law . . .
>
> A week later the same young men, with two other brothers and an uncle, captured in like manner another refugee wife of Sihayo, in the company of the young man with whom she had fled. This woman was also carried back, and is supposed to have been put to death likewise; the young man with her although guilty in Zulu eyes of a most heinous crime, punishable with death, was safe from them on English soil – they did not touch him.[89]

The third incident occurred in September, when two men were detained while on a sand bank of the Thukela River near the Middle Drift. Sir Bartle Frere described this matter in a despatch to Sir Michael Hicks Beach, Secretary of State for the Colonies:

Mr. Smith, a surveyor in the Colonial Engineer Department, was on duty inspecting the road down to the Tugela, near Fort Buckingham, which had been made a few years ago by order of Sir Garnet Wolseley, and accompanied by Mr. Deighton, a trader, resident at Fort Buckingham, went down to the ford across the Tugela. The stream was very low, and ran under the Zulu bank, but they were on this side of it, and had not crossed when they were surrounded by a body of 15 or 20 armed Zulus, made prisoners, and taken off with their horses, which were on the Natal side of the river, and roughly treated and threatened for some time; though, ultimately, at the instance of a headman who came up, they were released and allowed to depart.[90]

By themselves, these incidents were flimsy grounds upon which to initiate an invasion of Zululand. Indeed, Sir Henry Bulwer himself did not initially hold Cetshwayo responsible for what was clearly not a political act in the seizure and murder of the two women.[91]

I have sent a message to the Zulu King to inform him of this act of violence and outrage by his subjects in Natal territory, and to request him to deliver up to this Government to be tried for their offence, under the laws of the Colony, the persons of Mehlokazulu and Bekuzulu the two sons of Sirayo who were the leaders of the party.[92]

Cetshwayo also treated the complaint rather lightly, responding:

Cetywayo is sorry to have to acknowledge that the message brought by Umlungi is true, but he begs his Excellency will not take it in the light he sees the Natal Government seem to do, as what Sirayo's sons did he can only attribute to a rash act of boys who in the zeal for their father's house did not think of what they were doing. Cetywayo acknowledges that they deserve punishing, and he sends some of his indunas [regimental officers], who will follow Umlungi with his words. Cetywayo states that no acts of his subjects will make him quarrel with his fathers of the house of Shaka.[93]

We should note that the original complaint carried to Cetshwayo from the lieutenant-governor was in the form of a request for the surrender of the culprits. The request was subsequently transformed by Sir Bartle Frere into a 'demand':

> Apart from whatever may be the general wish of the Zulu nation, it seems to me that the seizure of the two refugee women in British territory by an armed force crossing an unmistakeable and well known boundary line, and carrying them off and murdering them with contemptuous disregard for the remonstrances of the Natal policemen, is itself an insult and a violation of British territory which cannot be passed over, and unless apologized and atoned for by compliance with the Lieutenant-Governor's demands, that the leaders of the murderous gangs shall be given up to justice, it will be necessary to send to the Zulu King an ultimatum which must put an end to pacific relations with our neighbours.[94]

We find the first mention of an ultimatum in this despatch. After considerable discussion and exchanges of views between Sir Bartle Frere and Sir Henry Bulwer,[95] it was decided to arrange a meeting with representatives of the Zulu king. The ostensible reason for this *indaba* was to present the long-awaited findings of the Boundary Commission to the Zulu people. In fact, the occasion was also to be used to present the king with an ultimatum.

By the time the ultimatum was presented, the two infractions by Sihayo's sons and the roughing up of Smith and Deighton had been joined by a number of more significant items.[96] One of these was Cetshwayo's apparent breaking of promises he had given to the then Mr Theophilus Shepstone at the king's 'coronation' in 1872. This farcical piece of theatre had been agreed to by Cetshwayo simply to satisfy the wishes of Shepstone and meant nothing to the Zulu people. Indeed, his real Zulu installation had taken place several weeks earlier when he had been acclaimed by his *izinduna* (regimental officers).[97]

In his report of the preparations for the installation, Shepstone himself says that during a marathon conversation with Cetshwayo, several points were discussed, two of which touched upon matters relevant to the ultimatum:

> 2nd.–The new laws to be proclaimed by me on Cetywayo's installation, the particulars of which, as given hereafter, were fully agreed upon at this meeting, and which amount to a kind of Bill of Rights, which may be pleaded by any Zulu subject suffering under oppression in future ;
>
> . . .
>
> 4th.–The position of the Missionaries and their converts in Zululand;[98]

When the time came for his pronouncement of the 'Bill of Rights', it was spelled out specifically:

1st. –That the indiscriminate shedding of blood shall cease in the land.

2nd. –That no Zulu shall be condemned without open trial and the public examination of witnesses for and against, and that he shall have a right to appeal to the King.

3rd.–That no Zulu's life shall be taken without the previous knowledge and consent of the King, after such trial has taken place, and the right of appeal has been allowed to be exercised.

4th.–That for minor crimes the loss of property, all, or a portion shall be substituted for the punishment of death.[99]

From this it might seem that Frere was correct. However, Shepstone goes on to describe the argument offered to him by one of the councillors concerning the deaths brought about during a 'smelling-out' by witch doctors, which he had included in his prohibition. Shepstone then admitted:

Although all this was fully and even vehemently assented to, it cannot be expected that the amelioration described will immediately take effect. To have got such principles admitted and declared to be what a Zulu may plead when oppressed, was but sowing the seed which will still take many years to grow and mature.[100]

Thus Shepstone himself, who extracted these supposed promises, did not take them sufficiently seriously as to expect them to be immediately binding.

In her discussion of the issue, Frances Colenso introduced two opinions that are also worthy of consideration here. The first was by John Dunn, who was present at the ceremony, and who commented: '. . . that no undertaking was made by, or even asked from, Cetshwayo. In the act of coronation, Mr. (now Sir T.) Shepstone gave to the king a piece of paternal counsel, and the conditions were in reality nothing more than recommendations urged upon his acceptance by the Special Commissioner.'[101]

The second opinion was that of Lord Kimberley, Secretary of State for the Colonies at the time of the coronation:

With respect to the so-called coronation promises, nothing had more astonished him in these papers than to learn that these promises were supposed to constitute an engagement between us and the Zulu nation. He happened to have had some concern in that matter; and if he had supposed that Sir T. Shepstone, in asking for these promises from Cetshwayo, had rendered us responsible to the Zulu nation to see that they were enforced, he would not have lost a mail in disavowing any such responsibility.[102]

A second addition to the ultimatum, which seems almost like an afterthought, required the surrender of Mbilini waMswati. Mbilini was the son of a Swazi king who unsuccessfully disputed the succession with his brother, resulting in his exile from the kingdom. He sought, and received, refuge from Cetshwayo and was granted land in the region of the Ntombe River in western Zululand. (It is entirely possible that Cetshwayo regarded him as a useful buffer between himself and the Boers of the Transvaal.) Here he took up residence on the Tafelberg, a flat-topped mountain overlooking the river. Something of a brigand, Mbilini made raids on anyone in his area, Boer and Zulu alike, accruing cattle and prisoners in the process. With the annexation of the Transvaal, Britain had also to deal with Mbilini, and, because Frere was convinced that the bandit chief was in the pay of the Zulu king, his surrender was included in the ultimatum. The light in which Mbilini was regarded is shown in a paragraph from a memorandum written by Sir Henry Bulwer:

> The King disowned Umbilini's acts by saying that Umbilini had been giving him trouble, that he had left the Zulu country in order to wrest the Swazi chieftainship from his brother, the reigning Chief, and that if he returned he should kill him. But there is nothing to show that he has in any way punished him, and, on the contrary, it is quite certain that even if Umbilini did not act with the express orders of Cetywayo, he did so with the knowledge that what he was doing would be agreeable to the King.[103]

Frere has been accused of chicanery by taking deliberate advantage of the length of time it took for correspondence to pass between South Africa and London to conceal his intentions from his political masters, or at least defer giving them the necessary information until it was too late for them to act.[104] The first intimation to the British government of his intention to make 'demands' on the Zulu was in a private letter to Sir Michael Hicks Beach written on 14 October 1878. But that letter only arrived in London on 16 November and by then messengers had already been despatched from Natal to the Zulu king to request the presence of a delegation at the Lower Tugela on 11 December for the purpose of receiving the Boundary Commission's findings. Had Hicks Beach then sent off an immediate telegraphic response explicitly forbidding any action other than the announcement of the boundary award, it might have arrived in South Africa just in time to prevent the ultimatum being presented – but only just. No prohibition was sent, however, and could hardly be expected to have been, for Hicks Beach had no means of knowing the last-minute urgency of the events that were already in train. Nowhere in

Frere's letter was there anything to indicate how soon he intended to act, nor was there anything to suggest how stringent his demands would be.[105]

Frere's first official notification was sent on 11 November (and received on 11 December) but mention of the ultimatum was again couched in such obscure terms as to be missed entirely:

> I propose to request his Excellency to communicate without delay the [Boundary] award . . . to the parties concerned.
>
> This will enable us to deal with the main question of our future relations with the Zulus, and I propose to request his Excellency to follow up the award in the boundary case with a statement of the guarantees which we consider necessary in order to ensure peace hereafter in our relations with the Zulus.[106]

A second mention a few days later still did not make matters entirely clear:

> 5. That the award in the matter of the boundary dispute to be at once communicated to Cetywayo and the Chiefs and council of the Zulu nation, together with a statement of the demands of the British Government for reparation for the past and security for the future, including the observance of the promises made by Cetywayo at his coronation.[107]

Frere's sharp practice did not remain undetected for very long. In a very detailed memorandum summarising the whole issue of the ultimatum, a copy of which was sent to Frere, Hicks Beach included the following statement:

> But on the 19th of December we received a short Despatch, dated the 16th of November, purporting to forward a great body of enclosures (which did not arrive until the 2nd of January), and showing that Sir Bartle Frere intended to accompany his award by certain demands on the King, which were very imperfectly and vaguely expressed in the Despatch, though their extent was made more plain from a Despatch of Lord Chelmsford's received on the 27th of December.[108]

By that time, of course, the ultimatum had almost expired and the columns of Lord Chelmsford were already poised on the Zulu border awaiting the order to cross.

Hicks Beach had earlier admitted his helplessness with regard to the Frere's actions in a telling note to his Prime Minister:

> I have impressed this [non-aggressive] view upon Sir B. Frere, both officially and privately, to the best of my power. But I cannot really control him without a

telegraph – (I don't know that I could with one). I feel it is as likely as not that he is at war with the Zulus at the present moment.[109]

Prophetic words indeed.

The Terms of the Ultimatum

The following are the terms that were included in the ultimatum delivered to the representatives of King Cetshwayo on the banks of the Thukela River on 11 December 1878.[110] No time was specified for compliance with item 4, twenty days were allowed for compliance with items 1–3, that is, until 31 December inclusive; ten days more were allowed for compliance with the remaining demands, items 5–13. The earlier time limits were subsequently altered so that all expired on 10 January 1879.

1. Surrender of Sihayo's three sons and brother to be tried by the Natal courts.
2. Payment of a fine of five hundred head of cattle for the outrages committed by the above, and for Cetshwayo's delay in complying with the request [!] of the Natal Government for the surrender of the offenders.
3. Payment of a fine of one hundred head of cattle for the offence committed against Messrs Smith and Deighton.
4. Surrender of the Swazi chief Umbilini, and others to be named hereafter, to be tried by the Transvaal courts.
5. Observance of the coronation promises.
6. That the Zulu army be disbanded, and the warriors be allowed to go to their homes.
7. That the Zulu military system be discontinued, and other military regulations adopted, to be decided upon after consultation with the Great Council and British Representatives.
8. That every man, when he comes to man's estate, shall be free to marry.
9. All missionaries and their converts, who until 1877 lived in Zululand, shall be allowed to return and reoccupy their stations.
10. All such missionaries shall be allowed to teach, and any Zulu, if he chooses, shall be free to listen to their teaching.
11. A British Agent shall be allowed to reside in Zululand, who will see that the above provisions are carried out.
12. All disputes in which a missionary or European is concerned, shall be heard by the king in public, and in presence of the Resident.
13. No sentence of expulsion from Zululand shall be carried out until it has been approved by the Resident.

Chapter 2

Isandlwana: Exordium

Has he luck?

Napoleon Bonaparte, 1769–1821

The Gunfight at Sihayo's

On 11 January 1879, coinciding exactly with the expiry of the thirty-day ultimatum to the Zulu king Cetshwayo, Colonel Richard Thomas Glyn's Third or Centre Column crossed the Mzinyathi (Buffalo) River at Rorke's Drift, accompanied by the general officer commanding, Lieutenant-General Lord Chelmsford, and his staff.

Chelmsford determined first to attack the homestead of the Zulu chief Sihayo kaXongo, located in the Batshe (Bashee) River valley about eight kilometres from the river crossing. This operation would serve two purposes: it would secure his left flank for the advance towards Ulundi and it would also serve as a lesson to Sihayo himself, whose brother and two sons were ostensibly one of the justifications for the ultimatum: they had crossed the Buffalo some months earlier, abducted two of Sihayo's wives who had absconded with their lovers and had murdered them.

After crossing the river, the column set up a sprawling camp on the left (or Zulu) bank of the Mzinyathi and, on 12 January, Lord Chelmsford ordered a large force forward under Colonel Glyn to assault Sihayo's homestead, which was nearby. This action poses two problems.

The first problem arises from the different modern accounts, at least one of which indicates that the only attack was against Sihayo's homestead,[1] while others state that this first attack was against a subsidiary homestead in a gorge and his main homestead was attacked some hours later or some combination of the two.[2]

The official version states:

At 3.30 a.m., a force under Colonel Glyn consisting of four companies of the 1/24th Regiment, the 1/3rd Natal Native Contingent and most of the mounted men left camp to reconnoitre the country to the eastward, where the kraal of the chief Sirayo was known to be situated.

Lord Chelmsford and his Staff accompanied this force, which, after a march of about five miles arrived at a ravine in the valley of the Bashee river.[3]

An engagement then took place at this location, and 'Sirayo's kraal, which lay further up the Bashee valley, was burnt later in the day.'[4]

A number of the participants left written accounts of these actions. One of these was Captain (local rank) Henry Harford, staff officer to the 3rd Regiment, Natal Native Contingent. He accompanied Captain George Hamilton-Browne with the 1/3rd NNC battalion into the gorge and gives a detailed description of the attack. He follows this account with these words: 'Now that the Cavalry, Mounted Police and 24th regiment had gone on to Sirayo's kraal, one of two companies of the [Natal Native] Contingent were sent off to capture some cattle, and after a short rest and a meal, the whole force returned to camp . . .'[5]

There was also a journalist present, in the person of Charles Norris-Newman. He left a more complete account: 'Just as this [first] engagement was finished the second force, consisting of the 2-24th and 2-3rd Natal Native Contingent, under Colonel Degacher, CB, which had started some [three] hours after us, came up and were taken on farther up the valley to Sirayo's principal kraal, called Loxie [Sokhexe] . . .'[6]

Norris-Newman was nearly correct, but not quite. Lieutenant Nevill Coghill was serving as orderly officer to Colonel Glyn. Although Coghill died at Fugitive's Drift on 22 January, his diary was later found on the battlefield of Isandlwana and several of his letters also survive. Of 12 January, he wrote:

According to the orders of the previous evening a party of the 1/24th and 2/3 NNC were to start at 5, and the 2/24th and 1/3 NNC to leave at eight by another route and join the first party at a certain point. This arrangement was however changed as in approaching within a mile or so of a krantz near Sihayo's kraal we heard the lowing of cattle and the Zulu chanting their war song and as it was evident that resistance would be made I was sent back to bring up the 2/24th and the 1/3 NNC.[7]

To conclude, there are the words of Lord Chelmsford himself, who observed the first action from the opposite side of the valley:

In passing by the Ngudu Hill we noticed that some herds of cattle had been driven up close under the Krantz where one of Sirayo's strongholds were said to be. I ordered Colonel Glyn with 4 Companies 1/24th & 1/3d Native Contingent to work up under the Krantz [and seize the cattle].

Colonel Degacher who had been sent for from the Camp when we found that the Krantz was occupied by the enemy came up towards the end of the affair with ½ battn. 2/24th and about 400 2/3d Native Contingent. This force went forward to Sirayo's own Kraal which is situated under a very steep Krantz which is filled with caves. I ordered Sirayo's Kraal to be burnt but none of the other huts were touched.[8]

From the foregoing evidence, it is clear that there were indeed two separate engagements in the Batshe Valley on that day. The first was the attack on a large group of Zulu who had taken a herd of cattle into a deep cleft in the steep cliffs of Ngedla Hill, which forms the eastern side of the valley. This was undertaken by the 1/3rd NNC (Major Wilsone Black), supported by four companies of 1/24th and most of the mounted troops, under the overall command of Colonel Glyn. The NNC made a frontal assault with companies of the 1/24th in support, while the mounted troops ascended the hill at the southern end to cut off any Zulu who were making their escape over the hill. The 1/24th ascended an adjacent spur with the same object in view.[9]

The attack into the cleft is described precisely by one of the combatants, who explains how they turned to their right flank to complete the movement:

> We paraded at 4.30 a.m. After going about six miles, we came across the Enemy in a large mountain surrounded by a dense bush. We crossed a river up to our knees in water, then extended in skirmishing order through the bush. We were then ordered to loose our Ammunition but not to fire unless they fired upon us. We hadn't gone very far before they commenced firing at us from the Rocks. We wheeled around to our right and let them have it proper.[10]

The route of the 1/24th, then, lay on the Rorke's Drift side of the Batshe until they reached a point opposite the cleft, then they crossed over and deployed ready for the attack. This is the point from which Lord Chelmsford watched the operation. There must have been uncertainty as to precisely where the enemy lay because, having advanced towards the cliffs directly ahead, they found that the firing came from their right, causing them to turn in that direction.

The second assault was by four companies of the 2/24th and part of the 2/3rd NNC (Commandant Cooper) under Colonel Degacher, which was brought up earlier than originally planned and which went further up the valley to attack and burn Sihayo's homestead itself.[11] This cautious action, it seems, was watched with some amusement by spectators of the 1/24th from the top of the cliff overlooking the homestead, because it was found to be deserted except for some old women.[12]

The second problem is the location of these two engagements. Most of the eye-witnesses are silent on their precise whereabouts but there are descriptions which might help us. The first is from Commandant Hamilton-Browne, who commanded a company attacking the first objective. He describes it thus: 'The Krantz was a precipitous mountain about 500 feet high, and where the enemy and the cattle were located was in a deep cleft running in a V shape, the foot of the hill being covered with boulders and rushes.'[13]

He emphasises the V shape several times in his descriptions of the site, in one of which he says: 'As we neared the place, I observed that I could send a party to the right and left of the V-shaped entrance.'[14] From this, it is clear that the V-shaped defile was at the rear of a wider mouth. Harford had this to say about the location: 'Eventually, on reaching the foot of a ledge of rocks, where they curved in a horse-shoe bend overhanging a steep valley, a somewhat grim sight presented itself.'[15]

From these descriptions, it seems that we must look for a wide-mouthed cleft in the hill which slopes upwards towards a cliff surrounding the cleft, but in which there is a narrower defile, into which the cattle were taken.

The first task in locating the site is to examine a large-scale topographical map.[16] From this, it is quite easy to determine that there is but one very deep defile in the western flank of Ngedla Hill, overlooking the Batshe River. This, however, is too narrow to fit the description because it would be impossible for it to hold the number of troops, in extended skirmishing formation, which were engaged.

There are also two other indentations in the hillside, one large re-entrant almost at the centre of the valley and a much slighter one about 1,500 metres to the south. The most southerly of these is again too narrow to fit the descriptions given, but that further north, which is also to the south of the narrow defile previously discussed, is a much better fit, having all of the required features: it has a wide mouth, extends to a depth of some 400 metres, after which there is a narrower defile about 250 metres wide and extending a further 150 metres into the hillside. Here there is a craggy cliff some 100 metres in height, accessible to the fleet-footed Zulu who tried to hold the British force off. Furthermore, the left flank of the re-entrant has a sufficiently easy gradient as would allow much easier access to the top of the hill, and is the most likely point at which some of the 1/24th made their ascent. Even

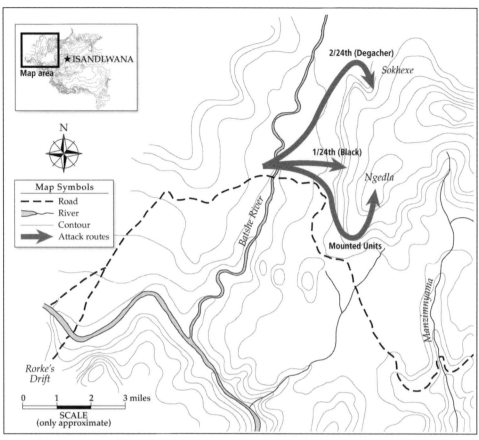

2 Engagement at Sihayo's

today the site is quite heavily covered with scrub and small trees and there are still many Zulu homes to be found on the lower level near the present road.

Whilst there is no tangible evidence that this is the site of the first engagement, it really is the only one of three possible sites that fits the descriptions given. It should also be mentioned that this indentation lies opposite an open area on the other side of the Batshe River, at a distance of about 1,500 metres, from where Lord Chelmsford and his staff could have viewed the skirmish.[17] There is no other such convenient vantage point along the whole western side of the valley.

The description of the site of the second engagement is drawn from an unusual source. In 1882, Bertram Mitford visited every battlefield in Zululand as a tourist and wrote an engaging account of his travels. His description of the location of Sihayo's homestead itself is as follows:

About an hour's ride [from St Augustine's Mission] brought us through the green valley of the Bashi and after several tedious detours . . . we entered the steep stony defile leading to the truculent old chieftain's former abode . . . The site of the kraal, which was easily found, is on a ridge, or rather spur, overlooking the approaches from the valley on either side; the cattle enclosure still stands, and is girt by a solid stone wall, around which, and thickly overgrown with tangles of weeds, are the clay floors of the huts, being all that remains of the same. On the other side of the ravine, in the rear, rises a huge wall of frowning cliff . . . and here, amid the stones and clefts, Sirayo's followers made a futile stand against the hated invader.[18]

Lieutenant Coghill also made a contribution here:

While this [the fight in the defile] was going on the 2/24th and 1/3 NNC were being moved round to attack the kraal itself wh[ich] was reported to be strongly fortified and loopholed . . . Its strength and the metal [sic] of its defenders were not to be tested for on arriving at the kraal it was found to be deserted . . . The kraal was burnt and we returned home with the cattle we had captured . . .[19]

The key word here is 'round'. Round what were the 2/24th and NNC moved? The answer is: the northern shoulder of Ngedla.

The last, and perhaps the most important, clue is provided by Captain William Penn Symons: 'It [Sihayo's homestead] was picturesquely situated in an angle of the hills 200 feet above the level of the valley, and well watered.'[20] Sokhexe is therefore not located within the western Batshe Valley at all, but rather, it occupies a high shelf on the northern flank of the hill, which itself is surrounded by a vertical cliff some twenty-five metres high, those same cliffs from which the 1/24th gazed down on their advancing comrades. As Mitford describes, it is approached from the northern valley by a steep, stony defile, now traced by a rather poor track, which winds its way almost to the summit of Ngedla. Also as Mitford describes, it looks almost due north across the Batshe river as it turns east to follow the northern face of Ngedla.

The first engagement lasted about one and a half hours and the force was back in its camp on the Mzinyathi by four in the afternoon. Interestingly, this small fight resulted in the capture of some cattle, which was highly regarded. Colour Sergeant Edwards again: 'If I get through this all right I shall have plenty of Prize money to draw as all that is captured is to be divided among the troops.'[21]

With regard to the cattle captured in this engagement, Lord Chelmsford was as pleased as was Edwards:

The cattle captured by this force up to date is 413 cattle, 235 sheep, 332 goats, and several horses.

The division of such booty will be made agreeably to the regulations sanctioned by His Excellency the High Commissioner, and reported by him for the sanction of Her Majesty.[22]

I have been able to visit the site of kwaSokhexe and was privileged to be shown round by Dlokodloko kaNgobese, a great-grandson of Mehlokazulu kaSihayo himself. The foundations of the stone cattle enclosure, indicating walls almost a metre in thickness, are still visible in the grass, showing it to be some thirty or forty metres in diameter. When it was at its full height, with embrasures for firearms, it might have seemed a formidable obstacle indeed; however, it is completely overlooked by the surrounding cliff and would thus have had little defensive merit against western arms: 'The position was strong had it not been that it was completely commanded from a cliff above, under whose shelter Sihayo had in the innocence of his heart erected an impregnable fortress.'[23]

One must also exercise caution when considering the military nature of the stone cattle pen. The mere fact that it was overlooked must indicate that it was originally not intended to have a military function. The addition of the extra height and embrasures was almost certainly defensive in nature, and equally certainly, was built as a response to the invasion. The area known as Sihayo's country was originally inhabited by baSotho people who were subsequently 'eaten up' by Shaka.[24] It was the custom of the baSotho to build stone enclosures for their cattle, whereas the Zulu always used wood.[25] Sihayo's people, therefore, were simply continuing a custom going back many generations.

The site around the perimeter of the homestead foundations is still occupied by the traditional Zulu round huts, rather more spread out than they would have been in 1879, and inhabited now, as then, by the descendants of Sihayo's people.

Topography of the Battlefield

The hill of Isandlwana stands some 130 metres (400 feet) above the surrounding countryside and looks, from a distance, very much like what students of heraldry call a 'lion *couchant*': a crouching lion. Those of a more superstitious bent, both then and now, compare it to the very similar design of the collar badges of the 24th (2nd Warwickshire) Regiment of Foot: the representation of a sphinx.

The route of the track used by the Third Column to reach the hill in January 1879 varies little from the dirt road that now runs from Rorke's Drift, a distance of about eighteen kilometres, other than that it now crosses the 'nek', or saddle, north of the hill rather than that to the south.

The theory that a new road was constructed for the passage of the Third Column, advanced by some local tour guides, seems unlikely. Given the fact that this alleged new road, or the part that was new, was constructed in less than a week the possibility is more an improbability. The composition of this road is also unlike anything the British might have constructed, since a part of it is still crudely paved from local stone and goes straight uphill from bottom to top, rather than following the contours as might be expected. Furthermore, its direction would have taken it across the lower Batshe River, an area of wide marshland even now.

More probably, attention was given to the several passages across streams and dongas, and through their small swamps, which the recent rains had turned into quagmires: 'No. 3 column at Rorke's Drift cannot possibly move forward even eight miles until two swamps, into which our waggons sank up to the body, have been made passable.'[26]

Map 2, based on that prepared in November 1879 by Captain T.H. Anstey, RE, and entitled 'Military Survey of the Country Around Isandhlwana', demonstrates that the route taken by the column was more or less the same as that taken by the present road and this seems conclusive.

Approaching Isandlwana from the west, that is, from Rorke's Drift, the track descended into quite a steep valley, at the bottom of which the Manzimnyama stream trickles from left (north) to right (south), then climbed steadily for nearly a kilometre to reach the southern end of the hill. Here, the hill called Isandlwana is separated by a saddle, or *nek* less than two hundred metres wide from a lower prominence to the south named by the British 'Black's Koppie',[27] and by the Zulu Mahlabamkhosi. This *nek*, now a visitors' car park, was used as a wagon park for the camp.

Looking east from Isandlwana, a plain some eight or nine kilometres wide extends to the south-east for about thirteen kilometres, to a group of hills which include Silutshana and Magogo; behind these, at a distance of about twenty kilometres from the camp, stand the higher hills of Isiphezi and Phindo. (The Zulu army made its penultimate bivouac to the north-east of Isiphezi on the night of 20/21 January.) The track across the southern *nek* continued across the plain south-eastwards towards Ulundi.

The plain naturally drains to the south and is intersected by several dongas, or dry watercourses, which in times of heavy rain have eaten into the floor of the plain to leave steep, often vertical, banks. Such dongas are a feature of much of Zululand. The plain is also studded with several small hills, the most notable of which stands, like some perfect but extinct volcano, only 2.5 kilometres from Isandlwana, and barely a kilometre from the escarpment to its left. This was known as the 'Conical Koppie', but to the Zulu it was Amatutshane.[28]

The plain is bounded to the south by a large mass of high ground known as the Malakatha range, which includes Malakatha itself at the north-western end and the higher Hlazakazi in the south-east. Behind these, still further south, the Mangeni River runs in a deep gorge to its westward confluence with the Mzinyathi (Buffalo) River.[29] Tucked below the most south-eastern edge of Hlazakazi, the Mangeni drops over picturesque falls into the start of the gorge. It was this place, at a distance of some sixteen kilometres from Isandlwana, that Lord Chelmsford proposed as the site for the next camp, to be established after Isandlwana was left behind.

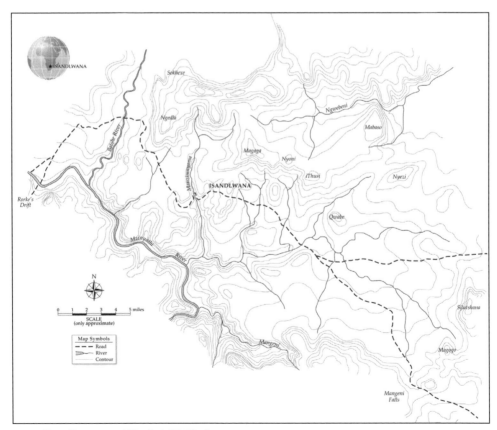

3 Isandlwana and Rorke's Drift Area

The northern side of the plain is bounded by an escarpment which rises sharply about 100 metres (about 330 feet) above the plain. Behind it, the plateau slopes gradually to the north-east, through the centre of which flows the rivulet of the Ngwebeni stream. Still further north more hills rise to the heights on which stands the small township of Nqutu.

At the eastern end of the lower plateau, the Ngwebeni stream suddenly turns south, taking a serpentine route between two hills which mark the eastern extremity of the plateau. The westernmost of these hills is Mabaso, the eastern edge of which drops suddenly into a steep ravine through which passes the stream before it turns north-east into more open country far to the north of Isiphezi Hill. This ravine, no more than ten kilometres from the Isandlwana camp as the crow flies, and the banks of the Ngwebeni further east, provided the site for the final Zulu bivouac on the night of 21/22 January.

Immediately to the north of Isandlwana itself lies another *nek* (over which the modern road now passes) about five hundred metres wide, which then rises as a spur joined to the plateau. The top of the spur is marked by a deceptively broad prominence known variously as Mkwene or Magaga, which lies at a distance of two kilometres from the northern *nek*, and which offers extensive views of the plateau behind the escarpment. Following the escarpment eastwards along its rim, two further prominences are found. First is the Nyoni ridge and still further east the rocks on the summit of Ithusi Hill stand like a cocks comb,[30] marking the point where the escarpment turns to run north-east, rather than east, towards Mabaso.

The camp was established some 150 metres from the eastern base of Isandlwana and extended right across its front to the south of the Ulundi track, a distance of about eight hundred metres. From north to south, the following units were camped in separate groups: 2/3rd NNC, 1/3rd NNC, 2/24th Regiment (seven companies), Royal Artillery (RA), Mounted Infantry and Volunteers. The camp of the 1/24th Regiment (five companies) was to the south of the track, on the eastern slope of Mahlabamkhosi. Behind each of these individual camps were parked regimental wagons, almost certainly including the vital ammunition reserve, which should have been easily identified by red flags attached to each wagon.[31]

The headquarters of the column, and Lord Chelmsford and his staff, were located between the hill and the camps, mid-way between the 2/3rd NNC and the mounted men. The hospital tent was located at the front of the southern *nek*, at the rear of the mounted men's camp. The remaining column wagons were formed into a wagon park on the southern *nek*.

The Zulu Impi

Virtually every study of the battle of Isandlwana on 22 January 1879 has given the names, and the roles, of the Zulu regiments which took part.[32] Some of them have addressed the issue quite specifically.[33] These attempts have enjoyed varying success. The Zulu army that confronted the camp at Isandlwana can be examined for four different characteristics: leadership, structure, numbers and deployment. This essay examines each of these four matters in some detail, so that the nature of the force that attacked the British camp can be better understood.

The Leadership

We should first examine the question of the Zulu leadership at Isandlwana. There are difficulties with our sources here because of the number of leaders named, and also the unfamiliarity of some forms of their names.[34] From the Zulu evidence, however, it is clear that paramount leadership lay with Ntshingwayo kaMahole,[35] supported by his lieutenant, Mavumengwana kaNdlela.[36] Other senior men are also named but were in subordinate positions commanding various regiments or sub-units:

> Cetywayo sent Untuswa to be his eyes, he was to place himself on some high ground and watch the battle.[37]
> Zibebu was there as a prince and also an induna, though a smaller one.[38]
> There were a few mounted men belonging to the chief Usirayo [Sihayo], who were made use of as scouts.[39]

Vumandaba kaMtati was said to have led the Mcijo regiment,[40] while the same source denies that Dabulamanzi kaMpande, King Cetshwayo's brother, was even present, even though he led the reserve regiments in the attack on Rorke's Drift later in the day.[41] Mehlokazulu kaSihayo was then only a young man and although his name has been given some prominence because of his widely quoted accounts of the battle, his was a relatively junior position in the Ngobamakhosi regiment.[42]

The Regiments

We should turn next to the composition of the Zulu army, in order to determine which regiments were engaged. In trying to make any sense of the multitude of names used by the Zulu to identify their military units, the researcher encounters substantial obstacles. In addition to their original given name, regiments were also given nicknames (*izithakazela*) and praise-names (*izibongo*), gathered as they progressed. Their name might also be derived from the military cantonment (*ikhanda*), or barracks at which they were based (or the reverse: an *ikhanda* name was often the locative form of the regimental name, e.g. the regimental name took the form *Uklebe*, and the *ikhanda* the locative form *Esiklebeni*). It could also be changed when a new king began his reign, or it might be absorbed into another unit to boost its declining numbers. At each of these stages, a different name might be used and it is here that the greatest difficulties arise. The Zulu generally state that as many as thirteen units were involved in the battle and these were as follows:

Zulu Units at Isandlwana

Units	A[43]	B[44]	C[45]	D[46]	E[47]	F[48]	G[49]	H[50]	I[51]
Nokhenkhe	√	√	√	√	√	√	√	√	√
Nodwengu	√		√	√		√		√	
Mbonambi	√	√	√	√	√	√	√	√	√
Mxapho[52]				√					
Ngobamakhosi	√	√	√	√	√	√	√	√	√
Mcijo[53]	√	√	√	√	√	√	√	√	√
Undi	√		√		√	√			
Dloko	√	√	√			√	√	√	√
Uve[54]	√		√	√	√				
Dududu		√							
Thulwana		√							
Indluyengwe		√							
Isangqu		√							

The problem that now arises is created by the amalgamation of regiments into so-called 'brigades' or 'corps'. The word 'corps' describes a group of regiments acting together rather than a single regiment.

As a regiment aged and its numbers diminished through death or illness, a younger regiment might be brigaded with it to bring it up to strength. This is why the table above apparently omits a number of regiments mentioned in our sources. As indicated above, a corps often took the name of its *ikhanda*, or cantonment, as is the case with the Nodwengu and Undi brigades here. We should now examine these two brigades in detail to see which regiments were incorporated in them, in order that we may complete our list of individual regiments. The regiments combined into corps are named in the following table.

Corps and their Regiments

Corps (*ikhanda*)	Regiment (*ibutho*)
Nodwengu	Isangqu[55]
	Dududu[56]
	Mbube
Undi	Thulwana
	Indlondlo
	Indluyengwe

As indicated above, these units took their brigade names from two *amakhanda* that stood on the Mahlabathini plain. (The former was the second Nodwengu *ikhanda* to be built there, the first being slightly further north, and the burial place of Cetshwayo's father Mpande kaSenzangakhona.) The latter, which name is more properly Ulundi, was the homestead of Cetshwayo and was also known as Ondini (the locative form of the proper noun Ulundi).[57]

This list should not be thought to be exhaustive; Julian Whybra also includes a number of other units which we should consider here. These are the Nkonkone, the Khulutshane and the Umsikaba.

The Nkonkone was incorporated into the Thulwana much earlier than 1879 and therefore should not be treated individually.[58]

The men of the Khulutshane were born *c.*1813 and formed by Dingane *c.*1833, making them sixty-six years of age in 1879.[59] Krige follows this but also says that it took part at Isandlwana.[60] This assertion must be based on her reference to Fynney, in which he assigns them to the Nodwengu corps, and who also, in a note, says that the latter took part at Isandlwana.[61] There is firmer Zulu evidence which says that it was incorporated into the older Imvoko, which was not at Isandlwana.[62] It would, in any case, have been too old to take part in this campaign.

The Umsikaba is given as an alternative name for Mpande's Mzinyathi regiment, a part of Mpande's Amaphela.[63] The Mzinyathi was listed by Fynney as part of the Uve but he also cites the Umsikaba separately to be a part of the Nodwengu corps. Worse, the regiment is nowhere mentioned in the *James Stuart Archive*. The only other reference I have been able to locate is a mention in a Zulu dictionary, where is said to be 'one of Mpande's regiments'.[64] If it was a regiment, and if it was present at all, the best we can do is to assign it, however small its representation might have been, to the Uve.

Whybra also names two obscure units, the Unqakamatye [Onqakamatshe] and the Umtulisazwi [Umthuyisazwe]. The first of these was an *isigaba*, or section, of the Mcijo,[65] while the second was one of the two wings or *uhlangothi* of the same regiment.[66]

Finally, Whybra includes the Umhlanga but this regiment is not mentioned anywhere in the *James Stuart Archive*, nor by Bryant or Krige. It is mentioned by Fynney[67] and by Samuelson,[68] but I rather suspect that it may not have existed at all, or was a section of another regiment.[69] It is not to be found in my Zulu dictionary. Its only Isandlwana reference in the primary sources is the now-discredited account of Zabange (see 'The Hazards of Primary Sources' earlier).

Finally, we can put this all together in a formal list of the regiments engaged:

Full List of Isandlwana Regiments

Corps	Regiment	Sub-units	Age[70]
	Nokhenkhe		33
	Mbonambi		31
	Mxapho		37
	Ngobamakhosi		28–30
	Dloko		40
	Uve	Umsikaba?	24–25
	Mcijo	Onqakamatshe	30
		Umthuyisazwe	
Nodwengu	Isangqu		46
	Dududu		39
	Mbube		39
Undi	Thulwana	Nkonkoni	44
	Indlondlo		41
	Indluyengwe		32

The Numbers

Let us now turn to estimates of the size of the Zulu *impi* or army at Isandlwana. A new regiment, or *ibutho* (pl. *amabutho*), was formed every few years as the number of young men became sufficient. The intakes were made up of youths of slightly differing ages, depending on the *intanga* (age group) to which they belonged as young boys. Each of these groups contained youths from every part of the country. Within the *ibutho*, boys were attached to an existing *iviyo* (company) or a new one was formed.

The Ngobamakosi. There were 80 companies *(viyos)* in this regiment. The *izinduna* grouped men in the *amaviyo*. These depended on numbers. They originated in cadetship. Thus members of a *viyo* grew up together . . . The *amaviyo* begin to be formed at the *amakanda*, but if small they may be added to by batches of others when they are called to headquarters, along with detachments from other *amakanda*.[71]

Each regiment was made up of two wings called *izinhlangothi*;[72] we will see shortly how these could be used separately in the example of the deployment of the Ngobamakhosi at Isandlwana. The regiment was further divided into sections called *izigaba* and into companies, or *amaviyo*. We cannot, however, be certain of the relationship between the *hlangothi* and *isigaba*, whether the latter were part of the former, or just an alternative sub-division. Mkando tells us that the Isangqu had only three *izigaba*.[73] We can say that, in the case of the Mcijo, there were twenty-three *amaviyo* in the *uhlangothi isicamelo* (left *uhlangothi*) and twenty-six *amaviyo* in the *isibaya esikhulu* (right and senior *uhlangothi*).[74] The two *izinhlangothi* were thus roughly equal in size with a total of forty-nine *amaviyo*.

It is with the *izigaba* and *amaviyo* that attempts to estimate the size of regiments must founder. Such estimates would be quite simple to calculate if their numbers were constant, but they were not. For example, Mtshapi lists twelve *izigaba* as being the full complement of the Ukandempemvu (Mcijo),[75] while Mpatshana describes the Undi corps as having five *izigaba* on the left side and six on the right side, a total of eleven.[76] Turning to the *amaviyo*, Mpatshana states: 'There were three to thirty *viyos* in an *isigaba*.'[77]

Furthermore, *amaviyo* varied in size from as few as forty men to as many as two hundred.[78] A more helpful range, given by a Zulu source, cites forty to fifty men,[79] with up to seventy men in those of the Ngobamakhosi.[80] With these variables, it is impossible to arrive at a definitive number of men in any specific regiment.

Finally, estimates are further confounded by the fact that an unknown proportion of each regiment at Isandlwana was absent. The reasons for this were twofold: either men failed to report to the king for some reason or part of a regiment remained elsewhere in the country; for example, while the Mxapho was said to be at Isandlwana, it was also present at the battle of Nyezane, which took place on the same day:[81] 'The force that was sent against Pearson was the Umpimga [Mpunga] regiment, plus the men belonging to other regiments who lived in the coast country.'[82]

Laband reminds us that the Ngobamakhosi, Thulwana, Mcijo and Mbonambi took part at both Khambula on 30 March and Gingindlovu on 2 April, although these two theatres were 160 kilometres (100 miles) apart.[83] Clearly, different elements of both regiments were used in each battle. Thus one might suggest that only 80 or 85 per cent of the full complement of the regiments may have fought at Isandlwana and probably much fewer of the Mxapho.

The only way to arrive at even a generous estimate is to use the iniquitous average. Thus, we might say that the average *iviyo* was composed of 45 men, with 70 for the Ngobamakhosi. We already know that the Mcijo had 49 *amaviyo*, and we can use Shilahla and Fynney for most of the remainder. This will give us the maximum number of men in each regiment available to fight. We know, too, that most of the Mxapho were at Nyezane and that perhaps another 15% of all warriors did not even appear at Ulundi. We therefore have to modify the numbers at Isandlwana accordingly:

Maximum and Likely Numbers of Men at Isandlwana

Regiment	Amaviyo	Maximum	Likely
Nokhenkhe	40	1,800	1,500
Mbonambi	40	1,800	1,500
Mxapho	15[84]	700	200
Ngobamakhosi	101	7,100[85]	6,000
Dloko	30	1,400	1,200
Uve	70	3,200	2,700
Mcijo	70	3,200	2,700
Isangqu[86]	6	300	250
Dududu[87]	20	900	800
Thulwana	50	2,300	2,000
Indlondlo	20	900	800
Indluyengwe	40	1,800	1,500
Total		23,600	21,150

A figure of about 21,000 is therefore not an unreasonable estimate for the size of the *impi*, of which some 5,500 made up the reserve, many of whom went on to attack Rorke's Drift.

Deployment
Let us now turn to the disposition of these regiments in the battle. They took their places in one of the four elements of classic Zulu deployment: the *isifuba* or chest, which occupied the centre (at Isandlwana, this may have comprised

two distinct groups), the two *izimpondo* or horns, which traditionally moved out from the centre to encircle the enemy (most importantly, one of the horns was often extended out of sight of the enemy, who would be unaware of their encirclement until it was too late) and lastly, the *umuva* or loins, which acted as a reserve. Each of these four elements is identifiable at Isandlwana, although their composition may be open to debate. We are fortunate to have the evidence of Zulus representing some of the regiments, and this gives vital information about how the regiments were deployed.

The Right Horn

By general consensus, the right horn consisted of the Nokhenkhe regiment and the Nodwengu corps, made up of the Isangqu, Dududu and Mbube.[88] This seems to disprove the theory that the horns were made up of the youngest men since the Nodwengu were all over forty years of age; on the other hand, it may simply reflect the apparent haste, imputed by some, with which the *impi* was brought to battle by its early discovery. The total involved was about 2,600 men.

The Chest

The chest or centre seems to have been divided into two groups, possibly because the Ngobamakhosi, being a very large regiment, was itself deployed as two separate wings. The right centre consisted of the Mxapho[89] and the Mcijo[90] regiments. Mhoti identifies his own unit as the 'Nxaka Matshe' (Onqakamatshe),[91] which was, as we have seen earlier, the senior wing of the Mcijo. This group crossed the plateau, constantly harassed by George Shepstone's two retreating mounted troops and the Natal Carbineers.

The disposition of the largest regiment, the Ngobamakhosi, is uncertain and it seems to have operated as two separate wings, one of which formed the left centre.

> There is a little red hill which overlooks Isandhlwana, within sight of the camp, and thence the Ngobamakosi, to which I belong, came in contact with two companies of mounted men. This was on the left, and about as far from the camp as the Court House is from Fort Napier; but we were on the height looking down. Some of these mounted men had White stripes up their trousers (Carbineers); there were also men dressed in black [Natal Mounted Police?], but none of the Native Contingent on the brow of this hill. The Ngobamakosi and Uve regiments attacked on this side.[92]

From the descriptions of Nzuzi and Uguku, the Uve regiment was a part of the left horn, but it is more likely that it was a part of the left centre.[93] These units moved along the escarpment and dropped down between the notch and the spur, confronting the left of the British camp. Taken together, the centre consisted of about nine thousand men.

The Left Horn

The second wing of the Ngobamakhosi formed a part of the left horn, attacking Durnford's group as they approached Qwabe ridge on the Isandlwana plain.[94] There is some confusion as to the precise whereabouts of the Mbonambi but none at all that they were a part of the left horn.[95] This being so, it is likely that they were the left-most unit.[96] There is also good evidence that some of the Undi corps, traditionally placed in the reserve, were also present in the left horn: 'On our left we were supported by the Umbonambi, half the Undi, Ngobamakosi, and Uve.'[97]

If this was so, then it is most likely to have been the young Indluyengwe regiment, who are known to have pursued the British troops down the Fugitives' Trail. After reaching the Mzinyathi River, some of the Indluyengwe crossed the river to rejoin their brigade in the fight at Rorke's Drift. This horn had a lot of ground to cover to both face and outflank the British right. It consisted of nearly six thousand men.

The Loins

The reserve consisted of the three regiments of the Undi corps (Thulwana, Indlondlo and Indluyengwe), together with the Dloko. However, we have already observed that the younger Indluyengwe were probably with the left horn, and so should not be treated as part of the reserve during the battle, although at least some of them rejoined their fellows later in the attack on Rorke's Drift. This would bring the reserve total down to about four thousand men.

Modern accounts of the movement of the remaining three reserve regiments state that they followed the right horn across the Nqutu plateau, turning south at the headwaters of the Manzimnyama stream to follow it down behind Isandlwana to the point where the stream intersected the track to Rorke's Drift, a point nearly a kilometre west of the hill. This tradition is based on the evidence offered by two Zulu informants. The first, and perhaps most important, was the 'Zulu deserter'. His statement has this to say:

> . . . the Undi corps and the Dloko formed a circle (as is customary in warfare when a force is about to be engaged) and remained where they were . . . these two corps, bore away to the northwest after a short pause, and, keeping on the southern side of the Sandhlwana, performed a turning movement on the right,

without any opposition from the whites, who, from the nature of the ground, could not see them.

The second statement comes from Umtegalalo, who states:

The Undi Corps, on seeing that the other four regiments had commenced the attack, as above, marched off to their right, and, without fighting, made for the north side of the Isandula Hill, being concealed by it until, their turning movement being completed, they made their appearance to the west of the Isandula at the spot where the waggon [*sic*] road crosses the neck.[98]

There are, however, both evidentiary and logical reasons why what has hitherto been regarded as a certainty may not be so. In common with all Zulu statements on which historians must rely, those above were subject to translation by white interpreters, and were often the result of interrogation by those same interpreters. It would not be unusual, therefore, to find at least parts of such statements to be confused, not only in their translation but in their interpretation. A case in point is given in the statement by the Nokhenkhe deserter: if the reserve was moving in the path of the right horn across the plateau, how then could they 'keep on the *southern* side of the Sandhlwana'?

The evidence of Umtegalalo is still more suspect. His version of affairs is brought into doubt by the unreliability of other parts of his statement; for example, by his placement of the Nokhenkhe in the centre, to the left of the Mcijo and on the right of the Mbonambi. In fact, he probably confuses the right horn with the reserve, and this may equally be true of the Nokhenkhe deserter.

Let us first consider the location of the reserve in their overnight bivouac. The Zulu deserter says that the order of encampment was: 'On the extreme right were the Nodwengu, Nokenke and Umcityu; the centre was formed by the Nkobamakosi and Mbonambi; and the left of the Undi Corps and the Dloko regiment.' This would place the reserve at the lower end of the Ngwebeni ravine, or still further downstream where the rivulet turns east into more open country, facing the Isandlwana plain, and not at the top or northern end of the Ngwebeni ravine, on the plateau.

Next, consider some contradictory evidence that may indicate this was not the route followed by the reserve: 'Behind us were the other half of the Undi and Dloko, who never came into action at Sandhlwana, but formed the reserve (which passed on and attacked Rorke's Drift).'[99] These words are ambiguous. Did Uguku mean that the reserve 'behind us' followed them towards the camp. If so, then the reserve also dropped down onto the plain, behind the Mcijo and did not completely cross the plateau. Alternatively, his words may mean that the reserve was behind them in the bivouac, indicating that they were indeed at the southern end of the ravine, or even further away.

More specific evidence is provided by Mehlokazulu kaSihayo, a junior induna with the Ngobamakhosi regiment: 'The men who fought at Rorke's Drift took no part at Isandhlwana; they were the men of the Undi regiment, who formed a portion of the left wing. When the camp at Isandhlwana had been taken these men came up fresh and pursued the fugitives right over the Fugitives' Drift into Natal.'[100]

The implication here seems to be that the reserve followed the route of the left horn, that is, across the plain, and not the plateau. Another witness is Commandant George Hamilton-Browne, who watched the battle from the plain with his 1/3rd battalion NNC. This is an extract, however, not from his book, but from his official report, dated 2 February 1879: 'During the whole engagement, I noticed large bodies of the enemy in reserve who never took part in the action.'[101]

Hamilton-Browne could not possibly have seen the reserve from his position on the plain had they been moving across the plateau and round the northern side of Isandlwana, indicating once more that the reserve could only be on the plain. Furthermore, he is given support in his view by an observer from the camp itself: 'I gave a look towards the front of the hill, towards where the General had gone in the morning, and saw a great many Zulus, evidently reinforcements, who were never in the fight.'[102]

The traditional deployment of the Zulu reserve, or 'loins', was to follow behind the 'chest' or centre and not one of the horns. One should note too that most of the reserve were not young men, three regiments being in their forties. This being so, since they allegedly arrived late at the bivouac and may have been camped as far as a mile behind the other regiments,[103] it seems odd that they would then travel up the Ngwebeni ravine to follow the stream across the plateau, and then turn south behind Isandlwana to reach this point, rather than simply cross the plain in the wake of the left horn.

This thesis is given modern support in an article discussing the 'Durnford Papers'.[104] A map of the Isandlwana battleground, seemingly annotated by Lieutenant Alfred Henderson of Hlubi's Troop of the Natal Native Mounted Contingent (NNMC), clearly shows the Undi corps and the Dloko regiment passing below Ithusi Hill on the plain, moving west towards Amatutshane and not on the plateau following the right horn. In a footnote to a discussion of the map, the authors wrote: 'There are a number of British accounts indicating a massive concentration behind the Zulu left horn, and a Zulu account that indicates that the concentration was part of the Undi corps.'[105]

The argument that, I believe, clinches the matter, is that it makes infinitely more sense if the reserve regiments were together crossing the plain behind the left horn, when the Indluyengwe, being much younger, linked up with it, while the older men remained behind. If this were not the case, one needs to explain how the Indluyengwe went to the left and the rest of the reserve went so far round to the right.

Finally, it is necessary to point out that it could not have been the reserve regiments that blocked the route to Rorke's Drift, thus forcing the fugitives to turn left from the *nek* and find their way over a very rough five kilometres to the Mzinyathi River. If one supposes that they did indeed move across the plateau behind the right horn, the distance they had to travel would have been such as to prevent them arriving at the Manzimnyama stream behind Isandlwana until it was too late to have performed such a function. The men who did this were those of the right horn itself.

To conclude, this paper has argued that the Zulu army at Isandlwana consisted of eight units, some of which were brigades consisting of multiple regiments. There was a total of thirteen individual regiments involved, numbering, as best we can estimate, about 21,000 men. The leaders of the *impi* were Ntshingwayo kaMahole, and Mavumengwana kaNdlela, with other *izinduna*, including Sihayo kaXongo, in lesser roles. Dabulamanzi kaMpande was not involved in the battle proper, being in command of the reserve, although he later went on to lead his regiments across the Mzinyathi River to attack the post at Rorke's Drift.

We have also been able to show the part played in the battle by each regiment, and to resolve some of the difficulties brought about by inconsistencies in our sources. Perhaps more importantly, a credible argument has been advanced that places the reserve on the Isandlwana plain and not on the plateau, as has hitherto been generally believed.

The Zulu Bivouac

In common with many others who have studied the Anglo-Zulu War, this writer has found the battle at Isandlwana a fascinating complexity of riddles. There are a substantial number of first-hand accounts by eye-witnesses, but often these accounts present further problems whilst shedding only a little light on the initial issues. Among the enigmas of that day, the identification of the location of the Zulu bivouac during the night before the battle might seem a trivial matter but its resolution will shed important light on the points of attack subsequently developed by the Zulu army.

We should perhaps begin by comparing the secondary narratives. These have identified the location of the bivouac as almost anywhere along the Ngwebeni stream. This rivulet rises some four kilometres north of Isandlwana hill and trickles for about six kilometres east across the Nqutu plateau, which itself falls gradually to the north-east. (Thus far, it has run roughly parallel to the escarpment of the plateau to the south.) At this point, its flow is interrupted by a gentle horseshoe curve round the north side of Mabaso hill, then turns south-east, squeezing through a narrow defile between Mabaso and another hill to the north, after which it resumes its north-eastern flow. There is thus a distance of more than eight, even ten, kilometres along the Ngwebeni where the *impi* might have rested.

The first modern opinion to be considered is as follows: 'Before sunset they had reached their objective, a rocky, bushy valley close under the north-east slope of the Ngutus about five miles from Isandhlwana and, of course, completely hidden from it.'[106]

Not very specific, but certainly sufficient to identify the Ngwebeni ravine. Next:

> It is true that there was no Zulu army in the vicinity [of Isandlwana] on the 15th, but on the 20th, as the British force began to set up their tents in a neat line 150 yards from the base of the mountain, the Zulu army was moving into the deep horseshoe-shaped valley of the Ngwebeni River four to five miles north-east of the camp.[107]

John Laband expressed the location in even more specific terms: 'During the evening of 21 January the army moved in small detached bodies to the steep and rocky Ngwebeni valley, which abruptly opens up under the Mabaso heights.'[108]

A less orthodox opinion was put forward by David Jackson: 'On the 21st . . . the "impi" moved westwards across the Nondweni valley and took up a position for the night along a glen running east and west in the Nqutu hills, the head lying three miles north of the camp but hidden from it by the escarpment and the plateau already mentioned.'[109]

The final example is diametrically opposed to that given by Laband and, by implication, Coupland and Droogleever, and is more unorthodox even than Jackson. The author suggested that new evidence[110] demonstrates that:

> . . . the Zulu army was not camped *en masse* in a gorge on the northern side of the Nqutu Plateau, but was bivouacked, in regiments, over a distance of about

four miles, all along the Nqutu Hills and the regiments attacked in the same strung-out line as that in which they were bivouacked. This would explain why the Zulu army appeared with such speed, already fanned out four miles wide, to encircle the camp.[111]

So much for modern narratives. It can be seen that there is a wide divergence of opinion on this matter but what is the evidence? Those who would have known best were the warriors who took part and we have some evidence of that location in their own words: 'On the 21st, keeping away to the eastward, we occupied a valley running north–south under the spurs of the Ngutu Hill, which concealed the Sandhlwana Hill, distant from us about four miles and nearly due west of our encampment.'[112]

And again: 'We slept the night before the battle in a valley rising from the Ngutu range, and running eastward towards the King's kraal.'[113]

Although the directions of the valley seem here to be contradictory, given the serpentine nature of the Ngwebeni around Mabaso hill, and the extensive character of the Zulu bivouac, the apparent inconsistency is easily forgiven.

The Zulu order of encampment is given by the Zulu deserter: the Nokhenkhe regiment was on the right, that is, it would have been one of the leading elements and would have had a position at the northern end of the ravine of the Ngwebeni, directly under Mabaso. The Ngobamakhosi regiment on the other hand, to which Mehlokazulu belonged, was a part of the left centre and would thus have been located towards the rear of the bivouac, where the Ngwebeni turns right to flow towards the north-east. Mehlokazulu would naturally, therefore, describe the valley as lying east–west.[114]

In a more recent publication, Ron Lock has resiled from his earlier position and has embraced the more orthodox view as to the location of the bivouac.[115] On the other hand, while not specifically referring to the bivouac, the latest offering of David Jackson indicates no such change of mind: 'Although new information has come to light in the interval, I have seen nothing that has significantly altered my previous interpretations.'[116]

He then locates the bivouac precisely where he placed it in 1965.[117] It is perhaps desirable to pause here and look more closely at the reason for Jackson's reluctance to accept the overwhelmingly preponderant view. His opinion is largely based on the evidence of two maps which form a part of what are known as the 'Durnford Papers',[118] held by the Royal Engineers Museum at Chatham. The conflation of the two original maps[119] into one in this article shows the alleged points of origin of the various regiments and, sure enough, they appear to be along the upper Ngwebeni Valley. The difficulty is, however, that the alleged author of the marking of the maps, Lieutenant A.F.

Henderson, commanded Hlubi's troop of the Native Mounted Contingent, and thus was with Lieutenant-Colonel Durnford on the plain. He could not, therefore, have had first-hand knowledge of the bivouac. One must assume, then, that Henderson was working with second-hand information since he could not have actually observed the position for himself.

Secondly, there is no reason why the map, as allegedly marked by Henderson, should not show apparent points of departure, rather than the real ones. It is almost certain that at some point during the subsequent attack, the regiments identified on the map would have passed near or through the points indicated, as part of their envelopment of the British force; if, as one must suppose, Henderson had drawn his information from his surviving fellow officers, then they may have assumed the Zulu bivouac to be what was, in fact, reported to be their position near the time of their discovery, while the truth is that those two places may well have been widely separated. The matter of the discovery of the Zulu army is of such crucial importance that its discussion has been deferred to a subsequent paper.

Next, a consideration of British forward observation. One of the maps to which reference has already been made has the title 'Military Survey of the Battle-Field of Isandhlwana'. This map shows the location of the vedettes, pairs of mounted Volunteers placed on prominent hills at a distance from the camp in order to warn of an approaching enemy.

Three vedettes were posted on the edge of the escarpment: from west to east, on Magaga Hill, the Nyoni ridge and on Ithusi Hill,[120] and a fourth on an unnamed prominence a mile or so south-east of Isandlwana.[121] Lieutenant Scott, Natal Carbineers, commanding the vedettes, and presumably with at least one other of his men, was located on Amatutshane. This hill, known then as the 'Conical Koppie', was never a good position for a vedette proper, since its peak lies below the level of the escarpment eight hundred metres to the north. It was, however, the perfect location for a command post, being able to see every vedette, and to be seen by them. The information on the map, however, is actually incomplete because it accounts for only four of the vedettes. Another vedette was posted further out on the plain directly in front of the camp. The post was beyond the range of the map, on Qwabe ridge, and Troopers Barker and Hawkins were located here.[122] Based on the evidence of the Mansel letter, another was located on a low prominence to the south-east of Isandlwana and this was probably the one shown on the Anstey map.

Lock states that the furthest vedettes were pulled back towards the camp. This assertion, he says, is supported by the testimony of Inspector Mansel of the Natal Mounted Police, in the letter to which reference has already been made.[123] This is not quite the case: what Mansel actually says is that he was ordered by Major Clery, staff officer to Colonel Glyn, to draw in the furthest vedettes, because in Clery's opinion, 'they were too far out'. Mansel began to comply but only went to the vedette to the right front to bring it closer to the camp. There he was diverted by the capture of an old Zulu, and the vedette positions were not changed. On the day of the battle, the vedettes appear to have been posted as they were the day before, with advanced vedettes on Qwabe ridge and Ithusi Hill.[124]

Next, consider the physical space that the *impi* would have required in bivouac, setting the minimum size of the army at an arbitrary twenty thousand, a figure which is generally accepted. Each warrior would have been armed with his shield, stabbing assegai, several throwing spears and perhaps a firearm of some description. In addition, there would have been at least some cattle to sustain the warriors. It is not, therefore, too much to demand an average area of about five square metres per warrior (or a square of a little over two metres (seven feet) a side). Simple arithmetic will then derive an area of some 100 hectares as the minimum area to contain this multitude. Looked at another way, assuming a depth of fifty warriors, the area required to contain the *impi* would be approximately 110 metres by 900 metres. This is not a small area, being almost as large as that occupied by the British camp, and not a small number of warriors to conceal.[125]

If one excludes any areas of bush or trees, of which there are precious few on the Nqutu plateau today, there is a view north to the Ngwebeni stream from two of the three vedette posts on the edge of the escarpment, the single exception being that on Magaga.[126] In particular, a vedette posted on Ithusi Hill would have had a perfect field of view to the hills which rise to the north on the other side of the stream. Would a sensible army commander place his men in such an exposed position for even a short time? The answer is: almost certainly not.

There is a large area of dead ground to the east of the Ithusi ridge, unseen from the Nyoni ridge, but open to the view of a vedette on Ithusi itself. Only to the north-east, where the stream flows behind Mabaso Hill, would their scrutiny be hindered. This area is sufficiently remote and sufficiently large to conceal the *impi* because immediately below Mabaso, the narrow valley (the 'ravine') opens up to a considerable extent, and could hold the army with ease, being in excess of two kilometres long.

From the Zulu point of view, the *impi* commanders would have chosen a secure location for the bivouac, where their presence would remain undetected. The principal reason for such caution is that originally the army was to rest there for two nights, it being stated by many Zulu participants that the attack would not take place on 22 January due to the inauspicious new moon.[127] (The reason for the delay was *not* the eclipse which occurred during the afternoon of the 22nd.[128]) The bivouac, therefore, had to be far enough away from the British camp to remain undetected by both the vedettes and any mounted patrols, while at the same time being close enough to enable a sudden descent on the camp. The Zulu leaders were far from being fools and the British camp would have been under close observation by their scouts from the moment the troops arrived. These same scouts would have noted the placement of vedettes and piquets, and the movement of any patrols. The original Zulu plan, then, was to remain hidden during the daylight hours of 22 January and to advance along the upper Ngwebeni stream during the following night to launch an attack on the camp on the morning of the 23rd.[129]

Next, let us consider distance. David Jackson does not explain how the Zulu were able to be in front (to the east) of Colonel Durnford after he had left the camp and travel a distance which we may estimate at some nine kilometres, arriving somewhat to the west of the Nyezi ridge.[130] If the Zulu were attacking the camp at Isandlwana from anywhere along a four-mile position along the upper Ngwebeni stream, not one warrior would have chosen to go via the southern side of Mabaso Hill.

Finally, we should return to the maps we have identified earlier. The second map is a companion to the first and is entitled 'Military Survey of the Country around Isandhlwana'.[131] This map clearly shows the location of the hidden Zulu force, using the identifier 'a.a.a.a.'. This is noted in the references as 'Valley in which the Zulu army bivouacked on the night of Jan'y 21st–22nd'. This is, I submit, irrefutable evidence of the location of the bivouac.

On the basis of all the evidence then, it would seem that the orthodox view should prevail. There is no evidence that the Zulu bivouac was anywhere other than where the Zulu said it was: in the Ngwebeni ravine behind Mabaso Hill.

Chapter 3

Isandlwana: Proelium

And you, good yeomen
Whose limbs were made in England, show us here
The mettle of your pasture.

Shakespeare, Henry V

Discovery of the Zulu Impi

This paper had its genesis in my inability to reconcile modern accounts of the discovery of the Zulu *impi* at Isandlwana with the primary sources, both Zulu and British.[1] The publication of a quite recent work on the battle of Isandlwana, however, and its re-examination of some of the evidence,[2] suggested that the discovery occurred elsewhere than the place advanced by more orthodox writers. This proved to be the catalyst for my own investigation into this vexing question.

The paper, then, attempts to determine the actual location of the discovery, based not only on the primary evidence but on the use of that crucial factor, time. The writer must state, as a prerequisite, that it is his opinion that the location of the Zulu bivouac on the night of 21/22 January 1879, was to be found in the ravine of the Ngwebeni stream, behind Mabaso Hill, and extending south then east along the stream from that point.[3]

The misconception concerning the discovery of the Zulu army is propagated in most modern narratives, which do little either to elucidate or eliminate the obscurity, merely echoing the error from one original source. Consider the following from Morris:

> For a time all was quiet. Then a group of Raw's men saw a few Zulu herding a small group of cattle up a slope some distance ahead. Kicking up their horses, they gave chase. The slope was a full four miles from the head of the spur, and

they were soon out of sight of Cavaye's men and most of their companions. The Zulu herders ran over the crest of the slope and disappeared, and the cattle slowed on the rise and stopped. One of the pursuers cantered up beside them, and in sudden alarm pulled his horse up just in time to prevent a tumble over the edge of a wide, deep ravine that lay just beyond the rise. Then, in astonishment, he stared into the ravine itself. Closely packed and sitting in utter silence, covering the floor of the ravine and perched on the steeply rising sides, stretched as far as the eye could see in both directions, were over 20,000 Zulu. The main impi had finally been located.[4]

The prose is perfect and the drama exemplary, but how much of it is substantiated by the evidence? Precious little, to be brutally frank. The fundamental error made by Morris was to assume that the discovery of the Zulu *impi* was made in the place in which it had bivouacked overnight, and this assumption has been followed by virtually every writer on the battle since 1965.[5]

David Jackson almost gets it right by sticking to the primary sources, but, in my humble opinion, he misinterprets the evidence before him by suggesting that the Zulu bivouac was to the north of the camp, on the upper Ngwebeni stream.[6] He is, however, only able to make his view of the primary evidence of the discovery fit the events by altering the location of the bivouac.

Shortly after his arrival at the Isandlwana camp, Colonel Anthony Durnford despatched two troops of Zikhali's Horse to reconnoitre the plateau to the north-east. The African horsemen were led by their troop commanders, Lieutenants Raw and Roberts under the command of Captain William Barton, commanding Zikhali's Horse.[7] They were accompanied by Captain George Shepstone, political assistant to Colonel Durnford (and unofficial chief staff officer), and his friend James Hamer, a civilian storekeeper with Durnford's force.[8] After some time pursuing their patrol, the discovery of the Zulu army took place but not, I suggest, as described by Morris. Let us review the primary evidence.

First, the official version, distilled from the only three eye-witness accounts:

It appears that Lieutenant Raw's troop of Basutos, which had been sent out to reconnoitre on the high ground north of the camp, had, after going some 3 or 4 miles, come on a herd of cattle which they had followed over a small rising ground. From the top of this they had seen the Zulu army about a mile off advancing in line, and extending towards its left.[9]

How is it possible to reconcile Morris's assertion that an observer saw them immediately below him in a ravine, 'sitting in utter silence', with this statement, which says they were seen a mile away and advancing in line?

Lieutenant Charles Raw's account of the event is as follows: 'We left camp, proceeding over the hills, Captain George Shepstone going with us. The enemy in small clumps retiring before us for some time, drawing us four or five miles from the camp when they turned and fell upon us, the whole army showing itself from behind the hill in front where they had evidently been waiting.'[10]

This statement makes no mention of a ravine, simply of a hill behind which the Zulu army was concealed. The distance of 'four or five miles' should also be noted, because the lip of Mabaso is more than six miles (ten kilometres) from Isandlwana as the crow flies, and the patrols were no crows.

Next, the account of James Hamer, who had ridden out in company with Captain George Shepstone and Lieutenant Raw, and was thus very close to the point of discovery:

> Very soon after the Mounted Native Horse had arrived they were sent out to cover [the] hills on the left of the Camp, Captain George Shepstone in command. I went along with him, and after going some little way, we tried to capture some Cattle. They disappeared over a ridge, & on coming up we saw the Zulu, like <u>Ants</u>, in front of us, in perfect order as quiet as mice & stretched across in an even line. We estimated those we saw at 12000.[11]

Once again, this does not in any way describe the discovery of an army concealed in a narrow, steep-sided valley; he says that the Zulu were 'in front of us', not 'below us', and nor does the phrase 'some little way' describe a spot over six miles off.

Finally, the evidence of Nyanda, a senior African non-commissioned officer of Roberts' troop, and himself a brother of Zikhali: 'We saw a handful (not many) of Zulu, who kept running from us. All of a sudden, just as Mr. Shepstone joined me on the crest of a ridge, the army of Zulu sprung up 15,000 men (if all there according to Mr. Drummond and Mr Longcast, interpreters).'[12]

Morris wants us to believe that a trooper looked into the steep-sided Ngwebeni Valley and saw the Zulu army camped below. In the only accounts by eye-witnesses, the evidence points to the mounted troop or troops crossing a ridge and finding the Zulu extended across their front, at some considerable distance, an impossible interpretation for a mass of warriors in a deep ravine only some seventy metres (220 feet) below them.

There is also a geographical difficulty: there is almost no 'slope' or 'rise' when approaching Mabaso from the south-west, the direction from which Raw and/or Roberts would have come, as any map will disclose. Mabaso, for all intents and purposes, is essentially a plateau until it drops down into the Ngwebeni ravine. It therefore becomes necessary to find a solution more compatible with the evidence.

When the Zulu army left Ulundi on 17 January,[13] its generals, Ntshingwayo kaMahole and Mavumengwana kaNdlela, could not have known that their adversary would set up his camp at Isandlwana, since the British did not begin the march from the left bank of the Mzinyathi River until the morning of the 20th. Their first inkling would have been later on the 20th when the Zulu were nearing Isiphezi and the Isandlwana camp was being established. Zulu observers would have reported the site of the camp almost concurrently with the planting of the first tent-pole. The Zulu leaders, established in their penultimate bivouac on the northern flank of Isiphezi, would then have given serious consideration to attacking the camp from the hills in the north-east because a direct approach across the plain would have been suicidal. It would also be an unexpected quarter from which an assault might be launched, as subsequently proved to be the case.

The suggestion that an attack into Natal be made through the Mangeni Valley, thus cutting off the British force from its supply base, presumably Rorke's Drift,[14] was probably never seriously considered by the Zulu leaders, if only because it would have involved crossing the Mzinyathi River, which Cetshwayo had specifically forbidden them to do.[15]

The departure of Dartnell's mounted men and the 3rd Regiment, NNC on their 'reconnaissance in force' on the morning of the 21st, innocent though it might have seemed, was the first step in the division of Chelmsford's force. The subsequent actions of Matshana kaMondisa and his people during the late afternoon effectively screened the movement of the Zulu army, in small groups at a time, from Isiphezi to the Ngwebeni Valley behind Mabaso Hill. (There is no evidence to support the view that Matshana was acting under the orders of the Zulu leaders to create a diversion to hoodwink the British, although the results of his actions were entirely the same.) This movement of the *impi* in small groups prolonged the time taken to complete the movement until late in the day, many arriving at the Ngwebeni after dark.[16] The most serious outcome, however, was Dartnell's decision to remain out of the camp overnight on Hlazakazi Hill, at the south-eastern end of the Malakatha range of hills, Commandant Lonsdale consenting to keep the NNC with him – this despite Chelmsford's order that they return to the camp before day's end.[17]

The closest the British came to an early discovery of the Zulu force was the patrol made by Lieutenant E.S. Browne with elements of the Mounted Infantry on the same morning.[18] Penetrating almost as far as Isiphezi itself, Browne's patrol was fired upon by groups of Zulu but he failed to recognise the army for what it was because it was split into small groups of men, widely dispersed.

A number of Zulu accounts state that the attack was planned for the morning of Thursday 23 January because the 22nd was considered a day of ill-omen due to the 'dead' or new moon.[19] Too much emphasis should not be placed upon this factor because on that same day Godide kaNdlela attacked Colonel Pearson's first column at Nyezane. Nevertheless, we must assume that initially the Zulu did not intend to attack the Isandlwana camp until 23 January and accordingly the warriors were not doctored as would otherwise have been the case.[20]

Imagine Ntshingwayo's astonishment, then, when at dawn on the 22nd, Chelmsford led six companies of the 2/24th, four guns and the Mounted Infantry to rendezvous with Dartnell at the base of the bare shoulder of Hlazakazi, some eleven kilometres (seven miles) from the camp, still further dividing his forces. The Zulu commanders saw the camp almost entirely deprived of its most formidable weapon, the mounted soldiers, and half of the infantry. No wonder that a group of unnamed Zulu chiefs was moved to say, after the battle: 'You gave us the battle that day . . . for you dispersed your army in small parties all over the country.'[21]

In so doing, Chelmsford also overlooked a promise he had made to himself the previous day: he would no longer make a thorough reconnaissance of the plateau to the north-east.[22] But it really was no longer necessary that he do so: he thought he now knew where the Zulu *impi* was, and set out to attack it.

A new thesis advanced in Lock and Quantrill's work argues that the battle began in the early morning of the 22nd, when the two furthest vedettes were driven from their posts, and, despite a forlorn attempt by their commander, Lieutenant F.J.D. Scott of the Natal Carbineers, never regained them.[23] As the authors state, two vedettes were indeed driven from their posts but I believe that they were on Ithusi Hill and the Qwabe knoll.[24] The Zulu thereby gained control of the dead ground between the Mabaso and Ithusi hills, and also the Isandlwana plain to the south-east of Mabaso as far as Qwabe. This allowed a still closer Zulu approach to the camp.

From this point, Lock and Quantrill's thesis that the battle had now begun founders on its biggest problem. Apart from movements observed from the camp which caused the troops to stand-to on two occasions, the battle proper did not commence until about noon. Why, if Ntshingwayo now had the initiative, did he not then continue his attack, rather than waiting for another five hours?[25]

The most recent synthesis of the battle suggests that the right horn moved out of the Ngwebeni ravine about 7 a.m. on the 22nd, leaving the remainder of the *impi* behind.[26] This movement was necessary in order to reduce the time it would take the regiments assigned to that wing to reach their final objective, the rear of the Isandlwana hill, and to allow them the necessary frontage. Mike Snook also insists that 'the further west its start point was the better: otherwise the route from Ngwebeni would be over fourteen kilometres in length.' This argument, surely, applies equally to the rest of the army in the valley, which would have to travel almost as far?

Snook argues that it was during this time that the right wing relocated to 'its own place of concealment behind the Ngedla heights'.[27] He too uses Barker's account to substantiate this movement, citing Whitelaw:[28] 'Whitelaw reported a large army advancing, "thousands" I remember him distinctly stating, and he was immediately sent back to camp with the report. This would be about eight a.m.'[29]

Their route from their 'place of concealment' was to be via the headwaters of the Manzimnyama stream, then following its course down to their final position about a kilometre west of Isandlwana. This would place them in an ideal position to closely invest the camp in combination with the left horn, which would cross the plain to close the pincer.

If, as I have suggested, Whitelaw and his partner were on Ithusi Hill, then he may well have seen the Zulu moving from the Ngwebeni ravine to take up new positions, but one wonders whether the right horn ever reached the Ngedla heights, if that was indeed their destination. In my opinion, they were simply observed advancing west along the Ngwebeni stream. There is some evidence for this view in the statement of Mehlokazulu.[30]

In the morning [of the 22nd] Tsingwayo called me and said, 'Go with three other indunas and see what the English are doing.' I called the indunas and started off at a good pace. We were all mounted. When we got to the range of hills looking on to Isandhlwana, we could see the English outposts (mounted men) quite close to us, and could also see the position of their camp. The outposts evidently saw us, for they commenced to move about,[31] and there seemed to be a bustle in the camp, as some were inspanning the wagons, and others were getting in the oxen. We immediately went back, and I reported what I had seen to our commander, Tsingwayo, who said, 'All right, we will see what they are going to do!' I went away and had something to eat, as I had had no food that morning. Presently I heard Tsingwayo give orders for the Tulwana and Ngyaza [?] regiments to assemble. When they had done so he gave orders for the others to assemble and advance in the direction of the English camp.

This statement makes it clear that it was not only the right horn (to which the Thulwana belonged) that moved: some of the other regiments also began to move forward. There is no doubting the place to which they were to move; it was not to be the Ngedla heights but the dead ground between the Mabaso and Ithusi hills and almost certainly onto the eastern end of the plain behind Nyezi. They seem not to have moved in any numbers towards Nyezi until about 8.30 a.m.[32] Further evidence of this forward movement from the ravine, if more is needed, is provided once again by Trooper Barker. After Whitelaw had returned from reporting his sighting,

> . . . numbers of Zulus being seen on all the hills to the left and front, Trooper Swift and another were sent back to report. The Zulus then remained on the hills, and about two hundred of them advanced to within three hundred yards of us, but on our advancing they retired out of sight, and a few of us went up to this hill [Ithusi?] where the Zulus had disappeared, and on a farther hill, at about six hundred yards' distance, we saw a large army sitting down . . . Hawkins and I were then sent back to camp to report a large army to the left front of the camp.[33]

Lieutenant Higginson, NNC, also saw large groups of Zulu on the plateau just before 10 a.m.: 'We found Captain Barry and Lieutenant Vereker watching some Zulus about half a mile from them in the plain before stated; we also saw large bodies of natives on the hills to the left front of the 2nd Battalion Natal Native Contingent. I remained there about half an hour watching the Zulus and then we returned.'[34]

The Zulu plan, I now believe, was to invest the camp more closely by moving out of the Ngwebeni Valley to occupy the newly created dead ground east of Ithusi and its northward ridge until the early morning of the 23rd.

Mid-morning the defect in the Zulu plan emerged: the camp was not to remain devoid of mounted men. Colonel Durnford arrived about 10.30 a.m. with, among others, five troops of the Natal Native Mounted Contingent, which included the three Basuto troops of Zikhali's Horse. Almost immediately, and as a result of the disturbing reports given to him by Lieutenant-Colonel Pulleine, Durnford sent back Lieutenant Wyatt Vause with one troop of Zikhali's Horse to provide additional security for his baggage train.[35] Perhaps half an hour later, needing more information to resolve conflicting reports from the plateau, and to remove a Zulu threat which seemed to be getting out of control, he sent out the two remaining troops of Zikhali's Horse with their commanding officer, Captain William Barton. As we have seen earlier, while Barton went with Lieutenant Roberts' troop, Captain Shepstone and his friend Hamer accompanied that of Lieutenant Raw.

Before his own departure eastward across the plain with the remainder of his command, Durnford despatched Lieutenant Higginson to the plateau for a second time, to pass on orders to Barton and Shepstone to support Durnford's proposed advance. Higginson never reached them:

> I rode off, followed by Serjeant-Major Williams, and on getting into the plain on the other side of the hill we saw the mounted Contingent about a mile from us; on coming within 200 yards of them I saw Captain Barry, with some of his outlying picquet, and at the same time saw a large number of Zulu coming from the rocks at the foot of the hill facing us. [36]

David Jackson estimates that Higginson would have taken about twenty minutes to reach Shepstone, riding at sixteen kilometres (ten miles) an hour.[37] Sir Garnet Wolseley estimated similar travel times by horse: '. . . when going at a good pace, a horse trots easily 8½ miles an hour . . . the gallop is at the rate of 12 miles an hour.'[38]

This gives us an opportunity to determine where Jackson thought Shepstone then was, because the distance Higginson could have travelled in that time must have been only about five kilometres. Examination of a map places his furthest point of travel near the ridge north of Ithusi Hill almost immediately after the discovery of the Zulu army, and nowhere near Mabaso.

Consider next the time taken for Higginson to return to the camp to warn Pulleine. He arrived at the same time as Captain Gardner, between noon and 1 p.m. A more exact time would be shortly after noon, about 12.10 p.m. If the discovery occurred just before noon, say about 11.50 a.m., how then could Higginson have ridden a distance of perhaps eleven kilometres (almost seven miles) in twenty minutes, a speed calculated to be thirty-three kilometres (twenty miles) an hour? General Wolseley, in the quotation above, gives the speed of the gallop as only twelve miles an hour.[39] Assuming Higginson began at Ithusi, however, he rode only about six kilometres (nearly four miles), and his speed was a much more acceptable eighteen kilometres (eleven miles) an hour. This surely is further proof that the discovery could not have occurred on the lip of Mabaso Hill ravine, which is five kilometres further to the north-east of Ithusi.

From the evidence previously reviewed, the mounted men had climbed a slight rise, but it was not Mabaso, as has previously been generally accepted (since there is little perceptible rise there) but the ridge extending north from Ithusi Hill. This is amply demonstrated by a statement of Henry Francis Fynn jr.: 'They observed the Zulu showing over a cock's comb rocky side of a ravine from the north-westerly direction (Sanhlwana being on the south from that point) and fired upon them. It was the Zulu army there concealed, and their plans thus disturbed, they rose like swarms of bees.'[40]

Ithusi has a prominent cock's comb rocky peak which overlooks the Isandlwana plain, but it also consists of a lower L-shaped ridge which stretches back several hundred metres across the plateau.[41] Furthermore, the view east from the Ithusi ridge gives one the impression of looking into a very broad valley stretching to Mabaso Hill, such is the height of the ridge above the eastern side of the plateau.

Despite what Fynney states in his contribution, Raw's men did not fire first. Both Raw himself and Nyanda both state that the Zulu fired on them, they returning their fire immediately afterwards. One must here question whether the Zulu, deep in the Ngwebeni ravine, would have been able to see, let alone fire at Morris' solitary figure above them, obscured as he would have been by the lip of the ravine.

There is still one more piece of evidence to place before the reader. Two maps were found by the writer in the Campbell Collections (previously Killie Campbell Africana Library) in Durban.[42] These are copies of the well-known map of 'The Country around Isandhlwana' by Anstey and Penrose of November 1879. They are here numbered 1 and 2. Both of these maps are annotated in pencil, some of which has been written over in ink. They are almost identical to the two other maps in the Royal Engineers Museum in Chatham,[43] which were the subject of the paper by David Jackson and Julian Whybra written more than twenty years ago.[44] (These maps were numbered 1 and 3.)

Jackson and Whybra attributed the handwritten notes on the maps to Lieutenant Alfred Henderson, who commanded the Hlubi Troop of the Natal Native Mounted Contingent, a part of Colonel Durnford's Second Column. It seems more likely that the notes were written by Evelyn Wood when he accompanied the French dowager Empress Eugénie during her memorial tour of South Africa in 1880, which included a visit to the Isandlwana battlefield as well as the site of her son's death.[45]

The new map 2 is the most significant because, like the Chatham map 1, it shows the locations of what purport to be Zulu bivouacs to the north of the Ngwebeni stream stretching in an arc from a point due north of Isandlwana to a second point to the north-west of Mabaso Hill. The westernmost unit is identified as the Nodwengu brigade and those at the easternmost are

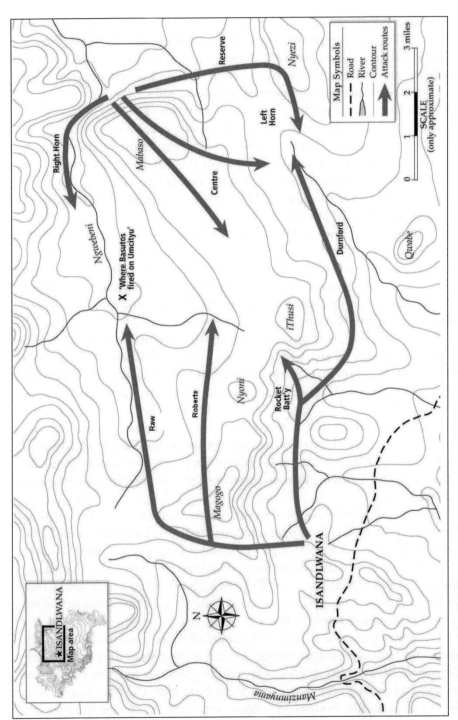

4 Discovery of the Zulu Impi

identified as the Undi and Uve. The map also shows an 'x' marked at a point below the centre of the arc on the southern side of the Ngwebeni. Unlike the Chatham map 3, however, this one has extensive handwritten notes down the right-hand side which explain the notations. The first three of these are relevant to our discussion of the discovery:

> The Zulu pointed out exactly the position of the Nodwengu in bivouac near a mealie garden, and indicated generally the remainder. The third line a.a shows the intended movements. The dotted lines that actually followed.
> x. I believe about where the Basutos fired on the Umcityu.[46]
> The Zulus attacked exactly as they bivouacked – all in line of Regiment except the Undi Corps which was ½ a mile in left rear of Ngobamakosi in bivouac and action.[47]

One might conjecture, from the Chatham maps, that the source of the information on the map was one or more of the three survivors from the plateau, Raw, Hamer or Nyanda – Raw being the most likely. This is no longer the case, at least for the first entry, which is attributed to an unknown 'Zulu'.

An explanation of the 'x' shown below the arc of Zulu regiments is also given, the annotator believing that point to be 'about where the Basutos fired on the Umcityu'. If the map is to be believed, it is certainly clear that the discovery of the Zulu army did not take place in the ravine below Mabaso Hill.

The notation continues by stating that the positions marked by the arc of Zulu regiments show the location of their bivouac.[48] This is somewhat extraordinary because the traditional view is that the regiments were in the Ngwebeni ravine further east on the night of 21 January. It does, however, explain Jackson's otherwise inexplicable reason for placing the Zulu bivouac there. It must also, however, be recognised that every one of the regiments supposedly bivouacked in their arc along the Ngwebeni would have been seen and reported upon after 6 a.m. on the morning of the 22nd by one or all of the three vedettes on the escarpment hilltops: Magaga (or Mkwene), Nyoni and Ithusi. That they could have escaped detection for the next twenty-four hours is inconceivable.

A possible alternative scenario is that the markings were meant to indicate their proposed bivouacs for the night of 22 January, since the state of the moon dictated that any Zulu attack should wait until the 23rd. Virtually every significant Zulu account, of which there are at least six, (the Nokhenkhe deserter, Mhoti, Mbonambi warrior, Nzuzi, Uguku and Mehlokazulu) makes this point, which is too many to discount.[49] Such an error in translation is perfectly possible. We might then speculate as to what followed. Following the departure of Lord Chelmsford with half his force at dawn on the 22nd, the Zulu commander, Ntshingwayo kaMahole, may have used the opportunity to commence a number of movements that would place his force in a more favourable position to attack the camp on the morning of the 23rd.

The first of these movements occurred soon after daybreak: two vedette pairs were driven from their posts about 6.15 a.m.[50] I have argued above that these vedettes were posted on Qwabe and Ithusi hills. This would have left a huge area to the east of the Ithusi and its ridge as dead ground, and still more on the plain eastwards of Qwabe. Neither can be observed from either of the two remaining vedettes on the plateau, on Magaga and Nyoni, nor the vedette to the south-east of the camp. This action would have allowed the regiments named to advance from the Ngwebeni towards their destinations. Their premature discovery by the patrolling mounted units of Raw and Roberts interrupted this movement and precipitated the battle while the Zulu were still in motion and unprepared.

From this argument, it follows that the case made by Lock and Quantrill that the battle began in the early morning of 22 January when the vedettes were driven off is no longer tenable, if it ever was.[51] Zulu evidence clearly indicates that Ntshingwayo was not planning to attack the camp on that day. It seems more likely that he was simply moving his regiments to a more favourable position for the expected attack on the 23rd. This is further demonstrated by the annotation that 'the Zulus attacked exactly as they [intended to be] bivouacked – all in line of Regiment except the Undi Corps which was ½ a mile in left rear of Ngobamakosi in bivouac and action.' The plan also called for the Nodwengu brigade to act as the right horn and drop down behind Isandlwana to attack across the southern *nek*, a movement which, although precipitated too early, was finally successful, thus forcing those fleeing the battle to escape down the Fugitives' Trail.

We can now finally reconcile the statements of the *Narrative* and the participants in the discovery much more readily, because, having breasted the Ithusi ridge, they were presented with the sight of part of the Zulu army, many still in the process of moving forward from the Mabaso ravine in preparation for the attack on the morrow, but previously hidden by the bulk of the ridge. The Mcijo regiment was already lying close under Ithusi itself: 'Just after the sun had come up on the Sunday, we crept towards the white men's tents. We crawled along in the grass with the white men shooting at us until we got within assegai-throw of them.'[52] (Gumpega uses the word 'Sunday' here to describe what was to him a special day, the day of the 'dead' moon: 22 January was, in fact, a Wednesday.[53])

We were lying in the hills up there, when one of our scouting parties came back followed by a number of mounted men; they were most of them natives, but some were whites. They fired upon us. Then the whole impi became very excited and sprang up. When the horsemen saw how numerous we were they began to retreat. We formed up in rank and marched towards the camp.[54]

The statement does not say: 'We were lying in a valley up there.' It is clear that many of the Mbonambi had already left the ravine and were awaiting the emergence of the remainder. It is also clear that the Mcijo (also known as the Ukandempemvu) regiment were on the plateau:

On the morning of the battle we heard firing of the English advance guard who had engaged Matshana's men and it being reported that the Ngobamakosi were engaged, we went up from the valley to the top of Ingqutu, which was between us and the camp; we then found that the Ngobamakosi were not engaged, but were quietly encamped lower down the valley. We saw a body of horse coming up the hill towards us from the Sandhlwana side. We opened fire on them, and then the whole of our army rose and came up the hill.[55]

This account makes it clear that at least a part of the Ngobamakhosi regiment had already left the ravine and was in the valley between Ithusi and Mabaso (and not the valley of the Ngwebeni, as has hitherto been assumed). Uguku ascribes the move to Mcijo inquisitiveness as to the rumoured involvement of the Ngobamakhosi; they were, in fact, ordered forward and found the Ngobamakhosi already there, lying quietly. Nor does Uguku suggest that the Mcijo moved back to the ravine when they found the rumour to be groundless. Finally, there is also an unstated period of time between leaving the ravine and the arrival of the mounted troops.

'However, as I said, the Natal natives fired upon our impi & our men could not be restrained from attacking them and our whole force advanced towards the camp, from the Nqutu range.'[56] These interpretations are also confirmed by the statement of Mehlokazulu:

The Zulu regiments were all lying in the valley I have mentioned, but the Umcityu made their appearance under the Nqutu range, and were seen by the mounted men of the English forces, who made at the Umcityu, not seeing the main body of the army. They fired, and all at once the main body of the Zulu army arose in every direction, on hearing the firing.[57]

From these descriptions, one can speculate that the Zulu had already begun to deploy to the area behind Ithusi, and that one regiment, perhaps more, was already lying in the grass there, including the Mcijo. It also seems likely that at the time of the discovery the Zulu right horn was making its way west along the Ngwebeni stream, well out of sight of the camp below the escarpment (but not those on Magaga, who fired on them as they passed by at a distance of 800 yards).[58]

The deployment was not only across the plateau: regiments resting lower down the ravine towards the plain, such as the Uve, chose not to go up to the plateau at all but attacked directly across the plain, probably from behind Nyezi, to which they had already advanced: 'Some of the enemy then came out of Isandhlwana and we were told of that by our spies. On hearing that we said we were not going to sit still on our mats, so we got up and after going about a mile we came up against them, on a flat bit of country near a small stream.'[59] This statement obviously refers to the confrontation with Colonel Durnford's troops as they moved east across the plain.

While he thought he was defining the area of the Zulu bivouac, Edward Durnford, brother of the dead Lieutenant-Colonel Anthony Durnford, wrote the following:

> Evidence taken on the spot fixes the exact position occupied by the Zulu army on the night of the 21st behind the hills on the left front of Lord Chelmsford's camp – the extreme right 3 miles N.N.E., and almost in direct prolongation of the line of the camps; the left about 6 miles to the left front, and E. of the camp. My informant is a distinguished officer who served throughout the campaign, and who, as an authority, is probably second to none.[60]

This describes almost exactly the position of the Zulu army at the moment of its discovery, which might explain his confusion: the chest was poised on the eastern side of the Ithusi ridge, while the left horn was near the Nyezi ridge, where it confronted his brother.

When the discovery is explained in this way, the statements of the various participants make sense, which they most certainly do not if one assumes the location of the discovery to be the lip of the ravine behind Mabaso Hill. Further, it explains why an otherwise astute historian like David Jackson could be misled into believing that these Zulu units, soon to be north of the British camp, had been in their overnight bivouac.

It is interesting to note that only two modern accounts use the primary sources to approach a correct, if still ambiguous, conclusion. The first is also the earliest, and was written by a professional historian:

The Basutos climbed the plateau and spread out over it. No Zulu were seen at first, only a herd of cattle. The Basutos rode on to round it up. Presently they came to the brink of a valley, and saw, about a mile off, what they had never dreamed of seeing. Thousands of Zulu were gathered there. Most of them were sitting on the ground, taking their ease. One body was moving westwards, probably taking up position to encircle the north flank of the camp at the appointed time.[61]

The second version pre-dated Morris by two years, and was consulted by him, according to his bibliography. The writer was C.T. Binns and this is his version of events:

Meanwhile Lieutenant Raw and his troop of Basutos, having advanced three or four miles in a northerly direction, had come across a herd of cattle which they followed over some rising ground. Reaching the top of the hill, to their amazement they saw a large Zulu force not more than a mile away and extending to their left; this was the Umcityu *impi*, of about 4,000 men. Unaware that the whole Zulu army was hiding in the near-by valley, but realizing his danger, Raw ordered a retreat, Shepstone meanwhile having galloped back to the camp to raise the alarm. Like a flash the whole Umcityu *impi*, roaring out their battle-cry '*Usutu*', sprang forward to the attack. The sudden advance of the Umcityu *impi* set the other regiments aflame, and they too rushed into action.[62]

A Battle Timetable

In three earlier papers, I have set out my views on the location of the Zulu bivouac, the composition and deployment of the Zulu army and the area where I believe the discovery of the Zulu forces took place, which then precipitated the battle. The principal features of the battle itself are now generally well known, although many particulars remain obscure. Not least of these unknown details is the approximate time at which the various events took place. Is it possible, for example, to determine at what time the battle began, how long the encounter lasted and when the camp finally fell? The authors of secondary narratives of the battle occasionally quote a time for some incidents and such times must have been based on a recorded account of some part of the disaster.

There are many accounts left by survivors, including those of a number of Zulu warriors. There are others by some who were not present at the battle at all, the best example of which is that by Captain Penn Symons, who was with Lord Chelmsford some twenty kilometres away but who wrote his own account based upon interviews with many of the survivors shortly afterwards.[63] Some of the survivors' accounts give specific times for various events that day but they vary widely for the same event. It is notable that most times quoted in the sources are to the nearest half-hour. There are some which mention a quarter-hour, but these are mostly in the *Narrative of the Field Operations*.

This paper attempts, as far as possible, a construction of the key events of the encounter, at the same time trying to assign more specific times to them. The time at which these key events occurred may then be used to determine a 'critical path' from which other times may also be estimated. Individual primary sources for the activities at Isandlwana itself, while valuable for constructing elements of what took place there, cannot tell the complete story from beginning to end because they describe only the events to which the narrator was a witness. On the other hand, the activities of Colonel Durnford's force may be followed from the beginning almost to the end and therefore should provide a more reliable base from which to proceed. His progress also has the benefit of having two observers, each of whom gave a detailed account of what occurred. The story may then be fleshed out by extrapolating times based upon the appropriate elements to complete the picture.

We should begin by defining the day of Wednesday, 22 January 1879 itself. The times of sunrise and sunset at Isandlwana differ little today from 1879, and we can say that the sun rose at 5.22 a.m. and set at 7.01 p.m. First light occurred approximately twenty-five minutes before sunrise and would thus be about 4.57 a.m., while last light occurred about twenty-five minutes after sunset, or about 7.26 p.m.[64] We also know that a partial eclipse of the sun occurred on that day, the maximum effect of which occurred about 2.30 p.m.[65]

The day began early with the departure of Lord Chelmsford and the 2/24th 'as soon as there was light enough to see the road'.[66] Drummer Sweeney, 2/24th Regiment, was more precise:

> At about 3:45 a.m. on the morning of the 22nd we were awakened by the Colour-Sergeant of our company at a place called Intaman [Isandlwana]. Our orders were not to make a noise or light a candle. At about 4:30 a.m. we received coffee and preserved meat. We marched out of camp about 5:10 a.m. to a distance of about 12 miles.[67]

Chelmsford's party was far to the east by sunrise and met Major Dartnell at the foot of Hlazakazi about 6 a.m. By that time the camp was already well astir, and day piquets and vedettes were in place.

It now becomes necessary to determine a reasonable time for the first key event based upon the available evidence. That event is the arrival of Lieutenant-Colonel Durnford at the camp because everything that followed flows from that point in time. Unfortunately, there are at least thirteen different times given in the sources for this event, which vary from 8.00 to 11.00 a.m.,[68] but, based on Durnford's earlier movements and his probable departure time from Rorke's Drift,[69] let us assume that Durnford and his mounted troops covered the sixteen-kilometre journey in about two and a half hours, arriving at Isandlwana about 10.00.[70]

Durnford's force came up to the camp at Isandlwana in three groups: first came Durnford himself with five troops of the Natal Native Mounted Contingent. Lagging behind him came the rocket battery under Brevet Major Francis Broadfoot Russell accompanied by two enlarged companies of 1/1st NNC: D Company under Captain Cracroft Nourse and most of E Company under Captain Walter Stafford. Finally, and bringing up the rear, came the baggage train, accompanied by Lieutenant Wallace ('Wally') Erskine and a few of Stafford's company left behind for the purpose.[71] Before reaching the camp, Stafford and the rest of his company were ordered back to provide additional support for the baggage train.[72]

Some time after his arrival, perhaps about 10.40, and following a briefing from Lieutenant-Colonel Henry Burmester Pulleine, Durnford sent Lieutenant Wyatt Vause with his No. 3 Troop, Zikhali's Horse, to provide additional support for the baggage train, which Lieutenant 'Harry' Davies says was four miles (6.5 kilometres) behind:[73] 'After riding through the camp we halted a few minutes and gave the men their biscuits. Col. Durnford sent for me and ordered me to ride back and meet our wagons as the Zulus were seen in our rear, and he expected they would try and cut them off.'[74]

About 11.00 am, after a quick meal taken while standing, Durnford also sent out the remaining two troops of Zikhali's Horse, under Captain William Barton, to reconnoitre the Nqutu plateau and clear away the bands of Zulu who were wandering about.[75] Lieutenants Charles Raw and J.A. Roberts commanded the individual troops. Durnford's political officer, Captain George Shepstone and his friend, storekeeper James Hamer, accompanied Raw, while Barton went with Roberts.[76] Raw says that Roberts was to pick up Captain A.J. Barry's NNC picquet company from the Magaga hill at the top of the northern spur and take them with him as support.[77] Another observer says that Raw himself was to take them.[78] In any event, Barry and his company certainly went with one of them. To replace Barry's men, Lieutenant Charles Walter Cavaye and his E company 1/24th were ordered to the top of the spur.[79] They must have left at much the same time as Barton's mounted troops, about 11.00.[80] It would have taken at least twenty minutes to march some 1,500 metres up to this position, arriving at the top of the spur about 11.20 or even later.[81]

About 11.15, Russell and the rocket battery arrived at the camp, accompanied by Nourse with his NNC company.[82] The next key event was Durnford's departure across the plain: 'Colonel Durnford . . . took with him to the front the remaining two troops [of the Mounted Contingent] and Russell's Rocket Battery, with a company of the Natal Native Contingent, under Captain Nourse, as escort to the battery.'[83]

The departure occurred between ten and twenty minutes after the rocket battery arrived at the camp, leaving them little time to recover their strength, and may therefore be determined as about 11.30 a.m.[84] The time of Durnford's departure is very important: from this event, one may estimate quite accurately the time of those which followed, particularly the time of the discovery of the Zulu army.

There next followed a series of conjunctions between bodies of men which must be timed so as to allow each meeting to occur appropriately. The three components of Durnford's force left virtually simultaneously but they travelled at very different speeds: 'Going at a canter, the rocket battery and escort were soon left behind by the mounted men.'[85] The men of the battery itself were mounted on horses but were accompanied by mules carrying the tubes and rockets. It consisted of Major Russell himself, one acting bombardier and eight other ranks of the 1/24th.[86] Captain Nourse's escort company of NNC numbered more than 120 officers, NCOs and men.[87] The NCOs and men were on foot, had already marched seventeen kilometres from Rorke's Drift that morning and had probably not eaten during that time. The white NCOs in particular would have been very tired.

Some time earlier, Trooper Barker, Natal Carbineers, had been sent back to the camp with a report of Zulu activity and on his return to his commanding officer, Lieutenant F.J.D. Scott, he came across the rocket battery.[88] The battery is reported to have travelled two miles (3.2 kilometres) before being overtaken by Barker and his mate.[89] The most likely point for this meeting, in view of what was to follow, is about 2.5 kilometres from the camp, placing them just south-east of the 'Conical Koppie' (Amatutshane). Barker told Russell about a Zulu advance on the plateau and, when asked for directions, pointed out the best route up the escarpment, where Russell was anxious to support the two troops of Zikhali's Horse sent out earlier.[90] This was by means of a feature now known as 'the Notch' and Russell turned the battery half-left to labour through a large donga on his way towards the steep western slope of Ithusi Hill.

When they were part way up the escarpment, the rocket battery was attacked by advance skirmishers from the Zulu centre which then went on to engage Nourse and his NNC a short distance away. (Their attackers could not have been the main Zulu force because Nourse was able to hold them at bay until Durnford returned to effect a rescue.) The battery had travelled no more than 4.5 kilometres when it was overwhelmed, leaving only four men alive.[91] The time calculated for this event is 12.15 p.m.[92] Nourse, his men being on foot, would have travelled more slowly, slowed down by the white NCOs. His engagement by the Zulu would still have occurred only minutes later, say at 12.25 p.m. Most of Nourse's African troops departed the scene after a few hasty shots, leaving him and the remainder of the company, most of whom were probably white NCOs, to defend their lives in hand-to-hand combat with the Zulu skirmishers.

The distances claimed for Durnford's foray after he left the camp were from as little as four kilometres (2.5 miles)[93] up to ten kilometres (six miles).[94] Four kilometres would have taken them only as far as Ithusi Hill and we know that they went farther than this. The best description of their route is given by Lieutenant Davies: 'We then proceeded round the pointed hill on the left front of the camp, and were about 2 miles beyond the ridge on the left front of the camp (we could not see the camp), and very near another ridge that you cannot see at all from the camp; this would make us about 3½ miles from the camp.'[95]

The 'pointed hill' is Amatutshane, which is little more than two kilometres (1.3 miles) due east of the camp; the 'ridge on the left front of the camp' is Ithusi Hill, a further two kilometres east. The last ridge is almost certainly Nyezi, which is about nine kilometres (5.6 miles) east of the camp. (It could not have been Qwabe because that knoll is visible from the camp and is too far south from their line of march.)

In the period from his departure at 11.30 to his rescue of Nourse at 12.35, a total of sixty-five minutes, Durnford crossed the plain to a certain point, engaged the advancing Zulu and returned. The time, however, must be scaled back slightly for two reasons: one, a brief conversation between Durnford and two carbineer messengers and, two, the time taken for the Zulu to advance about a kilometre from their first sighting until Durnford began his retreat. In total, these delays might have occupied about ten minutes, bringing the elapsed travel time back to fifty-five minutes. The calculated furthest point of his outward journey brought him to within two kilometres of Nyezi ridge, or a total of 7.5 kilometres (4.7 miles), from which point the Zulu could be seen advancing.[96] This distance accords very well with Davies' estimate of fifteen hundred yards.

The time now, according to our calculations, was 11.30 plus sixteen minutes to pass his future meeting point with Nourse, then a further fourteen minutes to reach his furthest point: very close to noon.[97] Here the two carbineer messengers caught up with Durnford's force:

> We were here overtaken by 2 Carbineers, who had been sent with a message from Lieutenant Scott, of the Native Contingent [*sic*], who was on picquet duty on the pointed hill to the left front of the camp. The message was to the effect that we had better return as the enemy were fast surrounding us.[98]

> Having proceeded between 5 and 6 miles, a mounted man came down from the hills on the left, and reported that there was an immense 'Impi' behind the hills to our left.[99]

The carbineers with Lieutenant Scott were probably somewhat to the east of Amatutshane, having been ordered to watch developments after reporting their activities earlier in the day.[100] Scott now realised the impending danger because: '. . . a few of us went up to this hill [Ithusi] where the Zulus had disappeared, and on a farther hill, at about six hundred yards distance, we saw a large army sitting down.'[101]

Scott then sent off the two messengers to warn Durnford of his predicament; they must have galloped about four kilometres before catching up with Durnford, taking about twelve minutes to do so. Raw's discovery of the Zulu army must, therefore, have occurred no more than a few minutes before the messenger's despatch, or about 11.45. Again, this accords well with the *Narrative*, which gives a time of noon.[102]

Now a brief digression. Some secondary accounts might lead the reader to suppose that, following their discovery, the Zulu charged the camp and overran it in short order. This was not so because of the long distances involved. There is also evidence that at least some units 'marched', rather than ran, towards the camp.[103] Smith-Dorrien described their gait as a 'very fast half walk, half run'.[104] The speed of their advance has, therefore, been calculated at eight kilometres an hour, an easy jog.[105]

To return to Durnford and his confrontation with the advancing Zulu army: 'It was during this conversation [with the Carbineers] that our scouts reported the enemy in sight. We looked up to the ridge on our front, and could see the enemy in great numbers about 1,500 yards [away], steadily advancing and firing at us.'[106]

The fact that a Zulu force was to their front, on what must have been Nyezi ridge, clearly demonstrates that some Zulu units did not go up to the plateau at all, but moved around the southern shoulder of Mabaso, then west across the plain. There is confirmation that the warriors were to Durnford's front, as well as on the edge of the escarpment: '[The messengers] had scarcely made the report when the Zulus appeared in force in front of us and to our left.'[107] It was clear to Durnford that he must turn back and he 'retired some little way, taking up a position in a "donga" or watercourse, of which there are several across the plain in front of Sandlwana.'[108]

This was not the final donga but one closer to the escarpment. This is described exactly by a Zulu warrior: 'The engagement now became very hot between the Mangwane (mounted natives) and us, the Mangwane being supported by the infantry who were some distance in their rear. We were now falling very fast. The Mangwane had put their horses in a donga, and were firing away at us on foot.'[109]

Durnford again shook his men into line and began to retire towards the camp:

> [He] gave the order for us to extend our men, and wait for the enemy to come within 400 yards of us, then Henderson's and my Troop to retire and fire alternately towards the camp . . . When we had retired about 2½ miles, and very near the pointed hill [Amatutshane], the enemy opened fire from the ridge that we had just a short time previously passed [Ithusi] . . . We continued our firing, and retiring, and just as we got round the pointed hill, I came upon Captain Nourse . . .[110]

The firing reported as being heard in the camp about noon caused the camp to stand-to again: 'About 12 o'clock we were turned out, as heavy firing was heard in the direction of Colonel Durnford's force.'[111]

Durnford's two troops of horse retreated for a total of about 3.5 kilometres (two miles), at the same speed as the Zulu advance: about eight kilometres an hour. As we have seen, it took him about twenty-five minutes to reach a point near Amatutshane, which, adding the further ten minutes for the delays before retreating, makes the time of the rescue of Nourse about 12.35 p.m.

> We retired steadily in skirmishing order, keeping up a steady fire for about two miles, when we came upon the remains of the Rocket Battery, which had been cut off and broken up. There was a hand to hand engagement going on with those that remained.[112]

When Durnford had gathered up Nourse and his few surviving men,

> The retreat was continued until we arrived at a 'donga' about half a mile in front of the camp. Here a few mounted men–Carbineers, Natal Mounted Police, &c.–reinforced our right.[113]

> We continued firing and retiring till we got to the watercourse, about 300 yards in front of the camp.[114]

Jabez Molife described how they then proceeded: 'After this we remounted & retreated 20 yds, always in a long thin line, then dismounted & fired, up again for another ten yards, dismounted & fired again, & so on ten yards at a time, firing always, slowly back towards the Camp.'[115]

The figures of ten and twenty yards are almost certainly incorrect and would have been nearer one hundred or two hundred yards, but even so the rescue and then the retirement to the large donga, about fifteen hundred metres from where Nourse was found, would have taken another fifteen or twenty minutes, bringing the time close to 1 p.m. Shortly afterwards, they were joined in the donga by other mounted men led by Captain Bradstreet of the Newcastle Mounted Rifles:[116] '. . . we were here joined by some mounted men, [I] supposed they were the Mounted Infantry, Mounted Volunteers and Police.'[117]

We have now established a coherent range of times for Colonel Durnford's activities, arriving about 10 a.m., departing about an hour and a half later and taking up his position in the large donga about 1 p.m. Furthermore, we have been able to estimate the time of the discovery of the Zulu army as about 11.45 a.m., not in the Ngwebeni ravine at Mabaso, but much closer to the camp, to the north of Ithusi. It is now time to turn to the remainder of the camp.

Just before he left, Durnford had seconded Lieutenant Higginson of the NNC from Pulleine and sent him up to the plateau to order Captain Shepstone to support his (Durnford's) march by riding parallel with him along the escarpment.[118] Before he was able to deliver the message, however, Higginson found that the discovery of the Zulu army had already taken place.[119] Most of Barry's men had fled at the first sight of them and Barry himself, with Lieutenant Vereker, were virtually alone and on foot.

> I left Serjeant-Major Williams with Captain Barry as he was without his horse, and as I knew that he would assist him back to camp if overpowered, he being a good shot, a good rider, and a very cool man under fire, I rode back to camp.[120]

In light of Higginson's actions later that day, we might take his reason for departing without further assisting the NNC officers with a grain of salt. Williams brought both Barry and Vereker into the camp safely.

The Zulu chest continued along the crest of the plateau after passing Ithusi Hill. These warriors, lead by the Mcijo, began to spill down from the escarpment onto the plain to the left front of the camp. Again assuming an advance at eight kilometres (five miles) an hour, they would have been engaged by the British artillery at long distance about forty minutes after their discovery, or about 12.25.

'Major Smith arrived as we were turning out and took command of the guns. We trotted up to a position about 400 yards beyond the left front of the Natal Contingent Camp and came into action at once on a large body of the enemy about 3,400 yards off.'[131] Smith had returned to the camp with Gardner and we have already determined that he arrived about 12.10, so our time accords well with that of Curling.[132] It was probably shortly after this that Lieutenant Roberts and some of his Zikhali's Horse, having sought shelter in a Zulu homestead, were killed by 'friendly' artillery fire.[133]

The slower Zulu approach from 3,200 metres to within four hundred metres of the infantry line, under increasingly heavy fire, must have taken a further thirty minutes, taking the time to 12.55 p.m., close enough to 1 p.m.

Here the Zulu advance on the whole front faltered under the withering fire from the defenders. George Hamilton-Browne, commanding the 1/3rd NNC, had been sent back to camp by Lord Chelmsford, and observed much of the attack from a low hill about five kilometres (three miles) from the camp. The British, he observed, were holding their own at 1 p.m.[134] The events which followed were extremely confused so that the determination of accurate times becomes, not surprisingly, more difficult. Nevertheless, sufficient clues are provided to enable our reconstruction to continue.

According to Curling, the guns were firing for at least fifteen minutes before Smith took one of them away for a short time to assist the right flank, which might have taken the time to about 12.45.[135] However, Hamilton-Browne also noted a movement from the plain: 'At about 1.30 p.m., I saw one of the guns alter its position.'[136]

It is entirely possible that Curling was confused by the heat of battle but it is also feasible that Hamilton-Browne's time may also be reasonably accurate, because he may have observed the movement of the gun back to its original position near Curling. Thus a compromise time of about 1.15 p.m. is likely for the second movement. Curling noted that shortly after Major Smith's return, 'we began firing case; but almost immediately the Infantry were ordered to retire', at which point the guns stopped firing. Hamilton-Browne also noted that the guns ceased firing shortly after the movement of the guns, perhaps about 1.40.[137] Thus the guns were firing for about one hour and fifteen minutes. Can we possibly determine how likely this was?

The guns had fired about forty rounds each, of which the last two had been case.[138] If this was so, and allowing about two minutes for each round, the firing time was about eighty minutes, so our time of seventy-five minutes is not unreasonable. There are also several reports of people in Lord Chelmsford's column hearing guns firing from the camp. Among these was Lieutenant-Colonel Harness[139] and Hon. William Drummond, Chelmsford's interpreter and intelligence chief. The latter was reported by Lieutenant-Colonel Crealock as occurring about 1.15, again a perfectly credible time.[140] An African also reported hearing them about half an hour later.[141]

It is time now to return to Durnford, still fighting in the donga. The Zulu left horn, meeting heavy resistance from the dismounted men in the donga, extended still further south, attempting to outflank them.[142] The resistance could not last for long: '[Durnford's force] made a stand for some time in a sluit which crossed the front of the Camp, but were driven out of it after a quarter of an hour or 20 minutes.'[143]

The stand was perhaps for a little longer than this, perhaps as long as thirty minutes because Durnford had time to go up to the camp and return, as indeed did Davies, who found the men leaving when he returned. The two elements which drove them back towards the camp were the threat of encirclement by the Zulu and a shortage of ammunition.

> After firing one or two volleys on the flank of the enemy on our left, my men called out they were short of ammunition. I took 15 with me to get ammunition; I managed to get some 200 rounds from the Carbineer's Camp, out of a box I found open in one of the tents. I tried to get back again to the sluit, but found everybody leaving it, and the Zulus very close on us.[144]

> A simultaneous forward movement was now made by all the Zulus, and many of our mounted men who had ridden in for ammunition were closely followed in by them.[145]

It is clear from the evidence that the Zulu began to enter the camp after Durnford's retreat from the donga, and this was about 1.30 p.m. About the same time, the right horn came over the northern *nek* and entered from the rear. This advance was almost certainly that observed by Hamilton-Browne:

> . . .when about half-past one I happened to glance to the right of the camp . . . By the road that runs between the hill and the kopje, came a huge mob of maddened cattle, followed by a dense swarm of Zulus. These poured into the undefended right and rear of the camp, and at the same time the left horn of the enemy and the chest of the army rushed in.[146]

Gardner went to Durnford to seek an explanation for his unfortunate retirement, which opened up the British right flank and enabled the Zulu to turn it. Durnford replied that 'he considered [his] position too extended and wished to collect all the troops together.'[147] The mounted men continued their withdrawal.

> One company of soldiers under a one armed man, he seemed to me to only have one arm (who shot four Zulus with his revolver) I saw as I neared the nek, march in good order up to the side of Isandhlwana among the rocks under the corner facing the tents on the right of the road leading into Zululand, taking the wounded as they were struck along with them and stood at bay there until the afternoon was far spent.[148]

From our timetable, one must wonder at Mhoti's words 'until the afternoon was far spent'. There is, however, a reasonable explanation. The Zulu had no sense of recorded time as we understand it. If, therefore, the final stand by Durnford lasted perhaps another half-hour, the time would have been about 2 p.m. or even later. By that time, the eclipse, which began shortly after 1 p.m., would have been well advanced, within thirty minutes of its maximum, and to Mhoti the dimmed light might have made the afternoon seem 'far spent'.

Some of the early escapees from the camp were able to use the track to Rorke's Drift before it was cut off. Among these were Lieutenant Adendorff of the NNC, and another, who are reported to have arrived at Rorke's Drift to warn Chard at about 3.15.[149] The seventeen-kilometre ride to the post could not have been carried out at a gallop, nor yet a walk, but probably a mixture of gaits, fast at first to escape the horror, then slower as they approached the Mzinyathi. Let us assume that they averaged nine kilometres an hour, thus taking perhaps two hours. In this case, they must have been two of the first Europeans to leave, departing about 1.15 p.m.; we should note that this time was before the right horn was able to cut the Rorke's Drift road.

It is worthwhile spending a moment on these two men because Morris stated that Adendorff's companion was a Lieutenant 'Vane', a fellow subaltern in Krohn's company of the 1/3rd Regiment, NNC.[150] Morris has the wrong name here because he is clearly referring to Lieutenant T. Vaines. However, he also had the wrong man because Chard himself said that the second rider was a 'Carabineer'.[151] Moreover, his name is given elsewhere as Trooper Sibthorpe.[152]

The problem of who left Isandlwana first, Adendorff or his men, will never be resolved. Perhaps one might just add that Captain Krohn, commanding the company to which Adendorff belonged, remained, to fall on the battlefield.

On the other hand, Sibthorpe, who probably met Adendorff en route rather than having left with him, must also have slipped away early and may well have been one of the vedettes. On the evidence of time it also seems unlikely that he could have gone with Captain Bradstreet to Durnford's donga.

As we have already seen, the Zulu right horn was established across the Rorke's Drift track about 1.20 p.m. It would not have taken them more than a few minutes to reach the *nek* from there. In the meantime, those elements which had attacked Cavaye and Mostyn had reached the bottom of the spur. They were joined by the Nokhenkhe regiment, driven back earlier, which now came across the northern, much wider, *nek* of Isandlwana, taking Captain Younghusband's company in flank. All this pressure, at every point, precipitated the final lunge into the camp.

It was about this time that the general retreat from the camp began, as evidenced by Private Westwood, Mounted Infantry: 'About 1.30 pm we found the Zulus were surrounding us, and I and my comrades thought we could do no more, and we had better get away.'[153]

This was also the time when the guns began to retire through the camp.[154] One cannot presume that the camp fell immediately. The close-quarter and brutal fighting which followed must have continued for some time, but it was to no avail. Slowly, each group was overcome by sheer weight of numbers. One further action remained before the Zulu triumph was complete: 'At one o'clock the Union Jack in front of the General's tent was pulled down and torn to pieces.'[155]

Conductor Foley may not be quite correct with his time, but he cannot be too far out – he gave the time of Durnford's arrival as 11 a.m., thirty minutes later than we have already determined, so this act might have taken place not long after 1.30 p.m.

'By 2 p.m. the only survivors of the force which had occupied the camp were those who were endeavouring to make good their escape to the Buffalo.'[156] The *Narrative's* statement may not be entirely correct, as we shall see shortly.

There was also a rather bizarre occurrence at about this time. Rupert Lonsdale, commanding the 3rd Regiment, NNC, had suffered concussion after falling from his horse on 9 January and had only returned to duty on the 20th. He and his 2nd Battalion were with Lord Chelmsford when he felt unwell and, giving as his reason the need to arrange supplies for his men, returned to the camp about 2 p.m.:

The statement as to the hour of this occurrence is supported by the facts that Commandant Lonsdale . . . met Lord Chelmsford about 5 miles from the camp not later than 3.30 P.M. As, after leaving the camp, his pony was so tired that he had to lead it most of the way, it must have taken him an hour and a quarter to get over these 5 miles.[157]

The time is also confirmed by Charles Norris-Newman: 'On arriving within 300 yards of it, at about 2 p.m., he [Lonsdale] found large masses of the enemy surrounding it, and in conflict with our troops. He had but just time, on discovering the state of matters, to turn and fly for his life: several shots were fired after him, and he was chased by many Zulus.'[158]

Lonsdale later reported that he had actually entered the camp but one might wonder if this was perhaps a little window-dressing:

> As I rode into Camp, I was in an absent state of mind for want of sleep and overwork. I don't know of what I was thinking, my thoughts were perhaps chiefly directed on getting something to eat, I had been a long time without food. I saw the movement of the Camp all around me and red coats surrounding me, suddenly I was brought to myself with a shock. A figure came out of a tent with a dripping assegai and looking all round, to my horror, I saw that every red coat had a black face above it![159]

From these statements, it is likely that some scattered resistance was still being offered by the British troops, individually or in small groups, even at this late hour, and that the Zulu were already looting the camp. The final testimony is an observation made by Hamilton-Browne: 'At this time, about 2.30 p.m., I could see that the resistance was over in Camp, and I retired as quickly as possible.'[160]

That may have been true of the camp proper but there was still resistance on the Fugitives' Trail. Snook has offered a convincing demonstration of the fighting cohesion of the British companies and particularly that of Lieutenant Anstey's F Company. Anstey's body was found with about forty men 'two miles down the Fugitives' Trail, where they were brought to bay on the banks of the Manzimyama [sic]'.[161] Theirs may have been the last organised resistance.

A further method of determining the time of the fall of the camp is by using the evidence of the fugitives. We have already examined the peculiar case of Adendorff and Sibthorpe. There is, however, more that can be done. By 1 p.m., many of the 'idlers'[162] had already begun to cross the southern *nek* to flee the camp; those men departing later would find their escape blocked by the Zulu right horn, forcing them off the track and down the hillside to the right of Mahlabamkhosi and on towards what is now known as Fugitives' Drift.

The time of departure from the camp of those who eventually reached Helpmekaar also provides evidence as to when order in the camp began to disintegrate. This calculation consists of three elements: the distance from the camp to the Mzinyathi, estimated at about seven kilometres (4.3 miles); [163] the actual crossing of the river; then the ride from the river to Helpmekaar, a distance of about twenty-four kilometres (nearly fifteen miles).[164]

The time for this has been calculated as follows: perhaps forty minutes to reach the Mzinyathi river (David Jackson has estimated thirty-five minutes for a distance of four miles at seven miles an hour[165]) then another fifteen minutes to cross the river, with all of the problems which that entailed. Some confirmation of this is provided by Wally Erskine:

> Immediately after this the Zulus rushed into the camp, and Captain Shepstone must have been killed then (about 4). I forgot to mention that just as I crossed the river a Zulu shot at me, the bullet passing within an inch of my ear. I felt my head to see if I was hit; it killed a conductor by the name of Dubois who was walking up the hill in front of me; this was about 5 o'clock.[166]

His times are wildly inaccurate, but the relative time of one hour between his 4 and 5 p.m., during which he must have departed the camp and crossed the river, is perfectly reasonable.

Lastly, the journey to Helpmekaar would have been covered at a slower pace – there is a steep climb up the Biggarsberg, as Erskine says – and allowing a speed of seven kilometres (4.3 miles) an hour,[167] this would have taken a further three and a half hours. In total, this allows forty minutes to reach the river, fifteen minutes to cross and then three and a half hours to Helpmekaar, a total of nearly four and a half hours. Essex estimated his arrival at between 5 and 6 p.m. while others reported 5, 6, 6.30, 7 and 7.30.[168] The mean time of arrival was thus about 6 p.m. and suggests a departure time of about 1.30 p.m. We have already seen that this was the time when the Zulu began to enter the camp.

While on the subject of the fugitives, a number of people reported seeing Adjutant Melvill at the river crossing and his watch is said to have stopped at 2.10 p.m.[169] The forty-minute ride down to the Mzinyathi meant that he left the camp about 1.30, which fits well with the time established above. It therefore seems quite likely that the action of his watch was stopped by immersion in the river. The same cannot be said of the time at which Colonel Durnford's watch had also stopped: 'Another evidence of the duration of the struggle is Colonel Durnford's watch (taken from his body on the morning of the 23rd). He was amongst those who formed the last group that fought it out; his death-wound caused the stoppage of his watch–the time, 3.40.'[170] It is more likely that Durnford's watch simply ran down and it may instead have stopped at 3.40 a.m. in the morning, or even the afternoon, of 23 January.

We may now sum up the results of this analysis by indicating that the discovery of the Zulu army by two troops of Zikhali's Horse occurred about 11.45 a.m. and that the battle was essentially over by 2.30 p.m. It has been said that the last British soldier to die, who had taken shelter in a shallow cave towards the summit of the east slope of Isandlwana, was shot after a determined defence 'when the shadows were long on the hills'.[171] David Jackson has ventured the opinion that this might have been 'about 5 p.m.'[172] but one might equally suggest that this too was the result of the pall cast over the battle field at the height of the eclipse, occurring about 2.30 p.m. That the sun should hide its face at this tragic moment seems a fitting tribute.

Notes on Time Calculations

The following notes are included as an appendix, rather than cluttering the main narrative with such matters. They describe in detail how the various times were derived.

1. Bearing in mind the fatigue of both men and animals in the rocket battery, it would at best have travelled away from the camp at about six kilometres an hour, making the elapsed time from their departure about forty-five minutes. The attack on the battery therefore must have occurred about 12.15 p.m. Nourse's company would have travelled more slowly, being on foot, say at five kilometres an hour, lagging behind the battery by about five hundred metres, and their confrontation with the Zulu would have occurred only minutes later, say at 12.25 p.m.

2. Assuming that Durnford's mounted men left the camp, 'at a canter', at about fifteen kilometres an hour,[173] then returned at about eight kilometres an hour,[174] it is relatively simple to find the approximate distance he travelled. It consisted of two components: one, the distance from the camp to the approximate position where he would eventually find Nourse, and two, the furthest point whose advance and return allowed him to cover the same distance at the two speeds mentioned earlier, in the time available.

    Nourse travelled about four kilometres (to the rocket battery's 4.5) and Durnford would have covered the same distance in only $((60\text{mins}/15^{\text{km/h}}) \times 4\text{km})$, which equals sixteen minutes. That leaves thirty-nine of the fifty-five minutes for the journey to his furthest point and back, which must be approximately the same distance. The single case which meets this requirement is a distance of about 3.5 kilometres: at fifteen kilometres an hour, the time taken is $((60mins/15^{km}/_h) \times 3.5km)$, which equals fourteen minutes. In the remaining twenty-five minutes (39 minus 14), and travelling at eight kilometres an hour, he must have travelled about $((8^{km}/_h/60mins) \times 25mins)$, which equals 3.3 kilometres. This is sufficiently close to the outward distance to suggest quite firmly that Durnford would have travelled an additional 3.5 kilometres, making a total of 7.5 kilometres (4.6 miles) from the camp before encountering the Zulu.[175]

3. The speed at which the Zulu advanced is not difficult to determine. Morris, in describing the Isandlwana camp site, says: 'The view of the approaches was as good as could be expected in a hilly country, and there was no cover for an attacking force within a mile and a half of the camp. An impi charging the camp would be visible for fifteen or twenty minutes in every direction save one . . .'[176]

Over Morris' distance of one and a half miles, or nearly two and a half kilometres, the Zulu would have to travel at nearly ten kilometres an hour to cover the distance in fifteen minutes, or nearly eight kilometres an hour to do so in twenty minutes. With the words of the Mbonambi warrior and Smith-Dorrien in mind, I have estimated that the Zulu advance came on at about eight kilometres per hour, which I believe to be the pace of an easy jog.[177]

The Eclipse

The battle of Isandlwana was marked by several coincidences that were treated by both sides as omens. There was, for example, the similarity between the silhouette of Isandlwana itself and the collar badges of the 24th Regiment, which took the form of a sphinx. For the Zulu, 22 January was a 'day of the dead moon', an unpropitious day for battle. By far the most dramatic omen, however, was the eclipse that occurred that afternoon. It has also been used to explain, in part, the collapse of the British line, suggesting that the darkness caused by the eclipse, combined with the smoke from the gunfire, obscured the Zulu warriors from the British rifles.[178] It is appropriate, therefore, to write a few brief comments about this matter.

The event is generally reported as a partial eclipse but at the point of greatest magnitude, off the south-west coast of Africa, it was, in fact, an annular eclipse.[179] A partial eclipse occurs when only a segment, or 'bite' of the sun is obscured. An annular eclipse, on the other hand, is much like a total eclipse, except that the moon at the time of the eclipse is too far away from the earth for its shadow to completely fill the sun's disc and therefore the moon obscures only the central portion, leaving a ring of the sun showing around the shadow, hence the use of the word 'annular', meaning ring-shaped. Because the track of the eclipse in 1879 ran some distance to the north of Isandlwana, and not directly overhead, it was observed in that area as a partial eclipse.

The question of the time of the eclipse is important but must be qualified by the difference in time between London and Isandlwana (or even Pietermaritzburg). To adjust London time to 'local' time in Pietermaritzburg in 1879, one must add two hours and fourteen minutes, rather than the present two hours.[180] The establishment of international time zones and the prime meridian at Greenwich have already been discussed in an earlier paper. The contemporary Pietermaritzburg times for the eclipse are:[181]

	Time
Eclipse began	13.09
Maximum obscuration	14.29
Eclipse ended	15.50

More modern, and precise, times of the eclipse as seen at Isandlwana, as opposed to those at Pietermaritzburg given above, are as follows:[182]

	Local
Eclipse began	13.10
Maximum obscuration (55.75%)	14.35
Eclipse ended	15.51

Several Zulu witnesses mention the eclipse, which occurred in the final stage of the battle: 'The tumult and firing was wonderful; every warrior shouted 'Usutu!' as he killed anyone and the sun got very dark, like night, with the smoke.'[183] Although this statement might appear to be ambiguous, referring either to the eclipse or the smoke, the author makes it clear that it was due to the eclipse.[184] The next Zulu witness is unequivocal: 'The sun turned black in the middle of the battle; we could still see it over us, or should have thought we had been fighting till evening. Then we got into the camp, and there was a great deal of smoke and firing. Afterwards the sun came out bright again.'[185]

Finally, the evidence of a young Zulu boy who was nearby, but not on the battlefield: 'After a few days, it came to pass that the sun darkened; there was silence – utter silence – throughout the land. Nevertheless the army was fighting at Isandlwana.'[186]

Of the many British and Colonial troops in the field that day, only two make mention of the eclipse: 'The sun was shining on the Camp at the time and then the Camp looked dark, just as if a shadow was passing over it.'[187] At the time, Mansel was some miles to the east of the camp, with the troops led by Colonel Glyn and Lord Chelmsford. The other witness was a Natal Carbineer:

> It must have been about 12 or one o'clock when I went out to relieve the first guard and had not been on [duty] long before the low boom of a cannon reached my ear, a second and a third followed. I drew my mate's (Harry Stirton) attention to the sounds. About this time an oppressive gloom pervaded the whole atmosphere. This was due to an eclipse of the sun but we never thought of that at the time.[188]

Symons was also with Chelmsford and would have been fairly close to Mansel. It is certainly odd that the phenomenon was not noted by any of the other officers in the vicinity, particularly Lieutenant Milne, a naval officer serving as aide-de-camp to Lord Chelmsford.

It is alleged that there was a witness in the 1/24th at Helpmekaar – Philip Gon has the following to say about him: '. . . and at Helpmakaar, Lieutenant Wilfred Heaton of 'D' Company noted in his diary that the eclipse of the sun began at 11:51.'[189] This is not so. Heaton's entries for the 22 January and later make no mention of the eclipse. An email enquiry to the curator of the museum holding the diary elicited the following response: 'In the diary . . . there is a *printed* reference [to] the eclipse made by the printers of the diary – what I am not sure is whether it was printed in South Africa – I would guess yes.'[190]

A more remote, and reliable, observer of the phenomenon was Commandant Friedrich Schermbrucker, the ex-British German legionary who led a volunteer force in the Luneberg area. In a letter to Colonel Evelyn Wood, commanding the Fourth Column, he brought it to Wood's attention: '9. Yesterday's partial eclipse of the sun (between 3 and 4 p.m.) is looked upon by the natives as a sign of Umbelini's power, who is reported to have particular power over that luminary.'[191]

The last apparent witness was a soldier in the 80th Regiment, also at Luneburg. Sergeant Anthony Booth, who was later to earn a Victoria Cross at the battle of Ntombe Drift said:

> We didn't believe [the news of Isandlwana] at first. Afterwards, they got us together and informed us that it was only too true. We shifted then into a smaller laager and waited there a few days.
> I remember the day very well, for there was eclipse of the sun.[192]

In light of the extracts quoted above, it is clear that the eclipse was observed by Zulus, people in Chelmsford's force and also further afield.

1. Site of the first engagement at Sihayo's homestead

2. Sihayo's Sokhexe: cattle enclosure foundations and cliffs

15. Remains of Fort Newdigate

16. Grave of King Cetshwayo kaMpande

From the data given in the earlier table, it will be seen that the moon obscured nearly 56 per cent of the sun's face, so that the available light would have been diminished accordingly. This still left more than 44 per cent of sunlight available and would have interfered with one's vision very little. Note too that this situation only obtained for a few minutes at maximum obscuration, before and after which more light was available.

On the question of smoke from firearms also contributing to loss of vision, I am disposed to discount this argument. There is reference to a smoke problem occurring at the battle of Khambula two months later, but in this case there were twice as many troops involved and they were more closely packed together in either the redoubt or the laager.[193] At Isandlwana, the six British companies were dispersed in a skirmishing line over a distance of more than two thousand metres, containing not many more than 570 infantrymen.[194] Simple arithmetic will show that with so few men even in a single line, the space between them could not have been less than four metres. In fact, the regulation infantry spacing was five yards, or a little less than five metres, between each man and the difference was made up by there being a substantial gap between one company and another.[195]

The final point to be made is that by the time the maximum effect of the eclipse occurred, around 2.30 p.m., it is highly likely that most of the British troops were either dead or fleeing for their lives down the Fugitives' Trail. It was therefore of little significance to the outcome of the battle if the light was obscured by the eclipse. Since most of the living combatants were absent from the field at that time, for one reason or another, the smoke issue is also superfluous.

Chapter 4

Isandlwana: Post Scriptum

En effet, l'histoire n'est que le tableau des crimes et des malheurs.

Voltaire 1694–1778

The Annotated Maps of Isandlwana

Within the extensive archives of the Royal Engineers Museum at Chatham there lies a collection of documents described as the 'Durnford Papers'. They refer principally to Colonel Anthony William Durnford, of Isandlwana fame, but also to other members of the Durnford family including his father and brother. A career in the Royal Engineers was a Durnford family tradition.

A number of those documents referring to Anthony Durnford were the subject of a most interesting paper published in 1990.[1] One of the documents discussed is an annotated copy of J.A. Brickhill's statement about his role in the battle of Isandlwana.[2] The authors cite the following entry and initials which suggest that the handwritten notes on that document were made by Lieutenant Alfred Fairlie Henderson, who had commanded Hlubi's troop of the Natal Native Horse during the battle:

> Col Durnford rode at the Head of the Column all the way from Rorke's drift & I did not lose sight of him until we were in the camp at Isandhlwana.
>
> There was a rumour that some Zulus had been in the camp that morning, had given up their arms, and were allowed to leave again – I saw nothing of them. AFH.[3]

A further two of the documents discussed are copies of two well-known maps originally prepared in November 1879 by Captain T.H. Anstey and Lieutenant C. Penrose of the Royal Engineers and published in the *Narrative of the Field Operations*. To acquaint the reader with the details of the Chatham maps, which received only cursory treatment in the Jackson and Whybra paper, I give below an overview of them.[4]

'Military Survey of the Country Around Isandhlwana', which is identified as map No. 1, covers the wider area of the battlefield and stretches from Rorke's Drift in the west to Magogo and Silutshana in the east, and from the Nqutu hills in the north to the Malakatha/Hlazakazi hills in the south. Prominently shown is the route of the track from Rorke's Drift over the southern saddle of Isandlwana and continuing eastwards where it divides, the northern path eventually leading to Ulundi and the other further south towards the Qudeni Forest. Among the printed features shown on the map are several letter groups which are identified in the key, the first of which states: 'a.a Valley in which the Zulu army bivouacked on the night of January 21st, 22nd'. The letters are to be found on the map along the Ngwebeni stream to the east of Mabaso hill in what has become known as the 'ravine'.

There are, in addition, a number of handwritten notes which have been added to the map. These notes purport to identify the positions of various named Zulu regiments prior to the attack on the Isandlwana camp about noon on 22 January and, by means of dotted lines and arrows, to indicate the direction of their movement southwards during that attack. The regiments are shown in an arc on the northern side of the Ngwebeni stream at the foot of the Nqutu hills and stretching from the western edge of Mabaso hill to a point almost due north of Isandlwana Hill, a distance of seven kilometres (a little more than four miles). There is an unbroken line, also marked 'a.a', which runs from the Nodwengu regiment on the extreme left of the arc south down the western side of Isandlwana and then east across the southern nek. There is also a mysterious 'x' marked a short distance below the centre of the arc of Zulu regiments. Finally, at a point well to the south of Mabaso Hill on the plain are the letters 'DH', written vertically, the 'D' on top.

The second map is identified as No. 3 and is the 'Military Survey of the Battle-Field of Isandhlwana', which shows the battlefield around Isandlwana Hill in more detail. It should be noted, however, that unlike the published version, the map does not include the diagram of the camp on the eastern flanks of Isandlwana Hill. It covers the ground from the Manzimnyama stream in the west to Ithusi Hill in the east, from the Nqutu escarpment in the north to the area below 'Black's Koppie', now named Mahlabamkhosi, to the south. Prominent in the centre of the map are the two major dongas running from north to south, in the westernmost of which Durnford made his unsuccessful attempt to halt the progress of the Zulu left horn.

There are handwritten additions to this map too, most of which are extended arrows showing the direction of attack by each Zulu regiment

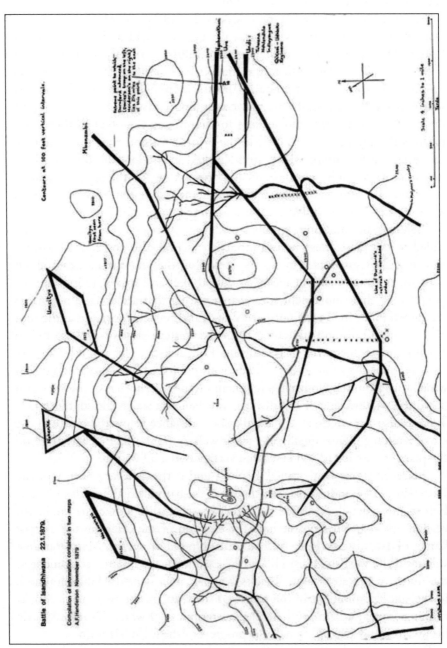

5 Isandlwana – Jackson & Whybra Map

or brigade on the camp itself. In addition, there are two vertical columns of small circles which show the locations of Durnford's horsemen as they retreated towards the last donga, accompanied by the words 'N.N. Horse under Durnford trying in vain to check the Uve'.

Jackson and Whybra observe that the notes on the two maps are in the same hand as that of the Brickhill annotations and that their identification as those of Henderson is supported by the entry in the RE Museum catalogue.[5] The handwritten notes on the maps are reproduced in the article, on a conflated map similar to No. 3, with the authors' advice that 'Nothing has been omitted'.[6] The two symbols from map No. 1 are defined in notations also found on the Brickhill account as (a) 'x': 'Umcityu first seen from here' and (b) 'DH': 'Extreme point to which Durnford advanced, Davies' troop on the left, Henderson's on the right, was 2½ miles to the east of this point'. (The position shown on the conflated map could not show its true position, so this was amplified by the authors in their comment.)

That is the position as it stood until recently and, sadly, not a great deal has been heard about the maps or their implications since the paper was published.

During a recent research visit to South Africa, this writer visited the Killie Campbell Africana Library (now known as the Campbell Collections) in Durban. Such visits have been almost an annual pilgrimage for the last eight years and this one was intended to be quite routine. Among the documents to be examined on this occasion, however, were two maps for which I knew the reference numbers but not what they represented. I had seen these references elsewhere and wondered what they showed. I was greatly surprised, therefore, to find that they were what I believed to be the same two Henderson maps that I had viewed in the RE Museum at Chatham in 2005 and 2006 (but had not been able to copy), and which I have described above.[7] I made photographic digital images of the new maps and brought them back to Sydney for study at my leisure.

On an impulse, on my return home I sent an email message about the maps to Julian Whybra, co-author of the paper under discussion, whom I knew would be interested in what I had found, and attached an image of one of the maps. I was astonished to learn from his reply that the map I had sent him was not the same as either of those in the RE Museum – numbered No. 1 and No. 3 (which I had not previously known) – but is identified as map No. 2. This new map is similar to No. 1 but has additional information on it, in the same hand, and thus may also be attributed to Henderson. Most important of all, it has extensive handwritten notes down the right side of the map which read as follows:

The Zulu pointed out exactly the position of the Nodwengu in bivouac near a mealie garden, and indicated generally the remainder. The third line a.a shows the intended movements. The dotted lines that actually followed.

x. I believe about where the Basutos fired on the Umcityu.[8]

The Zulus attacked exactly as they bivouacked – all in line of Regiment except the Undi Corps which was ½ a mile in left rear of Ngobamakhosi in bivouac and action.[9]

DH. Approximate position of Colonel Durnford when Hlubi hearing the firing of mounted and other contingents of Basuto persuaded him to retire.

The other notable feature of the map is that the Zulu regiments, except for the Nodwengu on the western side and the Undi and Uve on the eastern side, are not named. The 'x' is also more clearly marked, but in the same position.

Whybra then sent me images of the Chatham maps 1 and 3, on receipt of which I found that the two maps 3 were also slightly different. Whilst the position and directions of the arrows are the same, the details of regiments on the eastern side of the Isandlwana plain are more extensive and clearer. Written in a column across the border of the map, and to the south-east of Ithusi Hill, are the names of the regiments 'Ingobamakhosi', 'Uve, Undi' (and in pencil) Corps and 'Qikasi Regiment'. To the right of these names, as if further explaining, are the names 'Tulwana, Indlondlo' and 'Indluyengwe' (making up the Undi corps) and 'Udloko' (the proper name of the Qikazi). The Undi corps and the Dloko regiment represented the Zulu reserve at Isandlwana. There are two other notations to be found which are also omitted from the RE Museum map 3, to be discussed shortly.

What, then, are we to make of all this?

We should first examine the provenance of the maps. Jackson and Whybra suggest that the probable source of many, if not all, of these documents could have been Frances Ellen Colenso, whose relationship with Anthony Durnford is well known, and who, in gathering material for her book in defence of Durnford,[10] might well have been in contact with the survivors, including both Brickhill and Henderson. Presumably, these documents were passed to Durnford's brother Edward, also then pursuing a campaign for the restitution of Anthony's name, and then by him to the Royal Engineers Museum.

If indeed the notations on the Brickhill statement were made by Henderson, this does not demonstrate conclusively that the notations on the Chatham maps were also made by him. Jackson and Whybra, however, are of the opinion that the hand is the same on all three documents. Furthermore, the same, or similar, hand also appears on the new Durban maps. Finally, the

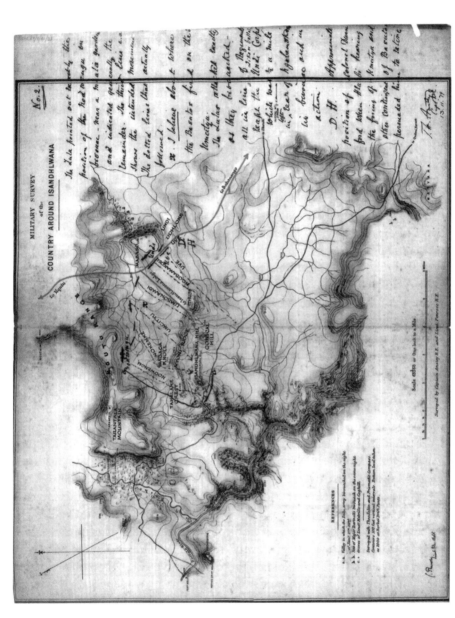

6 Isandlwana – Durban Map 2

RE Museum catalogue attributes both the maps and Brickhill notes 'possibly' to Henderson. It is difficult to go much further than that without scientific examination of the handwriting. The provenance of the Durban maps is still to be discovered but one might postulate that they came from the Colenso family papers, even from Frances Colenso herself.

Next we should consider the new information provided by the Durban maps. Of crucial importance are the comments on map 2, in particular the first sentence: 'The Zulu pointed out exactly the position of the Nodwengu in bivouac near a mealie garden, and indicated generally the remainder.' It might have originally been thought that the Zulu locations on the map were provided to Henderson by his brother-in-arms Lieutenant Charles Raw, the only white officer who was both on the plateau and survived the battle. Clearly this notion is now invalid because the source for this particular item, at least, was a Zulu. Did Henderson speak Isizulu? It is known that he did, as shown in his obituary: 'It was his extensive knowledge of the Zulu language, his wide experience of Dutch habits and his familiarity with every part of Natal that made him an extraordinarily useful man in these wars.'[11] Like many young Natal colonists, Henderson probably learned the Zulu language before his mother tongue, by virtue of being nursed in infancy by African servants; Henry Charles Harford is another example.[12]

The notation continues by stating that the positions marked by the arc of Zulu regiments show the location of their bivouac. This is somewhat extraordinary because the traditional view is that the *amabutho* were in the Ngwebeni ravine further east on the night of 21 January. It must also be recognised that every one of the regiments supposedly bivouacked in their arc along the Ngwebeni would have been seen and reported on the morning of the 22nd by one or all of the three vedettes on the escarpment hilltops: Magaga (or Mkwene), Nyoni and Ithusi. That they could have escaped detection for the next twenty-four hours is inconceivable.

A possible alternative scenario is that the markings were meant to indicate their bivouacs for the night of 22 January, since the state of the moon dictated that any Zulu attack should wait until the 23rd. Such an error in translation is perfectly possible. Virtually every significant Zulu account, of which there are at least six, (the Nokhenkhe deserter, Mhoti, Mbonambi warrior, Nzuzi, Uguku and Mehlokazulu) makes this point, which is too many to discount lightly.[13] We might then speculate on what followed. After the departure of Lord Chelmsford with half his force at dawn on the 22nd, the Zulu commander, Ntshingwayo kaMahole, may have used the opportunity to commence a number of movements that would place his force in a more favourable position to attack on the morning of the 23rd.

The first of these movements occurred soon after daybreak: two vedettes pairs were driven from their posts about 6.15 a.m.[14] I have argued elsewhere that these vedettes were posted on Qwabe and Ithusi hills.[15] This would have left a huge area to the east of the Ithusi ridge as dead ground, and still more on the plain eastwards of Qwabe; neither can be observed from either of the two remaining vedettes on the plateau, on Magaga and Nyoni, nor the vedette to the south-east of the camp. This action would have allowed the regiments named to advance from the Ngwebeni ravine and under the Nqutu hills towards their final destinations. Their discovery by the advancing mounted units of Raw and Roberts interrupted this movement and precipitated the battle while the Zulu were in motion and unprepared.

From this argument, it follows that the case made by Ron Lock and Peter Quantrill that the battle began in the early morning of 22 January when the vedettes were driven off is no longer tenable, if it ever was.[16] Zulu evidence clearly indicates that Ntshingwayo was not planning to attack the camp on that day. Had he been going to do so, why then did he wait from early morning until noon to begin?[17] It seems more likely that he was simply moving his warriors to a more favourable position for the expected attack on the 23rd. This is further demonstrated by the annotation that 'the Zulus attacked exactly as they [intended to be] bivouacked – all in line of Regiment except the Undi Corps which was ½ a mile in left rear of Ngobamakhosi in bivouac and action.' The plan also called for the Nodwengu brigade to act as the left horn and drop down behind Isandlwana to attack across the southern *nek*, a movement which, although precipitated too soon, was almost successful, failing only to close the ring completely, and thus allowing those fleeing the battle to escape down the Fugitives' Trail.

The explanation of the 'x' shown below the arc of Zulu regiments is also explained rather differently on map 2, because the notes state that the annotator believed that point to be 'about where the Basutos fired on the Umcityu'. Whether this refers to Raw's or Roberts' troop is only to be conjectured: perhaps it was Roberts, who is said to have been half a mile north of Raw.[18] If so, this would have placed Raw on the Ithusi ridge at the time of the discovery. If the map is to be believed, it is certainly clear that the discovery of the Zulu army did not take place in the ravine below Mabaso Hill as described by Donald Morris and many after him.[19]

The notation showing the initials of Davies and Henderson ('DH') is now also described more fully: 'Approximate position of Colonel Durnford when Hlubi hearing the firing of mounted and other contingents of Basuto persuaded him to retire'. The letters indicate that Lieutenant Davies' Edendale troop (D) was on the left and Lieutenant Henderson's troop of

Hlubi's Basotho (H) was on the right. The position they reached is almost exactly that given by Davies himself: 'We then proceeded round the pointed hill on the left front of the camp, and were about 2 miles beyond the ridge on the left front of the camp (we could not see the camp), and very near another ridge that you cannot see at all from the camp; this would make us about 3½ miles from the camp.'[20]

This ridge has been determined by the author as almost certainly Nyezi, which is about nine kilometres (5.6 miles) east of the camp. It could not have been the nearer Qwabe because that knoll is visible from the camp and is too far south from their line of march.

We should now turn to the Durban map No. 3, which is almost identical to the Chatham version. The difference is two further notations: the first is to be found at the bottom of the map in the valley to the south-east of Mahlabamkhosi. There is marked a cross and the note 'Last stand 1/24th'. Julian Whybra has suggested this point may relate to Q.M. Pullen's call to the passing soldiery to rally on him,[21] which might have been witnessed by a galloping Henderson in passing and who later assumed this was the last stand of the 1/24th. This is unlikely because (a) the point on the map is well away from the Fugitives' Trail, which was on the other side of 'Black's Koppie' and (b) Henderson went to Rorke's Drift and would not therefore have used the Fugitive's Trail. Nevertheless, it is perfectly feasible that later survivors on the *nek*, finding their way down the Fugitives' Trail now blocked by the Zulu right horn, turned south and moved down the eastern side of Mahlabamkhosi where they could have been intercepted by elements of the left horn. A glance at a map shows that, under normal circumstances, this route offers as good a means of reaching the Manzimnyama stream, and eventually the Mzinyathi River, as the traditional trail itself. It is therefore quite possible that a 'last stand' occurred here.

To the north, halfway up the escarpment between Magaga (or Mkwene) Hill and the Nyoni ridge is another 'x', this time with the note '1 co. 2/24?' This can only be a reference to Lieutenant Pope's G company, because every other company of the 2/24th was out with Lord Chelmsford. However, this also seems unlikely since G Company had been on picquet duty until 6 am, after which it took its place with the other companies when told to 'stand to'. We know that the company was at the southern end of the British line during the battle, separated at some distance from Durnford's party in the donga. An explanation offered by Julian Whybra on this notation suggests that it may relate either to Porteous' initial support of the guns (and erroneously written as 2/24, hence the question mark) or a glimpse Henderson had, as his and Davies' troops picked up rocket battery survivors, of Pope's or Dyer's composite company beyond the 'Conical Koppie'.

One final important point to note about this map, and its corresponding cousin at Chatham. The location of the Undi brigade and Dloko, which composed the Zulu reserve, is shown quite clearly on the plain to the east of Isandlwana, and not in its traditional position following behind the right horn on the plateau. This supports the view that the reserve did not take the circuitous route across the plateau but instead crossed the plain, a contentious alternative argued by this writer in 2004.[22]

To sum up, if the notations can be taken as genuine, and there is no current evidence to suggest they are not, then the Durban maps, combined with those at Chatham, throw new light on the circumstances surrounding the battle of Isandlwana, particularly on the discovery of the Zulu army by Zikhali's mounted troops under Raw and Roberts. The extent to which the diagrams of bivouacs and the direction of movements coincide with the other well-known Zulu evidence is unclear as yet, and there are still some obstacles to the development of an acceptable solution, but this is surely a beginning. Once again, the battle of Isandlwana poses more problems than appear to have been resolved.

An Addendum

Following the publication of the paper above in 2007, I received a communication from Ron Lock and Peter Quantrill, co-authors of *Zulu Victory*, arguing that the notations, at least on the Durban maps, were written by Evelyn Wood and not by Alfred Henderson. Their evidence for this assertion was a letter written by Edward Durnford to Wood dated 4 October 1880.[23] On my last visit to the Killie Campbell Library, in July 2008, I examined this letter closely and found some very pertinent matters which offer quite convincing evidence for the Lock and Quantrill thesis. For example, the letter begins:

> I return with many thanks the two maps you so kindly lent me.
>
> I see you note the mounted natives under Col. Durnford as 'Hlubi's Basutos'.
>
> The two troops under his immediate command were 1 troop Basutos (Hlubi's) & 1 troop of Edendale men. The 2 troops under Capt. G. Shepstone were Sikali men.

The last paragraph is a reference to the notation on Durban map 3 that identifies the two parallel lines of circles as the positions of 'Hlubi's Basutos under Durnford trying in vain to check the Uve'. Durnford goes on to suggest: 'May not the position of the Undi & Uve Regts (map 2) have been on the eastern side of the plateau? Zulu accounts say they slept in the valley of a small stream & the remaining Regts as shewn in the valley.' Here Durnford refers specifically to what he calls 'map 2', which is identical to the name of the Durban 'Map No. 2', and refers to the notation showing the Undi and Uve as the rightmost units in the arc of regiments, and slightly north-west of the point Durnford's force reached before it retired towards the camp. He is arguing that the two Zulu units should be shown in the Ngwebeni 'ravine' where the *impi* slept on the night of 21 January 1879.

> The position eastward of the plateau would agree with the description of the first attack on Colonel Durnford. 'Having proceeded five or six miles, a mounted man (Trooper Whitelaw, N. Carbineers) came down from the hills on the left, and reported there was an immense "impi" behind the hills to our left, and he had scarcely made the report when the Zulus appeared in force in front of us and to our left. They were in skirmishing order but ten or twelve deep, with support close behind. They opened fire on us at about 800 yards, and advanced very rapidly.'
>
> That reads as if they came <u>round</u> and over the hill (2800). I don't think Colonel Durnford was <u>persuaded to retire</u> by Hlubi. (Note map 2).

Durnford here cites a passage from Lieutenant W.F.D. Cochrane's statement (in WO 32/7713) in support of his argument to place the Undi and Uve in the Ngwebeni ravine rather to the west of Mabaso (which he refers to as '2800' and is actually its height above sea-level). He concludes by disagreeing with the Durban Map 2 notation that '. . . when Hlubi hearing the firing of mounted and other contingents of Basuto persuaded him to retire'.

What are we to make of this? The letter certainly refers to details to be found on the two Durban maps but what about their cousins in the Royal Engineers Museum?

The first thing to note is that the two parallel lines of circles on the RE Museum map are identified as 'N.N. Horse under Durnford trying in vain to check the Uve'. Thus the Durnford letter could not have been referring to this map because it refers to 'N.N. Horse' and not 'Hlubi's Basutos'. Wood may not have known the correct names of the two troops of horse that Durnford took with him, but Henderson, having command of one of them, most certainly did.

A second point is that on the Durban map 2, the Undi and Uve are shown as the right-most units in the arc of regiments. On the RE Museum equivalent, the right-most are the Indlondlo and the Uve, while to their immediate left are the Undi and Ngobamakhosi. Once again, Edward Durnford could only have been referring to the Durban map.

It would seem, therefore, that Edward Durnford had seen only the two Durban maps, and that these had possibly (but not certainly) been annotated by Evelyn Wood, perhaps from information he gathered when he returned to Natal. We know that he left South Africa with Lord Chelmsford in late July 1879 but returned to Natal in 1880 when he escorted Empress Eugénie on her visit to the site of the Prince Imperial's death. His visit lasted until the following July, during which time he and his charge visited Hlobane, Khambula and the site of the Prince's death. Since Edward Durnford's letter was written in October 1880, this was perhaps the only opportunity that Wood could have had to annotate the maps, although he makes no reference to them in his autobiography. Nor does Wood mention visiting Isandlwana during that time. The only reference that he did so is given in the Lock and Quantrill paper known as 'The Missing Five Hours':[24] 'We arrived at Isandhlwana on 5th June [1880] . . . General Wood interviewed several Zulus who had taken part in the battle . . . We left for Rorke's Drift on 8th June.'[25]

He also made a visit in 1881, in company with General Buller and several staff officers, because he tells us so himself:

We off-saddled on the Nek where Colonel Durnford fell, surrounded by the heroic Natal Police who died with him, and I described to my five Staff Officers how all the Zulu Corps, from right to left, attacked: the Nodwengu, Nokenke, Umcityu, Umbonambi, Ngobamakosi, Uve, to the Undi on the extreme left. I knew the ground, having spent some hours on it in 1880, guided by men who fought as foes on January 22nd, 1879. The stories of a mounted officer of the Ngobamakosi Regiment, a Natal Mounted Policeman, and a Basuto agreed in all respects.[26]

But where do the RE Museum maps fit in? They are too alike in their details to have been generated independently. One might speculate that Edward Durnford made copies of the two maps for his own use and these eventually found their way into the RE Museum. If so, it will be noted that he modified some of the entries on the maps to correspond with his own views as represented to Wood.

A sub-strand of the arguments presented here emerged in the form of a substantial paper written by Lock and Quantrill entitled 'The Missing Five

Hours', a reference to the apparent inertia of the Zulu army following its early morning movements, between 7 a.m. and noon on 22 January 1879. This was followed by the opening of a very extensive thread on the on-line Zulu War forum www.rorkesdriftvc.com/forum/viewtopic.php?t=2069, a long debate that continues to this day.

The Messages

In a letter to Lieutenant-General Lord Chelmsford, His Royal Highness George, Duke of Cambridge and commander-in-chief of the British Army had, through the adjutant-general, General Ellice, asked a series of pointed questions about the circumstances surrounding the defeat at Isandlwana. One of these questions related to the matter of messages which had passed during that day:

> 6. Did you at any point after [9 a.m.], and before Commandant Lonsdale reported to you that the Camp was in the hands of the enemy, receive any reports, native or otherwise, which led you to suppose that an action was going on near the Camp; and if so, what steps did you take?[27]

Lord Chelmsford replied that he had received only one message that day, at about 9.30 a.m., from Lieutenant-Colonel Pulleine, following which he ordered Lieutenant Milne, RN, one of his aides-de-camp, to observe the camp through a high-powered telescope for some ninety minutes. Milne had seen nothing untoward. Chelmsford had also, he said, 'sent back to camp at 9.30 a.m. one of the Native Contingent battalions' which would allow at least one of its mounted officers 'to bring me any intelligence of importance'. Other than that single message from Pulleine, 'I received no report whatever previous to Commandant Lonsdale's report that the camp was in the hands of the enemy, or that led me to suppose that an action was going on near the camp, or that it was in any danger.'[28]

The issue of messages that were sent to Lord Chelmsford that day is worthy of much more attention than seems to have been given to it hitherto. For that reason, this paper will attempt to trace every message that was addressed to him after the arrival of the centre column at Isandlwana in an attempt to find out why they did not reach the general, either in a timely fashion or, apparently, at all.

On the morning of 21 January 1879 two reconnaissance forces left the British camp at Isandlwana. The first left at dawn and consisted of eight companies from each of the two battalions of the 3rd Regiment, NNC, led by its commandant Rupert la Trobe Lonsdale, who had made a solid name for himself in the Ninth Frontier War in the Eastern Cape in 1877/8.[29] Their objective was a thorough reconnaissance of the Malakatha hills to the south-east of Isandlwana, reported to be the site of 'Matshana's Stronghold'.[30] The second party, consisting of most of the mounted men from the colonial volunteer units and the Natal Mounted Police, was led by Major John Dartnell, Natal Mounted Police, and it moved off about an hour later in the direction of Isiphezi Hill. By the end of the day the two forces had come together on Hlazakazi Hill, at the south-eastern end of the Malakatha range of hills, about twenty kilometres (12.5 miles) from the camp. After a confrontation, Dartnell was convinced that he had found the Zulu army that had been purportedly marching towards them.

About 3 or 4 p.m., Major Gossett and Captain Buller, two of Lord Chelmsford's aides-de-camp who had accompanied Dartnell, arrived near the camp and met the general before reaching it.[31]

> I was with the Lt General that afternoon when these officers brought the Lt General information that Major Dartnell with the Mounted Troops had come up with a body of the enemy, but he did not consider he was strong enough to attack them until Comm't Lonsdale's force arrived; further that Major Dartnell intended to remain out that night & watch the enemy with his own & Commandant Lonsdale's force.[32]

Lieutenant Milne also left an account of the message brought by these officers:

> Major Dartnell sent in for instructions as to what he was to do; in the meantime if no orders [to the contrary] were sent he intended to bivouac on the ground he had taken up, and watch the enemy.
>   Orders were immediately sent to Major Dartnell to attack it, and when he thought fit. Food also was sent to his force.[33]

According to Lord Chelmsford, permission for reinforcements for Gossett's force was denied because 'the day was far advanced',[34] but since Chelmsford had also sent out food, he clearly gave Dartnell tacit permission to stay out. This despite the fact that: 'My orders to that officer were distinct, that he was to return to camp after completing his reconnaissance, and I was much vexed at my orders not being attended to.'[35] He did not, as he perhaps might have done, order Dartnell to return to camp, leaving a small party of mounted men to watch the Zulus. But that alternative only derives from hindsight.

A second message, delivered about 8.30 or 9 p.m. by a Lieutenant Davey, brought further information:

> Major Dartnell was under the impression that he would not be at liberty to attack the enemy in the morning without instructions, and that the General therefore wished that Lieutenant Davey would be found and directed to start as early as possible in the morning, and inform Major Dartnell that he was at complete liberty to act on his own judgment as to whether he should attack or not. I eventually . . . conveyed to him the General's instructions, which I made him repeat over for me before I left him.[36]

This second message was entirely overlooked by Lord Chelmsford in all his reports. Perhaps an hour before midnight Dartnell sent the last of his three messages to Lord Chelmsford, still more insistent than the previous one:

> About 1.30 a.m. on the 22nd, a messenger brought me a note from Major Dartnell to say that the enemy was in greater numbers than when he last reported, and that he did not think it prudent to attack them unless reinforced by 2 or 3 companies of the 24th Regiment. I took this note to Colonel Glyn, C.B., at once, he ordered me to take it on to the General.[37]

As a result of these appeals, Lord Chelmsford also became convinced as to the whereabouts of the Zulu army; he left about 4 a.m. on the 22nd with the column commander Colonel Glyn and six of the seven companies of the 2/24th Regiment,[38] four guns under Lieutenant-Colonel Arthur Harness and the Mounted Infantry, leaving behind only those needed for vedette duty or whose riders or horses were unfit. Brevet Lieutenant-Colonel Henry Burmester Pulleine was left in command of the camp.

About 8 o'clock on that morning, there was increasing Zulu activity on the plateau above Isandlwana and, after ordering the camp to stand-to, Pulleine sent off the first message of that day. It is referred to as 'No. 1' in subsequent contemporary correspondence:

> Staff Officer.— Report just come in that the Zulus are advancing in force from left front of Camp (8.5).
> H. B. PULLEINE, Lieut.Col.[39]

This message was received at 9.30 a.m. by Captain Henry Hallam-Parr, staff officer to Colonel Glyn, who passed it to Major Clery, Glyn's principal staff officer: 'After receiving [it], I at once handed it to the General. The

General read it and returned it back to me without a remark. As he issued no orders on it, I asked him if he wished anything done on it. He replied there was nothing to be done on it.'[40]

The morning wore on and Captain Alan Gardner, director of transport to the column, was sent back to Isandlwana by the General:

I was sent back with an order from the General between 10 and 11 a.m. that day into camp, which order was addressed to Colonel Pulleine, and was that the camp of the force out was to be struck and sent on immediately, also rations and forage for about 7 days.[41]

I left the force with the General about 10.30 a.m., and rode back to Islandana [sic] Camp with the order to Lieutenant-Colonel Pulleine to send on the camp equipage and supplies of the troops camping out, and to remain himself at his present camp and entrench it.[42]

Gardner reached Isandlwana shortly after midday and was, in the circumstances, lucky to have reached it without incident because the Zulu army by then had been discovered – not at all where Lord Chelmsford either expected it to be or was himself located. The attack on the camp had already begun. As a result of this order Pulleine sent a second message to Lord Chelmsford:

Staff officer,
Heavy firing to left of our Camp. Cannot move Camp at present.
H. B. Pulleine Lieut.Colonel.

In his official evidence to the court of inquiry into the disaster at Isandlwana, Gardner was to recall: 'I may mention that a few minutes after my arrival in camp, I sent a message directed to the Staff Officer, 3rd Column, saying that our left was attacked by about 10,000 of the enemy.'[43] Gardner's message, which was only marginally more informative than Pulleine's, actually read as follows:

Heavy firing near left of Camp.
Shepstone has come in for reinforcements, and reports the Basutos falling back.
The whole force at Camp turned out and fighting about one mile to left flank.
Alan Gardner,
Captain, S.O.

There is some mystery as to the movements of both this message and that of Pulleine.[44] Pulleine's message was reportedly handed by the general to his assistant military secretary, Lieutenant-Colonel Crealock, on the following day, 23 January.[45] Gardner's own note, identified as 'No. 2' in the correspondence, while addressed to Major Clery, was apparently never received by him, but by Major Gossett about 3 p.m. on 22 January, who in turn handed it to Lieutenant-Colonel Crealock the next day.[46]

Clery was later asked to report on these two messages, to which he responded:

> With reference to the memorandum from the Deputy Adjutant-General, dated Pietermaritzburg, 24th February 1879, covering a minute . . . calling on me 'to report fully when and how I received reports Nos. 1 and 2, and what action I took with them, especially report 2', I have the honour to state in reply, with regard to report No. 1, that I never received this report, nor any similar report to this effect, nor was I aware, up to now, that any such report, had been received by the Lieutenant-General Commanding, or was in existence. Never having received this report, therefore, I beg to state that I took no action on it.
>
> With regard to report No. 2, I never received this report, nor any similar report to this effect, nor was I aware, up to now, that any such report had been received by the Lieutenant-General Commanding, or was in existence. Further, I received no report of any kind whatever from Captain Gardner that day, nor was I aware, up to now, that Captain Gardner had sent back to the force absent from the Camp any report of any kind on that day.[47]

As was seen at the beginning of this paper, Lord Chelmsford denied having seen the second of Pulleine's messages. He gave a second denial in another memorandum: 'Before the first and only report received from Lieutenant-Colonel Pulleine during the 22nd of January 1879 was received, I had ordered, as mentioned by Major Clery, 2 companies 2/24th and 4 guns under Major Harness, RA, to move back about 2 miles on the road towards the Camp.'[48] And yet, in that same short note he implied that he had seen it:

> After Captain Gardiner [sic] had delivered the message regarding the sending out of the tents and camp equipment to Lieutenant-Colonel Pulleine at about 11.30 a.m., it would seem that the latter officer sent a message back to the effect that he was not able to carry out the order at that time. This message was not received until quite late in the afternoon of the 22nd January 1879, and as it contained no allusion to any danger from attack, or any request for assistance, I feel that my assumption that no danger was anticipated must be correct.[49]

One must also wonder just how, and when, Pulleine's second message came into His Lordship's possession so as to allow him to pass it to Crealock on the 23rd. It is futile, however, to speculate on what might have happened had these two messages been read together, with reference also to Pulleine's first message. Gardner had taken about an hour and a half to ride from the area within which Chelmsford was moving to the camp at Isandlwana and it must have taken at least that long for any messages in reply to reach the Mangeni area, making the time not earlier than 1.45 p.m., by which time the disaster was almost complete.

All but one of the remaining messages came from Commandant George Hamilton-Browne, commanding the 1st Battalion, 3rd Regiment, NNC. His memoir was published in 1912 and his references to his messages in that work are not entirely reliable.[50] However, he wrote an official report of his proceedings that day dated 2 February, which must be more trustworthy.[51]

Hamilton-Browne and his battalion were despatched to the camp by Lord Chelmsford to assist Pulleine in the movement of the 2nd Battalion tentage.[52] Since Pulleine's report was received at 9.30, the lieutenant-general believed that the NNC battalion was sent off about 10 a.m., with which time Hamilton-Browne concurs. Hamilton-Browne had only 'moved the battalion round the base of the first hill' when he came across two Zulu scouts who, under his probably heavy persuasion, told him that the camp was to be attacked. He sent off Lieutenant Pohl to give this intelligence to the general, when the time was about 10.30 or 11 a.m.

The key part of Hamilton-Browne's report deserves to be quoted in full:

When I had advanced about three miles I saw the enemy advancing in large masses to attack the left of the Camp, and I saw the guns open fire on them.

I then sent Serjeant Turner to the General with this news, but neither himself or Mr. Pohl could find him, but reported these facts to officers they met on the road. I still pushed forward, but found at about 1 p.m. that I was cut off, as large bodies of the enemy were between us and the Camp. I then moved to my left, so as to try to get into the right of the Camp and advance some distance.

I then sent another message to the General informing him of the position the Camp was in, and also my movements.

At about 1.30 p.m., I saw one of the guns alter its position and fire towards the front of the enemy, and also noticed that heavy firing was going on in the front and left of the camp. I still pushed forward, but in a short time saw that the guns had ceased firing, but that heavy fighting was going on in the Camp; at the time I saw the gun alter the direction of its fire, I sent Captain Develin with this message to the General or any Staff Officer he could meet, 'For God's sake come back, the Camp is surrounded, and things I fear are going badly.'

Thus Hamilton-Browne sent no less than four messages to Lord Chelmsford between perhaps 10.30 a.m. and 2 p.m. and there is some evidence that at least two of them, and perhaps a third, may have been received by Lieutenant-Colonel J.C. Russell, commanding the mounted men:

> 15. Lieutenant-Colonel Cecil Russell, 12th Lancers, now joined us, and informed me that an Officer of the Natal Native Contingent had come to him (about 12 noon, I think) when he was off-saddled, and asked where the General was, as he had instructions to tell him that heavy firing had been going on close to the camp – our whereabouts was not exactly known, but the 2nd battalion 24th companies were still in sight, and Colonel Russell pointed them out and said we were probably not far from them; this officer, however, did not come to us.[53]

This must have been Lieutenant Pohl since he was sent off some time after 10.30 a.m. Russell himself, when required to report on the matter, responded thus:

> When I quitted the Isipisi Valley, I off-saddled for half an hour. At the end of that time, I believe about 1.15 o'clock p.m., a mounted European of the Native Contingent came up and said that he was sent to tell the General that the camp was attacked. We could not tell him where the General was, but he was told whereabouts he had been in the morning.[54]

The 'European' may well have been Sergeant Turner. This was not all; Russell then went on:

> I directed the Mounted Infantry to move quietly along outside the hills, while I went personally to the place where we left the General to try and gain information of his whereabouts, and ascertain his wishes. In this I was unsuccessful, so I rejoined the squadron, the officers of which informed me that they had seen the guns in camp firing, meeting a second mounted European, who also said that he was sent to inform the General that the camp was attacked. As soon as I approached the place where the movements of the morning began I sent out Lieutenant Walsh and Captain Davy,[55] each with an escort, to try to find his Excellency, and give him the information which we had received.

This was probably Hamilton-Browne's third, unnamed, messenger. Lord Chelmsford's ADC, Lieutenant Milne, also states, 'We then went on to look for bivouacing [sic] ground for the night, and had not gone far when one of the Mounted Natives came and reported heavy firing at the camp.'[56] According to Milne's reported times this occurred after 1.30 pm. This incident might be supported by the evidence of Norris-Newman: 'At this juncture one of our mounted natives came galloping down from the opposite ridge, whence the camp could be seen, and reported to a Staff-officer that an attack was being made on the camp, as he had seen heavy firing and heard the big guns.'[57] Still another officer also reported what must have been the same incident: 'When thus engaged a native came with a report from Commandant Browne who was with his native battalion watching the road between us and the camp that a large force of Zulus was in their front near Isandhlwana.'[58]

These reports seem also to relate to Hamilton-Browne's third messenger whom he did not name. Yet how could the lieutenant-general remain in ignorance of this message when one of his aides-de-camp knew about it?

Captain Develin was more fortunate in the delivery of Hamilton-Browne's fourth message:

Suddenly a body of about 1,000 natives appeared in the plain below, in the direction of the camp, and were pronounced to be Zulus by the native sappers.

Captain Church, 2-24th Regiment, suggested to Colonel Harness that if he would let him have a horse he would ride forward and find out. This Colonel Harness did. Captain Church galloped towards the natives. A European officer rode out to meet him, and said, 'The troops behind me are Commandant Brown's Contingent, and I am sent to give you this message, 'Come in every man for God's sake; the camp is surrounded, and will be taken unless helped at once.' Captain Church returned as fast as he could, and delivered the message to Colonel Harness, who was then in conversation with Major Black and Major Gosset, ADC, who had come up.[59]

What followed is reported by Major Gosset himself:

While talking to [Colonel Harness], Church of the 2/24th rode up in a very excited state and said the camp had been taken. I did not believe the report, but at the same time felt uneasy and saw that those around me shared the feeling. Harness on hearing Church's report said, 'I presume under the circumstances I had better move towards the camp.' I said, 'I do not know, but send an officer back with me and he can carry to you the General's instructions.' The General and Staff were some distance behind. I made my report. Harness was ordered back [to the new camp site] and the General mounted and rode towards the camp.[60]

Harness' own version of this event is as follows:

While I was going to the new camping ground I received a message from the camp saying that the camp was surrounded by Zulus and, unless it had assistance, must be taken. Upon this I went about and meeting [Lieutenant-Colonel] Cecil Russell who commands the cavalry, with a force of mounted infantry, I proposed with his escort to take the guns back to camp. We had no sooner agreed upon this than the general came up; he had received a report of the state of the camp but nothing like so strong as the message I received.[61]

While neither Chelmsford nor Crealock mention this incident, and thus throw no light on which version is correct; there is confirmation for Gosset: 'In the meantime news came that Colonel Harness had heard the firing, and was proceeding with his guns and companies of infantry escorting them to camp. Orders were immediately sent to him to return and rejoin Colonel Glyn.'[62]

The penultimate message was delivered personally. Rupert Lonsdale, commandant of the 3rd Regiment, NNC, had fallen from his horse about 9 or 10 January and suffered concussion as a result.[63] He did not return to duty until 'before the move to Isandlwana',[64] perhaps about 18 or 19 January. During the late morning of the 22nd, Lonsdale decided to return to the camp. His reasons for doing so are unclear, he himself stating: 'My chief object being to enquire about rations for my Regiment.'[65] Major Gossett also related this as the reason: 'At about midday I met Captain Lonsdale,[66] who said that his Native Contingent had been without food for 24 hours and he wanted to ride to the camp to make arrangements for them.'[67] Yet Lonsdale gave a different version to Norris-Newman: 'It appeared that in pursuing a mounted Zulu he had become separated from his corps, and had therefore ridden quietly back to the camp at Isandwhlana [sic].'[68]

It is probable that Lonsdale became disorientated as a result of lack of food and heat stress which, combined with his recent concussion, induced him to return. Whatever the cause, however, the result remained the same:

As I rode into Camp, I was in an absent state of mind for want of sleep and overwork. I don't know of what I was thinking, my thoughts were perhaps chiefly directed on getting something to eat, I had been a long time without food. I saw the movement of the Camp all around me and red coats surrounding me, suddenly I was brought to myself with a shock. A figure came out of a tent with a dripping assegai and looking all round, to my horror, I saw that every red coat had a black face above it! I had sufficient presence of mind not to check or increase my pace but gradually turned my pony round; so soon as I was facing my direction out of Camp, I jammed my heels into the pony's side. But the little beast would not move. The natives were rushing towards me. Again I frantically dug my heels in and the pony broke into a canter. Had the Zulus thrown nothing but their assegais at me I should have been done for, but the majority fired rifles and missed. So I got away from the Camp. After proceeding some miles I came across a European Sergeant of one of our Native Contingents, and gave him the message which was afterwards delivered to Captain Church.[69]

Lord Chelmsford had already begun his return to the camp.

When within about 6 miles of the camp I found the 1st Battalion Native Contingent halted, and shortly after Commandant Lonsdale rode up to report that [he] had ridden into camp and found it in possession of the Zulus.[70]

The general now sent for the remainder of his force and began the march back to Isandlwana. With the camp now seemingly lost Hamilton-Browne sent his final message: 'After some time, about 3 p.m., I saw the Mounted Infantry, and sent Captain Hays [sic] to them with a message. I then halted till the General arrived.'[71]

In a later letter calling for a report of that day from Lieutenant-Colonel Russell, Colonel Bellairs mentioned the Hayes message: 'Captain Hayes NNC is said to have been sent with an important message by Commandant Browne for the Lieut. General Commanding, which never reached [him] tho' it is reported that he delivered the message to the O.C. Mounted Infantry.'[72]

In the subsequent report which the deputy adjutant-general requested,[73] Russell made the following comment on this message:

Previous to joining the Native Contingent, though at what particular time I do not remember, a written memo was put into my hand, sent by Comm'dt Browne to the effect that 'there was a large force of the enemy between him and the Camp'.

This note I am under the impression was addressed to the Officer Commanding Mounted Corps. In any case, I am certain that I communicated it to the General.[74] I do not remember whether it was brought by Capt. Hayes or not. This is the only written note which I can remember to have received. It was unfortunately lost in the subsequent confusion.[75]

This, of course, directly contradicts his earlier words, unless he was being deliberately pedantic, relying upon the caveat that it was a 'written note' as opposed to one delivered verbally.

From the foregoing, it is easy to see that there was considerable confusion in the sending and receipt of messages that day, although had they all been received by the general or his staff he must have perceived the danger to the camp much earlier than he did. On the evidence, however, it is also clear, such was its distance from Isandlwana, that Lord Chelmsford's force would have been unable to prevent the overrun of the camp. The only occasion when this might have been possible was on receipt of Pulleine's first message at 9.30 a.m., but it was so sketchy as to have been almost useless, as it so proved.

The Several Captains Barton

The frequent, but not invariable, practice of contemporary official reports and commentaries to name officers without a forename or initial avoided confusion in most cases by simply including the officer's regiment or unit.[76] Where there happened to be two officers of the same name in a unit, their rank would also distinguish them. This apparently careless attitude to identification succeeded most of the time but when officers of auxiliary units became involved the propensity for confusion increased.

There were three captains with the surname of Barton who served concurrently in the Zulu War and who have thereby provided just such an example of uncertainty.[77] One of these, Captain Robert Johnston Barton, Coldstream Guards, may be disposed of quickly and without ambiguity. Robert Barton was a special service officer appointed second-in-command of the Frontier Light Horse (FLH) with which he served until he was killed at Hlobane.[78] His commanding officer, Lieutenant-Colonel Redvers Buller, was greatly affected by his death, lamenting 'my second in command, poor, dear, affectionate little Bobby Barton was killed.'[79]

The careers of the two remaining officers, however, are closely interwoven and it is the object of this paper to bring some light to bear on what is currently a very confused matter. The two officers were Captain Geoffry Barton,[80] 7th (Royal Fusiliers) Regiment and Captain William Barton, commanding Zikhali's Horse under Colonel Durnford. William Barton, we must assume, was a colonial gentleman since there is no record of him in Hart's Annual Army Lists.

We have a record of service for the first of these two men: 'Served throughout the war, first as Staff Officer to Durnford's Column, and, subsequently, in command of the 4th Batt. NNC, till the end of the war, taking part in the battle of Ginghilovo . . .'[81]

Another, more complete, record, however, includes some odd details, as will be shown shortly:

Barton, Geoffrey [sic] (1844-1922). Captain, 7th Fusiliers. Service in 2nd Ashanti War, 1874. On special service throughout 1879, first as Staff Officer to Colonel Durnford of No. 2 Column and commander of the Natal Mounted Contingent, and subsequently as commander of the 4th Battalion, NNC, successively with the Eshowe Relief Column, the 1st Division and Clarke's Column. Present at Isandlwana and Gingindlovu. Brevet Major.[82]

He is also mentioned as 'For general Staff Duties, Captain [no initial] Barton, 7th Foot'.[83] Further, a Captain Barton, 7th Foot, again with no initial, is listed as staff officer to Colonel Durnford.[84] Thus far there seems to be no difficulty but the seeds of confusion have already been sown: in Laband's brief entry above, the words 'commander of the Natal Mounted Contingent' and 'Present at Isandlwana' appear. If, however, we now pass to the period after May 1879, again there is no confusion: Captain Geoffry Barton is commandant of the 4th Battalion, NNC.[85]

Most of the problems arise with the battle of Isandlwana, when a Captain Barton is also listed by MacKinnon and Shadbolt as being associated in some way with the Natal Native Mounted Contingent (NNMC): 'Colonel Durnford now sent two troops of mounted natives, under Captains Shepstone and Barton, onto the hills to the left . . .'[86]

Perhaps the first modern writer to propagate the confusion was Donald Morris who consistently confuses the two men.[87] Laband perpetuates the misunderstanding in his biographical note cited earlier in which the reference quoted also confuses the activities of two men, without any reference to the only one of them who was present at Isandlwana, Captain William Barton.[88] From where did this new man spring? Or is this really Captain Geoffry? The fundamental question to be resolved here is whether, in fact, there were indeed two Captains Barton, and if so, just what positions did they hold, and where?

In Orders of Battle for Durnford's Second Column most modern authors associate Captain W. Barton with the NNMC.[89] Indeed, the very problem confronting us is tantalizingly canvassed by David Jackson who advises that Captain W. Barton is 'not to be confused with his regular army namesake, the staff officer of the 1st Regt NNC . . .'[90]

A close examination of the record demonstrates conclusively that both officers existed and performed the functions that they are supposed to have done, although only one of them was at Isandlwana.

Let us first deal with Captain William Barton. Although his antecedents are obscure, there is a brief glimpse of his earlier life but its veracity is perhaps as uncertain as its origin:

A man named Barton, with some Basutos, did real good service in covering the retreat of the fugitives [at Isandlwana]. I fancy many owe their lives to him. He is an Irishman, and has been fighting for seven years in South America against the Indians in those parts, and I suppose, attracted by a chance of fresh adventures, came here and got together 200 or 300 Basutos, who were formed into an irregular cavalry. When all was up and a certain number got into a water-course clear of the Zulus, he, being on that flank, moved his men into position to cover the flight. He retired firing, keeping his men together, and was, in fact, the last to cross the river.[91]

We can trace his service with the NNMC through the following steps. A letter from the then Major J.N. Crealock, assistant military secretary to Lord Chelmsford, to the Colonial Secretary of Natal identifies a number of appointments as officers to the Natal Native Contingent. Among them, as a lieutenant, is 'W. Barton Esq.'.[92] This was followed by an official promulgation in General Order No. 203 of 21 November 1878 which has the following entry:

4. The following names of gentlemen selected for appointment as Officers, to serve under the Officer Commanding Her Majesty's Forces in South Africa, have received the approval of His Excellency the High Commissioner and Commander in Chief:
As Lieutenants:
W. Barton . . . R.W. Vause . . .[93]

The fact that both the Barton and Vause appointments were promulgated in the same general order is significant, as will later be seen. A week later General Order No. 209, dated 28 November 1878, announced: 'W. Barton, C. Raw and J.A. Roberts will be attached, as Lieutenants, to the Natal Mounted Contingent . . .'[94]

Finally, and probably containing a typesetter's error, came General Order No. 231, dated 21 December 1878: 'Lieutenant C.[?] Barton, Natal Native Mounted Contingent to be Captain, dated 20 December, 1878.'[95] This apparently rapid promotion to captain occurred concurrently with those of a number of other officers of the NNC at this time, so Barton's appointment should not be considered unusual.

We should next follow the path of Captain Geoffry Barton in the Zulu War in a similar fashion. General Order No. 218, dated 9 December 1878, contained the following:

Lieut.-Colonel Durnford RE, is appointed to command a column now in course of formation, consisting of 1st Regiment, Natal Native Contingent, 2½ Squadrons Mounted ditto, ditto. A rocket battery.

The following officers will be attached:–

Captain Barton, 1-7th Regt., arrived from England, to act as Staff Officer to the Column.[96]

There is no doubt about the permanence of this appointment as Durnford himself wrote in a letter to his mother: 'Captain Barton, 7th Fusiliers, is my Staff Officer, and George Shepstone, the same who was with me [at Bushman's River pass] in 1873, is with me again . . .'[97] So it is clear that there were indeed two Captains Barton with the Second Column. This begs the question, however, whether both, or just one, were at Isandlwana.

There is firm evidence that William Barton was there. After the battle, and while crossing the Mzinyathi (Buffalo) River at Fugitive's Drift, Private Westwood, 80th Foot, became separated from his horse and was in imminent danger of drowning. Private Samuel Wassall, of the same regiment, was riding down to the river bank on the Zulu side when he saw Westwood struggling in the fast-flowing river.[98] He immediately dismounted and plunged into the water, eventually bringing Westwood back to the bank, where he pointed out that Westwood would be better advised to cross at a ford higher up, which he subsequently did. This action, for which Wassall later received the Victoria Cross, was witnessed by Captain William Barton who was riding directly behind Wassall as they made their way to the river. Barton gave a statement in support of an award of the Victoria Cross to Wassall, ending with the following signature:

Wm Barton, Captain
Com'g 'Zikhali' Squadron
Natal Mounted Contingent
No. 2 Column.[99]

This document establishes beyond doubt that Captain William Barton was at Isandlwana but it goes further. He himself indicates his function: he did not command the whole of the Mounted Contingent but only the troops containing Zikhali's men, that is, three troops out of six.[100]

This also resolves an otherwise potential problem raised by the relative ranks of William Barton and Captain George Shepstone, who was Durnford's political assistant. When two troops of Zikhali's Horse were sent up to the plateau to scout and clear away Zulu bands Shepstone went with Lieutenant

Raw while Barton accompanied Lieutenant Roberts. The question of command is raised by the account of James Hamer, a commissariat storekeeper with Durnford: 'Very soon after the Mounted Native Horse had arrived they were sent out to cover [the] hills on the left of the Camp, Captain George Shepstone in command.'[101]

One might infer from Hamer's words that Shepstone was in command of Raw's troop by virtue of his rank but it soon becomes plain that Shepstone had command not just of Raw's but of both troops of horse because Hamer also uses the words: 'After his having given orders to the Captain of the Native Horse to retire gradually, Geo. Shepstone (and myself) rode as hard as ever we could back to the Camp & reported what we had seen.'[102]

Barton was the only other captain present but Shepstone clearly outranked him. This may have been in part the result of the close friendship between Durnford and the Shepstone family, perhaps the most prominent family in Natal, but must also have derived from Shepstone's greater experience and his long association with Durnford stretching back to the Bushman's River Pass episode in 1873. We can see this relationship at work when Durnford, Shepstone and Hamer had dinner together on the night before the Isandlwana disaster.[103] Shepstone was probably also de facto staff officer to Durnford.[104] On the other hand, George Shepstone would not have been able to assert any superiority if the officer involved had been Captain Geoffry Barton. As a captain in the regular army of long standing he would have heavily outranked Shepstone, who would certainly have deferred to an Imperial officer.

There is another reference to William Barton's service with the NNMC: Wyatt Vause made an entry in his diary for 22 March 1879 in which he mentions: 'On going to saddle up in the morning, found my horse standing in a pool of blood, caused from kicking against the head of a nail. Fortunately, Capt. Barton had two horses and kindly lent me one of his . . .'[105]

Barton probably spent much of his time on very routine duty, as did Wyatt Vause. Unlike Raw, William Barton was not at Hlobane or Khambula. In early March he was at the office of the resident magistrate of the Upper Thukela, Albert Allison, 'making arrangements for the re-assembly of Sikali's Horsemen belonging to the N.N.C.'[106] Allison wrote to him on 8 March telling him that Zikhali's men would re-assemble some days hence and that he (Barton) would be notified in due course.[107]

William Barton, like all NNC officers, was on a six-month contract with the British military authorities in South Africa.[108] Since both he and Vause were appointed by the same General Order, dated 21 November 1878, he was due for discharge with Vause in May 1879: 'Stopped in camp all morning preparing for journey down as my 6 months would expire on 20th.'[109]

After leaving the service on 20 May, Barton returned to his previous obscurity and unlike a number of others did not pander to public demand for his version of the disaster. His only other mention is in the account of Charles Norris-Newman, in which Barton is quoted as saying that: '. . . his mounted men really fought well at their first charge [at Isandlwana], and until all their ammunition was exhausted; they were then compelled to fall back on the camp, where they sought a fresh supply of ammunition.'[110] He was awarded his South African Medal on 10 March 1882.[111]

On 10 January, Durnford had marched out of Kranskop for Sandspruit with the part of the 1st and the whole of the 2nd Battalions taking with him five troops of Native Horse and the Rocket Battery while the rest of the 1st Regiment remained behind with the sixth troop of horse (Jantze's men).

At Sandspruit, the veteran Major Bengough was sent with his 2nd Battalion NNC towards Elandskraal with orders to cross the Mzinyathi on the 22nd, leaving the 1st Battalion at Sandspruit. Durnford was ordered up to Rorke's Drift and he took with him the five troops of NNMC, the Rocket Battery and three companies of the 1st Battalion.[112] The three companies had been combined into two under Captains Stafford and Nourse because the third company commander, Captain Hay, being the senior, was left behind to act as paymaster.[113]

A letter included in the recent donation of Colonel Pearson's personal papers to the National Army Museum in London proves conclusively that Durnford left Geoffry Barton at Kranskop and so the latter could not have been present at Isandlwana:[114] 'In compliance with this memorandum (No. 15) Colonel Durnford left at 4 a.m. today with 250 horsemen, 1400 of the N.N. Contingent, & the rocket battery, en route for the Sand Spruit Valley; leaving me in command at the Middle Drift.'[115]

Confirmation, if any is required, is to be found in a newspaper column dated 17 January 1879 referring to an earlier report of the day before:

The whole of the 2nd Battalion and two companies of the 1st Battalion Natal Native Contingent, the Mounted Contingent, and the rocket battery are ordered off at an hour's notice to Helpmakaar, under the command of Major Bengough, Captains Russell, RA, Nourse, Henderson and [W.] Barton. Colonel Durnford and Captain Shepstone are going with the column. Captain [G.] Barton returns to Kranskop, and will probably go with the 1st Battalion to the Middle Drift.[116]

This posting is also confirmed in an undated Return of Troops from Assistant Military Secretary Crealock, but which forms part of a group of documents dated late January 1879. This return shows the 1st and 3rd battalions, 1st Regiment, NNC, together with the 3rd Natal Native Pioneers, located at Kranskop under the command of Captain (Geoffry) Barton.[117] The earliest modern writer to appreciate that Captain Geoffry Barton was not at Isandlwana is Dr Paul Thompson: '[Durnford] left the remainder of the No. 2 Column under his staff officer, Captain G. Barton, of the 7th Fusiliers.'[118]

Barton continued serving with the Native Contingent. General Order No. 38, dated 20 February 1879, announced that he was 'appointed to act as Staff Officer at Greytown'. [119] As we have seen earlier he then went on to command the 4th Battalion NNC until the end of the war,[120] taking part with his men at the battle of Gingindlovu. He was destined for still greater things. He received his South Africa Medal and later took part in the Second Boer War (1899–1902) eventually rising to the rank of major-general. He was made Knight Commander of the Victorian Order in 1906 and died in 1922.[121]

The Queen's Colour

The gallant attempt by Lieutenant Teignmouth Melvill to save the Queen's Colour at the collapse of the camp at Isandlwana has been related many times and will not be repeated here. Despite the mystery of how his action was precipitated, at the order of Colonel Pulleine as romantically portrayed,[122] by someone else's order or on his own initiative, the fact is that the attempt failed, for which Melvill subsequently paid with his life. This sacrifice was treated rather contemptuously by General Sir Garnet Wolseley, who said: 'I am sorry that both of those officers [Melvill and Coghill] were not killed with their men at Isandhlana [sic] instead of where they were: I don't like the idea of officers escaping on horseback when their men on foot are killed.'[123] This criticism was unfair to both of these gallant men because neither had a direct command and thus had no men under them. Melvill was adjutant of the 1st Battalion, hence his proprietorial interest in the Colour. Coghill had been aide-de-camp to Sir Bartle Frere and had sought his permission to rejoin his regiment when war seemed inevitable: 'He left Pietermaritzburg on January 6th and reached his regiment at Rorke's Drift on the 10th. Colonel Glyn . . . appointed him his Orderly Officer.'[124] Discounting the courage and sacrifice involved in the Colour's loss, however, the tale of its recovery nevertheless contains still more mystery.

On 21 February, Colonel Glyn, commanding the Centre Column, wrote a report from Rorke's Drift giving details of the loss and subsequent recovery of the Queen's Colour of the 1/24th battalion. The following is an extract:

It was not for some days after 22nd that I could gather any information as to the probable fate of these officers. But immediately I discovered in what direction those who had escaped from Sandlwana [*sic*] had crossed the Buffalo, I sent, under Major Black, 2/24 Regt., a mounted party who volunteered for this service, to search for any trace that could be found of them. This search was successful and both bodies were found where they were last seen, as above indicated. Several dead bodies of the enemy were found about them, so they must have sold their lives dearly at the last.

As it was considered that the dead weight of the Color [*sic*] would cause it to sink in the river, it was hoped that a diligent search in the locality where the bodies of these officers were found might lead to its recovery. So Major Black again proceeded on the 4th inst. [February] to prosecute this search. His energetic efforts were, I am glad to say, crowned with success and the Color with the ornaments, case & co. belonging to it, were found, though in different places, in the river bed.[125]

Thus there were two expeditions led by Major Wilsone Black, the first of which found the bodies of the two officers, while a subsequent search located the Colour itself. The extracts which next follow are the words of Captain (local rank) Harford, staff officer to Colonel Durnford of the 1st Regiment, NNC, who places himself at the centre of the action he describes, while at the same time contradicting Colonel Glyn's own account of events. The reader will perhaps forgive the extended quotations, which are necessary to develop the argument.

It was now clear that measures should be taken in hand at once to search for [the Colour], and I reported this to Major Clery. Colonel Glyn, however, for some reason of his own, declined to allow the search party to be organised by the 24th, and I, on the other hand, felt very unwilling to carry out a mission which – subaltern only, as I was – I considered would be anything but creditable to the Regiment, they being actually on the spot . . . So I talked matters over with Major Black and asked him to use his influence with Colonel Glyn, and see what could be done.

. . . Major Black's interview, happily, ended in Colonel Glyn giving him permission to go out in command of our Contingent, and his face beamed with delight when he came out to tell me the news . . .[126]

Harford and Major Black departed on the reconnaissance at once: 'As we had all had our frugal meal, and the afternoon was before us, he [Black] at once said, 'Come along, we'll saddle up and you show me the way', so he and I went off on a most enjoyable and interesting ride.'[127] It was during this 'interesting ride' that they stumbled on the two bodies:

> Suddenly, just off the track to the right of us, we saw two bodies, and on going to have a look at them, found that they were those of Lieutenants Melvill and Coghill! Both were clearly recognizable. Melvill was in red, and Coghill in blue, uniform.
>
> Our search over, we set to work at once to cover the bodies with large stones and bits of rock for protection, till proper interment could take place, after which we rode home, as it was getting dusk.[128]

Having returned with the news, both were anxious to follow up their success, this time in the company of others:

> Soon after sunrise the following morning our little cavalcade of officers and N.C.O.'s of the Contingent, headed by Major Black in command, and myself, moved quietly away . . .
>
> Scarcely had we taken a few steps than I stumbled on the Colour case mixed up with a heap of other things, and picking it up I said to Harber, who was closest to me, 'Look here, here's the case! The Colours can't be far off!' We all three then had a look at it, put it on a conspicuous boulder, and went on. Then, as Harber was returning to his position, I noticed a straight piece of stick projecting out of the water in the middle of the river, almost in line with us, and said to him, 'Do you see that straight bit of stick sticking up in the water opposite to you? It looks to me uncommonly like a Colour pole.' He waded straight in, up to his middle, and got hold of it. On lifting it out he brought up the Colour still adhering to it, and on getting out of the water handed the standard to me, and as he did so the gold-embroidered centre scroll dropped out, the silk having more or less rotted from the long immersion in the water.[129]

The next account, of the same events, is that of the journalist Charles Norris-Newman:

> . . . I sat up a long time with Major Black 'yarning'. Our chief topic was the recent wonderful recovery of the bodies of Lieutenant Coghill, ADC, and Adjutant Melville [sic], 1-24th, as well as of the missing Queen's Colour of that regiment. The Major, who had himself taken the principal part in the exploit, gave me very willingly the details of it as follows. On the 4th of February, Major Black, accompanied by Commandant Cooper and several other officers of the Natal Native Contingent, went out in search of the body of Adjutant Melville,

who was reported to have had the colours of the 1-24th with him when last seen to cross the Buffalo. About 300 yards on the Natal side of the Buffalo river they found the bodies of Adjutant Melville and Lieutenant Coghill, ADC, lying among some boulders, where they had fallen. In the Buffalo river, some distance ahead (about 300 yards), Major Black recovered the colours, with the staff broken, in a rather dilapidated condition.[130]

Two newspaper reports also announced the finds, both of which seem to resemble Norris-Newman's account, the first in particular, which was probably his report:

We are informed on reliable authority that on 4th February 1879, Major Wilsone Black (accompanied by some officers of the Natal Native Contingent, names unknown) went out in search of the body of Adjutant Melville [sic], who was reported to have had the colours of the 1-24th with him when last seen to cross the Buffalo. About 300 yards on the Natal side of the Buffalo River. Major Black found the bodies of Adjutant Melville and Lieutenant Coghill ADC, lying among some boulders, quite dead, where they had fallen. In the Buffalo River, some distance ahead (about 300 yards), Major Black recovered the colours, with the staff broken, in a very dilapidated condition.[131]

The second account is more general in nature, but the echoes from Norris-Newman can still be detected:

This morning we learn the gratifying news that Major Black – hearing from a fellow officer that Lieutenant-Adjutant Melville [*sic*], of the 1-24th regt., was last seen on the Buffalo River, endeavouring to swim across with the colours of the regiment, in company with Lieut. Coghill – went out to the spot, and succeeded in finding the bodies of the two officers 300 yards this side of the Buffalo. In the river, they found the colours much dilapidated.[132]

There is yet one more account to be considered, although its inclusion here is solely for the purpose of exposing the way Victorian gentlemen were quite beyond shame when it came to insinuating themselves into a good story. Commandant George Hamilton-Browne, 1st/3rd Natal Native Contingent, has thus far made no appearance in this tale. Here is his own determined attempt to remedy the shortcoming:

I immediately reported the story [of Melvill and Coghill at the river] to Colonel Glyn and Harford and myself determined to go down the river-bed and look for the colours. Major Black was also very keen on the job. A few days afterwards the river went down and a party of my officers started off to try and find the lost flag. I was awfully disgusted, for just as I was mounting, Colonel Glyn called me and told me I could not go as he wanted me.[133]

In these latter accounts the events of two separate days seem now to have been condensed into only one. Further, Major Black appears to have appropriated the credit and Harford is not mentioned by name at all, while Commandant Cooper makes an appearance for the first time.

From the accounts of both Glyn and Harford it is clear that the discovery of the bodies of Melvill and Coghill and the Colour took place on different days and those days were most probably consecutive, as Harford says. Thus the bodies were found on 3 February 1879 and the Colour on the following day. It is most unlikely that Harford's description of the first expedition, seemingly consisting only of himself and Black, and which could be thought ambiguous, is correct. Considering the great danger felt along the whole border at that time, and the evidence of bands of Zulu close to, or even on, the banks of the Mzinyathi, they must have taken an escort with them, probably from officers and NCOs of the disbanded 3rd Regiment, NNC. Harber was a captain with the 1/3rd Regiment, while Cooper commanded the 2nd Battalion of the same regiment.[134] It is very probable that other interested officers also went along, having heard about the proposed expedition. There is no doubt that the second expedition was somewhat larger because the bodies had been found and there was every chance of recovering the Colour. It is also very likely that Harford exaggerated his own involvement in the discovery.

All of this seems to be confirmed by the recent discovery of an entry in a ledger, or perhaps digest, kept by the 1/24th Battalion, and almost certainly based on a report by Lieutenant-Colonel Black.[135]

On the 4th February Lieut. Colonel Black who in a previous reconnaissance [on the 3rd] had discovered the bodies of Lieuts Melvill & Coghill set out with the following officers of the NNC: Captains Harber, Gubbins, Greaves, Underhill and MacIntosh; Lieutenants Trow, Hillier, Harford, Murray, Shepherd, Barry, Higginson, Godfrey, Goldsburg, Pohl, Sutherland, Long, Ryder and Raw to try and find the lost Queen's Colour of the 1/24th Regiment. The party raised a cairn over the bodies of Lieuts Melvill and Coghill, and descended into the glen through which the Buffalo runs in deep curves about 400 yards lower down the stream than where Melvill crossed. Hillier found the Cover, Trow the Crest, and finally about 50 yards above Harber raised the Colour from the water, it having been jammed between the stones. The party returned to Rorke's

Drift and gave over the Colour to Col. Glyn which was next day escorted by the above party to Helpmakaar and restored to the two Companies now representing the 1/24th Regiment.[136]

An interesting sequel to the discovery of the lost colour occurred later in the war. William Russell, correspondent for *The Times*, was at the Lower Drift on the Thukela River on 9 July and had just received news of the victory at Ulundi a few days earlier:

I slept on a stretcher in the barewalled, squalid room in which we had dined, with some sense of dignity in my position as sole guardian of the colours of Her Majesty's 3rd Buffs and Her Majesty's 99th Regiment, which had been duly deposited with Colonel Walker when the regiments crossed the Tugela – pregnant commentary on the use of regimental colours in such a war as that which may now be regarded as at an end.[137]

Chapter 5

Rorke's Drift

En effet, l'histoire n'est que le tableau des crimes et des malheurs.

Voltaire 1694–1778

The Hero of Rorke's Drift

Much has been written about the courageous defence of Rorke's Drift, to the extent that any words of mine would be entirely superfluous. However, a common perception of those not familiar with the engagement is that Rorke's Drift was dominated by one character: Lieutenant John Rouse Merriott Chard, Royal Engineers. This assessment has been fostered, for the general public, by the film *Zulu*, made in the 1960s and yet still universally popular, with its scenes of heroism on both sides. The fact that the film altered the real natures of the characters seems to be immaterial: Henry Hook, for example, is shown as a wild young man with a bad soldiering record, who was regarded as a drunk and a malingerer. The facts are that Hook was nearly thirty years of age at the time of the battle, a teetotaller and was awarded good-conduct pay just prior to the battle taking place.[1] Colour-Sergeant Bourne, rather than being the middle-aged man portrayed in the film, was actually only twenty-six years old, and was given the affectionate sobriquet 'the kid' by the older soldiers in the company. The two leading stars portray Chard as a man with a typically British stiff upper lip while Lieutenant Gonville Bromhead is the upper-class snob who belatedly recognises Chard's courage and leadership.

Those who have read more closely about the engagement will hardly be in a better position to judge, since both Chard, a Royal Engineer, and, to a lesser extent, Bromhead, commanding B Company, 2/24th Regiment, are usually extolled as the heroes of the hour. Virtually every account of the engagement, from Coupland[2] to Laband,[3] gives the lion's share of the praise to these two officers.

What, then, are we to make of the opinion, for example, of Sir Garnet Wolseley, who referred to Chard with the words: 'a more uninteresting or more stupid-looking fellow I never saw.'[4] Such was Wolseley's contempt for him that he presented Chard's Victoria Cross to him while passing by in the field. Wolseley described Bromhead in similar terms: 'Bromhead . . . is a very stupid fellow also.'[5] When he subsequently awarded Bromhead his VC, it gave Wolseley another opportunity to vent his spleen: 'I have now given away these decorations to both the officers who took part in the defence of Roorke's [sic] Drift, and two duller, more stupid, more uninteresting even, or less like Gentlemen it has not been my luck to meet for a long time.'[6]

Wolseley was not alone in his criticism of these two men. Major Clery, staff officer to Colonel Glyn, commanding the Centre Column, had this to say:

Well, Chard and Bromhead to begin with: both are almost typical in their separate corps of what would be termed the very dull class. Bromhead is a great favourite in his regiment and a capital fellow at everything except soldiering. So little was he held to be qualified in this way from unconquerable indolence that he had to be reported confidentially as hopeless. This is confidential as I was told it by his commanding officer. I was about a month with him at Rorke's Drift after Isandlwana, and the height of his enjoyment seemed to be to sit all day on a stone on the ground smoking a most uninviting-looking pipe. The only thing that seemed equal to moving him in any way was any allusion to the defence of Rorke's Drift. This used to have a sort of electrical effect on him, for up he would jump and off he would go, and not a word could be got out of him.[7] When I told him he should send me an official report on the affair it seemed to have a most distressing effect on him. I used to find him hiding away in corners with a friend helping him to complete this account, and the only thing that afterwards helped to lessen the compassion I felt for all this, was my own labour when perusing this composition – to understand what it was all about. So you can fancy that there was not one who knew him who envied him his distinction, for his modesty about himself was, and is, excessive.

Chard there is very little to say about except that he too is a 'very good fellow' – but very uninteresting . . .[8]

In fact, neither Wolseley nor Clery had a good word to say about almost anyone; however, while Wolseley consigned his caustic comments to his private journal, Clery was a self-confessed gossip and cheerfully acknowledged the fact in his correspondence.[9] Nevertheless, the criticisms do not stop there. Colonel Evelyn Wood, commander of the Fourth, later Flying, Column is reported to have told Wolseley that Chard was 'a most useless officer, fit for nothing'.[10]

Lest these accounts be thought too critical, there is corroborative evidence from a fellow Royal Engineer officer with first-hand knowledge of Chard's qualities:

> Chard got his orders to leave the 5th Company [Royal Engineers] for good and departed yesterday. He is a most amiable fellow and a loss to the mess, but as a company officer he is so hopelessly slow and slack. I shall get on much better without him and with Porter as my senior subaltern. Chard makes me angry, with such a start as he got, he stuck to the company doing nothing. In his place I should have gone up and asked Lord Chelmsford for an appointment, he must have got it and if not he could have gone home soon after Rorke's Drift, at the height of his popularity and done splendidly at home. I advised him, but he placidly smokes his pipe and does nothing.[11]

One of the survivors of Isandlwana, Lieutenant Henry Curling, RA, met the two men while he was at Rorke's Drift in the days after the battle and is quoted as saying:

> It is very amusing to read the accounts of Chard and Bromhead. They are about the most commonplace men in the British Army. Chard is a most insignificant man in appearance and is only about 5 feet 2 or 3 in height.[12] Bromhead is a stupid old fellow, as deaf as a post. Is it not curious how some men are forced into notoriety?[13]

Finally, there were also men in the ranks with an opinion: 'The men spoke very highly of Chard and another man named, I think, Milne, but I am not sure.[14] Of Bromhead they did not speak well.'[15] How, then, could two such men manage to bring off this miracle of heroism and endurance? Let me state now that this paper does not attempt to suggest that either of these two officers lacked courage. They both evidently shared this quality in abundance, as did the men under their command. The incongruity lies rather in, first, the capacity of Chard in particular, as senior officer, to make the decision to stand rather than to evacuate the post; and second, in his having the organisational skill to manage the defence arrangements – these factors fly in the face of the damning opinions of their military colleagues and senior officers.

On the first issue, fight or flight, they may really have had little choice. They apparently discussed the two options on the spot, especially in light of the order to stand, as Clery said: '. . . they all stayed there to defend the place for there was nowhere else to go.'[16] But let us consider the two men more closely.

First Bromhead. He was born in Versailles in August 1845 of a prominent military family and was thirty-three years old at the time of the battle. (His older brother, Brevet Major Charles James Bromhead, was then serving with the 2/24th Regiment at the Brecon depot and arrived at Rorke's Drift in March 1879.) The younger Bromhead had been commissioned as ensign into the 2/24th in April 1867, rose to lieutenant in October 1871 and was still in that rank at Rorke's Drift nearly eight years later. From his length of service in the rank of lieutenant, one might assume that he was not a brilliant soldier but that may be misleading.

Unlike many of his contemporaries in the regiment, Bromhead did not use purchase as a means of promotion,[17] except initially to gain entry into the army as ensign. A calculation of the average length of service before non-purchase promotion from lieutenant to captain by the twelve captains of the 24th in late 1878 shows that the shortest period of service prior to promotion was by A.G. Godwin-Austen (seventy-five months) and the longest was G.V. Wardell (127 months). In comparison, in January 1879 Bromhead had served only eighty-seven months.[18] This point is supported by an analysis of service of the seven subalterns senior to him, including Teignmouth Melvill. On 22 January 1879, H.M. Williams had served 123 months while Charles Pope had served only ninety-five. We should not, therefore, use Bromhead's length of service as an indicator of his ability. It must also be remembered that seniority was the key to promotion, not ability, and promotion normally came only when another man in a higher position in the seniority list either retired or died, in which case everyone below him moved up one 'step'. This is why the *Army List* was a publication to be found almost anywhere the army was serving.[19]

On the basis of service seniority, Bromhead was junior to Chard and in this position his alleged limited intellectual and military skills would not necessarily have proved an obstacle, although his supposed deafness, if true, might have done so. If someone else were to devise the strategy and issue the orders, then he was probably a man who could issue those orders to his subordinates and see them carried out. In this he was almost certainly aided by his senior NCOs, Colour-Sergeant Bourne and Sergeant Windridge. Both of these men were commended by Chard in his official report, as was Lance-Sergeant Williams, who was mortally wounded. Three other sergeants were also present: Sergeants Gallagher, Maxfield and Smith. Maxfield, of G Company, was killed while a patient in hospital but the other two receive no mention, despite their both being in B Company.

Now Chard. He was born in December 1847 and at thirty-one he was two years younger than Bromhead;[20] this refutes Coupland's remark that 'they were both scarcely out of their teens.'[21] He was commissioned into the Royal Engineers in July 1868 and before going to Natal he served in Bermuda and Malta. He arrived in South Africa on 5 January 1879 and only reached Rorke's Drift on the 19th, three days before the fight. Thus he had been a lieutenant even longer than Bromhead, ten years without promotion.

An analysis of some of Chard's contemporaries, however, shows that promotion in the Royal Engineers was even slower than in the line regiments.[22] Let us take, for example, three of the captains who served in South Africa concurrently with Chard. Captain Walter Parke Jones was promoted lieutenant in March 1864 and captain in October 1877, a service of 163 months as a lieutenant. Captain Bindon Blood was commissioned lieutenant in December 1860 and captain in August 1873, a total of 152 months. Finally, Captain W.R.C. Wynne, who died after his return from the siege of Eshowe, was made lieutenant in June 1862 and captain in February 1875, a total also of 152 months. These compare favourably with Chard's 126 months' service in January 1879. In the 1879 *Annual Army List*, there were still forty-eight lieutenants senior to him, so it is once again unreasonable to use Chard's long service in a lieutenant's rank as an indicator of his ability.

But is it possible that this man, described in such unhappy terms as those quoted earlier, had the decisiveness, resolve and organisational ability to arrange such a competent defence in just one hour? The answer is: possibly. He would certainly have been able to shape the orders to carry out the strategy but he still may not have had the initiative to develop it. Where else, then, were these characteristics to be found?

They did not come from Colour-Sergeant Frank Bourne, the ranking NCO, as one might assume from the movie. In reality, at only twenty-six years of age,[23] Bourne was an excellent soldier, as his career demonstrates, but he was simply too young and too inexperienced for such confidence to be placed in him. Wood and Buller later discussed the defence with General Sir Henry Ponsonby, private secretary to Queen Victoria: 'But the puzzle to them was – who was the man who organised it – for it showed genius and quickness neither of which were apparently the qualifications of Chard.'[24]

The answer lies with another, one with much more military experience than either of the two officers. Sub-Assistant Commissary James Langley Dalton was just the man for the moment. Dalton was born in 1833 and was thus in his mid-forties at Rorke's Drift. He had already enjoyed one career in the army, having enlisted in the 85th Foot in November 1849 at the age of seventeen. He was subsequently promoted corporal in 1862, and sergeant in 1863. Four years later he became a clerk and was promoted master-sergeant, then served with Wolseley at Red River in Canada in 1870. After twenty-two years' service, he retired in 1871 with a long service and good conduct medal. In 1877, he was in South Africa, where he volunteered for service in the British Commissariat during the Ninth Frontier War.

When Lieutenant Adendorff arrived at Rorke's Drift about 3.15 p.m. on 22 January, Chard was working at the ponts at the river. Having delivered his warning message, Adendorff then rode up with Chard to the mission station, about 800 metres distant, while Adendorff's companion, Trooper Sibthorpe of the Natal Carbineers, went on to Helpmekaar. On their arrival at the post, preparations for the defence were, it is recorded, already in progress,[25] apparently in response to a similar message sent by Captain Alan Gardner and received by Bromhead only minutes earlier.[26] This version, however, does not entirely correspond with events as recorded by Henry Hook:

> Suddenly there was a commotion in the Camp, and we saw two men galloping towards us from the other side of the river, which was Zululand. Lieutenant Chard of the Engineers was protecting the Ponts over the river and, as Senior Officer, was in command at the Drift . . . Lieutenant Bromhead was in the Camp itself. The horsemen shouted and were brought across the river, and then we knew what had happened to our comrades . . . At the same time, a note was received by Lieutenant Bromhead from the Column to say that the enemy was coming on and that the post was to be held at all costs.
>
> . . . There was a general feeling that the only safe thing was to retire and try to join the troops at Helpmekaar. The horsemen had said that the Zulus would be up in two or three minutes; but luckily for us they did not show themselves for more than an hour. Lieutenant Chard rushed up from the river, about a quarter of a mile away, and saw Lieutenant Bromhead, orders were given to strike the camp and make ready to go, and we actually loaded up two wagons. Then Mr Dalton, of the Commissariat Department, came up and said that if we left the Drift every man was certain to be killed. He had formerly been a Sergeant-Major in a line regiment and was one of the bravest men that ever lived. Lieutenants Chard and Bromhead held a consultation, short and earnest, and orders were given that we were to get the Hospital and storehouse ready for defence, and that we were never to say die or surrender.
>
> Not a minute was lost. Lieutenant Bromhead superintended the loopholing and barricading of the Hospital and storehouse, and the making of a connection of the defences between the two buildings with walls of mealie-bags and wagons.[27]

Hook's account of the preparations for flight has the ring of truth. There is no drama or romance; just the facts stated simply and clearly. There was also no reason for Hook to have invented what he related since he had nothing to gain by so doing. Chard may at first have been in favour of flight: he was an engineer not a soldier and he obviously reposed little confidence in Bromhead's ability to hold the post, even though he, Chard, was in command as a result of his seniority.

The initiative was provided by Dalton, who counselled against flight and instead explained how the post could be held and probably pointed to the work that had already been done. Work on the defences was already in hand before Chard's arrival, as verified by Surgeon-Major Reynolds' statement:

> Just at this period Mr. Dalton's energies were invaluable. Without the smallest delay, which would have been so fatal for us, he called upon the men (all eager for doing) to carry the mealie sacks here and there for defences, and it was charming to find in a short time how comparatively protected we had made ourselves. Lieutenant Chard arrived as this work was in progress and gave many useful orders as regards the lines of defence.[28]

Once Chard agreed to stay, his engineering training came into play, a stream of orders was issued and the process of constructing the defences continued apace.

From this point on, the vital decisions having been taken, the defence itself was a matter of grim determination and courage, obviously characteristics with which Chard was endowed to the full and which carried him through the long hours of the defence, backed up by Bromhead and in particular by Dalton, who, even after he had been wounded, still continued to assist.

Dalton's role was not a matter known only to Hook. In commenting above on Chard, Wolseley continued: 'I hear in this camp also that the man who worked hardest in defence of Roorke's [sic] Drift Post was the Commissariat officer [Dalton] who has not been rewarded at all.'[29] This was not to remain so. Dalton received his own well-deserved, but belated, Victoria Cross on 16 January 1880, almost twelve months later to the day.

An interesting event occurred some months later when Ulundi had been won and Natal was settling back to enjoy the peace:

> After the war, the company of the 24th that had defended Rorke's Drift was marching into [Pieter]Maritzburg amidst a perfect ovation. Among those cheering them was Mr. Dalton, who, as a conductor, had been severely wounded there. 'Why, there's Mr. Dalton cheering us! We ought to be cheering him; he was the best man there,' said the men, who forthwith fetched him out of the crowd, and made him march with them. No one knew better the value of this spontaneous act than that old soldier . . . Mr. Dalton must have felt a proud man that day.[30]

The NNC at Rorke's Drift

This paper came about as a result of reading a work by Ian Knight concerning Rorke's Drift.[31] The words that gave the writer pause were in relation to the unit of the Natal Native Contingent (NNC) which was left at the mission station and which subsequently deserted before the Zulu attack: 'This was a company of the 2nd Battalion, 3rd Regiment, Natal Native Contingent, under Captain William Stephenson – or Stevenson, even the spelling of the name is in doubt.'[32]

Knight's assignment of these men to the 2nd Battalion, 3rd Regiment, NNC, however, struck a false chord, because seemingly the full complement of the 3rd Regiment, NNC was at Isandlwana on 22 January; eight companies of each battalion under Commandant Lonsdale were on an extended reconnaissance of the Malakatha hills to the south-west of Isandlwana, while the remaining four companies, two from each battalion, were in the camp itself.[33] Since the complement of each battalion was ten companies, Knight seems, at first sight, to be in error in thus assigning the people at Rorke's Drift to the 2/3rd Regiment.

There was indeed a small element of the NNC left at Rorke's Drift and its official role was to guard the ponts over the nearby Mzinyathi (Buffalo) River, orders having been given to that effect to Lieutenant Chard by the commanding officer, Major Spalding, on the morning of 22 January:

> 1. The force under Lt Col Durnford, RE, having departed, a Guard of 6 Privates and 1 NCO will be furnished by the detachment 2/24th Regiment on the Ponts. A Guard of 50 armed natives will likewise be furnished by Captain Stephenson's detachment at the same spot. The Ponts will be invariably drawn over to the Natal side at night. This duty will cease on arrival of Captain Rainforth's Company, 1/24th.[34]

Normally a company of NNC contained only a hundred men and was under the command of a captain, with two lieutenants, three sergeants and three corporals, all being white.[35] As far as it is possible to ascertain, the unit at Rorke's Drift had only a captain and at least one NCO, apparently lacking lieutenants or other NCOs despite the number of men to be commanded. An officer named 'W. Stephenson' is mentioned as being appointed as a captain to the 2/3rd Regiment, NNC and, lacking any evidence to the contrary, we must assume that this is our man.[36] (The discrepancy in the spelling of his name was not an uncommon phenomenon at that time: most correspondence was prepared by dictation to clerks, who spelled the names as they thought best. Indeed, the most common error was in the presentation of forename initials, when they were given at all.)

Only six captains are named by David Jackson as commanding seven companies of the 2/3rd NNC on the reconnaissance,[37] but this number excludes Captain Orlando Murray, whose company left the reconnaissance and brought back some captured cattle to the camp. Two more, Captains Barry and Erskine, were left at the camp. In fact, no less than ten captains were originally assigned to the 2nd Battalion, including Stephenson.[38]

Thus, I would list the following officers as being assigned to the 2nd Battalion on 22 January: Captains Barry, Erskine and Murray (at Isandlwana), Beverley-Davies, Greaves, Gubbins, Mackintosh, Nelson and Underhill (on the reconnaissance) and finally Stephenson at Rorke's Drift. Clearly, therefore, one of the companies on the reconnaissance must have been led by a lieutenant.

The next problem is the size of the unit at Rorke's Drift, variously reported as 100,[39] 350,[40] and even 2,000.[41] It is likely that the second figure, quoted by Reverend Smith, was closest to the mark because 100 men would not have made a lot of difference to the size of the barricade which needed to be built round the post, whereas 350 would certainly have done so.[42] The figure of 2,000 is, of course, nonsense.

Who were these men? Their presence was certainly recognised, since Major Spalding had left orders for their employment. The most likely answer is that they were indeed a part of the 3rd Regiment, and may even have been a part of the 2nd Battalion, as Knight says. The reason for their being left behind at Rorke's Drift may be explained by the fact that the complement of the regiment had been greatly exceeded, despite the fact that it took time for the levies to arrive.[43]

The African levies were to assemble initially at Sandspruit (modern Pomeroy) by 18 December 1878. The resident magistrates, however, began to call up the men well before, but even so only 1,452 out of 2,000 had come forward by that date. Levies to make up the shortfall continued to arrive, even after the regiment had moved from Sandspruit to Rorke's Drift, a movement that took place on 2 January. Allow me to quote from what may be regarded as the definitive work on the Contingent:

> 294 men from [the resident magistrates] were turned over to the military on January 10th, and more continued to flow in from various quarters until the number reached 450. Ultimately the 3rd Regiment was over strength by some 300 men, whom the Lieutenant General proposed to leave at Rorke's Drift for road work and other duties while the column advanced into Zululand.[44]

Evidence for this over-manning is provided by a letter written by Lonsdale's staff officer, Captain Henry Harford, to William James Dunbar Moodie, the resident magistrate of the Klip River district on 14 January 1879: 'In case Com't Lonsdale has forgotten to send a line about the Natives, could you kindly prevent any more joining. They are dropping in, in half-dozens, & we are now some 300 over our strength. If you would kindly see to this I should be obliged.'[45]

It can be seen from the foregoing that Reverend Smith was pretty close to the mark and that the NNC at Rorke's Drift did indeed number about three hundred. The confusion and late arrival of these men also accounts for the lack of officers and NCOs. Stephenson was probably given command of this group at the last moment, his original company then being commanded by his senior lieutenant. One might speculate that he was specifically selected to stay behind to care for the levies still appearing, since Lord Chelmsford was well aware of them, as is shown in the quotation above. The functions of the unit, whatever their composition, is fairly clear. They were to be used for road-building and guarding the ponts across the Mzinyathi River, a task ordered by Major Spalding.

While preparing the barricades for the defence of the post, the unit worked well: 'The Native Contingent, under their Officer, Captain Stephenson, were working hard at this with our own men and the walls were rapidly progressing.'[46] The arrival, and subsequent sudden departure, of the men of the Natal Native Mounted Contingent, probably elements of several troops under the command of Lieutenant Alfred Henderson, prompted an immediate response from the terrified NNC: 'About the same time [as the mounted men left] Captain Stephenson's detachment of Natal Native Contingent left us, as did that officer himself.'[47] As they left, shots rang out:

Instantly the natives – Kaffirs who had been very useful in making the barricade of wagons, mealiebags and biscuit boxes around the Camp – bolted towards Helpmakaar, and what was worse their Officer and a European Sergeant went with them. To see them deserting like that was too much for some of us and we fired after them. The Sergeant was struck and killed.[48]

Reverend Smith places this incident later, when the Zulu attack had started, and thus, perhaps kindly, blamed the Zulus for the death. He also identified the NCO as a corporal:

The garden must have soon been occupied, for one unfortunate Contingent corporal, whose heart must have failed him when he saw the enemy and heard the firing, got over the parapet and tried to make his escape on foot, but a bullet from the garden struck him, and he fell dead within 150 yards of our front wall. An officer of the same corps who had charge of the 350 natives before referred to, was more fortunate, for being mounted, he made good his escape and 'lives to fight another day.'[49]

There were, of course, valid reasons why the African mounted men left: they had already endured the horrors of Isandlwana and the destruction of the British camp, followed by their narrow escape from the closing horns of the Zulu army. As one of them later said, their leader Colonel Durnford was cut off from them and there was nothing further they could do.[50]

During the flight from Isandlwana, another NNC officer referred to a Captain Stevenson as being at Helpmekaar when he arrived there: 'I found that Captain Stevenson, of 2nd Battalion 3rd Regiment Natal Native Contingent had brought Lieutenant Purvis up from Rorke's Drift.'[51] Higginson's statement might also reveal something of Stephenson's character, as the missionary Otto Witt also claimed to have escorted Purvis from the post just before the Zulu arrived.[52] Since both Higginson and Witt later proved to be somewhat strangers to the truth, it is difficult to determine which of them was speaking with veracity.

Finally, a word about the NNC departure from the post in the face of the advancing Zulu force. These men had only recently joined the levies, almost certainly at Rorke's Drift itself, and since the unit was poorly provided with officers and NCOs, their training would have been virtually nil. We cannot be certain as to how they were armed but given that the rest of the NNC had only ten men in every hundred armed with rifles, most of them old muzzle-loaders, at best they would have had only thirty firearms between them; more probably, they had nothing but their traditional weapons. In these circumstances, then, it is hardly surprising that they chose to decamp when they saw the Africans under Lieutenant Henderson depart – and they were fully armed *and* mounted.

What is to be deprecated is the departure of Stephenson himself, which was hardly the action of an officer and a gentleman. We should note that most of the other officers of the Contingent chose to stay at Isandlwana with their British Army comrades and shared their fate, even after their own men had also fled, as the Zulu army began to surround and enter the camp. Clearly, Stephenson was not of the same stamp as his NNC comrades Captains Krohn and James Lonsdale, 1st Battalion, nor Barry, Erskine and Murray, 2nd Battalion.[53] Also choosing to stay, and perish, were Lieutenants Avery, Holcraft and Jameson, 1st Battalion, and Gibson, Pritchard, Rivers, Vereker and Young, 2nd Battalion. In fact, of the NNC officers present on that day at Isandlwana, only three of the 3rd Regiment made their escape.[54]

The circumstances of Stephenson's subsequent treatment by the authorities is lost to us, other than a bald announcement in a local general order: '6. The services of Captain Stevenson, 2-3rd Natal Native Contingent, are dispensed with, being no longer required.'[55] Strangely, the variant spelling is repeated in the case of this officer, who can only be the same as that under discussion. It was a better outcome than he deserved.

The Blame Game

The publication of a work on the Zulu War that entertains the notion that there was a cover-up by Lord Chelmsford's senior officers concerning Isandlwana, of which Chelmsford himself may or may not have been a part, brings to the fore the matter of culpability.[56] Valid or not, the thesis offered by Lock and Quantrill is interesting in its own right, but it was really only the tip of the iceberg. 'After a lapse of several weeks following the Isandlwana affair, it dawned upon some honest mind of the headquarter staff that since Colonel Glyn was in orders "to command the 3rd column" perhaps some part of the odium of that business which was accumulating regarding that affair could be transferred from the general's shoulders to his.'[57]

The suggestion was a sycophantic one certainly, yet under the circumstances then prevailing it was not wanting in audacity. The attempt, too, was entered upon with a certain amount of skill, for it was insidiously cloaked in the form of apparently routine enquiries as to how certain regulations had been carried out.[58]

The court of inquiry into the disaster at Isandlwana on 22 January 1879, initiated by Lord Chelmsford, was only the public face of the subsequent examination of what had taken place, and a poor one at that. Behind the scenes, other examples of military political manoeuvring can be observed, in which subtle insinuations were made, and refuted, in writing. There was something of a scramble to determine who was to blame, and for what. For a brief time there was, for example, a somewhat spiteful cloud over the matter of Brevet Major Henry Spalding's departure from Rorke's Drift to Helpmekaar on the afternoon of the 22nd, only two hours before the attack on the post, and, coincidentally, during the final stages of the battle at Isandlwana.[59] In fact Spalding was deputy assistant adjutant-general and temporarily in command at both Helpmekaar and Rorke's Drift so that his departure from one to the other should not have been regarded as unusual. Only very late in the day did Lord Chelmsford come to his defence:

I was under the impression until very lately that the orders I had personally given to Colonel Glyn to have a work made at Rorke's drift previous to our leaving it, had been partially carried out. It will be seen now that such was not the case & that the orders sent by Colonel Glyn to Helpmekaar for a detachment to march at once to this point never marched. It does not appear however why the company already at Rorke's drift did not commence the work.

It was in consequence of the non-arrival of this detachment that caused Major Spalding to go to Helpmekaar to hasten its departure & this was the reason of that officer's absence from Rorke's drift when the attack was made.

I refer to this latter point in justice to Major Spalding, as I have heard that remarks have been made relative to his absence from this post at the time – Helpmekaar was also under his command.[60]

The prime candidate for responsibility for the Isandlwana disaster itself was to be Colonel Anthony Durnford, commander of the Second Column, who was alleged to have taken command of the camp from Lieutenant-Colonel H.B. Pulleine, 1/24th Regiment. As has been said elsewhere, Durnford was both convenient and dead. Since the secondary candidate, Pulleine, was also dead, it was to be Colonel Glyn, officer commanding the Centre Column, who was to come under heavy scrutiny, despite his having been with Lord Chelmsford throughout the day of 22 January.

Richard Thomas Glyn had been the commanding officer of the 24th Regiment since February 1872 having served, first with the 82nd Regiment in the Crimea, and the 24th during the Indian Mutiny, and in the more recent Ninth Frontier War.[61] Lord Chelmsford appointed him to the command of the Centre Column for the invasion of Zululand, in which both battalions of his regiment served.[62] His command was, in fact, only nominal because Chelmsford himself accompanied the column and assumed effective command. Glyn's staff officer, the gossiping Major Clery, observed:

That [Chelmsford] should take command was of course to be expected, but it of course had the effect of practically effacing the nominal commander of the column and his staff.[63]

. . . of course the general took command of the whole column . . . And being a small camp and living in the middle of it he saw everything and looked into everything himself. Colonel Glyn and his staff however were *allowed* to work the details – posting guards, etc.[64]

The development of a smear campaign can be seen in the flow of memoranda and reports that passed between the principal players in the drama. Most of the extracts that follow are drawn from letters or memoranda derived from War Office records.[65] Some of the quotations are quite extensive but they are necessary in order to show the extent of the enquiries that were made, and the potentially serious threat to careers. One note of caution when reading the correspondence: Colonel Bellairs was in Pietermaritzburg and Colonel Glyn, for the most part, was at Rorke's Drift some 320 kilometres (200 miles) away over very poor, or non-existent, roads. Mail delivery, therefore, might take up to four or five days depending on the weather. We do not, therefore, know the exact order of receipt of the various items of correspondence. There were three distinct threads to this correspondence, most of which overlap.

Glyn's 'Inadequate' Reports

In early February 1879 Colonel Glyn submitted his report of the actions of 22 January to Colonel William Bellairs, deputy adjutant-general.[66] Only one day later, even before it could have been received, the campaign to besmirch the colonel began with a somewhat innocuous memorandum, but with a nasty sting in the tail, written by Bellairs to Glyn:

> Lieut. Chard's report of the enemy's attack of the 22nd ultimo on Rorke's Drift post has been received, but none from you of the movements of your column from the day of its leaving to the time of its returning to Rorke's Drift, or the occurrences which took place in the interval. Please to be particular in giving the time of your taking up the position at Isandhlwana. Furnish a sketch showing the formation of the camp; how the guards and picquets were disposed; where the alarm posts were placed; whether they were occupied in the evening and morning, the position of the wagon laagers, &c. All with reference to the instructions on these heads laid down in Field Force Regulations, paragraphs 16 to 21.[67]

Glyn was too wily a bird to be caught so easily and his response one week later quoted chapter and verse on military communications protocol.[68] He pointed out that the usual daily reports had been submitted to Lord Chelmsford's assistant military secretary, Brevet Lieutenant Colonel John North Crealock, who, Glyn said, was 'acting as Deputy Adjutant-General on the spot'. He went on to point out that, in fact, his report of the events of 22 January had already been sent to Bellairs.

Meanwhile Bellairs had sent a further note on the 8th, then a more insistent demand on 18 February, which again crossed with Glyn's earlier reply:

1. Your attention is called to my memorandum of 8th instant, requesting that further evidence might be taken regarding the action of the 22nd ultimo. No further reports have as yet been received from you.

2. Also to a minute addressed to you on the 7th instant, calling for report from yourself on the same subject. Your report of the 6th has since been received, but, as you will perceive by the minute referred to, it is not as full as desired as to time, and does not enter into details enquired about. Be good enough to supplement your account as soon as possible.

3. Have the goodness to return a report on the Rorke's Drift post defences, sent back to you on the 31st ultimo, with marginal notes for your instruction, and to report how far the said instructions have been carried out.[69]

Glyn's introduction of Crealock's name into the correspondence was bound to provoke a response from that officer, thus providing a second thread.

The Involvement of Crealock

Accordingly, on 20 February Crealock passed the following observations to his general, introducing new matters for enquiry and also an early advice of his own lack of any culpability:

On perusing the accompanying statement of Colonel Glyn's, I notice the following :

(1.) That no mention is made of the receipt or non-receipt of information during the 22nd from the Officer Commanding the Camp at Sandhlwana.

(2.) As I have already mentioned, Major Clery showed me an official memorandum about 9.45 a.m., 22nd, received by Colonel Glyn from Colonel Pulleine. I read it, but it was not handed over to me as documents belonging to the General.

(3.) I think it will be found in the evidence before the Court that an order was sent to and received by Colonel Pulleine. In answer to the memorandum referred to above, Colonel Glyn should, I think, be asked to record what orders were sent then; they certainly were more than had reference to starting a portion of the Camp, if the evidence I refer to is correct.

(4.) In Colonel Glyn's answer to Deputy Adjutant-General's memorandum, 8th February 1879, he refers to an acting Deputy Adjutant-General, and that all his reports, &c., were sent to him. This evidently refers to myself. It is very desirable that this matter should be set right. As you are aware, I was not acting Deputy Adjutant-General; when I promulgated a general order I signed it for the Deputy Adjutant-General, and the copy was sent on to the Deputy Adjutant-General.

(5.) There has never been a question of my acting in such a capacity; if I had received such authority, I certainly should not have satisfied myself by at times signing a document for him, and being the simple recording channel of certain documents.

(6.) I wish to place on record that on our joining Colonel Glyn's Camp I explained to Major Clery, which he will remember, my views of the General's position there with reference to Colonel Glyn's authority. The words I used were (repeating a remark of the General's to Mr. Strickland at Maritzburg) 'It is an accident the General's being here, and no interference with matters of detail will take place.' All reports were to be made by Colonel Glyn to the General, and orders I believed would be given for the general movements of the Column by the General.

In practice this was the case; the only knowledge I, or other officers of the General's personal staff had, of the arrangements of the Column, was the Daily Order Book.

The General's Staff was not consulted in any matter connected with the pitching of the camp, its outposts, or its site, and, were it desirable to do so, proof could be easily shown of it. The personal staff, to my certain knowledge, were neither authorized to nor did they take any initiative in any matters which, if they had been Officers of the General Staff of Adjutant-General or Quartermaster-General would, I consider, have been their duty to have done.

(7) I am not, nor have I ever been, in possession of the information referred to by Deputy Adjutant-General in his memorandum to Colonel Glyn.[70]

The result was that on that same day Chelmsford sent off the following to his deputy adjutant-general, in which he subtly introduced the question of blame, while at the same time refuting any possible future charges of having done so.

1. The memorandum of Lieutenant-Colonel Crealock, together with this one of mine, should be sent to Colonel Glyn. It appears to me very fairly to represent the position occupied by myself and staff during the time that I was in the Field with No. 3 Column.

2. I have no desire whatever to shift any of the responsibility, which properly belongs to me, on the shoulders of the Officer Commanding No. 3 Column.

3. At the same time I am anxious to make it clear that, by accompanying No. 3 Column, I did not accept the responsibility for the numerous details which necessarily have to be considered by an Officer Commanding a Column in the Field.

4. On arriving at the Camp of No. 3 Column, I myself explained personally to Colonel Glyn that I did not wish to interfere in any way with the Command

of the Column, but that of course I should be only too glad to talk over with him all matters connected with it. I believe that I also said the same to Major Clery, the Senior Staff Officer.

5. As regards the movement of the Column, and the several reconnaissances [*sic*] made by portions of that Column, I was entirely responsible. My orders, however, were always conveyed to Colonel Glyn in plenty of time for him to consider over and reflect upon them, and I consider that I have a right to assume that if Colonel Glyn considered that any such order was in any way likely to be injurious to any portion of his force, or that my proposed movements were in any way hazardous, he would have, at once, brought the fact to my notice.

6. I go further, and say that I consider Colonel Glyn was bound to inform me if, at any time, his own judgment dissented from the movements I was anxious to carry out.

7. No such objection was ever made, and I assume, therefore, that which was ordered by me received his approval.

8. As regards outposts, patrolling, and the ordinary precautions for the safety of the Camp, I consider that for all these arrangements Colonel Glyn was entirely responsible – had I interfered in such it would have been tantamount to my taking direct Command of the Column, a position which I deprecated from the very first.

9. I should wish Colonel Glyn to reply fully to these two memorandums separately, so that there may be no doubt regarding the relative positions occupied by that Officer and myself during the time that I was present with No. 3 Column.[71]

Lord Chelmsford had here introduced the third hare, that of his expectation that Glyn would inform him if he (Glyn) dissented from any of the lieutenant-general's orders.

Glyn and Dissent
Bellairs sent Lord Chelmsford's memorandum and attachments on 21 February to Glyn, who discussed the issues with his staff officer Major Clery.

Colonel Glyn is a guileless, unsuspicious man, very upright and scrupulously truthful yet of a slow, not to say lethargic, temperament; so when this document arrived he regarded it in the way an easygoing man would solve a problem that he did not quite see his way to solving. So he chucked the paper over to me with the remark, 'Odd the General asking me to tell him about what he knows more about than I do.' But the moment I read it, *I* (being the villain of the piece) saw at once that there was a trap, so I told Colonel Glyn what I suspected. He then, I think, for an instant suspected that I was a villain for supposing such a thing possible, but all the same he allowed me to write his reply. I did so at no very great length, but the jist [sic] of it all was, 'Ask the General; he knows all about it himself.' Of course this was all put in the most decorous and respectful language.[72]

This is the resulting masterpiece to Bellairs, drafted by Clery in Glyn's name:

Your memorandum of the 21st instant, returning your previous memorandum of the 7th instant with my reply thereto has just been received.

The reply furnished by me to your memorandum of the 7th February, was to explain to you what I presumed you were unaware of, that the information on the different points you alluded to as not having been supplied, was as I believed already in the knowledge of His Excellency the Lieutenant-General Commanding.

Your subsequent memorandum of the 18th, acknowledging my report of the 6th instant, on the events of the 22nd January 1879, was since received, and in it you call attention to the omission of information on the points referred to in the above quoted minute of the 7th, and requesting a supplementary report supplying this information. I lost no delay in complying with those instructions, and sent you detailed information on the different points mentioned in your memorandum referred to of the 7th by the next mail. I also enclose a sketch I had in the meantime had prepared from memory of the ground and camp at Isandhlwana, as I proposed should be done in my previous reply to your memorandum of the 7th February.

In reply to the Minute of His Excellency the Lieutenant-General Commanding I regret exceedingly that he should think from the manner in which the above information was conveyed to you that I sought to evade any of the responsibility devolving on me as Officer Commanding No. 3 Column. I have no desire to do so, and I consider that during the time His Excellency was present with the 3rd Column, I was as fully responsible for the numerous details which necessarily have to be considered by an Officer Commanding a column in the field, as I was before His Excellency joined the column, and as I have been since he left it.

On arrival at the camp of No. 3 Column, His Excellency personally explained to me that he did not wish to interfere in any way, with the command of the column.

My senior Staff Officer, Major Clery, states that His Excellency more than once expressly stated the same to him. Major Clery further wishes to add that on one occasion when through some misapprehension, His Excellency's wishes with reference to a matter of detail were erroneously construed by the Officer to whom they were conveyed as an order, the Lieutenant-General at once repudiated the fact of their having been meant as an order. On another occasion when Major Clery referred to His Excellency for instructions on some matter of detail connected with the movement of the column, the Lieutenant-General replied, 'that is for Colonel Glyn to settle. I do not interfere in these matters. I want you to take me on with you.'

As regards outposts and the ordinary precautions for the safety of the camp, I consider for all these arrangements I was solely responsible. I lay as much stress as I am able on these different points, as I am anxious to remove from the Lieutenant-General's mind the impression that I regret he seems to labour under, that I seek and have sought to evade any responsibility that devolves upon me.

With regard to part of para. 5 and to para. 6 of His Excellency's minute, I regret very much to say that hitherto I have not understood that my duties in such matters were such as he represents them. I was certainly not aware that if I happened to consider that if any proposed movement of the Lieutenant-General Commanding were in any way hazardous, that I should have at once brought the fact to his notice, nor that if my judgment dissented from a movement the General had ordered I was bound to inform him of it. I was certainly not aware that my position called on me, or entitled me to do this, and indeed I was under the impression that it would have been presumptuous on my part to have done so. I might add that even had I understood this position towards His Excellency in this matter, as I appear not to have done, yet considering that the only intelligence department of the force was entirely at the disposal and under the control of His Excellency and his Staff, and being aware that His Excellency was obliged to consider in all he did the movements and interests of the other columns of the Army, I certainly would always have been very diffident in volunteering an opinion adverse to a movement decided on by His Excellency without having been referred to for an opinion on the matter.

Though I am thus compelled to dissent from what His Excellency advances in these two paras, I must express my great regret if the erroneous views I appear to have entertained of my position was due to a misunderstanding of mine, but having been ordered by His Excellency to reply on this matter I can only state what was the case, and greatly regret my error if I am answerable for it.[73]

It will be seen here that Clery and Glyn provided a provocative response to Lord Chelmsford's suggestion that Glyn might dissent from any of his orders. His Lordship had little choice but to acknowledge the truth of Glyn's words:

I quite accept this statement as a fair and honorable explanation of the relations which existed between myself as Lieutenant-General Commanding the Forces, and Colonel Glyn, C.B., commanding the column. The only difference of opinion which exists between us is that relating to paras. 5 and 6 of my memorandum. I leave the point in question to be decided by those before whom all the papers connected with the events of the 22nd January will be laid.[74]

Also on 26 February, Glyn replied separately to Bellairs with the following:

With reference to your memorandum, dated the 18th instant, calling attention to your previous minute of the 7th instant, in which latter it was pointed out that certain information connected with the 3rd Column when encamped at Sandhlwana had not been furnished, I beg to state that a reply to that minute was forwarded without delay explaining that the information on the different points noted had been supplied at the time and as they occurred to His Excellency the Lieutenant-General Commanding in the Field. It was further mentioned, that though no sketch of the ground at Sandhlwana was in my possession or obtainable here, I would have one prepared from memory with as much accuracy as possible should he desire it. I have had that sketch prepared in anticipation and forward it.

Regarding the different points mentioned in your minute of the 7th inst., I now send you replies in detail as supplementary to my report, according to His Excellency's wishes.

1. I fear it will be impossible to state the exact time of the taking up the position at Isandhlwana as, owing to the difficulties of the road, the different portions of the force only arrived there gradually. For about a week previous to the advance a very strong working party had been employed in repairing this road, but still only about half the repairs required had been completed. Several bad places existed through which each wagon in turn had to be assisted; so that the delay of each entailed a corresponding delay on all behind it.

I am therefore unable to state now the exact time of the arrival of the head of the column, but the Lieutenant-General took on a part of the mounted force to reconnoitre soon after their arrival, which was about mid-day as well as I remember. The delay was so great in getting the wagons through the last sluit that the 2/24th Regiment and about 35 wagons could not be brought across it that night and had to be halted about a mile in rear of where the rest of the force took up its encampment.

These wagons and the 2/24th Regiment moved up into camp the following morning.

2. The formation of the camp is shown in the annexed sketch, done from memory. The red dotted line shows the disposition of the line of out-posts by day; the blue dotted line the same by night. Each battalion supplied its own front and rear guards which, in addition to the outpost line, was considered sufficient security for the front of the camp. Additional provision, however, was made for the protection of the rear of the camp through which the road ran where the 1st Battalion 24th Regiment furnished a permanent guard by day and night, and the Natal Pioneers furnished a guard as well by night. Further, the camp of the Natal Pioneers was placed on this ground for its protection.[75]

3. The alarm posts of each Infantry Battalion was [*sic*] appointed to be in front of the line of its own tents. The battalions on the flanks of the camp having special regard to their outer flanks. Special arrangements were made with the officers commanding the mounted troops and Royal Artillery, for the distribution and action of their men, horses, and guns in case of alarm. This was reduced to writing, and a copy retained in possession of each of these officers.

4. As regards the occupation of the alarm-post, a modification was made of the instructions contained in para. 20, Field Force Regulations – two companies per battalion mounted at retreat as an in-lying picquet. They were then inspected by the F.O. of the day. They again paraded in front of their own camp at tattoo, under the Regimental Captain of the day. This force lay down fully accoutred with its arms at its sides ready to turn out at a moment's notice and occupy the alarm post. The troops were not in the habit of turning out under arms two hours before sun rise; but the whole camp was roused at 4 o'clock a.m., about an hour before sun rise. The heavy fatigue duties that were almost constant from the time the force crossed the Frontier made it desirable to give the men as much rest as possible, and the above arrangements were held to fulfil the spirit of the regulations.

5. The instructions contained in para. 18, Field Force Regulations, regarding · the formation of a wagon laager for oxen, were not complied with. As was previously stated, a large portion of the wagons had to be left behind, about a mile from camp, on the 20th, and remained for the night under the protection of the 2nd Battalion 24th Regiment. The remainder as they arrived in camp were ordered to be formed up in rear of their regiments. This was partly caused by the fact that in accordance with instructions from His Excellency the Lieutenant-General Commanding, half the wagons of the force were under orders to off-load their contents next morning and proceed back to Rorke's Drift to bring up more supplies; so that the stores off-loaded had to remain in charge of the corps they belonged to; this work was not finished till late on the 21st, and the empty wagons were then collected near the road towards the rear of the camp in readiness to start on their return journey at daylight the following morning.[76]

In a third memorandum, dated 26 February, Glyn responded at some length to Crealock's comments, again through Bellairs, although the prolixity and references to Clery's name make one suspect that the latter was the author of this too: the small salvo regarding irregular behaviour by senior officers is more typical of Clery than of the stolid Glyn.

With reference to a minute from Lieutenant-Colonel Crealock addressed to His Excellency the Lieutenant-General Commanding forwarded with your memo of the 21st instant, I beg to reply as follows:

I regret the omission made by me in my report on the occurrences of the 22nd January in not mentioning the receipt of information during that day from the Officer Commanding the Camp at Isandhlwana.

One communication only was received from that Officer on that day. It is now before me, and the hour of its being sent from Camp is entered on it as 8.5 a.m.; the contents are as follows

'Staff Officer. – Report just come in that the Zulus are advancing in force from left front of Camp (8.5).

H. B. PULLEINE, Lieut.-Col.'

The hour of its reception is entered as 9.30 o'clock, with the initials H. P. (Hallam Parr).

This memorandum was received by my Senior Staff Officer, Major Clery. I saw him hand it at once to the Lieutenant-General, who was close to him, before he showed it to me. This, no doubt, was irregular; Major Clery received the General's instructions on it. Major Clery states this memo was never handed over to Lieutenant-Colonel Crealock or any of the Head-quarter Staff as a document belonging to the General.

It is stated by Lieutenant-Colonel Crealock that he thinks it will be found in evidence before the Court (of enquiry into the loss of Isandhlwana, I presume) that an order was sent and received by Lieutenant-Colonel Pulleine in answer to the memo referred to above. I beg to state, with reference to this, that no order of any kind was sent by me or by my order or with my knowledge in answer to this memo.

Further, my Senior Staff Officer, Major Clery, assures me that no answer was sent by him or with his knowledge to this memo. He adds, that he is the more confident about this as when the Lieutenant-General handed him back the memo above referred to, he asked His Excellency, 'Is there anything to be done on this?' His Excellency at once replied, 'There is nothing to be done on that.' I might also state that I have a distinct recollection of hearing His Excellency reply to this effect to either Major Clery or Lieutenant-Colonel Crealock, for I was close by all that time.

The only order, to my knowledge, sent to the Officer Commanding the Camp at Isandhlwana that day was one issued by order of the Lieutenant-General to send out the tents, &c., of the force with the Lieutenant-General to the place where that force was to form a fresh encampment. Major Clery took the Lieutenant-General's instructions to this effect down in his note book, and tore out the page on which they were written and sent it into Camp. Major Clery informs me that he read over this message to the Lieutenant-General before sending it, to make sure he quite understood what His Excellency required done. He further adds that this message had reference to nothing except what concerned moving a part of the Camp. Captain Allan Gardner, 14th Hussars, was given this message to take into Camp, and Major Clery states that he read this message over with Captain Gardner, as he gave it to him, to ensure his knowing its contents should any accident happen to it.

With regard to Lieutenant-Colonel Crealock being referred to on matters connected with the Adjutant-General's Department concerning the forces in the field, I was informed by Major Clery immediately after arrival of the Lieutenant-General at Helpmekaar, that Lieutenant-Colonel Crealock had instructed him that all such matters could be temporarily referred to him for the Lieutenant-General's immediate decision, instead of sending them to Colonel Bellairs, C.B., at Pietermaritzburg. This appeared so natural that it never occurred to me to question it.

As a matter of fact, such was the course invariably pursued, while the Lieutenant-General remained with the column; and I was under the impression that the Lieutenant-General was aware that such was the case. On now referring to Major Clery, he states that this arrangement was made by Lieutenant-Colonel Crealock in the latter's tent at Helpmekaar.

With reference to Lieutenant-Colonel Crealock's statement regarding his explanation to Major Clery on the subject of the Lieutenant-General's position, Major Clery states that he has a very distinct recollection of the conversation, and that his memory of Lieutenant-Colonel Crealock's words is exactly as he expresses it, i.e., 'It is an accident the General's being here, and no interference with matters of detail will take place.'

Lieutenant-Colonel Crealock is perfectly correct in stating that the Lieutenant-General's Staff was not consulted in any matter connected with the pitching of the camp, its outposts, or its site. Reference was in one instance made direct to the Lieutenant-General himself regarding the relative positions two corps were to occupy, and His Excellency's decision was adverse to the arrangements made by my Staff Officer, and in this I concurred.

Lieutenant-Colonel Crealock is also quite correct in stating that, with the exception of his own case above referred to, none of the Lieutenant-General's Staff were regarded by me in the light of officers of the Adjutant-General's or Quarter-Master-General's Department.[77]

On receiving a copy of Glyn's waspish response, one can imagine Chelmsford's gorge rising; he could not let the matter rest there so he sent the following on 4 March:

Colonel Glyn is in error when he states that on seeing the message sent by Lieutenant-Colonel Pulleine, that I replied, 'there is nothing to be done.' It was on receipt of this information that I sent my Naval Aide-de-Camp, Lieutenant Milne, with a powerful telescope to the top of a high hill from which the camp was distinctly visible. Lieutenant Milne remained up there for an hour and a half, and came down and reported that he could not see any signs of an enemy near the camp, but that the oxen had been driven into camp. This measure I considered a precautionary one, very proper under the circumstances.

One hour before Lieutenant Milne descended the hill in question, I had ordered Commandant Brown's [sic] Battalion to return to camp across country. This officer has furnished a report by which it will be seen that he discovered the presence of the enemy when on his way back to camp, and sent several officers to inform me of the fact; none of these reports ever reached me until I myself was on my way back to camp late in the afternoon. I shall at once make enquiries as to how these reports did not reach me, and forward the result when received.[78]

A very long statement was also written by Clery, this time in his own name, as senior staff officer to Colonel Glyn, which described in great detail the actions of the Centre Column from its advance from the Mzinyathi (Buffalo) River on 20 January until its return to Rorke's Drift on 23 January.[79] This report included the small landmine that Clery, and not Lord Chelmsford, had left the 'defend the camp' orders for Pulleine, a matter about which Chelmsford had earlier expressed himself as most grateful.[80] This further example of Clery's verbosity forced Lord Chelmsford on to the defensive – on 19 March he wrote to his political masters in London:

Before the first and only report received from Lieutenant-Colonel Pulleine during the 22nd of January 1879 was received, I had ordered, as mentioned by Major Clery, 2 companies 2/24th and 4 guns under Major Harness, RA, to move back about 2 miles on the road towards the Camp.

On receipt of the report, I sent Lieutenant Milne, RA with a powerful telescope up to the top of a hill from which the Camp was plainly visible, and half an hour after I ordered a battalion of the Native Contingent, under Commandant Browne, to move back to Camp.

No signs of an enemy in the neighbourhood of the Camp were seen by Lieutenant Milne, although he remained on the look out till 11 o'clock a.m., and no fresh report, to confirm the first one, came in.

Major Harness, RA, was in the main road, and would have intercepted any messengers that came from the Camp. But one report, however, it would seem, and that written at 8 a.m. (at least three hours before Lieutenant-Colonel Durnford became engaged), was ever sent, and I can only infer from this fact that the necessity for assistance did not become apparent to the defenders of the Camp until it was too late.

After Captain Gardiner had delivered the message regarding the sending out of the tents and camp equipment to Lieutenant-Colonel Pulleine at about 11.30 a.m., it would seem that the latter officer sent a message back to the effect that he was not able to carry out the order at that time. This message was not received until quite late in the afternoon of the 22nd January 1879, and as it contained no allusion to any danger from attack, or any request for assistance, I feel that my assumption that no danger was anticipated must be correct.

I have been desirous to avoid making any statement that might be construed into a defence of my conduct on the day in question, as I was anxious that the evidence should speak for itself – but the inference to be drawn from Major Clery's evidence is so damaging to myself that I felt bound to afford explanation regarding a point, on which that officer appears to have misapprehended my action, and my reasons for that action, for fear lest, if it passed without remark, I might be supposed to acquiesce in its accuracy.[81]

Between them, Glyn and Clery had successfully defeated the campaign against the commander of the Centre Column while at the same time quietly sheeting home much of the responsibility to Lord Chelmsford himself. In England questions were also being raised at a number of levels, the most potentially damaging perhaps being those raised by HRH George, Duke of Cambridge, commander-in-chief of Queen Victoria's armed forces. But that is another story.

Chapter 6

Intermission

My argument is that War makes rattling good history; but Peace is poor reading.

Thomas Hardy 1840–1928

The NNC Withdrawal from Eshowe

This paper discusses a little-known aspect of the Zulu War, that of the withdrawal from Eshowe by the 2nd Regiment of the Natal Native Contingent led by Major Shapland Graves. Major Graves was an officer of the 3rd (East Kent) Regiment (the 'Buffs'). He had been commissioned into his regiment on 28 February 1856 and was promoted to lieutenant 6 July 1859, captain 15 May 1866 and major on 11 October 1876. By the time of the Zulu War, he had served in the army for twenty-two years.[1]

Graves had already been in Natal for some time when preparations were made for the Zulu War. He was serving as Protector of Immigrants, a government post involving the care of the many Indian people then arriving in the colony, when in December 1878 he was appointed commandant of the 2nd Regiment, Natal Native Contingent.[2] In a document entitled 'Distribution of Troops in the Field' dated 16 January 1879, Major Graves is also shown as having command of his own 1st Battalion.[3] This was not an unusual circumstance in the NNC: Commandant Rupert Lonsdale had also been in the same situation when first appointed to the 3rd Regiment. Commandant William John Nettleton had command of the 2nd Battalion.[4]

About 9 a.m. on 28 January 1879, Colonel Charles Knight Pearson, commanding the First Column then at Eshowe, received a telegram from Lord Chelmsford advising him of the disaster at Isandlwana which had occurred six days earlier. He was given the choice of holding his ground, which even then was being fortified by the efforts of Captain Wynne, RE, or withdrawing his column to the Lower Thukela.[5]

After a conference with his officers, the consensus was that they should withdraw, and Pearson initially concurred, but then changed his mind and determined to stay on, as a means of making a point to the Zulu king. Perhaps another item which tipped the scale in favour of holding out was the imminent arrival of a supply column under Colonel Ely. In order to conserve rations, Pearson also decided that the mounted men and the two battalions of the NNC would withdraw to the Thukela River. The NNC units left Eshowe about noon on that same day, 28 January, while the mounted men started some two hours later.[6]

The manner of the withdrawal by the NNC was less than exemplary. The first intimation to the public of a problem came from a newspaper report as early as 1 February: 'Opinions and accounts differ as regards the suddenly developed determination of these [NNC] people to go home, on reaching this side of the Tugela. Some of our volunteers, who accompanied them as far as the drift, attributed their dispersion to the apparent precipitancy of what looked like a retrograde movement . . .'[7] This was gilding the lily. Another report of the same day, this time part of a letter from a member of the mounted corps which also returned, was more specific: 'We made a forced march, leaving Etshowe at 2.15 p.m., and reaching the drift at 10.30 p.m. No enemy had appeared before Etshowe. If the Mounted Police troops and Native Contingent had left together at 5 p.m. properly organised, and marched in proper order, the natives would have better understood the meaning of the movement.'[8] Still more explicit was a report two days later: 'It is . . . an evident essential to efficiency that the officers should know the language and have the confidence of the natives. The march back from Etshowe appears to have been anything but a creditable movement.'[9]

Thus far, the responsibility for the untidy nature of the withdrawal seems to have been laid at the door of the African troops of the Contingent. On 18 February, however, the emphasis began to change when the following newspaper item appeared:

I believe the whole responsibility of [the Contingent's] sudden panic and consequent wish to go home, lies with the way in which the order for the retreat of the N.N.C. on the Tugela was carried out. By all the accounts which I can glean from those present at the time, a most injudicious haste, such as leaving all baggage, even to blankets and such articles as might easily have been carried on the persons of the owner, was used in packing them off, the expression 'everyone for himself' having even, it is said, more than once been used. The retreat of the Contingent consequently was conducted without order or method, the whites all herding together, and leaving their men – natives – to their own resources.[10]

The next event was the publication of a general order in the *Times of Natal* which quietly announced the appointment of another officer to the command of the 1st Battalion, NNC: '2. Captain Barton, 7th Foot, will proceed to Stanger to take over the command of the 1st Battalion, Natal Native Contingent from Major Graves, 2-3rd Foot, the latter officer having been appointed to other duty.'[11] What was left unsaid was that Graves was also in command of the whole 2nd Regiment and that, if he left, then the regiment itself was seemingly without a commanding officer.[12]

On 13 March, the *Natal Colonist* published a 'skit', or what today would be called a satirical sketch, to which some prominence was given, though no names were mentioned. The following is a key extract:[13]

Chit-chat

A play for the times – in one act

Dramatis Personae

Citizens – voices – passengers – a fool of quality – a judicious observer

Scene 1 – a back room – anywhere

Enter three citizens of repute and the judicious observer.

1st Cit. – I see the gallant winner of the Etshowe races has returned to town.

2nd Cit. – Yaas! Couldn't eat fire, so they've sent him back to protect the General's last base.

3rd Cit. – What! Has he gone back to his office?

2nd Cit. – Yaas! Shows moral courage don't it? (laughter).

The relevance of some of these barbs is not immediately apparent but the article was sufficient to fuel the fires of ugly rumour and would have future repercussions. The reference to the 'Etshowe races' was clearly the almost indecent haste of the NNC withdrawal to the Thukela while the inability to 'eat fire' implies a lack of personal courage in the face of the enemy. The significance of 'going back to his office' will become apparent shortly.

By this time, rumours were rife in Durban as to the identity of the officer concerned. Nothing further was heard until ten days later, when an exchange of correspondence was reported between Colonel William Bellairs, deputy adjutant-general, and the editor of the *Natal Witness*. Not having achieved his object by private means, Bellairs went public and arranged for the correspondence to be published in the *Natal Colonist* and *Natal Mercury*.[14]

The letters revealed that Colonel Bellairs had demanded, on behalf of Lord Chelmsford, that the *Witness* divulge the name of the officer who had made

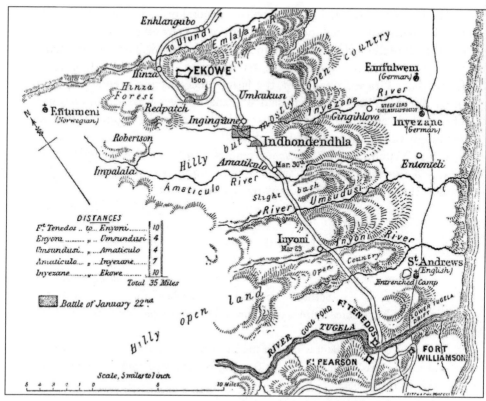

7 The road from the Thukela to Eshowe

an accusation of cowardice towards a fellow officer. Included in Bellairs' letter was a paragraph that publicly identified the accused gentleman:

> Under these circumstances, Lord Chelmsford feels bound, in justice to an officer wrongly attacked, to publish the accompanying copies of telegrams, showing that the removal of Major Graves was in consequence of his being required to resume his duty as Protector of Immigrants, and his services in command of a battalion of the Natal Native Contingent not being urgently required at the time.

In his reply, the editor of the *Witness*, Mr Statham, refused to divulge the name, and included some further pertinent questions:

> I may, however, venture to draw His Excellency's attention to the fact that, whereas in General Order No. 38,[15] Captain Barton, 7th Foot, is appointed to

certain duties at Greytown, in General Order No. 43, issued only six days later, Captain Barton, 7th Foot, is directed to proceed to take over the command of a certain native regiment from Major Graves, who is there stated to be 'appointed to another duty.'[16] And I may further beg to be informed as to the nature of the 'other duty' to which Major Graves has been appointed, and the number of the General Order in which his appointment is to be found.

The two telegrams to which reference was made, dated 20 February, were also published in the same article.

(From Colonial Secretary, Maritzburg, to H.E. Lord Chelmsford, Durban.)
Are Major Graves' services any longer required by Your Excellency as Commandant of a Natal Native Contingent Regiment?

(From Lord Chelmsford, Durban, to Colonel Law, Fort Pearson.)
I have just received the following telegram from the Colonial Secretary: – 'Are Major Graves' services any longer required by Your Excellency as Commandant of a Natal Native Contingent Regiment?'
Please communicate its contents to Major Graves, and tell him that I cannot conscientiously say his services are required, as his battalion will only be on the passive defensive. I think therefore, he ought to rejoin his proper appointment.[17]

In fact, Lord Chelmsford was being particularly disingenuous by arranging the publication of these telegrams, because on the 19 February he had written a private note to Colonel Charles Mitchell, Colonial Secretary of Natal, as the latter explained to Lieutenant-Governor Sir Henry Bulwer:

Following close on Gallwey's cipher despatch of yesterday comes this note of Lord Chelmsford's.
It is, I submit, useless to allow a man in whom the General has lost confidence to continue in Command and perhaps the course indicated is the best to leave an open exposure.
Will Your Exc'y give me instructions in time to save today's post.[18]

This was the note the general had written to Colonel Mitchell:

Can you help me to get Major Graves out of his present position by asking me officially whether he can be spared to go back to his proper position as Protector of Immigrants?
He is a failure as a C.O. and is impetuous.

In the retreat from Etshowe, he evidently lost his head and brought the natives and their European leaders back as a disgraceful rabble.

I do not, of course, wish to dismiss him, but it is certainly in the interests of the colony that he should be removed. I can replace him with a good officer.

If you would telegraph the question, I could send it on to Graves and say that I do not feel justified in retaining his services.

This will let him down easy.[19]

On 18 March 1879 the following notice appeared in the *Natal Government Gazette*:

His Excellency the Lieutenant Governor directs it to be notified that Her Majesty's Secretary of State for the Colonies has been pleased to confirm the following appointments, viz.:–

Major Shapland Graves,
3rd Regiment, 'The Buffs' to be Protector of Immigrants in this Colony.[20]

Graves' own account of the march, as presented to Lord Chelmsford (or more properly, the deputy adjutant-general, Colonel Bellairs), is lost but another was written for the Natal attorney-general. The report is dated 12 March 1879 and therefore the events are likely to have still been fresh in Graves' mind. It is a long, rambling document, sometimes almost incoherent, but, since it also illustrates the detail of the march, it is re-produced here in full.

About 10 am on the 28th January 1879 at Etshowe, Zululand, I received an order to proceed to Lt. Colonel Pearson's tent; on arriving there, I found all the Commanding Officers of Corps assembled for a Consultation on a telegraphic message received from his Excellency the Lieutenant-General Lord Chelmsford from Pietermaritzburg to the following effect: that Colonel Durnford's Column had been cut up & he himself killed. All previous orders issued to Col. Pearson for the conduct of the campaign were now at an end; that he might use his own discretion, as to remaining where he was or retiring on Natal, as he might expect to be attacked by the whole Zulu army; and that he was not to expect any help from him, the General.

The gravity of this intelligence was so great that it was deemed expedient to retire on the Lower Tugela, 'Fort Tenedos' having been attacked, as reported by Lieutenant Kingscote the night before and an inroad to Natal was thought very probable.

However shortly after, the idea of abandoning Etshowe was rejected, and it was decided to send away the Mounted Men and Native Contingent only,

who were ordered to leave all baggage behind and the tents were not even
to be struck.

I immediately issued the necessary orders for the March, giving permission
to any white man to remain behind who chose to stay, as the March was to
be a forced one & on to the Tugela, and likely to be fatiguing. Several of my
Battalion availed themselves of this & remained at Etshowe.

Both battalions paraded and then marched out to an open space in front
of the tents with the intention of being formed up with all the white men in
front, which was deemed the best way of proceeding as, in case of attack, we
feared the Natives would only think of themselves, so many being unarmed;
this Conclusion was come to by Captain Hart & myself, from what we had
seen at 'Inyanzane' on the 22nd.

At 12 noon we moved off from camp, preceded by a guide kindly placed at
my disposal by Mr Peterson, to show us a short way by which we avoided the
Hinza forest and kept in sight of Lieutenant Colonel Eley's column which was
halted on the main road & this path, only about 3½ miles from Camp, causing
a saving of at least 5 miles in distance.

I had instructions from Col. Pearson to get down to Lt. Col. Eley [sic] &
give him the information received from the General as quickly as possible,
in order that he might make all haste to Camp for fear of his being cut
off; in consequence of this, I moved off at the head of the Column. It now
appears that Comm't Nettleton met with an accident just at this time and
in consequence of this his Batt. did not move off at the same time as mine.
I did not see that this was the case, or it would have been rectified. When
this Batt. did march off, the men endeavoured to make up for lost time, and
thus several of those on foot (white NCOs) got blown before they reached Lt.
Col. Eley's party. The pathway above mentioned is all down hill, and steep in
many parts, consequently the line of men was of considerable length. Before
leaving Lt. Col. Eley, I ordered Capt. Shervington to take back with him to
Etshowe any NCOs who showed signs of fatigue or who wished to return.
With the Europeans together, having ordered them all to the front, we started
once more, still down hill, passing wagons en route for some way after we left,
until we got to the Inyanzani river, 8½ miles as we came from Etshowe, which
we crossed then and halted for one hour and a half, to give time for any who
might have come on instead of returning with Capt. Shervington, who was
behind. Commandant Nettleton then came up and informed me that several
NCOs were fatigued and not coming on as well as they could. While resting
here Major Barrow with 300 mounted men passed us. I stopped him and said
I wished to him to remain with us, in order that we should go to the Tugela
together. However he made an excuse of the large number of led horses he had

charge of and that he wished to get through the Amatakulu before dark, but he agreed to wait for us after he got through that bush, & if he saw any signs of the Enemy, he would let me know. To this I assented. I then asked him for some of the led horses but only got from him six to mount some of the most tired of the NCOs, several more horses being lent by our own officers. I was thus enabled to help on the most fatigued; to this point I put the distance down at 8½ miles. So after a brief rest we resumed our journey, Europeans all together. The fact of removing the white men from the Companies broke them up to a considerable extent. I mean the natives, and which under these circumstances could not be helped. About 4 miles on we again halted, and all then partook of biscuits or anything else that they had, the Natives having found plenty of mealies seemed to satisfy themselves. After this halt we moved on to the Ford across the Amatakulu river, a distance of two miles more. When we reach this Ford it had to become <u>dark</u> and after crossing we halted again, having left several officers on the opposite bank to see all the NCOs over, but as it was then <u>so dark</u> and Major Barrow who, according to agreement, should have been close by on the ridge, we moved up to it, which was clear of the bush alluded to before. Then we halted again, and waited for a report from the rear, which was shortly brought by Captain Burnside, saying that all the NCOs had crossed, but a party of 13 say they will not march another step for any b—— officer and that they can take care of themselves, or words to that effect.

On receipt of this report I sent off two mounted officers to try and overtake Major Barrow and request him to send back 100 men to help us but I regret to say they did not overtake the Mounted men. At this time I imagined Major Barrow might have gone on to the Umzindoozi & waited there.

The NCOs who refused to march any further were told that the rest of the Column was waiting for them only a little way on, but all the same they said they would remain there and stay for the night. Whereupon I thought it best to bivouack for the night and try and get these men on.

Before deciding to do this, I asked Captain Hart, my Staff Officer, what he would advise. His reply was 'If the NCOs will come on, I should wait for them, if they refuse to come on tonight, I should not wait for them'. I was then informed that they meant to stop where they were. Under the circumstances, we deemed it expedient it to move on slowly, so as to give them time to catch us up if they chose, and hoping to meet some Mounted men with led horses at the same time.

We soon afterwards reached the Umzindoozi, which is only about 4 miles from the Amatakulu and then we halted again for a considerable time, and then continued our March, so slowly did we go that before we reached the next river, about 7 miles from Camp, Capt. Gough on foot overtook us & said that he, with several officers, had brought on the 13 NCOs & left them at this side of the Umzindoozi; when they said they really meant to stay. I must here add that although all danger from attack from the rear was at an end, besides Major Barrow had acted as an advanced guard, and would have fallen in with the Enemy, had any been about. The only danger I apprehended therefore was in front & that only on account of Lt. Kingscote's reported attack on 'Fort Tenedos' & as I was only about 7 miles from this Fort, I thought the best thing to do now was to move on there and send back horses to bring these refractory men in.

All was done that under the circumstances could be done for these NCOs; horses were offered them, but as in my opinion they had some ulterior object in view, they chose to stay behind to make themselves out as being badly treated & in order that if they were not discharged, that they might get quit of serving with Natives any more; besides, the work was much harder than they expected. There is one unanimous opinion amongst the officers, who tried all they could to get them on from the Umzindoozo, that they did not exert themselves as they should have, and that if they chose, with the help of the officers and a few horses that were offered them, they were able to march if they liked.

I think under these circumstances, to go on to Camp and send back, was the best that could be done, where we arrived at 2:30 a.m., having taken 14½ hours to March 30 miles. The greater part of the distance being done in the dark, there was a little moonlight early in the night, after that it was quite dark, only starlight.

Immediately after coming to Fort Tenedos, I sent Capt. Hart with orders to Major Barrow to send 100 men with horses as soon as possible to go and bring these NCOs to Camp and it was arranged that the party was to be sent off at 4:30 a.m.; that would be at daylight. This duty was not performed as well as I should have wished, however all the NCOs who remained behind under charge of a Lieutenant Ellis, who took the duty upon himself, came into Camp safely. So that I am happy to state that no casualty of any kind occurred during the march, and beyond fatigue, which we all suffered from owing to the tediousness of the journey, no one was a bit the worse. Some, of course, were foot sore for a few days, and to prove that these NCOs were not injured or had any cause of complaint when the Lt. Gen'l arrived some few days afterwards at Fort Pearson, not one man of either Battalion made a complaint to him, at his inspection.

I have now stated all the particulars of this March, and the more I inquire into the conduct of some of the NCOs, the more it appears, on an occasion of this sort, every man should exert himself to the utmost. The Natives would have helped them on, if they were not too proud to accept assistance, but no, their grievance was, that they <u>were not mounted</u>, and by making this to do they felt sure that they would not be asked to go on foot with Natives again.

I could say a great deal more on the subject of these men, who were of all Nations I may say, picked up anyhow in Cape Town and other places in the old Colony. I need not say that it has caused me more regret than I ever experienced during my whole life having had the command of the <u>two Batts.</u> of the Native Contingent.

A great deal, I believe, has been said about this March, and a great deal has been said about everything connected with this war, so to refute the sayings of a lot of excited people would give one plenty to do without doing anything else. My opinion is that some spiteful persons have set reports going which are utterly untrue, and which never lose on repetition.

Had these NCOs been under the Articles of War, a better discipline could be maintained. The severest punishment that could be inflicted was dismissal, to this they did not object in the least, after their insight into Zululand.

Although Major Barrow did not stay with us, or wait for us, yet he acted as a rear guard, I may say, to the 'Inyezani' and from there to Camp as an advanced guard.[21]

Thus Graves was deftly set aside to a position from which any further action on his part could do no further harm to the military authorities. Unhappily for Graves, it was not the end of the matter and these events eventually led him, after the conclusion of the war, to pursue a civil action for libel in the Durban Court. That story is told in a later paper.

Hlobane: A New Perspective   Huw M. Jones[22]

On 28 March 1879, the British were roundly defeated as they tried to take cattle belonging to the Qulusi from the plateau of Hlobane. On the following day, the main Zulu *impi* attacked the British laager at Khambula and was decisively repulsed, a victory which overshadowed the earlier debacle. This paper sets the action at Hlobane in its geographical and historical context using a previously unnoticed source to clarify the movements of the British and Zulu forces, illuminate the relationship between colonial units and imperial officers and illustrate the intrigues initiated by the latter to cover their mistakes.

The rugged country where the Mfolozi Mhlope (White Mfolozi), Mfolozi Mnyama (Black Mfolozi) and Mkhuze rivers have their headwaters has for long been the cockpit of south-eastern Africa. In the late eighteenth century, when it was occupied by the Ngwane of Masumpha Zondo and a less cohesive grouping of Zwane and Mazibuko peoples known as the Ngwe, the Ndwandwe and Mtetwa vied for control. The Ngwane under Matiwane kaMasumpha were forced out and in consequence caused the Hlubi polity centred on the rolling landscape between the Ncome and Mzinyathi rivers temporarily to disintegrate. As the Ndwandwe defensive zone roughly drawn along the middle reaches of the Mfolozi Mhlope crumbled under the probing of the Mtetwa, a small group of Khumalo under Mzilikazi Khumalo was prompted to plunder its smaller neighbours to the west under Nyoka Zwane before coming into further conflict with the groups locked into the kloofs of a massive spur of the Khahlamba dominated on its southern side by Ngcaka Mountain overlooking the upper Phongolo River. Here the Nyawo, Shabalala and Kubheka peoples, who looked for stability towards the related Ngwane Dlamini polity north of the river, were plundered and quietened. Not many years later Ndwandwe refugees followed the same route on to the upper highveld, ejected by forces now controlled by Shaka kaSenzengakhona Zulu. Attempting a return in 1826, they were met at Ndololwane on the western edge of the area and dispersed. As the larger refugee groups rolled through, the original small groupings largely survived, the craggy landscape providing shelter from the military and political attentions of the increasingly dominant Zulu polity to the south.

For many years the area remained relatively isolated, the western end of a border zone between the Zulu and Ngwane Dlamini now becoming better known as the Swazi. Refugees who sought sanctuary with the Zulu were placed on the edge of this *cordon sanitaire*; rebel Swazi princes were settled at Bhadzeni near the Dumbe Mountain in 1847 by Mpande kaSenzangakhona Zulu. Mpande had viewed with apprehension the return of the Hlubi under Langalibalele kaMthimkulu and the need to keep them as well as others, such as the Mazibuko and the people of Nyamayenja waSobhuza Dlamini, aware of the potential of Zulu power even though he acknowledged they were not his subjects. Continuing requests for land from trekboers arriving west of the Mzinyathi River were also cause for disquiet. Mpande responded by placing important groups and reliable *izinduna* in localities of strategic importance, strengthening the north-western border area by moving the Ntombela under Lukwazi kaMazwana into the eastern foothills of the Zungwini Range south of the Bivane River and the Mdlalose under Sekethwayo kaNhlaka into the lands along the upper Mfolozi Mhlope. Immediately to their rear, in the deep kloofs of the linking series of plateaux running north-westwards from Ntendeka in the west through Hlobane and Ityenteka to Mashongololo, Mpande moved the Qulusi homestead, Baqulusini, which had become his responsibility on the death of Mnkabayi kaJama Zulu. This was the focus for a group of refugees of royal origin who came under Zulu protection, but retained their privileged status and to this homestead the Swazi were attached.

Tensions lead to war
As polities consolidated and border zones shrank to boundaries more precisely defined, potential for conflict increased. This is not the place to rehearse the causes of the Anglo-Zulu War of 1879, save to note that for several years previously the area had been marked by tensions, which became more obvious as the British upset the balance of political power by annexing the South African Republic (ZAR) in 1877, taking control of the upper Phongolo area from its burghers. On the other side of the boundary, the situation also changed with the arrival in 1866 of another Swazi refugee, Mbilini waMswati Dlamini, the first-born son of Ngwenyama Mswati.

He settled in the hills north of the confluence of the Ntombe and Phongolo rivers, immediately establishing a close personal and dominant position in Zulu politics. After spending three years at Ulundi, in 1878 Mbilini established another homestead, Ndlabeyitubula, on the south-eastern slopes of Mashongololo. From here he raided the south-western borders of the Swazi country as well as the districts of Utrecht and Wakkerstroom.

Even as the British appeared magisterially to resolve border problems, their relations with the Zulu deteriorated to the point when, in late 1878, it became obvious to Cetshwayo that war was inevitable. Mbilini was still the dominant personality in the area and Cetshwayo was content to allow him to assume military control. Through his spies and mounted scouts who regularly patrolled as far north as the Mkhondvo River, Mbilini was aware of British troop movements. Most obvious were the continuous wagon trains from Newcastle through Utrecht carrying supplies for a forward commissary at Balte's Spruit. The arrival of the administrator of the Transvaal, Sir Theophilus Shepstone, in Utrecht at Christmas 1878 would not have gone unnoticed. Africans living on farms in Utrecht and Wakkerstroom districts were pressed into service and drafted to Utrecht to be kitted out with arms. Since his surrender was one of the conditions of the British ultimatum to the Zulu, Mbilini left his homestead above the Ntombe and moved to Ndlabeyitubula. On 1 January 1879 the wagon route to Balte's Spruit was choked with troops. Clearly visible from the Zungwini range was the British camp at Conference Hill, not far from the banks of the Ncome, as were attempts by the troops to ford what was assumed by their commanders to be the Zulu boundary; they were finally successful on 6 January, five days before the ultimatum was due to expire. Mbilini did nothing to impede the progress of this force, No.

4 Column under Brevet Colonel H.E. Wood, 90th (Perthshire Volunteers) Light Infantry, attempting only, albeit unsuccessfully, to deter waverers such as Tinta Mdlalose and the border *induna* Mbemba from defecting with their people, cattle and weapons. Instead he took control of the Qulusi and of the Ntombela, now led by Mabamba kaLukwazi and his principal *induna* Ndabankulu Ntombela, as well as the Kubheka under Manyonyoba kaMagonondo who lived in the Ntombe Valley north of the Phongolo. Mbilini's defensive strategy was that in which he had been sedulously trained in the Swazi polity: given the obvious military superiority of the enemy, offer as little resistance as possible and withdraw to prepared positions in the mountains. By early March, homesteads had been cleared of people and cattle; men were trained and drilled in the use of captured weapons. For his central defensive position, Mbilini selected the series of plateaux stretching from Ntendeka to Mashongololo above Baqulusini. Here on the flat plateau of Hlobane, the Qulusi ranged their cattle from temporary homesteads built on the terraces around its precipitous sides.

When circumstances were opportune, Mbilini struck with ferocity in the sudden dawn raids that were a feature of Swazi offensive tactics. A British convoy from the hamlet of Derby bound for Luneburg became bogged down during the heavy rains of early March and several wagons were looted. The remaining wagons were collected at the drift across the Ntombe, but the convoy was inadequately guarded and Mbilini attacked at dawn on 12 March, killing seventy-nine soldiers and civilians and seizing arms and ammunition. By the time reinforcements arrived from Luneburg, the Qulusi had disappeared. Stung by the defeat at Ntombe Drift and lured by reports of thousands of cattle grazing on Hlobane, Wood was pressured into an assault on this plateau which he incorrectly believed to be the main locus of Qulusi opposition. Poorly crafted plans, based on inadequate intelligence and compounded by inept soldiering, marked the British defeat in the action at Hlobane on 27/28 March 1879.

Wood's accounts
Accounts of the action have relied heavily on Wood's autobiography published in 1906.[23] He used his official despatch written on 30 March 1879, of which there are, in fact, two versions.[24] That published officially contains two important sections omitted from the abbreviated version which received wide publicity in the newspapers of southern Africa and Britain. One gave Wood's reasons for proceeding against the Qulusi, setting out why he thought a Zulu *impi* from Ulundi would not reach him before the action took place, and a second covered his order to Lieutenant-Colonel (local rank) J.C. Russell, 12th

(Prince of Wales' Royal) Lancers, and his assertion that Russell went to the wrong location; a footnote commending the courage of Major W.K. Leet, 13th (Somerset) Light Infantry, was also omitted. In addition to being released to the press, the abbreviated version was used by Norris-Newman in his account of the Anglo-Zulu War compiled in Pietermaritzburg in 1880[25] and by Williams in his biography of Wood published in 1892.[26] Certain aspects of the action were described by Wood and published as articles in *Pearson's Magazine* in 1895.[27] In *British Battles on Land and Sea*, edited by Wood for publication in 1915, his autobiography was the principal source of a description of Hlobane with changes introduced to counter some of the criticisms of his command expressed, albeit *sotto voce*, shortly after the action was fought.[28]

Wood's despatch is essentially a description of his own movements with commendation for certain individuals, not an overall report based on those of the unit commanders. It is incomplete because Wood adopted the role of interested spectator, taking no part in either the main assault on Hlobane plateau commanded by Brevet Lieutenant-Colonel R.H. Buller, 60th Rifles, and the repulse from there, or in Russell's advance onto and retirement from the lower plateau of Ntendeka. In a brief memorandum reporting his actions, Wood elided the events at Hlobane and Khambula so as to mask the severity of defeat and elaborate the decisiveness of victory and both versions of the despatch are internally inconsistent and vague in certain important aspects. Subsequent commentators have accepted Wood's accounts without demur, but as Major-General M.W.E. Gossett pointed out in 1906: 'by a fluke he [Wood] rec'd information of the enemy's advance on Kambula [*sic*] & he dovetailed the two actions in his report, so as to show himself to the best advantage.'[29]

Releasing the news
By 7 p.m. on 29 March, immediately after the Zulu had been driven from Khambula, Wood wrote a short memorandum on the events of the previous two days[30] as well as a somewhat incoherent letter to the high commissioner, Sir Bartle Frere, fortuitously then in nearby Newcastle:

> Your two kind letters were put into my hands as 20,000 were attacking us. We have lost about 7 officers and 70 men killed and wounded, but entirely defeated the enemy who suffered severely. This makes up for yesterday when we successfully assaulted the Inhlobane army but being caught up by the Ulundi army suffered considerable loss. Please spread the news of our fight today. To our grief Piet Uys was killed yesterday. I will write further particulars later. My horse was killed yesterday falling on me. Poor Ronald Campbell, Lord Cawdor's son, [killed?] when behaving most gallantly. The Zulus came on from 1.30 pm to 4.30 pm.[31]

On the following day he completed his despatches on Hlobane, accompanied by the reports of the unit commanders and other statements relating to Russell's conduct, and on Khambula. Utrecht had no telegraph at this time and the line of communication was through Newcastle. Frere, despondent at the news of 'reverses suffered by Buller's Patrol to the Hlobane Mtn', was writing to Wood when the latter's note arrived. 'Most heartily', responded Frere, 'do I thank God & congratulate you, on what from your brief account seems to have been so very brilliant & decisive a victory.'[32] He was also quick to respond to Wood's plea 'to spread the news': on 31 March he sent a letter to Colonel W.O. Lanyon, now administrator of the Transvaal, forwarding 'extracts from despatches received from Colonel Wood VC, CB, reporting the result of an attack on his camp at Kambula, by a force of Zulus, estimated at 20,000 men, comprising regiments which were the elite of [the] Zulu army'; as Frere congratulated Chelmsford on 'this decisive victory', there was no mention of Hlobane, only a condolence on the death of P.L. Uys, leader of the Burgher Force. Lanyon had Frere's letter and its enclosures published in Pretoria in a *Government Gazette Extraordinary* on 3 April in English and Dutch. The memorandum and despatch were published in full, duly attested as true copies by T.S. Hutchinson, landdrost of Wakkerstroom, and Capt R.A. Knox, 4th (The King's Own) Regiment, commanding the troops at Newcastle. The Hlobane despatch appeared in the abbreviated version with Knox attesting only that it was a 'correct copy, but not verified'; the postscript referring to Leet somehow became attached to the English copy of the Khambula despatch, although it was correctly placed at the end of the Dutch translation.[33]

Rumours that Wood had suffered a very serious reverse began to circulate in Pietermaritzburg on the evening of Monday 31 March, Government House admitting only that Wood had seen a force of some 20,000 Zulu whilst on patrol. So serious were they that the correspondent of the *Cape Mercury* cabled his office that he 'dare not wire, except officially confirmed'.[34] Wood's memorandum had been telegraphed by the resident magistrate in Ladysmith to the colonial secretary in Pietermaritzburg at 9.30 am on 1 April and the news began to circulate there immediately. In Durban, the *Natal Mercury* announced at its office at 2 pm that day that 'the Zlobane [*sic*] mountain was attacked on the 28th, and taken, but 20,000 Zulus surrounded it and recaptured the cattle, after great loss on our side', followed by a report that Khambula had been attacked and the Zulu driven off. This appeared in the issue of that paper on 2 April with a statement released earlier that day by the deputy adjutant-general (DAG), Colonel W. Bellairs, army headquarters being then in Durban. In Pietermaritzburg, the *Times of Natal* also carried

Wood's memorandum on 2 April with a postscript from a letter transmitted through Ladysmith that Captain Ronald Campbell, Llewellyn Lloyd and Piet Uys had been killed. On the same day, Bellairs also released Wood's official Khambula despatch and it was printed in the *Natal Mercury* on the next day, 3 April.

To those in Natal waiting for news, the situation was confused; on 5 April, the 'special commissioner' for the *Cape Times* reported from Durban that he had no details of the Hlobane action, but there was no doubt that Buller's force 'was surrounded and that those who saved their lives did so by cutting through the ranks of the enemy'.[35] Not until a one-page 'extra' to the *Natal Mercury* appeared about 6 April with a report from the correspondent of the *Times of Natal* by-lined 'Kambula Hill, March 29, 1879 and March 30, 1879', as well as a list of those killed issued by Bellairs on 5 April, was there any firm information of what had happened at Hlobane. In Pietermaritzburg, the *Times of Natal* provided news from 'the authorities' on 4 April quoting a reliable source at Khambula giving some details of the attack on the laager, followed by even fewer about Hlobane; it also published Wood's despatch on Khambula. Only on 11 April did the *Times of Natal* publish Wood's Hlobane despatch, copied from *Die Volksstem* of 4 April and prefaced by the note: 'It appears by some accident not to have been transmitted with Brigadier-General Wood's report of the attack on the camp, which it seems it accompanied.'

In Cape Town, the despatch covering the action at Khambula was published in the *Cape Argus* and the *Cape Times* on 2 and 3 April and speculation about what had happened at Hlobane was rife. On 3 April a leading article in the *Cape Times* considered that the Zulu army's strength had been underestimated and that it was possible that the 20,000 who had surrounded Wood were Swazi commanded by Mbilini. Further consideration on the next day led to the thought that Hlobane had been a repeat of the Uys 'experimental patrol' carried out in February and that Wood had possibly 'remained in defence of the camp'. A telegram from Cape Town dated 15 April reported that 'no details are yet at hand concerning the disaster at Zlobane [*sic*] Mountain.'[36] Not until 17 April was Wood's Hlobane despatch published in the *Cape Times*, to be followed the next day by paeans of praise for Wood and the astounding conclusion that:

> The attack upon the Inhlobane Mountain, so modestly described by Colonel Wood, was one of the most daring feats in the annals of modern warfare. It was daring, we fear, unto rashness, but the feature on which we would lay the most stress is that the 'fighting column' has made up in personal bravery for

paucity in numbers . . . The siege of the Inthlobane [*sic*] Mountain and the attack upon the Khambula camp may almost be regarded as one engagement; and whilst we have to mourn over the loss of so many brave men we have also to rejoice over an undoubted victory.[37]

The *Cape Times* followed this with more adulatory references to Wood and by early May contended with its rival paper in Cape Town that no blame had been or could be attached to anyone for the Hlobane defeat.

It is clear, however, that Wood's Hlobane despatch and attachments were with Bellairs in Durban at least by 5 April. That day he telegraphed the news of Hlobane and Khambula to the Secretary of State for War, quoting from Wood's despatches and adding telegrams from Chelmsford about the action at Gingindlovu.[38] In Chelmsford's absence with the column he had taken to relieve Eshowe, Bellairs decided to send the despatches to London immediately. On 5 April, he formally forwarded them to the War Office, having made arrangements on his own initiative to arrange for the mail steamer to leave Cape Town a day earlier than advertised and for it to call at Sao Vicente in the Cape Verde Islands instead of Madeira so that the telegram could reach London earlier. The *Dublin Castle*, scheduled to sail from Cape Town on 8 April, was ordered to leave with despatches at 9.20 pm the previous evening. At 11.20 pm on 22 April, the ship reached Sao Vicente, from where the news was telegraphed to Britain.[39] *The Times* carried the news on the following day that Wood had successfully attacked the enemy position on Hlobane mountain:

> Unfortunately in bringing off the large number of cattle captured, he was delayed owing to the extreme difficulty of the ground, and assailed in his turn by a large body of the enemy estimated at 20,000 strong, who endeavoured to cut off his retreat. That the safety of Colonel Wood's detachment was imperilled is evident, and they cut their way through with heavy loss, losing Captains the Hon RE Campbell and R.J. Barton of the Coldstream Guards, both special service officers, besides a long roll of colonial officers and men whom we can ill spare.

There followed the description of the success at Khambula, thus following a scenario which could only mislead and confuse. Wood's Khambula despatch was published in *The Times* on Friday 2 May and the abbreviated Hlobane despatch followed a day later. A staff writer on *The Times* reflecting on the Hlobane despatch over the weekend commented on the following Monday that it 'lacks clearness'. 'We are left in ignorance', he wrote, 'of the reasons which led to the attack on the Zlobani [*sic*] mountain. According to one account, it was for the purpose of directing attention from Lord Chelmsford's advance on Ekowe [*sic*]; but there is good reason to believe it was with a view to clearing Luneburg district, which for months past has been infested by Umbelini's men . . .'[40] On 17 May *The Times* published an account of 'The Battle of Zlobane' by its own correspondent who had taken part; significantly it was written after the action at Khambula on 30 March and prefaced by the statement that 'After two days' severe fighting, Colonel Wood has gained a complete victory . . .'[41] By this time, Bellairs' memorandum of 5 April with Wood's compete despatches and attachments had been published on 7 May in a supplement to the *London Gazette,* that relating to Hlobane first.[42]

Managing the news
The staff writer of *The Times* was not the only one to puzzle over the abbreviated Hlobane despatch. Strangely, Lord Chelmsford himself, having returned to Durban on 9 April, commented to the Secretary of State for War that he had 'not observed in Colonel Wood's despatch any reference to the reason why he considered it desirable to attack on the 28th'.[43] Yet in the full version of his despatch Wood wrote that 'I considered that the great importance of creating a diversion of the Ekowe [*sic*] Relief Column justified me in making a reconnaissance in force, and moreover . . . it was improbable that Cetewayo's army could leave Undi [*sic*] till the 27th inst.' Could the commander-in-chief have been reading the abbreviated version and why and by whom had this been prepared?

According to Lanyon, the omissions in the Hlobane despatch as published in the *Transvaal Government Gazette* were made on the instructions of Frere through whom the accounts had been received in Pretoria. On receiving his copy of the gazette in Khambula, Wood had immediately protested to C.E. Steele, acting colonial secretary of the Transvaal, that a paragraph had been omitted without anything to show that it had been left out. 'By this omission', wrote Wood, 'not only is undue prominence given to my personal action, on the 28th, but an injustice is done to the arrangements I made, for conducting the retreat in an orderly manner.' In response Lanyon had a letter sent to the Transvaal press emphasising 'that what was published was only an extract from Wood's official despatch' and he published a notice, No. 48 of 1879, to this effect in a subsequent gazette.[44] This was the only omission to which Wood objected and, as far as is known, he made no further protests. The paragraph omitted contained his instruction to Russell to withdraw to Zungwini Nek and Wood's pointed contention that in moving to the wrong place Russell failed to cover Buller's withdrawal and was responsible for the deaths of some eighty of Hamu's people. Laying the blame on Russell was one of Wood's manoeuvres to shift responsibility for the disaster at Hlobane from himself to others; this first move failed, but he was soon to have Russell disgraced.

In camp at Khambula, little was said about Hlobane. On 15 April a general parade was held to read a letter from Lord Chelmsford at which Wood thanked everyone for their part in the action on 29 March. As one correspondent noted, however, 'In allusion to the Hlobane matter very little was said. He [Wood] spoke of it feelingly enough and in deploring our heavy loss of 28th instant [*sic*] stated that no fault could be attributed to anyone but himself, if anyone was to blame for the untoward occurrence.'[45] 'Manliness' was one description of Wood's reticence in speaking of the reverse at Hlobane.[46]

It could be said that despatches written close to the events they describe are inevitably uneven. And in the circumstances of Hlobane, the loss of Campbell was not only a severe emotional shock for Wood, but that of a staff officer competent in preparing reports. Major-General Sir Archibald Alison, head of army intelligence, described the despatches at the time as gibberish, Lieutenant-Colonel J.N. Crealock, military secretary to Chelmsford, attributing this to the loss of Campbell.[47] In the light of subsequent events and detailed analysis, however, it is difficult to attribute Wood's ambiguous memorandum and despatch solely to his mental state or written competence, which was not, in fact, inconsiderable.

It could also be said that, given the hitherto lamentable sequence of campaign disasters, affecting Wood's column no less than others, the desire to laud the rout of the Zulu at Khambula is fully understandable. But there are certain aspects of the content of his despatch which lead one to suspect that Wood's motives were not that simple, that he knew of matters best left unsaid.

Another account
The task of unravelling the consequences of the action at Hlobane, let alone its course, is by no means complete. Some of the inconsistencies in Wood's accounts have been noted in a recent article.[48] But the information in a source which has never, as far as I am aware, been consulted with reference to the Anglo-Zulu War provides a different perspective on three assertions made in Wood's version of events: that Wood knew of the presence of the Zulu *impi* only on his return westwards at 10.30 am on 28 March; that the Border Horse was marching away from the action when encountered by Wood; and that it displayed cowardice in the face of the enemy. The memoir of C.G. Dennison, who took part in the action at Hlobane as second-in-command of the Border Horse and the only officer in that unit to survive, throws new light on these assertions.[49] Written shortly after the end of the second Anglo-Boer War, it

comprises 170 pages of typed text covering Dennison's career to the end of the first Anglo-Boer War. This period is barely summarised in Dennison's book, *A Fight to a Finish,* published in London in 1904, which deals with his experiences during the second Anglo-Boer War.[50] His experiences at Hlobane are totally omitted, probably because, however much Dennison suggested otherwise, it implicitly blamed Wood for the fiasco and Wood was by then Field Marshal Sir Evelyn Wood, VC, GCB, GCMG, commanding 2nd Army Corps.[51] The memoir provides answers to several questions (imagination and supposition having hitherto sufficed), brings to light the major mistake which Wood made and demonstrates how he manipulated the record of events.

Dennison was born at Cradock in the Cape Colony and brought up in Grahamstown before moving to the Orange Free State with his family whilst still a small boy. Both his father and a brother were killed in action during the Frontier Wars.[52] In 1865 he served under Captain E.S. Hanger as a trooper with the Bloemfontein Mounted Rangers, a voluntary burgher corps, taking part in the Second Basuto War (1865–6).[53] About 1869, he moved with his wife and family to Rustenburg in the western ZAR and on its formation in 1871 joined the Rustenburg Schutzen Corps; by 1877 he was a lieutenant, one of the only two officers, the other being the commandant.[54] When a commando against the Pedi was raised in May 1876, Dennison commanded the president's bodyguard and Lieutenant-Colonel F.A. Weatherley and his family came over from Eersteling to join President T.F. Burgers and watch the proceedings. It was probably on this occasion that Dennison first met Weatherley who asked him in 1878 to be second-in-command of a volunteer force he expected to lead, and later that year Weatherley raised a unit generally known as the Border Horse. Towards the end of January 1879, fifty-five men, comprising A troop, were ready to march to Eersteling in the Zoutpansberg under Dennison's command, but the day before he was due to leave, Dennison heard that his wife was seriously ill in Rustenburg and he left Pretoria to look after her; the troop marched without him.[55] Towards the end of January 1879, Weatherley received a letter from Colonel H. Rowlands, VC, commanding both imperial and local forces in the Transvaal and then at Derby near the Swazi border, asking him to march as soon as he could with as many men as possible for Makati's Kop[56] in the direction of Luneburg.[57] On 30 January Weatherley issued orders to B troop to parade that morning 'in full marching order for active service and . . . proceed to Luneberg [*sic*] to join the Transvaal Column'. Alerted the previous day, Dennison hastened back to Pretoria and left with the troop as second-in-command to Weatherley. Before following B troop of the Border Horse to Hlobane, it is necessary to have a closer look at its commanding officer, now Commandant Weatherley, whom Wood described as a 'rebel' – 'or said to have been'.[58]

Weatherley's career
Commenting immediately after its printing of Wood's Hlobane despatch, the *Cape Times* noted that: 'It seems to us as a singular omission that in Colonel Wood's despatch the death of Colonel Weatherley finds no place. We are perfectly sure that it was an omission and nothing more and that the brave soldier's memory will have justice done to it.'[59]

But this was a deliberate omission designed by Wood to preserve his reputation; in Dennison's forgotten memoir, Wood's negligence in the field, followed by a deliberate cover-up and the vilification of a dead officer with no next-of-kin able to support his memory, can now be clearly identified. Weatherley was the perfect candidate for the role of scapegoat: not only was he dead, but his life had been recently marked by scandal and intemperate behaviour. Born in Newcastle-upon-Tyne in 1830, he was the son of Ilderton Weatherley, a shipowner. Educated for four years at the military academy in Dresden,[60] family influence secured for him a commission as a lieutenant in the 4th Austrian Imperial Tuscan Dragoons quartered in Italy.[61] Here he was engaged in clearing the Apennines of brigands and disbanded soldiery from the 1848 war.[62] Returning to Britain, Weatherley commanded a troop as a captain in the Tower Hamlets Militia and made personal representations for a cornetcy in the Light Dragoon Regiment then serving in the Crimea, the war there having broken out in September 1854. At the age of twenty-four, he was somewhat old for a commission of this nature, but the nomination of the Earl of Cardigan was sufficient to secure a cornetcy without purchase in the 4th (The Queen's Own) Regiment of Light Dragoons on 30 March 1855.[63] Very shortly afterwards, Weatherley obtained his lieutenancy in the regiment by purchase on 26 June 1855.[64] Arriving in the Crimea with his regiment on 13 August 1855, he was present at the battle of Tchernaya and the siege and fall of Sevastopol. In dramatic circumstances, Weatherley ran away with a rich heiress, Maria Louisa Martyn, daughter of Lieutenant-Colonel Francis Mountjoy Martyn, 2nd Life Guards, and on 5 January 1857 they were married in Windsor.[65] Four months later, the Sepoy Mutiny erupted in India and Weatherley, possibly because of the circumstances of his marriage, exchanged on 5 June 1857 into the 6th Regiment of Dragoon Guards (Carabiniers) then stationed in Meerut.[66] In India he was involved in operations in the Rohilkhand and Awadh. By late 1861, prospects for promotion in the Carabiniers were limited and on his behalf Lord Raglan asked the commander-in-chief 'to be good enough to favor [*sic*] his views if it lies in your power?' It did, and at a cost of £1,100, HRH Prince George sanctioned the purchase of a troop by Weatherley with a captaincy in the 6th (Inniskilling) Regiment of Dragoons on 28 January 1862 and he served for a further six years before retiring in April 1868 by the sale of his commission.[67] Retiring to Brighton, he was appointed on 31 March 1875 to command a corps of the Sussex Artillery Volunteers with the rank of lieutenant-colonel; he was subsequently promoted to command the brigade of four corps of artillery.[68]

Weatherley and southern Africa

In mid-1871, Edward Button, a Durban butcher, discovered gold on the farm at Eersteling in the Zoutpansberg initiating the first gold rush in the ZAR. He formed The Transvaal Gold Mining Company Limited in Britain in August 1872 with a nominal capital of £50,000 'to purchase the estate called Eersteling' and among the seven initial subscribers who took ten £10 shares each was Weatherley, who became a director.[69] On the death of his father-in-law in January 1874, Weatherley was left £42,000 which he invested unwisely. Much went to finance a twelve-stamp battery and an engineer sent from Britain, but the Eersteling mine did not flourish and the prospectors and miners soon left for the fields near Lydenburg. In mid-1875, one of the directors, A.R. Roche, went out to inspect the property, but he became ill and although he reached Eersteling, was forced to return and shortly died.[70] These adverse circumstances, and a need to economise because of his poor investments, were the reason for Weatherley's departure early in 1876 to become managing director at Eersteling at a monthly salary of £45.[71]

Relationships between the ZAR and the neighbouring Pedi polity under Sekhukhune woaSekwati had deteriorated to the point when in May 1876 President T.F. Burgers led a commando against him into the mountainous country south of the Olifants River. The republic was in such parlous financial straits that Burgers asked the management of the Eersteling company for their spare arms and ammunition, which were duly provided. Weatherley offered his services and joined Burgers' commando. The campaign was a failure, but in payment for the arms and ammunition, Weatherley obtained a concession from the president granting the company mineral rights over most of the government land in the Zoutpansberg. The fortunes of the ZAR declined further when Sir Theophilus Shepstone crossed its border on 4 January 1877 intending to annex it to the British Crown. Taking up residence in Pretoria, Shepstone sounded public opinion and among those most active in furthering annexation was Weatherley. Labour and transport difficulties had contributed to the failure of the Natalia Mine at Eersteling and Weatherley, disenchanted with the prospect of living in the remote and unsettled Zoutpansberg, had established himself in Pretoria. Prominent in public life, he became commandant of the Pretoria Mutual Protection Association formed on 7 April from British residents anxious lest annexation should be forcibly opposed.[72] He was there to greet the arrival of the 13th (Somerset) Light Infantry on 4 May, calling for three cheers in its honour[73] and was a steward at the first race meeting held in the republic.[74]

The establishment of a British administration in April, however, was not the fillip to his fortunes that Weatherley anticipated. Due to be ratified by the Volksraad at its sitting in February 1877, the threat of annexation took precedence in the debates and ratification of his concession was held over for the next session – which never took place. Repeated representations to Shepstone, now British administrator, to confirm the concession went unheeded and in Weatherley's difficult financial position this was a bitter disappointment. If Weatherley had a fault, it was the gullibility of the vain. On 1 August 1877 heading the signatures to a memorial to Shepstone praising the efforts of Weatherley 'in saving the town from any serious consequence' was the adjutant of the Pretoria Mutual Protection Association, one Gunn of Gunn, later to play a significant role in Weatherley's downfall.[75] Weatherley believed that his considerable military experience was to be made use of by the new British administration. Lieutenant-Colonel E. Brooke, RE of Shepstone's staff and Weatherley became close colleagues on the military commission considering defence. Raising an African police corps, often referred to as the 'Zulu Battalion', in the Transvaal (as the republic was now known) was discussed and Weatherley confidently expected to become its first commandant. He had prepared all the details for Brooke and understood from both Brooke and Captain Sir Morrison Barlow, special commissioner in the Waterberg and Zoutpansberg based at Eersteling, that Shepstone had approved the appointment. So confident was he that he resigned his commission in the Sussex Artillery Volunteers, losing significant benefits.[76]

When Weatherley called on Shepstone to thank him for the appointment, to his amazement Shepstone denied asking Brooke to let Weatherley know that the appointment had been made. A bitter correspondence followed, Weatherley asserting that his honour had been seriously compromised. Barlow described it as a 'monstrous misunderstanding' and, although he denied that Brooke had ever told Weatherley that he did have the command, he said that he had thought it a fait accompli since there had been much discussion in Pretoria to this effect.[77] A public meeting called on 4 December to consider the question of a volunteer force resolved to serve under Weatherley and no one else.[78] Frere, W.C. Sargeaunt (a senior civil servant in the Crown Agents sent from London to ascertain the financial probity of the Transvaal and who had been Colonial Secretary in Natal from 1853 to 1857), the commanding officer and officers of the 13th (Somerset) Light Infantry and eventually the Secretary of State for the Colonies all became involved.[79] Piqued by

Shepstone's refusal to ratify his concession or to appoint him to command a volunteer force, Weatherley offered his services and those of five hundred men from the Transvaal in January 1878 to help the Cape government in its wars on the frontier; his offer was sarcastically declined.[80]

Weatherley's animosity against Shepstone now became used by the administrator's political opponents, typified by J.F. Celliers, editor of *Die Volksstem*, and others with more personal motives such as the charlatan Charles Stewart, commonly known as the Gunn of Gunn.[81] As Shepstone himself wrote: 'Weatherley was thrown into the arms of and made champion of the Disaffected party.'[82] Two petitions to replace Shepstone as administrator with Weatherley were prepared and presented to the government: they carried 3,883 signatures, of which only sixteen were proved to be genuine, with a further five in doubt.[83] Weatherley flatly denied involvement and he was supported by the testimony of J.W. Glyn who protested during Stewart's trial on charges of fraud, conspiracy and forgery, at the attempt by the prosecution to connect Weatherley personally with the petitions. Glyn emphatically denied Weatherley's 'having been connected with this matter in any way',[84] the latter having seen the first petition only after it was circulated and the second possibly not at all, since he had left for Cape Town before it was printed.

Fulminating against 'the apathy and neglect displayed by the present situation', Weatherley visited Cape Town in mid-May 1878 to see Frere, not about the petitions, but the apparent slight on his honour by Shepstone's actions. It was now, however, that the real reason for his problems surfaced. His marriage, never a happy one, had been dominated by the temper of his wife. He determined to leave southern Africa and asked his wife to sell their house in Pretoria and join him in Cape Town with the children. She replied that, as Stewart was now in prison on charges connected with the forged petitions, it would be quite wrong to abandon him. How plucky, thought Weatherley, and returned to Pretoria, only to find from his sons, Poulett (aged 18) and Rupert (aged 13), that their mother's support for Stewart had clearly gone beyond the bounds of propriety. For some time Weatherley continued to believe in his wife's honour, even though he now had serious doubts about Stewart's assumed identity; he was a man who had always sought the peaceful option in his troubled marriage. The liaison, however, continued to flourish and became even more flagrant – to the point that Weatherley left the marital home and brought an action for divorce against Mrs Weatherley. In addition to pleas referring to property, additional pleas were filed – of connivance: that Weatherley had allowed the liaison to flourish; of condonation: that a confession of guilt had been secured using undue influence; and collusion:

that Weatherley and his lawyer had made arrangements with Mrs Weatherley for a divorce. And so in November 1878, the case came to court, with Maria Louisa Weatherley accused of adultery on various occasions between June and October 1878 with Charles Grant Murray Somerset Seymour Stuart Gunn. Weatherley realised by now that he had been duped and on 26 October 1878 wrote a fulsome letter of apology to Shepstone saying that he had been 'led into all sorts of errors by designing people, of which I am now heartily ashamed'. In a subsequent letter explaining his situation, Weatherley thought that Shepstone would accuse him of weakness, 'but I don't think', he wrote, 'you can imagine without having tried it, the sort of life I have led, and how a man will do anything for peace.'[85]

The Border Horse
With Shepstone's acceptance of his apology, Weatherley once again considered leading a volunteer force. British forces were being withdrawn from the Pedi country and the Zoutpansberg became exposed to the possibility of hostile raids. With the concurrence of Colonel H. Rowlands, VC, commanding both imperial and local forces in the Transvaal, it was decided to station a volunteer force at Weatherley's company property at Eersteling, Barlow's headquarters.[86] As Weatherley was dragged into the divorce court, he asked Lord Chelmsford for employment and was immediately appointed commandant of a volunteer unit, Shepstone sanctioning the recruitment of 150 volunteers for Weatherley's Border Lances[87] for service in the Zoutpansberg or elsewhere for six months from 18 November 1878.[88] Each volunteer with a horse would be paid eight shillings, each volunteer provided with a government horse five shillings, both receiving free rations and forage; until they reached the front, pay was to be three shillings per day in lieu of rations. Their uniform was a blue 'jumper', cord breeches, red sash, riding boots and a white hat; they carried Martini-Henry rifles.[89] Weatherley's knowledge of continental armies and fluency in their languages attracted many French and German volunteers to what became generally known as the Border Horse. As we have seen, A Troop of the Border Horse left for Eersteling in mid-January 1879 and B Troop left Pretoria for Luneburg on 30 January.

Soon after the troop arrived in Luneburg a combined patrol was made on 2 February to the caves of the Kubheka in the Ntombe Valley with the Swazi Police under Lieutenant W.F. Fairlie. Rowlands' Transvaal column having been amalgamated with Wood's No. 4 Column, the Border Horse was ordered to move to Wood's camp at Khambula where it arrived on 2 March. The first two weeks of March were marked by heavy rains, which severely curtailed the raiding and patrolling activities of the column. Not until 14 March was the Border Horse involved in any offensive activity when it formed part of the column commanded by Buller which left Khambula for Nhlangwine to bring in followers of Hamu kaNzibe Zulu who had just defected to the British. Out for two nights, this patrol met with no opposition. The troop did not take part in the three days' patrol to the Ntombe valley from 24 to 26 March.

Losing the way to Hlobane

On 26 March, however, regimental orders were issued by Lieutenant V.H. Lys, RN[90] for a 'reconnaissance' to Hlobane; all available men were to parade at 8 a.m. the following day with seventy rounds of ammunition, a blanket and rations for two days. The troop was the last unit to leave Khambula in Buller's column, which was to carry out the main assault on Hlobane from the east. There was thick mist that morning but the men were cheerful and looking forward to their first action against the enemy. Buller arrived at the designated bivouac under the southern face of Zungwini Mountain at noon followed by the Border Horse half an hour later. He told Weatherley where he should unsaddle and added that he would give him the order when to move on. Having breakfasted, the men snoozed and relaxed. About 4 p.m. a bugle sounded and Dennison asked Weatherley whether they should respond to the call 'boot and saddle', but the latter said that it was not necessary as Buller had said that he would send the order when to move. As the column moved off, Dennison again questioned whether the troop should move, but Weatherley still refused to move without a direct order from Buller, emphasising that it was Buller who was in command.

As time went by, the men became increasingly restive until Weatherley was roused to order them to upsaddle. Dennison places the blame squarely on Weatherley for this misunderstanding, noting that Buller had originally spoken only with kind intent and had not sent an order since the troop was resting only a few hundred yards from the main column. Dennison's memoir agrees with his report written after the action noting that the circumstances why the Border Horse were not with the column 'arose through our Col. not having received orders to march from our first camping ground'.[91] Buller himself wrote that he could not understand why 'he [Weatherley] waited for individual orders and did not saddle up when he heard the trumpet sound "Horses in"'.[92] It should be remembered that Weatherley was a former cavalry officer with considerable campaign experience and eight years older than Buller; it is entirely likely that he viewed Buller's actions as the deference due to one of his age and experience and was waiting for another kind gesture in recognition.

The Zulu Impi

In his Hlobane despatch, Wood relates how he met Weatherley on the morning of 28 March 'coming westward, having lost his way the previous night' and directed him to turn about and join Buller's column which could be seen near the summit. As Dennison tells the story, the sun was setting as the troop set off from the Zungwini Nek bivouac on the previous evening in the tracks of the main column, but soon a misty rain began to fall and only the fires of Buller's second bivouac guided their march. On cresting a ridge, however, the lights disappeared and the troop rode on in drizzling rain for a further two hours. Suddenly, cresting yet another ridge, Weatherley saw what appeared to be stars and thought that the weather was breaking. Dennison identified the lights as camp fires, probably those of a Zulu *impi*. Taking Lance-Corporal E. Bernhardt and Trooper L. Barth, both Germans from British Kaffraria, Dennison went forward on foot and ascertained that it was indeed a Zulu *impi* and bound for Khambula. Returning to Weatherley, Dennison reported his findings and suggested that, as the troop was quite lost, it should remain where it was until the direction in which Hlobane lay could be ascertained. Before daybreak, flashes presumed to be those of firearms were seen to the north and the troop mounted quietly and moved off. As dawn broke Hlobane loomed to the front and loud and continual firing was heard. Just under the foot of the mountain the troop caught up with a group of men galloping across their front – Wood with his personal staff and escort. Weatherley reported the position of the *impi* to Wood, Dennison adding that he judged that it was a strong force. But Wood retorted that the report was nonsense – as he had sent out a patrol the day before and there was no *impi* about, Weatherley and Dennison were mistaken.

Here we not only have a glimpse of Wood's arrogance, but evidence to refute the deliberately misleading assertion in his despatch and autobiography that he met Weatherley and the Border Horse moving westwards away from Hlobane. The troop was coming from the south and not, as Wood wanted others to infer, from the east and away from the action which was by this time evident. His innuendo that the Border Horse was running away from the action has successfully persisted. Selby, for example, asserted that: 'The unit was made up for the most part of English settlers in the Transvaal, who were no great warriors, and they still showed reluctance to join the fight, so Wood rode on ahead with his escort to show them the way.'[93]

Wood laid the blame for his reverse at Hlobane on the sudden and unexpected arrival of the main Zulu *impi* from Ulundi. In his memorandum after the action, he claimed that: 'We assaulted the Inhlobane successfully yesterday, and took some thousands of cattle, but while on top, about 20,000 Zulus, coming

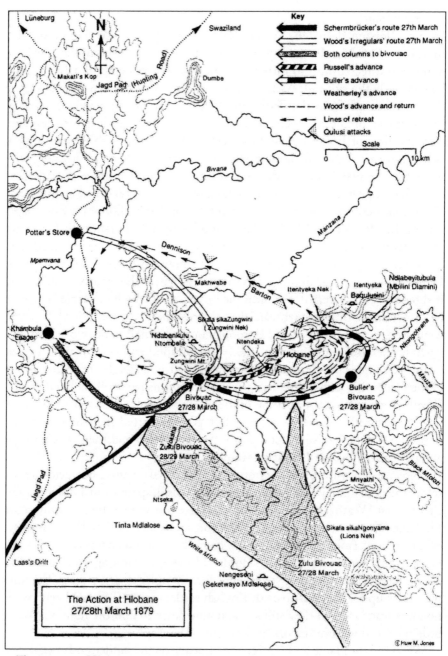

Key

Schermbrücker's route 27th March
Wood's Irregulars' route 27th March
Both columns to bivouac
Russell's advance
Buller's advance
Weatherley's advance
Wood's advance and return
Lines of retreat
Qulusi attacks

Scale
0   10 km

Lüneburg
Swaziland
Makati's Kop
Jagd Pad (Hunting Road)
Dumbe
Bivana
Manzana
Potter's Store
Mpemvana
Dennison
Makhwabe
Barton
Itentyeka Nek
Itentyeka
Ndlabeyitubula (Mbilini Dlamini)
Baqulusini
Nkongowana
Khambula Laager
Sikala sikaZungwini (Zungwini Nek)
Ndabankulu Ntombela
Ntendeka
Hlobane
Mkuze
Zungwini Mt
Bivouac 27/28 March
Buller's Bivouac 27/28 March
Tokatha
Zulu Bivouac 28/29 March
Tshoba
Mnyathi
Black Mfolozi
Jagd Pad
Ntseka
Tinta Mdlalose
White Mfolozi
Sikala sikaNgonyama (Lions Nek)
Laas's Drift
Nengeseni (Seketwayo Mdlalose)
Zulu Bivouac 27/28 March
KwaNobamba

© Huw M. Jones

The Action at Hlobane
27/28th March 1879

8 The action at Hlobane

from Ulundi, attacked us, and we suffered considerable losses, the enemy retaking the captured cattle.'[94] In his despatch, however, Wood noted that it was Mtonga kaMpande Zulu who first saw the *impi* advancing in the 'normal attack formation', but, in contradiction of his memorandum, 'exhausted by its rapid march, did not close on Colonel Buller, who descended after Uhamu's people the western point of the mountain'. By 1915, Wood made it clear that it was he who had sent Mtonga 'as a matter of precaution . . . up the height to the south'.[95] Although it is clear that the Zulu *impi* played no significant role in the action, according to Wood its arrival encouraged the Qulusi who 'emerged from their caves and harassed the retreat'; 'the main Zulu Army being exhausted by their [*sic*] march, halted near where Vryheid now stands.'[96] As *The Times* writer observed, the despatch lacked clarity, one of the ambiguous claims being that the Zulu *impi*, having surrounded the retiring British troops, did not attack because it was tired and hungry from its forced march from Ulundi. The evidence of Troopers C. Hewitt and G. Mossop, both of the Frontier Light Horse (FLH), that Zulu were found dead at Khambula taking mealie meal from the camp pots and the information obtained later that the *impi* had had no food for three days has been used to support Wood's contention that its energy was nearly spent by the time it arrived at Khambula laager.[97] As Laband has suggested, however, the *impi* was without food only on the morning of 29 March.[98] Supporting this position, Dennison's evidence suggests that it rested and had food on the night of 27/28 March probably between Ntabankhulu and the range running westwards from Mnyathi mountain, of which Sikala sikaNgonyama (Lion's Nek or Leeuwnek) is the principal feature. There is also evidence that during the march it fed reasonably well since Mnyamana Buthelezi, who was in command, took a hundred head of cattle from Hamu kaNzibe Zulu's herds for this *impi*.[99]

Cowardice
Wood states that the Border Horse 'got off the track' and implies that they were moving so slowly that he and his escort had to go ahead. Nearing the screes and krantzes marking the edge of the plateau, they came under heavy fire. Wood's political assistant, L.H. Lloyd, was fatally wounded by his side and Wood's horse, which he was leading, quite irrationally when the others had been left behind because of the difficult ground, was killed. Wood then directed Campbell to order Weatherley 'to dislodge one or two Zulus who were causing us most of the loss'.[100] Since the Border Horse did not advance as rapidly as Campbell wanted, he and others of Wood's personal escort jumped from cover and dashed into the rocks where Campbell was immediately shot dead. Wood wasted little time in relaying this story since P.L. Uys, Junior

(Vaal Piet), having been heavily involved in the desperate fighting at what became known as 'Devil's Pass' and having left Khambula laager at 5 p.m. on 28 March, was able to tell H.C. Shepstone on the following day in Utrecht that Wood had ordered a couple of men to dislodge some Zulus who had killed four horses and that they had refused; there followed in his statement an account of the death of Campbell and Lloyd.[101] Thus Wood prepared the scene for his demolition of Weatherley's reputation in order to draw attention away from his own mismanagement of the situation. The staff writer of *The Times* took up Wood's innuendo and although noting 'Colonel Weatherley, a colonist of distinction', who 'fell gallantly fighting to the last, cutting down Zulus with his right hand while grasping his son, a young lad, with the other', wrote that his 'men showed some disinclination to face the enemy'.[102]

Two years later, after revisiting the site, Wood wrote another account with the intention of recommending two of his personal staff and escort, Lieutenant H. Lysons and Private E. Fowler (both 90th Light Infantry, Wood's own regiment), for the Victoria Cross and the accompanying letter noted that in his original despatch the incident in which Campbell had been killed had been written 'in language calculated to spare the reputation of another dead man'. Although even now he did not mention Weatherley by name, he directly accused him of cowardice in the face of the enemy:

> I observed to Captain Campbell that all the fatal shots came from one rock, and directed him to order an officer to take some men and turn the Zulus out. He received the order three times, but would not leave the cover where he was shelter-ing close to where my second pony was – the one I rode had been shot – and about ten feet below me and on my left. Captain Campbell called out 'Damn him! he's a coward. I'll turn them out', and ran forward. Mr. Lysons called out 'May I go?' I shouted 'Yes! Forward the Personal Escort', and of the eight which composed it, all who were disengaged, some four in number, went on. His Royal Highness will, I hope, understand my reluctance to tell all this. The man whose heart failed had been unfortunate, which kept me silent, and, moreover, I was averse to write about myself, which I could not fail to do if I explained all the circumstances.[103]

For Wood this was a traumatic experience; he had become 'greatly attached' to Campbell since he had joined his staff at Utrecht shortly before Christmas 1878.[104] In a letter to Crealock written in February, Wood said that he had been ill, but 'Campbell nursed me tenderly'[105] and in the letter quoted above Wood wrote that if Campbell had lived he would have been the first to be recommended for the award of the Victoria Cross. Wood never mentioned Weatherley by name in his article in *Pearson's Magazine* eulogising Campbell, always referring to 'the

Irregulars' and the 'officer in command'.[106] At this stage of Wood's retelling of the events, Weatherley was said to have told Campbell that 'it was impossible to force the passage through the rocks.' This opinion, Wood said, he rejected as several wounded men were exposed to Zulu fire and he then repeated the order only to be met with renewed objections, whereupon Campbell, 'determined to secure the safe removal of the wounded', ran up to the entrance of the cave formed by the boulders and was killed. After Lloyd and Campbell had been buried lower down the mountain, Weatherley, according to Wood, sought and received permission to follow Buller's track, having lost, in Wood's words, 'only six men killed and seven wounded, in the half hour that it was under fire'.[107]

According to Dennison, however, after Wood had dismissed their report about the Zulu *impi*, Weatherley and Dennison then discussed the best way to ascend the mountain – place piquets on a nearby hill commanding the ascent and advance on foot until the order could be given to bring the horses. This was countermanded by Wood who insisted that as the rest of the column had taken their horses the Border Horse should do the same. The Border Horse with Dennison in the lead then followed the direct route to the path which Buller had taken earlier and which was 'shewing red on the summit'. Wood, however, directed the unit to the left towards a horseshoe krantz of great height with huge boulders at its foot in which there were clearly a large number of the enemy. They headed towards a stone *isibaya* with a large number of cattle, Dennison remarking with some point 'whether they gave rise to the order or not I cannot say.'[108] Here, from the concentrated fire which came from the rocks at the base of the horseshoe, Bernhardt and Barth were killed and several others wounded including Sergeant-Major J.S. Fisher and Dennison's batman, Trooper J. Cameron.

As the Border Horse worked forward from rock to rock, Dennison was called back to Weatherley, standing with his son Rupert a little way from Wood, who was attending to the dead body of Lloyd. He was told that Wood had ordered a charge and, although amazed at such a senseless order in a place where the only way to progress was 'baboon fashion', went forward to relay the order to the troop. As he did so Campbell rushed forward calling 'Forward Boys!' and immediately had the top of his skull blown off. His body was recovered by men of the Border Horse assisted by Lysons and Fowler who were later awarded the VC on Wood's recommendation. In his own dramatic account, Wood makes out that he and his escort were in front and that the Border Horse were '200 yards behind us' and 'taking cover under rocks below us', a situation which makes little sense in a military context unless one is intent on drawing attention to 'Campbell's difficulty in inducing the men to advance'.[109] Not unnaturally, Dennison resented Wood's slur that the Border Horse hesitated to move forward. The *Cape Argus* correspondent's report supports Dennison's narrative, relating how 'Colonel Wood gave the order to Colonel Weatherley to send men and clear the rocks. The call for volunteers was promptly met, and Lieutenants Poole [*sic*] and H. Parminter, of Weatherley's corps, along with Captain Campbell, rushed forward leading the men on.'[110] Ashe and Wyatt-Edgell's account also supports the fact that the Border Horse were performing well and attributes any delay in responding to Campbell's order to the fact that its troopers 'were engaged with several Zulus at close quarters'.[111]

Cut off

Dennison's memoir also provides detail, hitherto missing, on the fate of the Border Horse and a troop of the FLH which became cut off. On Campbell's death, Wood retired with his personal escort and a wounded trooper of the Border Horse, Andrew Hammond, leaving, according to Dennison, no orders for the volunteers who found their own way on to Hlobane plateau. Here they halted whilst Weatherley went to look for Buller and receive orders. Shortly after he left, a hatless trooper of the FLH rode up looking for him and gave Dennison the message that, as they were surrounded by a large Zulu *impi*, the Border Horse were to return to camp. This, it should be noted, was not the main Zulu *impi*, but the Qulusi who had sprung the trap by emerging from the edges of the plateau and had also brought substantial reinforcements from the Ityenteka plateau to the east.

On Weatherley's return, the unit fought its way down without casualties and at the foot of the mountain halted to make a stretcher for Fisher. Here they were overtaken by Barton and a troop of FLH with the message not to delay as 'the mountain is surrounded'. As they began to move, the FLH were now about one kilometre ahead. Rounding the shoulder of the mountain, Dennison's description confirms that they were riding along the foot of the mountain with the right flank of the main Zulu *impi* by this time along the ridge north of Nyembe Hill with only the valley of the stream between them. Ahead, Barton and the FLH rode directly between two stone homesteads where Zulu hidden in ambush fired into them at point-blank range. Here, in the vicinity of modern Boomlaer, many of the FLH were killed in the confusion and the survivors turned round to retreat eastwards. Again the *Cape Argus* correspondent supports Dennison's account, recording that Weatherley was ordered down the mountain to cover the return by that route and that Barton and his troop of FLH went down to join Weatherley.[112]

As they reached the Border Horse, Barton brought his men under control and both units retired together in good order firing controlled volleys although their horses were now blown and very weak. Weatherley, Dennison,

Lieutenant W. Pool and supernumerary Lieutenant H.W. Parminter rode behind their men cutting their blanket straps to lighten their loads. Several men were unable to continue and were caught and killed by the pursuing Zulu. Trumpeter W. Reilly dismounted from his 'knocked up horse', fired on the enemy close by and then shot himself. By now, few men had any ammunition left and so it was not possible to turn and make a stand, although Barton suggested doing so as Ityenteka Nek was reached and they saw Qulusi lining the heights on either side of the *nek*. As the men reached the *nek* they scattered and immediately Dennison saw the reason – the descent on the other side was precipitously steep and panic set in. Some men disappeared whilst about twenty obeyed the order to keep together.

On the right of the *nek* forward progress was blocked and Dennison led by jumping his horse down. It was here that Parminter was killed. The others led their horses down, Barton and four men close by, with Weatherley not far behind leading his horse with the bridle rein linked in his arm, one hand helping his son and the other holding his drawn sword. As they reached the foot of the mountain, Dennison turned with two men to help Weatherley and his son, but they were too late. The pursuing Zulu had caught up with the survivors and, as Weatherley's sword flashed, Rupert with a piercing wail fell dead on his father. Wielding his carbine as a club to good effect, Dennison managed to mount with Barton close at hand. Firing his carbine with its smashed stock from the hand, Dennison broke the Zulu cordon to his front and caught up with some twenty-seven men, mostly FLH with Regimental Sergeant-Major B. Winterfelt strongly urging them on. As they rode north-westwards towards Potter's Store on the Mpemvana River, Trooper P. Martin panicked and was killed. Here Sergeant C. Brown and Corporal J. Archer of the Border Horse saved one of the unhorsed troopers of the FLH as he was about to be overtaken and killed. Eventually the survivors were pursued by only three Zulu who were waylaid and shot. Just before sundown, a drenching rain set in, but the lights of the camp fires at Khambula gave them the direction. Delayed by the outer piquets, the survivors eventually reached camp where Dennison got out of his wet clothes and between the blankets to be brought a hot drink and food by the Indian mess cook.

Dennison's account conforms with his original report, providing further circumstantial evidence that the two columns retired from Hlobane around the south side of Zungwini Mountain and not through the re-entrant west of the present Zungwini station. From the north side of Ityenteka Nek, even in the desperate confusion, British troops moving along the eastern edge of the Zungwini range would have been visible and a clear objective in the desperate ride to get away from the Zulu and Qulusi. But Dennison and the others thought that their best chance of reaching Khambula was by way of Potter's Store and the Jagd Pad (Hunting Road). Buller's patrol to bring in stragglers that night did not include Dennison and the survivors of the Border Horse and certainly not Weatherley's elder son, Lieutenant C.P.M. Weatherley, who took no part in the action.[113]

After a restless night, Dennison was unable to face the breakfast table, where the cook had laid just one place, and he ordered breakfast in his tent. Afterwards, he went with one of the surviving NCOs to Weatherley's tent to make out the casualty return and as he did so Buller came in, shaking his hand and congratulating him on his escape. Buller asked how he had fared and told him not to bother with the return as Cetshwayo's *impi* was expected at Khambula about noon. When Buller commented that it was a pity they had not known about it in time the previous day, Dennison replied that they had, and told Buller what had been seen and reported to Wood. Buller responded saying, 'I believe you, Dennison. What a sad mistake, but say nothing for the present, lie low', and they walked together to Wood's tent where Buller left and Dennison then reported what had happened after they parted the previous day. When Wood asked why Weatherley had not returned to camp when ordered by him to do so, Dennison replied that he had not heard such an order and did not think that Weatherley had heard it either. Dennison suggests that Wood was so upset by Campbell's death that he may have intended to give the order, but had forgotten to do so. Wood was uneasy and did not respond to Dennison's reference to having seen the Zulu *impi*. That morning, on Buller's instructions, Dennison prepared a report for him. Noting only that the Border Horse had missed the main column during the night and been ordered by Wood to join the main point of the attack on Hlobane Mountain, the report makes the point that Weatherley received an order to return the way he had come, and describes the chaos of the retreat. A final sentence, clearly added on instructions, gave the reason why the Border Horse were not with the main column. Dennison's report was appended as Annexure A to Buller's report with the retort that:

I never knew where Col. Weatherley was on the 28th and never sent him any order whatever. His orders on the 27th were to conform to the General Movements of the leading troop in the Column but to march independently. He was fully aware of what we were going to do and I cannot understand why he waited for individual orders & did not saddle up when he heard the trumpet sound 'Horses in'.[114]

Shortly after the attack on Khambula, Dennison was ordered to Pretoria to report to Rowlands. On arrival, he was given command of the Border Horse and saw immediate service in the ongoing campaign against the Pedi.

Dennison's veracity

It is pertinent to ask whether Dennison's recollections of Hlobane are at all accurate or whether he simply interpreted the situation from the point of view of a colonial officer piqued by the distrust and condescension shown by an imperial officer. Certainly Dennison suggests that Wood gave no credence to his report on the immediate presence of the Zulu *impi* because Dennison was a colonial officer and that officers such as Wood had a 'false idea of their superiority over men of no Sandhurst training but of a lifelong practical experience'.[115] In the introduction to his book, Dennison notes that 'it is written by "only a Colonial"; my story is plain history of facts that defies contradiction'. He was clearly irked by the superiority assumed by imperial officers regardless of their military experience, but made no effort to expose Wood. This one can only attribute to the mores of the day, to the realisation that 'influence not service counts most' as he wrote in his book.[116] Dennison goes so far as to say, 'I do not consider that Colonel Wood was to blame but acted as no doubt half the generals in the British army would have done under the same circumstances.' In fact, he blames Buller, Uys and others for pushing Wood into action after the disastrous losses at the Ntombe drift on 12 March engineered by Mbilini waMswati, their adversary at Hlobane.[117] There is a clear correlation between the detail provided by Dennison and that of other sources.

Dennison was not, of course, alone in either his compliant attitude to authority or his assertion that serious mistakes had been made at Hlobane. The staff writer of *The Times* went only so far as to say: 'For once Colonel Wood's brilliant good luck appears to have deserted him.' R.O.G. Lys, the nephew of the adjutant of the Border Horse killed at Hlobane, was serving with No. 4 Column as an intelligence officer and 'soon came to the conclusion', however, 'that this British officer [Wood] possessed too nervous a temperament ever to make a successful leader of men; and lacked that calm and resolute judgement which is so essential in a country like South Africa where one is constantly surprised by unforeseen circumstances'.[118] Whilst Wood went on to have honours and rewards heaped upon him, Weatherley's only surviving son, Cecil Poulett Mountjoy Weatherley, attested as a private in the Middlesex Regiment on 19 January 1883.[119]

Envoy

Only the Zulu *impi* assaulted Khambula laager.[120] That day, although suffering from a superficial flesh wound in the chest, Mbilini carried on with his previously prepared plans and led the Qulusi forces up the Bivane Valley, raiding homesteads and farms in the upper Phongolo Valley and collecting huge herds of cattle numbering some three thousand head on the way.[121]

On the night of 4 April two companies of the 2nd battalion of the 4th (The King's Own) Regiment, on their way from Utrecht to relieve the garrison at Luneburg, laagered for the night at J. Alcock's farm fearing attack by the Qulusi *impi*. Mbilini judged the detachment too strong to assault and continued rustling cattle and horses. Alerted to the plight of the incoming detachment, a patrol of six mounted men was sent from Luneburg under Captain J.E.H. Prior, 80th (South Staffordshire) Regiment, on 5 April. Coming upon a group of six men driving some twenty horses eastwards along the right bank of the Phongolo River, Prior recaptured the horses and pursued the men. Two got away, but after a furious chase one was unhorsed and killed, whilst a second, although seriously wounded by an African auxiliary called Sinakwe, managed to escape. The latter was Mbilini, who managed to ride back to his homestead above the Ntombe River and was then carried to Ndlabeyitubula, but died before reaching there.[122] Effectively, co-ordination and drive drained from the resistance he had generated and organised, particularly after the death of Mabamba Ntombela that winter. The Kubheka put up sporadic defiance from their homesteads above the Ntombe, but many of the Qulusi, including Memezi waMswati, Mbilini's brother, withdrew to the Ngwagwa Hills[123] north of the Phongolo which had been for some years the home of Ndida kaMlokotwa, a Qulusi induna. Although a hard core of resistance held out on the Ityenteka plateau under Mcwayo Zwane, Seketwayo Mdlalose surrendered on 25 August at Fort Cambridge, near the confluence of the Mfolozi Mhlope and Nsengeni (or Sandspruit) rivers. The Qulusi *izinduna* Msebe kaMadaka and Mahubulwane Mdlalose surrendered at Ntseka Hill to Lieutenant-Colonel B.C. Russell, 13th Hussars, on 1 September. Not until 22 September was Manyonyoba Kubheka finally forced into submission and, with some of his people, exiled to the Batshe Valley.

Whilst surveying the boundaries of the new political units into which the Zulu country was to be divided, Lieutenant-Colonel the Honourable G. Villiers climbed Hlobane on 25 September, finding most of the homesteads in the area deserted.[124] Having had his authority and territory extensively enlarged by the British, Hamu Zulu began a systematic campaign against the Qulusi and those who had fought under Mbilini's overall command. The action at Hlobane was to be the last defiant gesture of the inhabitants of this mountainous upland before they were brushed aside by a new dispensation and most traces of their occupation obliterated as the face of the country assumed new patterns of settlement.

17. Presentation of the ultimatum (*ILN*, 8 February 1879)

18. Recovery of the Queen's
Colour (*ILN*, 29 March 1879)

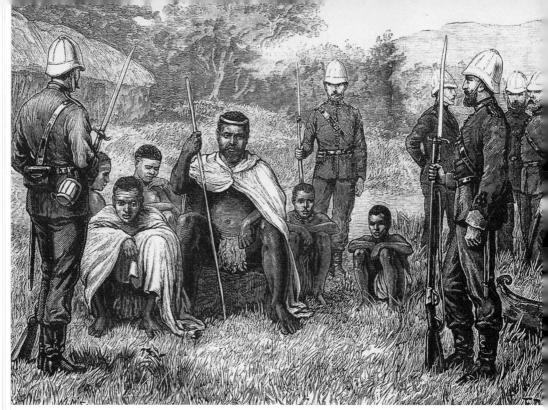

27. Captive King Cetshwayo (*ILN*, 18 October 1879)

28. Captain A.N. Montgomery
(Keith Smith Collection)

Chapter 7

The Second Invasion

Governments never have learned anything from history, or acted on principles deduced from it.

G.W.F. Hegel 1797–1856

The Road to Ulundi

The small group of horsemen paused on the brow of the hill, their mounts immediately putting their heads down to snatch at the russet tufts of grass at their feet. The men looked around them, noting the thick blue tint to the air that almost obscured the distant views and was so very different from the normally clear sky. The heavy scent of burning assailed their nostrils, giving confirmation, if any were needed from the distant plumes of smoke, that grass fires were burning everywhere. Those experienced among them knew that this was an annual winter task of the Zulu, burning off the old grass that would then be replaced by the new, sweet, spring growth. But the Zulu also knew that this action now had a second purpose: it would deprive the advancing British troops of the fodder essential for their animals.

The foregoing is a fictional account but it is certain that similar scenes would have been played out on the march of the 2nd Division as it made its tortuous way towards Ulundi from 1 June to early July 1879. The precise route followed by the division is not as well known as perhaps it should be. This is largely the result of the inaccessibility of much of the documentation and a propensity on the part of most modern narratives to abbreviate the description of its course, preferring instead to dwell in detail on the two most prominent occurrences during the course of the invasion: the death of the Prince Imperial at the beginning and the concluding battle of Ulundi.

The precise details of the journey, particularly the early movements of Wood's Flying Column, are difficult to determine because the names of many of the geographical features by which they were then known were largely based on guesswork and were often transliterations of Zulu names. Even those parts of the advance marked by a number of features that are well known, including the sites of the Prince Imperial's death, Forts Newdigate and Marshall, and the plateau of Mthonjaneni, still pose problems in determining the exact route taken. The purpose of this paper is, therefore, to examine contemporary sources, together with modern maps, to determine exactly the route taken, day by day, and to discuss some of the issues involved in coming to a conclusion concerning the problems encountered.[1] As an aid to their location, the contemporary names of these geographical features, and their modern equivalents, are given in a note at the end of the paper.

The force that was to march on Ulundi was the 2nd Division under Major-General Newdigate, composed of two brigades (under Colonels Glyn and Collingwood) and the Cavalry Brigade (under Major-General Marshall), together with the separate Flying Column, a reinforced version of newly promoted Brigadier-General Evelyn Wood's old Fourth Column. 'I am calling your command "a flying column" so as to keep you separate from Newdigate who will command the 2d Division S. African Field Force.'[2]

The actual launch of the invasion was deferred for some time pending the discovery of a satisfactory route for the very many wagons that made up the division's convoy. The several changes of mind that occurred as reconnaissance progressed led to the first two choices of a start-point being abandoned before a third was finally agreed upon. Although he did not say as much, Lord Chelmsford must have been anxious to advance by a route other than that used in the first invasion, thus avoiding the battlefield of Isandlwana and its still-unburied dead. He gave different reasons for the change of path, despite the very circuitous nature of the new line.

> Rorke's drift was abandoned by me as a line of advance on account of the Greytown-Helpmakaar road, after Insandlwana [*sic*], being considered dangerous by the native waggon drivers & leaders who when the news of the disaster reached the Colony, abandoned their wagons and ran away.
>
> It had also the disadvantage of being exposed on the right flank to attack from the Indeni [Qudeni] Forest direction which it was impossible to watch properly.[3]

Wood himself favoured a more direct line to the north of the Inhlazatye mountain but the lieutenant-general gave his reasons for not using that route:

If we advance from the Utrecht base by a road south of the Inhlazatye [mountain], we are at once on the line of retreat of any force raiding across the Tugela, and can really give Natal very effective assistance. If however we take the Northern road and a raid be made into Natal I feel sure that I should be blamed for my strategy and very properly so. Kindly consider then how we can best work to the South of the Inhlazatye, and yet not leave the frontier North of that mountain completely unprotected.

I am willing to admit that the Babanango road is the worst of the two, but I am certain that I am right in determining that our main line of advance shall be made upon it – and with the force at our disposal, and at this season of the year we ought to have no difficulty in making any line practicable for our convoys.[4]

The initial divisional headquarters was located at the village of Dundee, then a mere scattering of farms that could scarcely be described as a village:

The name Dundee rather leads one to believe one will see some flourishing little town, instead of which it properly belongs only to a single farm. The place really consists of two tin stores and about half a dozen farms scattered about in the hills round, though there will probably be a town there some day as there is coal worked on the farms.[5]

Supplies were brought forward from Durban to Dundee via Pietermaritz-burg and Ladysmith and then on to Conference Hill, which lies on the Zululand border formed by the Ncome (Blood) River. This lies almost mid-way on the modern Dundee–Vryheid road (R33), at its intersection with the road running north to Utrecht (R34).

After considerable communication with Colonel Wood and more recon-naissances by Buller's Frontier Light Horse, it was decided that a better place to cross the Ncome was at Landman's Drift and supplies were then re-directed there instead of to Conference Hill. Lord Chelmsford has argued that no supplies were subsequently moved from Conference Hill: 'The supplies at Conference Hill were never moved back, but when General Wood returned to Koppie Allein with empty waggons half of them loaded up at the supply depot and half at Landman's drift. Conference Hill is about 8 miles from Koppie Allein with a good road between the two.'[6] If they were not moved from Conference Hill to Landman's Drift, they were certainly moved from Conference Hill to Koppie Allein, as we shall see.

A month later a third departure point was selected when reconnaissances demonstrated a superior line commencing at Koppie Allein on the Ncome River:

Bettington took a line from Conference Hill south of Bemba's kop and appears to think that a waggon track is to be made by it.

He came back on a line apparently due East (?) to Koppie Allein. If we could cross the Blood river at this latter point we should save a good many miles; and Bishop Schroeder writes me word that the road runs over the north end of the Ngutu Mt, which seems to show that an advance in that direction is practicable. I will have it carefully explored by the mounted men at Conference Hill, and let you know the result.[7]

Finally a route was found that satisfied his lordship, and with which Wood also concurred: 'The line of our advance from the Blood river to Ibabanango runs almost in a B line, in a south-easterly direction, over the neck between the Inceni and Itelezi mountains, between the Ityotyozi and Tombokata rivers to the southern slopes of that mountain [Babanango].'[8] This then was the route that was to be followed by the 2nd Division, accompanied by Lord Chelmsford and his staff, and shortly to be joined by Wood's Flying Column. The movement of the division to Koppie Allein was commenced on 27 May and by 31 May all its components were in place on the starting line.[9] Contrary to Lord Chelmsford's view expressed above, stores at Conference Hill were also re-located: 'Conference Hill was no longer to be the base of operations; the advance was by another road; and all the piles of stores collected, with so much trouble and expense, were to be moved to Koppie Allein twelve miles lower down the river.'[10]

We should begin tracing the route by first following Wood's movement from Khambula to the Ityotyosi River, where his column linked up with the 2nd Division. In the sub-headings that follow, the daily mileage travelled is that quoted in the *Narrative of the Field Operations*.

5 May, Khambula to Segonyama Hill, 15 miles
The location of Wood's first camp at Segonyama is difficult to identify precisely although its position is given in the *Narrative* as being 'some 10 miles due south of Kambula'.[11] During a recent visit to Kew's National Archives, however, I located a contemporary map of Zululand that actually shows, not only Segonyama, but many of the more problematic locations further along the route.[12] The map shows the hill to be about three miles almost due north of Wolf Hill on a farm called Arcadia. We can also opine that he was compelled to make an initial substantial detour because the *Narrative* also says that: 'the distance travelled by Wood's column on 5th May was about 15 miles.' The route from Khambula to this spot could not have been directly south because this would have taken the column, and more particularly the wagons, through

some very difficult hill country. Thus he actually travelled about twenty-four kilometres (fifteen miles) to cover a distance of sixteen kilometres (ten miles) as the crow flies, an excellent day's march when the average distance travelled by ox wagons per day was often less than ten miles, and an indication that the country he crossed was relatively easy. Wood almost certainly first travelled east from Khambula until he reached the old Jagt Pad or Hunting Road, which runs south to Conference Hill. A spur track running parallel to it passes through a place marked on the map as 'Wolf Hill'.[13] Some four miles north of present-day Vryheid (which did not then exist) his line would have eased to the south-west, to the upper reaches of the White Mfolozi River, the valley of which would have taken him towards Segonyama.

The distances cited above, and the route thus followed, would place Wood's camp at the knoll close to the Vryheid Agricultural School, about four kilometres north-west of Stilwater and nearly six kilometres north-north-east of Wolf Hill – the distances dovetail perfectly.

It is surprising that Wood chose to stay here for so long but that he did stay is confirmed by a letter he wrote from there to Lord Chelmsford on 10 May. This long stay was due to the uncertainty of their route; even at this late stage Wood was still reviewing the possibilities: 'I have been talking to a Zulu trader who laughed at the idea of finding a road between the Incanda and Mundhla. I shall know more when Buller comes.'[14] The short move to Wolf Hill was probably forced on him due to deteriorating hygienic conditions at Segonyama, as occurred twice at Khambula, and not necessarily because the road into Zululand had by then been determined.

12 May, Segonyama Hill to Wolf Hill, 3 miles
Wolf Hill was located, according to Laband and Thompson,[15] between the Dundee–Vryheid road and the parallel railway line, just over three kilometres east of the Strathcona railway station. Indeed, there is an unnamed hill at this place with an extensive plateau, and this is very likely the spot that Wood named Wolf Hill. I visited this place with the owner of the property in 2007 but visibility was very limited because of a morning mist. The owner later showed me some artefacts he had found there after burning off the grass but they seemed to suggest that the site had later been used during the Boer War. (The battle of Scheepersnek was fought near this spot in May 1900.) It will be noticed that Wood stayed here almost another two weeks.

25 May, Wolf Hill to Munhla Hill, 12 miles
Wood's next march took him from Wolf Hill to Munhla Hill, a distance of more than nineteen kilometres (twelve miles). Laband and Thompson

locate this camp near the present-day eMondlo,[16] now a substantial African township. The *Narrative*, however, is quite precise as to where the camp lay: 'The site of the new camp was on a ridge between the Munhla and Incanda hills.'[17] There is indeed a hill here still known as Nkanda, but what about Munhla? It is perhaps too facile but the name is surely a British corruption of 'eMondlo'; there is a hill called eMondlo to the east of the eponymous township and some eight kilometres (five miles) from Nkanda. This should place Wood's camp somewhere in the middle of the township, and it is therefore no wonder that Laband and Thompson could find no traces of it, although they place it somewhat further to the north-west.

Once again there is substantial high ground between the two camps and Wood must first have marched south-west towards Conference Hill and then turned south-east through easier country, keeping Bemba's Kop (Shalala) on his right, to reach Munhla Hill. The distance between the two camps is about fourteen kilometres (nine miles) as the crow flies but the detour would have added at least five kilometres to that distance.

1 June, Munhla Hill to Umyamyene River, 8 miles

On 1 June, Wood moved forward again 'in a southerly direction' and set up a camp that night at a river called in the *Narrative* the Umyamyene, having travelled a distance of thirteen kilometres (eight miles).[18] Wood himself, however, names this river as the 'Umvunyana' and not 'Umyamyene'.[19] The river that best fits this location, and which has an almost identical name, is the Mvunyana, although the precise location of the camp on its bank is unlikely to be precisely resolved.

2 June, Umyamyene River to Ityotyosi River, 10 miles

Laband and Thompson are unable to assist us on this stage because there is a gap in their maps at this point. However, the Ityotyosi (or Jojosi) is easily traced on a modern map and it has a confluence with a river now called the Vumankala. Since this is very close to the site of the death of the Prince Imperial, it is surely near here that Wood encamped, so that we can probably equate the 'Tombokala' with the Vumankala River. (The Ityotyosi River, after its confluence with the Vumankala, joins the Mvunyana some five kilometres – three miles – further east.) The straight-line distance, however, between Munhla Hill and this river is twenty-two kilometres (fourteen miles), and yet the *Narrative* claims the distance travelled to have been twenty-nine kilometres (eighteen miles). The discrepancy can only be explained by the circuitous nature of the route taken to accommodate the wagons.

We should next follow the route of the 2nd Division from its start-point at Koppie Allein. On 31 May Major-General Newdigate moved the 1st Brigade and N/5 artillery across the Ncome River in preparation for the march the next day.[20]

1 June, Koppie Allein to Itelezi Hill, 7 miles
The invasion proper began on Whit Sunday, 1 June, and Captain Montague left us a vivid word-picture of the advance:

> The promised advance had already commenced – the 1st Brigade crossing the long-looked-at Blood river, and winding slowly across the grass-land beyond. The drift over the river bore signs of having been hurried through; the sides were steep and sloppy, and the black mud in the bottom, increasing continually, threatened to swallow up each succeeding waggon. Far on the left were the Lancers, dotted about; nearer at hand, the advancing infantry, clearly marked by black lines drawn across the veldt. Beyond, again, the swells of grass-land, then yellow, reach up for some miles to a broken ridge of flat-topped hills, grass-grown to their summit; that on the left, 'the Incenci' – both the 'c's pronounced hard; that on the right, Itelezi – later on a station from which the heliograph flashed its messages far on towards the front. Between these two hills is a neck, or saddle-back, yellow with the everlasting grass; and on this neck our first camp was pitched, succeeded by the more permanent erection, 'Fort Warwick.'[21]

Molyneux, Lord Chelmsford's aide-de-camp, described the first laager:

> Three laagers were formed, in plan something like the 'three of diamonds'; an infantry brigade in each of the outside squares, and the cavalry, oxen, and natives in the centre one. It did not answer, in consequence of the stupidity of the foreloopers, and afterwards an oblong of two hundred and eighty yards by one hundred and forty was adopted to contain the whole of the Second Division and the cavalry; this was easier formed, and covered less ground.[22]

It was on this day that the Prince Imperial met his death. As a consequence, the day of 2 June was spent in recovering his body, arranging an ad hoc funeral service, then beginning the transport of the hastily embalmed body back to Pietermaritzburg and Durban.

3 June, Itelezi Hill to Ityotyosi River, 9 miles
The advance resumed on 3 June and Colonel Brown had some remarks about this day.

The division marched about 9 miles, over undulating ground, perfectly open – not a bush to be seen. The grass seems better than in Natal. There were a few mealie fields about. The mounted men scouted all round, and the division marched with two battalions in column and a battery at full intervals between them, the mule transport and ammunition column next, and the ox-wagons after, 10 or more wagons abreast.[23] The rear brigade followed in the same formation as the leading one, and Bengough's natives kept on the flanks of the wagons. The laager was formed about 800 yds. from where the Prince Imperial's body was found, which was at the junction of four dongas. The laager was an oblong one . . . divided by a traverse of ammunition and staff wagons, the cattle on one side, the greater part of the horses on the other, the tents round the outside beyond the shelter-trench, which was close to the wagon wheels . . . The camp was near the Ityotyosi River.[24]

The division advanced to the Ityotyosi River and camped 'within half a mile of the spot where the Prince had been killed'.[25] We have already observed that Wood's Flying Column had camped close by on the previous day: 'Wood's column . . . was now on the left front of the Division, on the farther side of the Ityotyosi.' An interesting pictorial view of the two camps, and their geographical relationship with the scene of the death of the Prince Imperial, was drawn by Melton Prior and appeared in a copy of the *Illustrated London News* on 19 July 1879.[26] The view looks approximately north from the hills overlooking the valley of the Ityotyosi and shows the camp of the 2nd Division on the front of a hill to the left or west of the death site; the hill is shown on the modern map as being named Mabulawayo. The site of Wood's camp is shown in the drawing as being 'three miles distant' to the north-east. From the contours of the land, this would seem to be on the left or further bank of the Vumankala river.

Further progress due south was now impossible owing to the many intervening dongas and high ground. The column therefore had to march some distance to the east before resuming a south-east route. The distances next covered were short, probably because much labour had to be undertaken at the dongas. From this point it will be necessary to distinguish between the two columns because Wood generally led one day ahead of Newdigate.

3 June, Wood: Ityotyosi to Inshalwan Hill, 2.5 miles
The Flying Column probably marched down the Vumankala River to the north side of Inshalwan Hill, a distance of only four kilometres (two and a half miles). The likely site of this camp was between the river and Mhlungwane Hill.

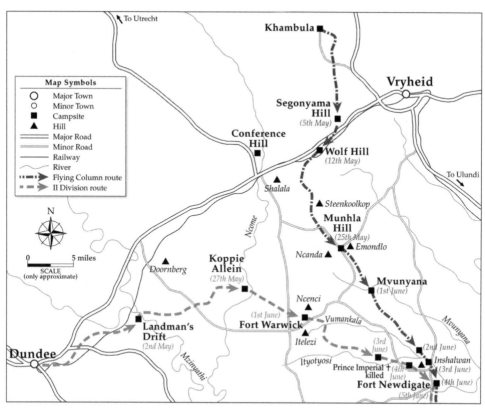

9 The Second Invasion – Start Points to Fort Newdigate

4 June, Wood: Inshalwan Hill to Fort Newdigate, 3.5 miles
The next day Wood marched on another six kilometres (three and a half miles) and established a camp on the Nondweni River, at the site to be known as Fort Newdigate. To achieve this they must have left the river and marched to the eastern side of Mhlungwane and then south, roughly following the line of the present Vryheid–Kranskop road which in those days was the traders' track running south from the Transvaal.

4 June, Newdigate: Ityotyosi to Inshalwan Hill, 3 miles
The *Narrative* is confusing here but the diary of the 2nd Division makes it plain that the division 'marched to the site of Wood's Camp of yesterday, about three miles [five kilometres], with rather bad drifts to cross'.[27] This is confirmed by Colonel Brown, who observed that 'as there were two bad drifts to cross, the 2nd Brigade had not moved off before the 1st Brigade was

beginning to laager.' It should be noted that Brown also says that the march did not begin until 12.30 p.m., which explains the short distance marched. It was dark before the laager here was completed but note: 'Lord Chelmsford always settled the laager for the 2nd Division himself.'[28] Wood must also have suffered the same problems when he had moved the day previously, which explains the short distance which he travelled. It was here that the fort to be called 'Newdigate' was to be built.

5 June, Wood: Fort Newdigate to Matyanhlope Hill, 6 miles
The Flying Column next moved south to a hill known as Matyanhlope 'on the right bank of the Nondweni'. This river cannot be correctly named because had he followed the Nondweni he would have travelled far to the south-west. Wood more probably moved south, striking the confluence of two streams, one of which was the Ntinini, then called the Upoko (uPhokhwe).[29] The distance travelled would have then placed him mid-way between the future Forts Newdigate and Marshall, some twenty-two kilometres apart.

On 5 June a skirmish took place between Buller's Frontier Light Horse and a large number of Zulus. This was said to have occurred 'near some kraals on the eastern side of the Upoko river,[30] and had obliged [the Zulu] to retire into some thorn bush on the lower slopes of the Ezunganyan hill'.[31] Buller was unable to winkle the Zulu out of their rocky fastness and was in the act of withdrawing when he was joined by some of General Marshall's cavalry under Colonel Drury Lowe. On ground entirely unsuited to regular cavalry, Lowe sent in his men with the only result being the unnecessary death of Lieutenant and Adjutant Frederick John Cokayne Frith of the 17th Lancers.[32] His body was returned to Fort Newdigate for burial.

The identity of Ezunganyan Hill poses something of a mystery but a possible site is ventured in a map by Paul Thompson.[33] He identifies it as a long north–south ridge to the south-east of the confluence of several streams with the Upoko River. My difficulty with this hill is that it is now called Sikhonkwane, quite unlike the name 'Ezunganyan'; my own preference, and not simply on the basis of a much closer similarity of name, is a hill some four kilometres north-east of this ridge, called Zungeni. A second raid was made on this hill on 8 June, during which a contemporary newspaper report stated: 'The Lancers and Dragoons, with two seven-pound guns, skirmished past the north-east end of the mountain, driving what Zulus there were before them; while Buller's command . . . went round the southwest end of the mountain into the deep donga-riven valley at the back, burning many kraals . . .'[34]

Now there is certainly a north-east side to Thompson's hill, but, just as certainly, there is no easily accessible south-west side simply because the ridge extends to the south by merging into still another hill called Mkhwakhweni, the whole running about six kilometres (three and a half miles) southward. Zungeni, on the other hand, has a well-defined south-west side which has a mass of dry dongas running down into a river valley just as described.[35]

Wood remained at Matyanhlope until 7 June when he took his column back to Fort Newdigate, having received orders that his column was to escort more than six hundred wagons back to Koppie Allein, and thence to Conference Hill and Landman's Drift, so that additional supplies could be brought up. This re-provisioning had been planned with some care by Lord Chelmsford as early as 19 May:

> The only chance therefore to get a proper supply to the Babanango or other intermediate post, will be by making two trips.[36]

> I have been thinking over the arrangements for the empty wagons coming back from Babanango and refilling with supplies. I am inclined to think that it will be an advantage for half to refill at Landman's Drift and half at Conference Hill as this camp is about halfway between each depot.[37]

5 June, Newdigate: Inshalwan Hill to Fort Newdigate, 3.5 miles
All the wagons from both columns were unloaded here ready to be sent back to Koppie Allein. 'For the protection of the stores here deposited, two stone forts were this day commenced, and the post was named Fort Newdigate.'[38] Lieutenant Charles Commeline, Royal Engineers, who assisted with the construction, left a crude diagram of the work:[39]

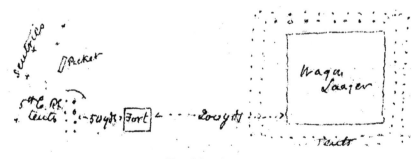

Fort Newdigate

This was also the date and scene of an unfortunate false alarm, the details of which will be found in the appendix, and which resulted in Fort Newdigate being assigned the unhappy sobriquet of 'Fort Funk'.

6 June, Newdigate: halted

7 June, Newdigate: Nondweni River to Ezunyangan Hill, 7 miles
On 7 June the 2nd Division moved forward eleven kilometres (seven miles) to make a camp 'on the left bank of the Upoko river near the skirmish of the 5th'. This camp must have been on the eastern bank of the Upoko or Tinini River, close to Ezunganyan Hill. Here it remained until 17 June when Wood returned, camping about a mile further up the Upoko.

7 June, Wood return to Koppie Allein
Wood left with more than six hundred empty wagons on this day to return to Koppie Allein, passing the 2nd Division on the same day. The wagons went on, either to Conference Hill or Landman's Drift, where they were loaded with the additional supplies required to maintain the force until its mission was completed.

8 June, Newdigate: halted
Despite it being Sunday, there was an attack by the mounted men and artillery guns on parties of Zulu, followed up by the infantry. During a search of nearby caves many relics from Isandlwana were found, including a mule wagon that was brought back into service. The time from now until the next move forward on 18 June was spent 'getting in fuel and giving the horses and cattle a chance of feeding a little better'.[40]

17 June, Wood returns to Ezunyangan Hill
On 15 June, Newdigate's operational diary recorded: 'The rations supplied to the men are ample and of good quality. The oats for the horses are indifferent. Many of the English Cavalry horses have fallen off in condition. The heavy Cavalry saddles and paraphernalia connected with them are ill adapted for service in the field in this country.'[41]
    On 17 June Wood's huge convoy arrived back with the additional supplies. These were dropped off with the 2nd Division, after which the Flying Column continued for a further mile before making camp.

> . . . Br. Gen. Wood arrived from Koppie Allein with the big convoy of provisions which is to keep the army supplied till the end of the campaign. He had 700 wagons and 9000 oxen guarded by his Column. Such a convoy has never before been seen in S. Africa and probably never will again and was indeed a wonderful sight.[42]

From this point on, the two columns would march in tandem, the Flying Column leading the way and the 2nd Division camping close to Wood's camp site of the previous night.

18 June, Ezunganyan Hill to Fort Marshall, 5 miles
Brown describes the route now followed: 'We . . . kept on the S.S.W. side of the hills which we had faced for the last 10 days. We passed Inthlabaumkosi [Nhlabamkosi] . . . on our right, and descending a steep grassy slope, found ourselves on the old wagon track from Rorke's Drift to Ulundi.'[43] This route is identical to the unmade road that still runs south from Fort Newdigate 'to the head of the Upoko river', where the Flying Column crossed to the eastern bank while the 2nd Division remained on the western side.

The late David Rattray's grand book of Lieutenant Lloyd's paintings and drawings contains a reference to the route from here. The text suggests that the column moved away from the Upoko River due to the impassable country along the river, taking a westward swing across the eastern flank of Alarm Hill.[44] This route is the same as the road shown in the contemporary map of Zululand. The column, however, did not march west but rather south-west at this point.

It was here that construction of a second fort began, to be named Fort Marshall. The fort stood at the junction of the Transvaal track and the trading road from Rorke's Drift to Ulundi and ironically the force was now only a little more than thirty-two kilometres (twenty miles), as the crow flies, from Rorke's Drift and only twenty-four kilometres (fifteen miles) from Isandlwana. Worse, they were now only sixteen kilometres (ten miles) or one day's march from the site of Lord Chelmsford's proposed camp site near the Mangeni Falls. Isiphezi hill, so long a signpost on the horizon for the Centre Column in January, stood just five kilometres (three miles) to the south-west.

The 2nd Division remained here for two days building the fort. Captain Montague, who to his disgust was left here temporarily as part of the garrison, left a word picture of the site: 'The situation of Fort Marshall was depressing and depressed. It lay in a basin. All round, the sky-line was high overhead. The sun shone on the rim of the bowl in which it was built fully half an hour before he warmed up the garrison, the damp, limp mass of tea-leaves in the bottom.'[45]

It now becomes difficult to locate with any precision the sites of some of the intermediate halting places of either column on their journey from Fort Marshall to Fort Evelyn and thence to the heights of Mthonjaneni. The route became increasingly difficult and extremely hilly. It is clear that they tried

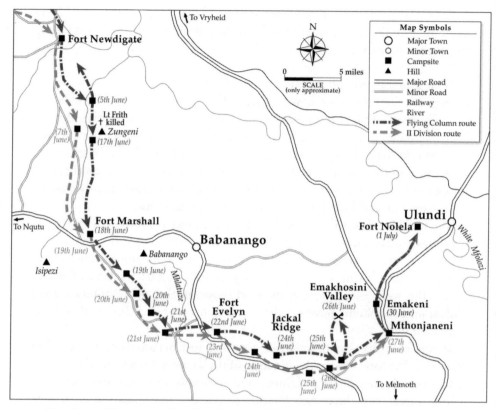

10 The Second Invasion – Fort Newdigate to White Mfolozi

wherever possible to follow river valleys, hence their use of the Mhlathuze River, and later they tried to follow the course of ridges. Modern maps show tracks that follow the course of the river downstream which might well reflect the actual route they took. Overall, however, it is reasonable to assume that they roughly followed the course of the modern Nkandla road before leaving it, near where Owen's Cutting is located today, to move north-west back towards the modern Babanango road and thence to Fort Evelyn.

19 June, Wood: Fort Marshall to Ibabanango Spruit, 5 miles
On the 19th Wood again moved forward, this time following the trading road, for a distance of eight kilometres (five miles) 'and camped between two branches of the Umhlatoosi river' while the 2nd Division crossed the Upoko and occupied the site of Wood's camp and Fort Marshall.

20 June, Newdigate: Fort Marshall to Ibabanango Spruit, 6 miles
The next day the 2nd Division resumed its own advance, camping about a mile in advance of Wood's camp, a total of ten kilometres (six miles), 'rain during the night and early morning [making] the steep ascent onto the hill very difficult . . .'[46] What hill was this? It was not the Babanango mountain because contemporary maps show that the force made a wide swing to the south and east to avoid the very high ground there.

> The native road [towards Ulundi] branched off to the left of our own soon after leaving Fort Marshall, and wound over the northern slopes of Ibabanango, while we followed the southern, soon leaving them altogether. This Zulu road was worn and trampled into many ruts and holes, and was some fifty feet in width, crossing the most impossible dongas, and climbing the steepest hills, intent only on finding the nearest cut. It was of course, for this reason, quite unfitted for the passage of waggons, and so was not used by us.[47]

Colonel Brown also noted: 'A great deal of grass about here has been burnt, as well as some mealie fields.'[48]
    It is likely that the route taken followed the minor road towards Nkandla that deviates to the south-east from the modern Babanango road (R68) at a point some three kilometres (two miles) from Fort Marshall. In the early stages of this road there is a steep passage between two hills which would have given the wagons some difficulty. Their camp would have been close to the mission near the Boer War Fort Louis, and a little way past Wood's camp.

20 June, Wood: Babanango Spruit to the headwaters of Mhlatuze River, 5 miles
Wood had taken his column on still further and 'encamped between two branches of the Umhlatoosi river'. On this same day Newdigate also moved forward ten kilometres (six miles) to close up on Wood's previous camp site.

21 June, Newdigate: Babanango Spruit to Mhlatuze River, 10 miles
On 21 June the division made a good march of sixteen kilometres (ten miles) to the upper reaches of the Mhlathuze River, 'leaving the Babanango Mountain on our left . . . On the banks of the Umlatoosi, our camp lay in a hollow, commanded by hills and precipitous cliffs, and one where, had the Zulus attempted an attack, we should have had some trouble. Extra precautions had to be taken, all of which were luckily not needed . . .'[49]
    At the same time, the Flying Column advanced just five kilometres (three miles) so that by nightfall they were on the left bank of the eastern branch of the Mhlatuze, while Newdigate was camped close by on the opposite bank.

Indeed they were now so close that Newdigate observed: 'Came upon the rear of Wood's Column, which was delayed by having to improve the drift over dongas near our camping ground.'[50] Brown also tells us that there was a violent thunderstorm about 5.30 p.m. and the 24th Regiment did not get to the laager until after 8 p.m. [51]

22 June, Wood: Mhlatuze River to Fort Evelyn, 4 miles

On this day the 2nd Division remained in camp while Wood moved his column six kilometres (four miles) further east to the site of a third fort to be named Fort Evelyn.[52] It being Sunday, a divine service was held, after which the troops took the opportunity to bathe in the stream and wash their clothes.

To assist in its construction Newdigate sent on 'two companies of the 58th Regt, the 2nd Co. of the Royal Engineers and one Company of Bengough's Native Battalion to construct the Fort . . .'[53]

The present site of the fort can only be found with difficulty and it is surrounded by a high wire fence; nor is there a modern sign indicating its position, as there are with Forts Newdigate and Marshall. It can be found a little more than two kilometres after the junction of the Owen's Cutting road with the main Babanango–Melmoth road (R68), on the left side of the road. The site is just two hundred metres past a farm turn-off to the right.[54]

23 June, Newdigate: Mhlatuze River to Fort Evelyn, 4 miles

'The Division marched from Umthlatuzi where it had halted on the 22nd Instant, and encamped on the left bank of the Seguini Spruit.'[55] This was the stream near which Fort Evelyn was being built. By now the invading force had reached the base of the foothills of the Mthonjaneni plateau and from here the road became increasingly difficult.

24 June, Wood: Fort Evelyn to summit of Jackal Ridge, 4 miles

Unfortunately, the hills shown on modern maps in this area are unnamed so that the location of 'Jackal Ridge' can only be surmised.[56] The ridge is, however, well-marked on the contemporary map of Zululand and begins at a distance of some five miles from Fort Evelyn. The most likely candidate lies about two kilometres to the west of another ridge called Nkongqolo, which is about the correct distance from Fort Evelyn. This is on the modern road to Mthonjaneni and is labelled 'Havemanshoogte'.

On the same day Newdigate led his 2nd Division over the same ground but was unable to complete the ascent of the steep approach to Jackal Ridge and thus made its camp halfway up,[57] a completed distance of only about five kilometres (three miles).

25 June, Wood: Jackal Ridge towards Mthonjaneni, 6 miles
The camp made here left Wood just thirteen kilometres (eight miles) short of Mthonjaneni itself, which was the highest point in that part of Zululand.

25 June, Newdigate: halfway up Jackal Ridge to summit, 4 miles
Newdigate was having a much tougher time. On this day his 2nd Division climbed to the top of Jackal Ridge but had only enough time to reach the top of the ridge beyond, which may well have been the same Nkongqolo mentioned earlier. Unusually, Lord Chelmsford 'dispensed with an entrenchment round the laager, as the natural strength of the position was great and the infantry had had a very hard day helping wagons up the hill'.[58] What was more, the men received an issue of grog and an extra half pound of meat for their dinner.

26 June, Newdigate: closes up to 1.5 miles from Wood
Newdigate brought his column on to within 2.5 kilometres (1.5 miles) of Wood's camp. Wood himself did not move forward, awaiting Newdigate. Instead he led his mounted units and elements of the Natal Native Contingent on a raid into the heartland of the country, the nearby Emakhosini Valley. Here the Zulu themselves burnt one of their oldest Zulu military *ikhanda*, probably Esiklebheni, in which was kept the *inkatha yezwe*, or sacred coil, a symbol of the Zulu nation, which was lost in the conflagration.[59] Colonel Brown observes that it was 'the third largest in the country and the oldest military kraal, having been built by Charka [Shaka]'.[60]

27 June, arrival at Mthonjaneni, 10 miles
By the 27th, both columns had reached the Mthonjaneni heights[61] after an easy march 'over fine open downs'. They were now able to look down over the Mahlabathini plain and the several huge Zulu cantonments, including Nodwengu and Ondini, which were only twenty-six kilometres (sixteen miles) distant. They were in sight of their objective. Their arrival did not go unnoticed: Zulu envoys arrived with a gift of 150 cattle, two elephant tusks and a letter written on behalf of Cetshwayo by Cornelius Vijn, a Dutch trader who had been made a hostage. Lord Chelmsford replied to the king as follows:

> You have not complied with all the conditions I laid down. I shall, therefore, continue to advance, as I told you I should but, as you have sent me some of the cattle, and state that the two cannon [from Isandlwana] are on their way, I consent not to cross the Mfolozi river to-morrow, to give you time to fulfil the remainder of the conditions.

Unless all my conditions are complied with by to-morrow evening you must take the consequences.

I return the tusks you send to show you I shall still advance. I will keep the cattle a few days to show I am willing to make peace if you comply with the conditions laid down.

I am willing that the men collected now at Ulundi, whom I have seen, should, to the number of a regiment (1,000), come to me and lay down their arms, as a sign of submission; they can do so at a distance from me of 500 yards and then retire. Their lives are safe; the word of an English General is sufficient to ensure it.

The arms in possession of the men around you now, taken at Sandhlwana, must be given up by them.[62]

Lord Chelmsford held his columns at Mthonjaneni during 28 and 29 June, sending back the mule wagons to Fort Marshall to bring up further supplies.

30 June, Mtonjaneni to Emakeni bivouac, 5 miles
In accordance with Lord Chelmsford's intention, the force moved down from the heights at 9.30 a.m. on 30 June, setting up an intermediate camp near to the Emakeni *inkhanda*.[63]

Marched from Camp at Emtonjaneni at 8.30 a.m. and formed laager in the Valley about 4 miles further on towards Ulundi. We carried no tents nor the men's valises nor any impedimenta that could be dispensed with. Ten days grocery and breadstuffs, Rations and 7 days preserved meat were carried in Regimental ox waggons. No mule transports except the Regimental Ammunition carts and two mule wagons with Lt. Col. Harness' Battery.[64]

One of Lord Chelmsford's aides-de-camp said of the camp: 'That night we bivouacked at Amakeni, a six mile march from Entonjaneni, but only three miles as the crow flies from that laager, which was in sight on top of the hill.'[65] The principal reason for choosing this place was that: '[It was] known to be the only watering place in the sandy bush-covered flat which extends from the base of the Entonjaneni heights to the banks of the Mfolozi.'[66]

The first camp, then, was not on the banks of White Mfolozi River, which was too far to be reached in one day's march, but was of necessity located near fresh water and wood. The camp site lies close to the Mgodi stream to be found about two kilometres south-west of the junction of the Melmoth–Vryheid road (R34) and the Ulundi road (R66). It was in the vicinity of the future Fort Victoria, which was to be built nearby on 9 August.[67] The following extract indicates its proximity: 'The convoy remains encamped, under escort of four companies of the 58th Regiment, on a spur between Entonjaneni and the White Mfolozi, where a fort has been constructed and named Fort Victoria.'[68]

Here again they were met by Zulu messengers, this time bringing the Prince Imperial's sword and another letter written by Vijn on behalf of the Zulu king.

1 July, Emakeni bivouac to White Mfolozi, 9 miles
Wood moved some fourteen kilometres (nine miles) almost to the river but Newdigate halted about a mile short of Wood's camp. On 2 July the latter moved his force further down towards the river. The columns here formed two laagers 'in a thick wood' on the hillside leading down to the river, that of the 2nd Division being about a half mile higher than that of the Flying Column.

'The next day [3 July], a fort [Nolela] was built on a knoll between the two laagers, and then the wagons of the Second Division were moved down and formed into two lines, one end of each line resting on a side of Wood's laager and the other ends converging on the fort.'[69] The nearby river bank was dominated by a low rocky hill on the southern side from which Zulu marksmen soon began to harass bathers and those who came down to collect water.[70]

Once again there was an alarm in the camp at midnight, this time causing Bengough's own NNC to bowl him over in their panic: '. . . as I staggered to my feet, I heard the voice of one of my officers, Captain Boord. "They are not worth a rap." "Who," said I. "Our men, sir!" was the reply and then the truth dawned on me. It was only another false alarm.'[71]

It was from this camp site that Lieutenant-Colonel Buller led his momentous reconnaissance across the Mahlabathini plain on 3 July, almost stumbling into a Zulu ambush, during which Lord William Beresford showed extraordinary courage. He turned 'to assist Serg't Fitzmaurice, 1/24th Foot (whose horse had fallen with him), mounted him behind him on his horse, and brought him away in safety under the close fire of the Zulus who were in great force, and were coming on quickly', for which action he was awarded the Victoria Cross.[72]

It was also from this camp that the troops marched out the next day (4 July 1879) to fight, and win, the battle of Ulundi, heralding the subjugation of the Zulu nation.

Fort Funk

During the early construction of Fort Newdigate there was a serious false alarm as a result of which numbers of the 2nd Division were wounded. Miles Gissop, with the 17th Lancers, recorded the details in his diary:

> We were alarmed about 8.30 pm by 2 shots fired by the outlying picket, we were all in the tents and the majority of us asleep, every one jumped up and seized his carbine, tents were dropped and we were in breathless haste ran into the Laager. The picket was called in. The Infantry to man the waggons, the order was given to 'Fire'. It was a beautiful moonlight night and it was said the enemy were seen advancing in 2 distinct Columns but whether such was true or not I cannot say. In the scare a Sergt of the Engineers was wounded, the effects from which he died. Before he died he made a statement to the effect that the bullet which hit him was fired by the enemy.
>
> A Fort was built there and was named Fort Newigate but was ever afterwards known to us and referred to by the Soubriquet [sic] of 'Fort Funk'. After two hours the Picket was again sent out and we went once more to roost, as comfortable as if nothing had happened.[73]

The alarm was also described by Lieutenant Commeline, RE, in detail:

> About 9 p.m. [on 6 June] as Porter and myself were sitting in our tent, two shots, rapidly followed by a third, were fired by the sentry of the picket close to us and our men made an immediate rush for the fort. Porter and I got them distributed round the low wall and meanwhile the picket fired three volleys so we concluded the enemy was pretty close. The alarm had been sounded by all bugles in the big laager and in a few minutes a heavy firing was commenced on the side furthest from us, being gradually taken up all round.
>
> The picket then returned into our fort saying that the enemy were coming on in thousands and from the firing on the far sides of the lager this seemed most probable. Chard and Jones had been dining in the laager and came tumbling into the fort just before the picket came in. The officer commanding the picket, who happened to be the senior present, then ordered that we should retire on the laager with the boxes of ammunition but no sooner did the men jump over the lower wall than they were received by a tremendous volley from the wagon laager and came tumbling helter-skelter back into the fort. We then lay as flat as possible behind the little 2 ft. wall while a regular hale [sic] of bullets whistled over us. How it was no one was killed I don't know and casualties only amounted to 1 sergeant, bullet through the thigh, 4 men slightly wounded in the face and 1 man two fingers shot off. Two of our horses were shot on the picket line. After

some 2000 or 3000 rounds had been fired at us there was a pause when we kept our bugles blowing the cease fire and shouted for doctors. Voices from the laager answered 'Alright' and then we stood up very thankful to be alive. A more unpleasant predicament is hard to imagine, as we naturally thought the Zulus were coming on in our front and were taken for them by our own people behind. And the same time it was a most disgraceful thing that the troops should thus have fired at nothing and it is even reported that an artillery battery fired one or two rounds. As far we know, there was not a Zulu within miles of us, a nervous sentry having probably fired at an ant heap or shadow. The officer who ordered the picket to fire volleys will probably hear more of it yet.[74]

General Newdigate's own official report was brief and he identified those responsible:

I attach great blame to Brevet Major Hesse,[75] who by firing volleys without seeing an enemy, alarmed the Camp, and also for retiring with his Picquets before he had even ascertained whether or not an enemy was at his front.

I also blame the Officer Commanding Regiment for allowing them to fire without seeing anything to fire at, and for permitting the Companies to fire independent firing contrary to my orders. I have given the most stringent orders upon this subject. It is of the greatest importance that the fire should be controlled. This can only be done by Volley firing.[76]

Old and New Names of Geographical Features

Doornberg	Doringberg
Ibabanango Hill	Babanango Hill
Inceni Hill	Inceceni Hill
Indeni forest	Qudeni forest
Inshalwan Hill	Mhlungwane Hill
Inthlabaumkosi	Inhlabamkhosi Hill
Itelezi Hill	Itelezini Hill
Ityotyozi River	Jojosi River
Munhla Hill	Emondlo Hill
Mzunyangan Hill	Zungeni Hill
Ngutu range	Nqutu range
Teneni River	Ntinini River
Tombokala River	Vumankala River
Umyamyene River	Mvunyana River
Upoko River	Uphokhwe River

Modern Maps Used in the Construction of the Invasion Route
The maps listed below are in the 1:50000 series issued by the Chief Directorate, Surveys and Mapping, South Africa.

2730DA Nkambule	Wood: Khambula south towards Vryheid.
2730DC eMondlo	Conference Hill; Wood to Munhla Hill.
2830AB Tayside	Landman's Drift east towards Koppie Allein.
2830BA Nqutu	Newdigate: Koppie Allein to iTelezini Hill.
2830BB Nondweni	Wood to Ityotyosi, Newdigate to Ityotyosi then both to Fort Newdigate.
2830BD Fort Louis	Fort Newdigate to Fort Marshall and the Mhlathuze river.
2831AC Babanango	Mhlathuze river to Fort Evelyn.
2831CA Nkandla	Fort Evelyn to Jackal Ridge.
2831AD Ulundi	Jackal Ridge to Mthonjaneni and Ulundi.

Lord Chelmsford and Sir Henry Bulwer

The reader might, with some justice, assume that the opprobrium that attended Lord Chelmsford after the military disasters at Isandlwana, Hlobane and Ntombe Drift, not to mention the death of the Prince Imperial, were the principal causes of his eventual supersession. In fact, this was not the case. The primary reason was his unsatisfactory relationship with the lieutenant-governor of Natal, Sir Henry Bulwer[77] – a relationship that began badly and only became worse.

As early as December 1878 Sir Henry had observed that Chelmsford was 'a good general officer: very, very careful, very painstaking, very thorough' but 'not very pleasant to deal with in official matters' and he even questioned whether he was 'in all matters quite open and frank with one'.[78] This last comment was subsequently proved to be correct. For his part, Lord Chelmsford quickly found that Sir Henry was strongly opposed to war with the Zulu nation:

> Were I certain that the Zulus were going to attack or to be attacked, I would ask that the Cavalry regiment from Malta and at least one Native Infantry regiment should be sent to reinforce me. I cannot, however, make any such statement. Sir Henry Bulwer on the contrary seems to lean to the opinion that the Zulus are not anxious to provoke a quarrel and appears to deprecate any military preparations.[79]

Bulwer was sincere in his beliefs concerning the pacific nature of the Zulu people, if not necessarily their king. Public opinion was initially with the lieutenant-governor, largely as the result of apathy. In October 1878 a correspondent wrote to the *Times of Natal*: 'We object to being compelled to fight in a cause which has in no way been brought about by any action of ours. We were submitted to disgrace in the Langalibalele affair, and do not wish a repetition of that disaster upon a larger scale. It is right that those who make wars necessary should do the fighting.'[80]

Sir Henry also had grave misgivings about the conscription of the proposed Natal Native Contingent (NNC), not least concerning the passing of the command of levies from local to imperial military hands. He strongly opposed the issuing of firearms to Africans, which were forbidden to them by law without permission, an issue that had precipitated the Langalibalele incident in 1873. He sensed the potential for armed rebellion if they were given such arms and military training. A combination of the Zulu and Natal Africans, many of whom were themselves Zulu in origin, was – in the minds of settlers and their leaders – too awful to contemplate. One must bear in mind that at this time the population of Natal was about 360,000, of whom less than 27,000 were Europeans and some 17,000 were Indians.[81] It was probably for this reason, as much as a shortage of the arms themselves, that the NNC was allowed only ten armed men in each company of one hundred, the remainder having only their traditional weapons. The ensuing debate between the Natal government and the military delayed the conscription of both officers and men of the Contingent.[82]

Chelmsford's frustration was almost palpable and he made his feelings absolutely clear in a letter to Governor Frere in September 1878:

> The fact is that Sir Henry Bulwer trusts no one, and wishes to settle every petty point of detail himself. But as he has essentially a small mind and cannot take a full grasp of the situation, the time of the Defence Committee, when it met, which has not been often, has been taken up with discussing details which should have been left entirely to the magistrates of districts.[83]

In this same letter he was able to report that he had finally met with the Executive Council, and addressed the Defence Committee on the previous day, 10 September 1878. He had been able to win over the members and agreement was reached on a satisfactory resolution of Natal's defence problems. Even so it is plain that the lieutenant-governor's pedantry continued to irk Chelmsford, who saw Bulwer as 'very particular, moreover, about the exact language in which his orders are clothed, and will discuss and alter *ad nauseam* every sentence, wasting most valuable time and trying the temper of his council most woefully'.[84]

Following the battle of Isandlwana in January 1879 the NNC was left in disarray. The lieutenant-general was extremely concerned that the men had seemingly deserted their units. He disbanded one regiment and the other two were rendered virtually useless. Sir Henry Bulwer initiated an inquiry into the 'desertions' and, based largely upon the responses from his resident magistrates after they had consulted the chiefs, re-stated his opposition to the NNC's existence. In a detailed memorandum, Bulwer identified inherent problems in the Contingent as the result of the apparent disregard by the lieutenant-general of his government's views.[85]

In a belated reply Lord Chelmsford answered the criticisms point by point, essentially arguing that the matters raised had been adopted virtually as the lieutenant-governor had required.[86] Referring, for example, to the principal bone of contention – the military organisation of the NNC rather than the tribal organisation favoured by Sir Henry – Chelmsford asserted that Bulwer, in a memorandum to Sir Bartle Frere, had substantially agreed with the sub-division of a large body of Africans, and the necessity for such sub-divisions to be led by Europeans.

Their correspondence was, in the normal course, copied to Governor Frere. On 7 March, Sir Henry Bulwer wrote to Frere indicating quite clearly that he was not to be mollified by Chelmsford's reply and had 'no desire to continue this controversy'. He therefore abstained 'from entering into any notice of the various points in the Lieutenant-General's Minute which, otherwise, I might be disposed to think require notice'.[87] This implacable response was one of the early catalysts that were eventually to bring about Lord Chelmsford's early departure.

As reinforcements began to arrive in March, Lord Chelmsford began planning for the relief of Pearson, still trapped in Eshowe and rapidly running out of supplies. In order that the expedition be more certain of success, the lieutenant-general asked for the co-operation of the column commanders in providing demonstrations that might divert the Zulu king's attention from the real British objective. In this regard, Chelmsford wrote to Colonel Evelyn Wood that, having just returned from Greytown and Kranskop, he had obtained as many African levies as he could 'out of the [Natal] Government along the Tugela border' and that: 'I hope to be able to send in large raiding parties with a hooroosh, directly you are in a position to resume the advance.'[88]

This letter does not make clear which body of troops would make the diversionary demonstrations but seems to refer to the Native Border Guard under the civil commanders of the various Colonial Defensive Districts, and thence the lieutenant-governor. The only African forces commanded by the lieutenant-general were the NNC and associated troops such as the Natal Pioneers and the mounted troops of the Natal Native Mounted Contingent.

Bulwer and Lord Chelmsford met at Pinetown on 11 March 1879 to discuss matters, including the demonstrations for which the lieutenant-general had called.[89] Bulwer left this meeting convinced that they had agreed that while the Border Guard would assemble for demonstrations, they would not be required to cross the river into Zululand. This restriction did not, of course, extend to the NNC. Bulwer then used the supposed agreement as the basis for orders to his district commanders that their levies were not to cross the Thukela River border but could be used on the Natal side for demonstrations.[90]

Only days later, Chelmsford wrote a second letter to Evelyn Wood, formally requesting his assistance with demonstrations and stating his intentions with regard to other areas and encouraging Wood to 'make any forward movement about the 27th of this month, so that the news of it may reach the neighbourhood of Ekowe about the 29th'. He added that 'I shall tell the border commandants to make demonstrations all along the line also, and if the river admits to raid across for cattle.'[91]

In his response to this request, Wood made arrangements for an assault on the nearby Hlobane mountain.[92] The attack was unsuccessful, as it coincided with the arrival in the vicinity of a Zulu *impi* intending to attack Wood's camp at Khambula. Ensuing events led to the disastrous British withdrawal from Hlobane mountain on 28 March and the battle of Khambula on the following day.

Although the evidence is scant, John Laband has argued convincingly on the basis of the above-mentioned correspondence and records of meetings that 'Chelmsford had early determined on proceeding behind Bulwer's back' by using border levies for these raids.[93]

In the meantime Major A.C. Twentyman, commanding troops on the Middle Drift of the Thukela from his Greytown headquarters, was planning just such a demonstration on 25 March using the NNC and the Border Guard. He requested that W.D. Wheelwright, commanding Colonial Defensive District No. VII (Umvoti), assemble his troops for a combined raid into Zululand. Mindful of his instructions that his men were not to cross the river, Wheelwright agreed to assemble his men but said that they would not cross until the Natal government had given him authority to do so. On 29 March Twentyman reported Wheelwright's refusal to cross the river to Deputy Adjutant-General Colonel Bellairs, and requested that Bellairs grant permission for Wheelwright's men to cross.[94]

On 2 April, Twentyman, concerned that permission to use the Border Guard had still not been received, reported to Colonel Bellairs that while the state of the river had prevented a crossing, a demonstration by more than 1,000 border levies and the NNC on the Natal side on 25 March had seemed to be effective: 'The Zulus all along the Border seem to fear our crossing, and everywhere the cattle have been driven over the hills towards the interior.'[95]

When Eshowe was relieved on 3 April, Special Border Agent Fannin reported another crossing of the NNC at Middle Drift. His report shows his anxiety about continuing raids and fear of Zulu reprisals, indeed of 'a disaster if any more of these raids are made, for Bishop Schreuder through his glass has seen a considerable number of Zulus about three miles from the ferry. They are evidently watching for a favourable opportunity to attack.'[96] The following day, Commandant A.N. Montgomery, temporarily commanding the NNC while Captain Cherry was ill, chose not to cross, to Fannin's relief: 'the Natives refusing to cross. I think it is fortunate it was not attempted, as the Zulus had assembled a considerable body of men to resist.'[97] Following the relief of Eshowe, Pearson and his men arrived back at the Thukela on the 7th but both Twentyman and Lord Chelmsford seemed intent on prolonging the tactic of demonstrations at the Middle Drift, even though its *raison d'être* had expired. In fact such raids persisted until 9 April and were resumed in May.

These various actions at the Middle Drift had an impact at higher levels. Despite the fact that the Border Guard and the NNC were under the command of the lieutenant-governor and Lord Chelmsford respectively, Bulwer's Acting Secretary for Native Affairs, John Shepstone, obstinately wrote to Major Twentyman at Greytown on 15 March, instructing him that he must ensure that the Native Contingent at Kranskop did not 'enter Zulu country against their will'.[98] Twentyman, then in his post for only a short time, duly passed on the instruction to Commandant Montgomery and Captain Cherry. As an experienced serving army officer the latter ignored it but Montgomery thought that, since he was a civilian commandant, he must comply and announced the restriction to his assembled men, who responded that 'they would follow him anywhere'.[99] Inevitably this matter was drawn to the attention of Sir Henry, who immediately recognised the error and wrote to Shepstone on 29 March:

> I cannot remember that I ever gave instructions to the S. for N. Affairs to write to the Commanders of these Battalions of the N. N. Contingent. In fact, it would be a breach of official etiquette for this Gov't to communicate with Captains Cherry or Montgomery except through the proper Military authorities, and I am quite sure I never could have authorised this being done. I am at a loss to understand the origin of this communication.[100]

Shepstone stubbornly responded that he was then, and remained, under the impression that Bulwer had instructed him to write to Twentyman, but went on to state that he must have misunderstood his instructions.[101] Bulwer then became aware of the request made by Twentyman to Wheelwright and yet another candid exchange of views between Chelmsford and Bulwer followed. On 9 April, the lieutenant-governor wrote to Sir Bartle Frere objecting strongly to the raids across the Thukela into Zululand:

> The burning of empty kraals will neither inflict much damage upon the Zulus, nor be attended with much advantage to us; whilst acts of this nature are, so it seems to me, not only calculated to invite retaliation, but to alienate from us the whole of the Zulu nation, men, women, and children, including those who are well disposed to us.[102]

In a second letter of the same day, this time to Chelmsford, Bulwer clearly expressed his anger at his betrayal over the Pinetown accord. He wrote that he had received information that Twentyman had requested the use of border levies under Wheelwright to make raids across the Thukela border, as demonstrations during the relief of Eshowe. While Wheelwright had assembled his men at the river, he had properly advised Twentyman that he would not send his men across into Zululand without the authority of the Natal government.

> I have to observe, with regard to this portion of Major Twentyman's request, that, whilst I fully agreed to your Lordship's proposal that the native levies assembled on the border for the defence of the border should assist, if necessary, in any demonstration that may be made, I have not authorised their being employed in making raids into the Zulu country.[103]

Lord Chelmsford wrote to the Secretary of State for War two days later advising him of the difficulties he had to endure with Bulwer and asking him to intercede:

> The interference of the Lieutenant-Governor of Natal with my plan of operations, however, opens up a very serious question, and I feel bound to point out that if my orders to the Colonial forces, which have been placed under my command by Sir Henry Bulwer himself, are to be referred to himself before being complied with, the satisfactory management of the military operations now being carried on becomes an impossibility.[104]

We should note here, however, that Chelmsford blurred the issue of command by suggesting that the border levies were under his control, which they were not. His report continued:

> the question now at issue is far more serious, and I would beg for the speedy decision of Her Majesty's Government, as to whether the Lieutenant-Governor of Natal, having once placed the services of certain Colonial forces at my disposal, has the power to prevent the orders issued by me to their commanders being obeyed.
>
> I need scarcely point out that if this power be vested in the Lieutenant-Governor, it will be impossible for me to accept the responsibility of the command of the Colonial forces now in the field for the defence of Natal, or to employ the Native Contingent battalions which have been hitherto associated with the British troops.[105]

Not content with this letter, Chelmsford also wrote on that same day, and in a similar vein, to the British Army Commander-in-Chief, the Duke of Cambridge: 'from my first arrival in Natal [Bulwer] has thrown every obstacle in my way whilst at the same time he has endeavoured by long memoranda, minutes & dispatches to make it appear that he has given me all the assistance I have asked for.'[106] On the following day, 12 April, Chelmsford addressed a brief note to Bulwer advising him that the matter of their differences had been referred to London.[107]

Bulwer responded with a tart explanation of his actions, based upon his interpretation of what had transpired at Pinetown,[108] and sent his own explanation, with copies of the correspondence, to British Colonial Secretary Sir Michael Hicks Beach.[109] Bulwer made two key points. The first was that the raids now brought to his attention had been proposed for dates *after* the relief of Eshowe and therefore could not have had any bearing on the success or otherwise of that venture. The second was to note the rather ambiguous manner in which Lord Chelmsford had referred to the African levies:

> The question, therefore, put by the Lieutenant-General, in the way that it is put, before the Secretary of State for War, by not distinguishing between the two descriptions of native forces, but, as is actually done in the last paragraph but one, by naming and associating the two together as if there were no distinction between them, fails I think to represent the real state of the case.[110]

In his counter-claim of 18 April, Chelmsford pointed out to Bulwer that 'there appears to be an unfortunate misunderstanding with regard to the conversation which I had the honour of holding with your Excellency at Pine Town', and that he had given no commitment such as was now being claimed by the lieutenant-governor.[111] Furthermore, he demanded that all African troops along the border be placed 'unreservedly' under his command and 'that I should be permitted to employ them, within or without the border, in whatever manner I may consider best in the interests of the Colony, and with due regard to its protection from invasion.'

Bulwer acknowledged this letter and grudgingly undertook to bring the matter to the attention of the Executive Council.[112] This he did, and in a letter a few days later he reluctantly capitulated,[113] enclosing a minute of the Executive Council deploring the use of the levies in cross-border raids but adding: 'that the Lieutenant-General, who is responsible for the operations of the war and for the defence of the Colony, should have the power of so employing the native levies on the border.'[114]

The dispute closed with a whimper rather than a bang, following a submission by F.B. Fynney, special border agent at the Lower Thukela, which included the words 'respectfully to state my conviction that in the event of our natives being met by a body of Zulus on their own ground, they would not stand against them, but make the best of their way back to Natal.'[115] In response to this advice, forwarded to him by Bulwer, Lord Chelmsford made a complete volte-face, replying in part that 'with such men it would be absurd to attempt any military operation across the border; and I should certainly have never pressed so strongly that the border forces should be placed at my disposal for that purpose had I been informed earlier of the real feeling amongst these natives.'[116]

While this ended a prolonged dispute between the two men, the mills of government in London were still grinding slowly and the fate of Lord Chelmsford was even then being determined. Sir Michael Hicks Beach sent off the following terse telegram to Bulwer on 19 May confirming that: 'The full command of any forces whether European or Native, which are called out for service, must of course be with the General, with whom the responsibility for the operations rests.'[117]

As Chelmsford was preparing to make his final assault on the Zulu king in late June, he received a telegram from the Secretary of State for War:

Her Majesty's Government have determined to send out Sir Garnet Wolseley as Administrator in that part of South-Eastern Africa in the neighbourhood of the seat of war, with plenary powers, both civil and military. Sir B. Frere instructed accordingly by Colonial Office. The appointment of a senior officer is not intended as a censure on yourself, but you will, as in course of service, submit and subordinate your plans to his control. He leaves this country by next mail.[118]

The Secretary of State gave these reasons in a subsequent letter:

> . . . though the orders given by the Colonial Office have instructed His Excellency to comply with your lordship's military demands, I must nevertheless express my sorrow that you should have been unable to settle this question amicably with His Excellency by personal or friendly communication without the necessity of resort to the Home Government . . . I have now to convey to you the intimation that Her Majesty's Government, having carefully considered the information at their command, have come to the conclusion that the satisfactory administration of affairs in that part of South-Eastern Africa in the immediate neighbourhood of the seat of war can, at the present moment, only be carried out by placing that administration in the hands of one person, holding plenary powers, both civil and military, and that they have selected Sir Garnet Wolseley to discharge these duties.[119]

Details followed in a personal letter from Hicks Beach to Sir Bartle Frere, in which he pointed out the dangers of such a dispute and 'the urgent necessity for a change':

> In fact, a dictator is required. Lord Chelmsford, if only because he has been one of the parties to the dispute, could not be the man; and we have decided . . . to send out Sir Garnet Wolseley for the purpose. He will be supreme over both Bulwer and Lanyon,[120] though of course he will leave to them as much as possible of the civil administration of their respective governments. In him also will be vested that part of your functions as High Commissioner which gives authority in Zululand and 'the seat of war' generally . . .[121]

Thus Bulwer stayed on undisturbed, while Chelmsford found himself subordinated to Wolseley. The lieutenant-general was unwilling to submit to the humiliation and resigned, but not before he had regained his *dignitas* with a final victory at Ulundi on 4 July 1879. Although Chelmsford came close to achieving his objective of ending the war, he faltered in the last stretch and chose to quit the field after he had won the final battle – though not the war itself, given that King Cetshwayo was still at large.

The Pinetown Accord

Since writing this paper some years ago, I have had the opportunity of undertaking further research on the topic. The original reference that underpins the work was given by John Laband and refers to a minute written by Lord Chelmsford, dated 15 March 1879.[122] The meeting between Lord Chelmsford and Sir Henry Bulwer took place on 11 March 1879 in Pinetown, then a small town near Durban, now a suburb in the larger Durban conurbation.

I have searched in vain for this particular document in the Pietermaritzburg Archive Repository on two separate occasions and at the Greytown Library, but during my last visit there in 2007 I did come across some material that reflected the substance of the agreement.

The nub of the accord seems to have been set out in a minute written by Bulwer on 15 March, just four days after the Pinetown meeting. Much of the material relates to Lord Chelmsford's recommendation for the raising of a reserve force of levies to supplement those already under the commanders of the Colonial Districts. There is also reference to the matter of the defensive levies crossing the border, which was not to be permitted. This was not true for the NNC, of course, which was under the control of the military authorities:

> The Lt General further considers that the Reserve Force may perhaps be useful in making demonstrations, and it is probable he may desire to use it for that purpose:– for instance, before making advance into the Zulu Country, the Lt General may consider it advisable that the demonstration should be made along our borderline with the view of diverting attention, &c.
>
> The Reserve Force will not be required to cross the border, but it may be required to make a demonstration immediately along the line of border.[123]

There is, however, a caveat, summarised in a circular written by John Shepstone, Acting Secretary for Native Affairs, dated 11 March 1879, the same day as the meeting. It is sufficiently brief as to be quoted in full and is addressed to William Douglas Wheelwright, commanding Colonial Defensive District No. VII. (Umvoti): 'I am directed by His Excellency the Lieutenant-Governor to inform you that should Zulu raids be made into this Colony the Natal Natives are free to pursue the Raiders if necessary, and if they wish to do so, across the Border.'[124]

Thus it seems clear that, while additional levies were to be raised at the request of the lieutenant-general, neither these nor the original defensive border levies were to be permitted to cross the border, even while making demonstrations. The single exception, raised by John Shepstone, was that when Zulu raiding parties crossed into Natal, they could be pursued across the border, provided the levies were prepared to do so.

Chapter 8

After the War

History: a distillation of rumour.

Thomas Carlyle 1795–1881

Lord Chelmsford and Whitehall

After his return to England after the Zulu War, Lord Chelmsford settled down to what he thought would be a quiet life in London. It proved not to be so: for the next several years he was pursued by correspondence from, and publications by, Lieutenant-Colonel Edward Durnford, who was anxious to exonerate his brother Colonel Anthony Durnford, killed at Isandlwana, for his alleged culpability for the disaster.[1] Whilst this correspondence was certainly an irritant, Chelmsford was sufficiently confident in his own position to fend off the accusations that he (Chelmsford) had covered up his own incompetence by blaming Durnford's brother for the Isandlwana disaster.

The same could not be said, however, of Chelmsford's dealings with the government he had served for so long. His allegedly premature withdrawal from the Mahlabathini plain came back to haunt him because much of his correspondence with Sir Garnet Wolseley at that time had been omitted from the official 'Blue Book' (now known as the British Parliamentary Papers, Command Series).[2]

Chelmsford wrote a letter to the Duke of Cambridge in February 1880, requesting that 'an accompanying letter and enclosures' be 'submitted for the consideration of the Right Hon. the Sec. of State for War'.[3] He also canvassed his expectation:

> [that] a searching enquiry may be made into the circumstances attending the mutilation of a most important telegram sent by me to Sir Garnet Wolseley through Major-General Clifford, and which, if the Blue Book be correct, was

published in the latter in that mutilated form for general information, and no doubt reached His Royal Highness in that distorted condition.[4]

The letter he enclosed complained bitterly at the treatment of his correspondence with Wolseley during this period. The nub of his complaint was that some of their correspondence had been omitted from the 'Blue Book':

> As the correspondence now stands it would seem as if my withdrawal of the troops under my command from the immediate neighbourhood of Ulundi, after the successful action of the fourth July 1879, was an event not contemplated by Sir Garnet Wolseley, and as if the responsibility for that step, which, it is alleged, delayed the pacification of Zululand, must rest on my shoulders.

His evidence supporting the application to correct the official record took the form of copies of key correspondence between the two men.[5] Among these documents is a telegram from Chelmsford to Wolseley which, his lordship complained, was 'mutilated and garbled . . . having been apparently so published by General Clifford for general information'.

Chelmsford labelled the first document he produced as 'A'. It is the memorandum he sent to Wolseley from the Mthonjaneni heights on 28 June, the essential detail of which is contained in Chelmsford's covering letter:

> It will be seen that in that memorandum I stated exactly what I proposed to do with the forces under my command and what assistance I expected to obtain from General Crealock's column; it disposes moreover summarily of the false impression which had apparently reached Sir Garnet Wolseley, that I reckoned upon that column joining the one under my command in its advance on Ulundi.
>
> It will be seen also that in that I informed Sir Garnet Wolseley that I did not consider it would be advisable to hold onto the Ulundi valley in the event of our operations being successful.

Document B is Wolseley's reply, in the form of a telegram received by Chelmsford on 'the night of 5th July'. The telegram, Chelmsford pointed out, offered no instructions to be followed in the event of a successful conclusion but only in case of failure, together with indications of Wolseley's own movements in concert with General Crealock's 1st Division on the coast.[6]

Document C was a telegram sent by Chelmsford to Wolseley on 6 July, in which: 'I state my opinion that "a hasty evacuation of the country I now occupy seems to me inadvisable" and I await "further instructions before carrying it out"'. Chelmsford claimed it was 'mutilated and garbled' by General Clifford when a copy was sent to London.[7] These alterations incensed Chelmsford because of their potential for incorrect interpretation, and he went to the trouble of reproducing his original message and that transmitted by Clifford side by side for comparison.[8]

The document is reproduced here exactly as written by Lord Chelmsford.[9]

Mutilated Telegram	Correct Telegram
Page 45, C. 2482.	Substance of telegram dispatched via Landman's drift and PMBurg, to Port Durnford from Lord Chelmsford to Sir G. Wolseley.
From Maj. Gen. Clifford, PMBurg, to Commandant, Cape Town. Friday, July 11, 1879.	Entonjaneni 6 July Your instructions sent through General Crealock received last night. They appear to contemplate of my being forced to retire and probably do not hold good . . .
The following from Lord Chelmsford, the camp at Entonjaneni, to the General Commanding, is published for general information:–	
July 6th. After the severe defeat inflicted on the Zulu army, I have returned to Entonjaneni, as the Zulus having dispersed in all directions, it is not possible to strike another blow at them for the present.	. . . after the severe defeat inflicted on the Zulu army. I have returned to Entonjaneni, as the Zulus having dispersed in all directions, it is not possible to strike another blow at them for the present.
I was also anxious to get the men under <u>canvas</u> again as the nights were cold with heavy dews.	I was also anxious to get the men under cover again as the nights are very cold with heavy dews.
	With your approval I propose to send back 2nd Division to Fort Newdigate with the wounded numbering some 90 odd, and to bring up another convoy of supplies should it be required;
The flying column to proceed towards you via Kwamagwasa and St. Paul's, a strong post being left at the former place, which like all my lines of communication will be garrisoned by troops of the second division.	The Flying Column to proceed to join you via Kwamagwasa and St. Paul's, a strong post being left at the former place which like <u>all other posts</u> on this line of communications will be garrisoned by troops of the second division

Mutilated Telegram	Correct Telegram
The posts I now hold secure the best grass lands in this part of Zululand that were beginning to fail. I expect to be at St Paul's on the 12 July with more than a fortnight provisions and hoped to find Crealock within communicating distance by the old Ondine, Empangeni. The cattle of this force will not live on the sea coast line.	The posts I now hold secure the best grass lands in this part of the country, but these are beginning to fail. A hasty evacuation of the country I now occupy seems to me inadvisable at the present moment, and I await your further instructions before carrying it out. The cattle of this column will not live on the sea coast.
N.B. The words underlined [above] are not to be found in the correct telegram on opposite side.	N.B. The words underlined [above] have been omitted from the mutilated telegram.

In essence, the telegram offers Chelmsford's reasons for the withdrawal, an action which he had foreshadowed in his memorandum of 28 June. It can readily be observed that Clifford's changes drastically altered the sense of Chelmsford's original telegram, and despite the fact that both versions were available to a reader of the Blue Book, a wrong interpretation was almost inevitable. A perfect example of such an interpretation was the quoting of Clifford's inserted words as part of the published criticism of Lord Chelmsford's command by the journalist Archibald Forbes: 'I have returned to Etonganeni, as, the Zulus having dispersed in all directions, it is not possible to strike another blow at them for the present. I was also anxious to get the men under canvas again. The best grass lands are in this part of Zululand, but they are beginning to fail.'[10]

This was not the first time that Clifford had altered Lord Chelmsford's telegrams, a matter to which his lordship had drawn the attention of the Secretary of State for War as early as June 1879:

I have just received your private letter dated 8 May, and cannot conceal from you that it has distressed me very much. I quite feel that you have every right to complain of the baldness of the telegram which was sent regarding the additional three regiments I asked for, but that was not my fault. I send herewith copy of the telegram I sent to General Clifford, and which he altered so as to leave out all the explanation I had put in.[11]

Document D was a copy of a memorandum from Wolseley's military secretary, Lieutenant-Colonel Henry Brackenbury, dated 8 July.[12] He used this memorandum to demonstrate that he had correctly withdrawn to Mthonjaneni because:

It will be seen from this memorandum that I had anticipated Sir Garnet Wolseley's wishes in withdrawing from Ulundi to Entonjaneni; and that my possible move as far as Kwamagwasa was not altogether unexpected as will be seen from the paragraph quoted below:–

'In case you have fallen back with your whole force to or towards Kwamagwasa before you receive this message, you need not to send Brigadier General Wood back towards Entonjaneni, but he may occupy any suitable position near to the place where this message finds him.'

The final exhibit was Lord Chelmsford's reply labelled 'E'. This had been printed in the Blue Book, but was included to show that Lord Chelmsford had valid reasons for his further withdrawal from Mthonjaneni.[13]

Chelmsford's attempt to redress what he clearly saw as an inequitable representation of his actions had positive results but the subsequent corrections proved less than satisfactory. His covering letter, together with the five enclosures, was printed in the next issue of Parliamentary Papers dated June 1880,[14] but much of his letter was excised, as shown in the original holograph. All references to the changes by Major-General Clifford had been removed and, while the telegram was printed in full, it was not in the two-column comparison format that Chelmsford had prepared. Much of the last part of the letter was withheld, with the instruction 'Letter to end here' written in the margin and the remainder crossed through. This omission consisted largely of an account of Chelmsford's stay at KwaMagwasa and the congratulatory telegram sent by Wolseley after the victory at Ulundi. Two paragraphs remained to defend his failure to pursue Cetshwayo:

The chance of capturing Cetywayo in such a country by means of mounted men, without any assistance from the Chiefs or people, was too remote to be taken into consideration; and it now appears that the King left Ulundi the day before the battle, and no-one but his then small following knew in what direction he had gone.

The details of the subsequent long hunt after Cetywayo conducted under Sir Garnet Wolseley's own immediate presence in the neighbourhood, and with all the advantage of assistance from Chiefs and people, show clearly how hopeless it would have been to have attempted it, until such the bodies of mounted men could safely traverse that most difficult and intricate country, not only without fear of molestation from the people, but actually fed and guided by them.[15]

It is clear that Chelmsford acquiesced in the heavy editing of his covering letter because included in his file is an undated note from Adjutant-General

Ellice to the Under-Secretary of State for War: 'I presume it will be unnecessary for me to communicate the contents of your note of the 5th instant to Lord Chelmsford, as his Lordship has consented (see letter enclosed) to the omission of that portion of his letter of the 20th February, which it was not thought advisable to publish.'[16]

The only employment offered to Lord Chelmsford after his return home was the command of the Western District in 1880. He 'asked permission to decline it on account of a limited private income, and also being anxious for an Indian command'.[17] On 1 January 1881, he sent a letter to the Duke of Cambridge, accompanied by a record of his service, in a bid to obtain an Indian command.[18] It is notable that he made mention of his Indian experience several times but did not mention his South African experience once. It ended with the plea: 'At the same time I would wish it to be distinctly understood that I am perfectly prepared to accept any appointment which may be offered to me.' He was never given another command, but was promoted to the substantive rank of lieutenant-general in April 1882.

Having once served as aide-de-camp to Queen Victoria, and retained her loyalty, Lord Chelmsford received the sinecure appointment of Lieutenant of the Tower, which he held from June 1884 to March 1889, and was Gold Stick at court to both Queen Victoria and King Edward VII. He was promoted to full general in December 1888 and finally retired from the army in June 1893. Lord Chelmsford died on 9 April 1905 at the United Services Club after suffering a seizure whilst playing billiards. He was just one month short of his seventy-eighth birthday.

Major Graves v. the Natal Colonist

This paper examines the further events following the disreputable withdrawal of the 2nd Regiment, Natal Native Contingent (NNC) from Eshowe to the Thukela River on 28 January 1879, the politics of which were set out in an earlier paper.[19] It will also be remembered that Major Shapland Graves' account of the withdrawal was reproduced in that paper.

The relevance of the civil case of libel now to be discussed is that the witnesses called provide a unique opportunity to view the inner workings of a regiment of the NNC. In no other instance is such a wide variety of detailed information made available, and the political manoeuvres behind the scenes are no less fascinating. Unfortunately the court evidence is so very substantial, having been given over the four days of the hearing, that it cannot be fully reproduced here so that only the general tenor can be indicated.

Major Graves' name continued to be common currency in the colony for some months after the withdrawal and on 13 September a subpoena was issued to several prominent persons, including Major-General Clifford (Inspector-General, Lines of Communications and Base), Charles Mitchell, (Colonial Secretary of Natal), Commandant Nettleton (commanding the 2nd Battalion, 2nd Regiment, NNC), and one 'Bovey Esquire, now or lately a Captain in the Natal Native Contingent',[20] to appear personally at ten o'clock on 9 October 'in a certain cause now depending in our said Court between Shapland Graves Plaintiff and John Sanderson Defendant, wherein the said Plaintiff claims the Sum of £1000 stg. as damages for Libel.'[21] Sanderson was the proprietor and editor of the *Natal Colonist*.

A belated press announcement was made in an attempt to exculpate Graves but it served mostly to alert the general public to what promised to be an interesting affair:

> Full inquiry has been made by the proper military authorities into the charges recently brought forward by certain newspapers and others against Major Graves. He has been honourably acquitted by the court of inquiry which was held. It was ascertained that the charges against the Major originated through certain statements made by a drunken member of the corps, who was dismissed. Major Graves' Solicitor is suing the *Witness, Advertiser, Colonist*, and *Cape Argus*, for heavy damages for libel in connection with the affair.[22]

In fact no such formal court of inquiry had been held, as will shortly be shown; the clumsy circumstances of the removal of Major Graves from his command earlier in the year were described in the earlier paper.

The libel case lasted for four sitting days: Thursday, Friday and Saturday, the 9, 10 and 11 October, and Monday 13 October. The first three days were taken up with the hearing of witnesses while the last was taken up with counsels' closing arguments, the judge's summing up and the jury's verdict.[23]

The plaintiff's counsel called thirteen witnesses, including Colonel Pearson, commanding the 1st Column, Major Percy Barrow, commanding the mounted men, and Major Graves. Colonel Charles Mitchell, Natal Colonial Secretary, was also briefly called. Of the NNC witnesses, two officers came from Nettleton's 2nd Battalion, one of whom, Captain Shervington,[24] had not been with the column but with Colonel Ely's supply train. Defendant's counsel called no fewer than nineteen witnesses, including the defendant himself, John Sanderson, and Commandant Nettleton, commanding the 2nd Battalion. It is notable that every other NNC witness for the defendant also came from the 2nd Battalion.

During his opening address for the plaintiff, Mr Harry Escombe set out the key issues confronting Major Graves:

The defendant on the 13th day of March 1879, in the said Natal Colonist newspaper, falsely and maliciously printed and published of the plaintiff the words following:– 'I see the gallant winner of the Etshowe Races has returned. Yaas! Couldn't eat fire, so they sent him back to protect the General's lost base. What! Has he gone back to his office? Yaas! Shows moral courage, don't it.' Whereby the defendant meant and conveyed to others the following meaning: 1st. That the plaintiff being such officer as aforesaid, left a place called Etshowe in an enemy's country and raced with his troops sent from Etshowe to the Tugela, to see who could first arrive at a place of safety, and that in such race the plaintiff was the first to arrive at the place of safety. 2nd. That plaintiff was a coward under fire and afraid of fire, and was sent back to Durban because of his cowardice and fear. 3rd. That plaintiff had been guilty of such unsoldierly conduct which made the resumption by him of his duties as protector of immigrants improper. 4th. Defendant in the same newspaper, and on the same date, further falsely and maliciously printed and published of the plaintiff the words following:

'For he who fights and runs away,
May live to fight another day.'

Whereby the defendant meant and conveyed to others the meaning, that plaintiff being a soldier had run away from the enemy.

He next read the plea of the defendant:

The defendant rests his defence in this action on the insufficiency in law to sustain the action of so many of the averments in the declaration as may be proved, and on the following averments of fact and the law relating thereto, or to such thereof as shall be proved:– 1. That the said words in the declaration mentioned, were and are a part of a play, printed and published in the said newspaper in the declaration mentioned, and which said play contained the said words in the declaration mentioned, was and is a fair and *bona fide* comment upon a certain irregular and disorderly march from the Fort Etshowe, in the Zulu country, to the Lower Tugela, of a certain regiment of the Natal Native Contingent, composed of natives of the colony of Natal, and officered by Europeans, then under the command of the plaintiff, and engaged with Her Majesty's troops in military operations against the Zulus, and upon the conduct of the plaintiff, as such commander, during the march, and upon the several matters and premises contained and referred to in the said declaration, and was printed and published by the defendant, as and for such comment, and without any malicious intent or motive whatever.

The method to be adopted in describing the remainder of the hearing will be to examine the most serious matters that were raised in evidence, since to follow the action chronologically would introduce much irrelevant material. The first issue to be reviewed is that of the court of inquiry which was said to have been held, and which was said to have exonerated Major Graves. In his own evidence, Graves testified:

> On the 2nd April, I asked for a Court of Enquiry into the charges which had been made against me in three of the [newspaper] columns. In the letter, I stated that a Court of Enquiry was imperatively necessary to clear away the stigma against my character. I received a reply to the effect that no official report having been sent in against me, no Court of Enquiry was necessary, but that as I intended taking legal proceedings against the columnist, I should have every opportunity of full enquiry.

Thus the statement in the *Natal Mercury* that '[Major Graves] has been honourably acquitted by the court of inquiry which was held' – information which could only have originated from the military authorities – was patently untrue, as was the press announcement quoted earlier.[25]

A second matter of a general nature refers to the withholding of pertinent documentary evidence by the Natal government. This emerges in two places in the evidence. The first is an exchange between counsel for the defendant and Colonial Secretary Mitchell, in which the latter 'declined to produce other letters that had passed because he believed their production would be detrimental to the public service of Natal'. The judge ruled that the Secretary 'could not be compelled to produce the documents'. Mr Escombe, for the plaintiff, asked if Major Graves knew of the existence of 'certain other documents', to which, after some discussion as to whether the witness should answer the question, the Colonial Secretary replied that 'Major Graves did not know of the existence of certain documents in his [Mitchell's] possession relating to the matter.'

The second occasion was the later examination of the defendant, Mr John Sanderson, by his own counsel, in which the following exchange took place:

> Q. Your sense of fairness also prompted you to publish Colonel Bellairs' letter to you with a statement that there was something kept.

A. I do consider, and did consider, that there was an attempt to throw dust in the eyes of the public, because I was satisfied that something had passed contrary to the correspondence which I had published, and which has not been made public to this day.

These two references clearly concern the written request made by Lord Chelmsford to the Colonial Secretary to ask him 'officially whether [Graves] can be spared to go back to his proper position as Protector of Immigrants' as a means of removing him from the command of the NNC regiment.[26]

With regard to the march itself, the first issue related to the command of the withdrawing column. In his written evidence Colonel Pearson stated that he had given no written orders to Major Graves but that Graves 'was senior in command both of the horses and Native Contingent'. This seniority was by virtue of the fact that Graves was still a serving army officer whilst Major Barrow was a volunteer. In such a circumstance, the serving officer was rated senior to those of the same rank who were not.

When the NNC left Eshowe at noon, Barrow and his mounted men were still absent on a reconnaissance, so Graves may well have been unaware that he (Graves) was in command of the whole withdrawal. Major Barrow and the mounted men left Eshowe about 2 p.m. In his own evidence, Barrow stated that his orders were also given verbally and was unequivocal that he 'was placed under the command of no one'. During the march Major Graves was allegedly reminded of his seniority with respect to Major Barrow when the latter declined to march with the NNC. Graves stated:

When [the mounted men] halted, there was an interview between myself and Major Barrow. Up to that time I had not known that he was coming. I asked him to accompany my force to the Tugela. He did not do so. He said that he would wait for me when he had got through the Amatikulu bush as he wanted to get through it before it got dark, and would send back any intelligence that he might receive of the enemy.[27]

It was at this point that Commandant Nettleton is alleged to have reminded Major Graves of his seniority:

I heard afterwards that Commandant Nettleton had asked Major Graves to order Major Barrow to form an advance and a rear guard of mounted men. The Major then said he would request Major Barrow to wait for them at the Amatikulu, and Commandant Nettleton said, 'Don't request, order; you are the senior officer.' The Major requested them to wait at a certain spot.[28]

Major Barrow, however, saw the event differently: 'Nothing was said to me by Major Graves about waiting at some point this side of the Amatikulu bush, nor at any point on the road. I did not indicate to Major Graves any particular point. I said I would halt as soon as I got through the bush.'[29] Thus the NNC and the mounted men retired as two independent commands, although Graves did state in his evidence that: 'I was, as senior officer, to assume the command at Lower Tugela.'

The next matter is the form taken by the march. Major Graves had ordered that all the Europeans were to march together at the front of the column:

> I decided upon this peculiar formation in consequence of the state of discipline, and [the officers'] inability to carry orders to the natives, or to get them to carry them out, at which I had had sad experience at the Inyezane. Besides, before I went into Zululand, it was my opinion that if we were successful the natives would be true to us; but that if the Zulus were successful, it was doubtful whether they would not join them.[30]

> When the officers were withdrawn from their command, the natives all broke up, and the companies ran into one another, and the men who could walk the fastest got in front.[31]

As a result of these actions, the column quickly spread out so that by the time Major Barrow caught up to it, 'there were some natives in front of Major Graves, and the body of non-commissioned officers were with him. I can't say at what distance the natives were ahead. From the rear men to those in front of Major Graves, I should say there was a distance of a mile or more.'[32]

Perhaps the most serious issue during the march, and afterwards, was the behaviour of the non-commissioned officers. It should be noted that while officers were mounted, the European NCOs were on foot and were thus unable to keep up the same pace as their African charges. The result was that, from a very early stage, the NCOs began to tire. Captain Shervington testified that he had been with Colonel Ely's column and that on meeting him a short distance from Eshowe, Major Graves had told him that 'he was to stop every man going down, and tell them that if they did not consider themselves able to march the distance to Fort Tenedos they were to return to Etshowe.'[33] Further on, and after a short break at a water-hole before the Nyezane, some NCOs refused to go on and became insubordinate: 'Witness had a company of natives with him in rear of the non-commissioned officers. The latter all fell out to drink at the waterhole. After waiting some time, he called on them to fall in again, but they refused, stating that they would not fall in for witness or for any — officer.'[34]

Some of the NCOs eventually continued the march while others remained behind. Some officers gave up their horses to those unable to walk and chose instead to walk themselves. Captain Gough, 2nd Battalion, for example, walked the whole distance to the Thukela, while Captain Maclean, 2nd Battalion, walked most of the distance.[35] Corporal James walked all the way by the side of Major Graves' horse.[36]

Major Graves was also alleged to have made an inflammatory statement regarding the recalcitrance of the NCOs although the evidence was often contradictory. Colour Sergeant Leeding gave evidence that he heard Graves say, 'every man for himself'. Richard Hazzard, also an NCO, heard him say: 'If you can't come on, then here's off; every man for himself and God for us all.' Thomas Brown, previously an NCO with the NNC, also stated that Major Graves said: 'Well, I'm off; every man for himself, and God for us all.' The NCO Thornton declared that he heard Captain Maclean say that he had been told that Major Graves said: 'Every man for himself, God for us all, and the devil take the hindermost', but in his own evidence Captain Maclean said only that Lieutenant Spiller had told him that Major Graves had said every man must look out for himself. Captain Hart, however, said that 'the Major's reply "we must go on; every man for himself" was false, and he was prepared to swear that it never occurred.'[37] In his own memoir, Hart chose to gloss over the retirement to the Thukela.[38]

From all of the evidence it is plain that the withdrawal was of a very untidy nature and that some NCOs were insubordinate in their refusal to march. On the other hand many encountered great physical difficulty on a march of more than thirty miles, much of it in the dark, and which was covered by many in about fourteen hours. As has been seen, some men were fortunate enough to be able to ride on the horses of others while their owners walked. NCOs also disposed of their uniforms, weapons and accoutrements in order to lighten their load:

> I saw a man on the road who had only a shirt on. I asked him what he had done with the other things, and he told me that his boots hurt his feet, and he could not wear them, and that the other things had got too heavy to carry. I reported this to Commandant Nettleton. This man had got a mount from the mounted men, and gave it up to someone else as it hurt more to ride than walk.[39]

The problems did not end when the column reached Fort Tenedos on the Lower Drift. A 'round-robin' letter, signed by the officers of the 2nd Battalion, was handed to Major Graves indicating their dissatisfaction with his command and that they wished to become separated from him. Discussing this document Captain Burnside, 2nd Battalion, declared:

> He recollected a paper being signed by the officers of Nettleton's battalion, and addressed to Major Graves. The letter was in Commandant Nettleton's own handwriting. It was sent round to the officers to ask if the officers approved of it. Witness did not approve of it and it was altered to suit the feelings and ideas of the officers. It was then re-copied by Lieutenant James, signed, and sent to Major Graves under cover, and a footnote by Commandant Nettleton.
>
> Mr. Escombe: Was the document the spontaneous act of the officers, or did it come from Commandant Nettleton?
>
> Witness: As he wrote it, I suppose it came from him.
>
> Mr. Escombe: Was there anything in the letter to show Commandant Nettleton's connection with it?
>
> Witness: Nothing.

Burnside subsequently signed the letter but it seems that it was rather through loyalty to Commandant Nettleton than any stronger cause, explaining '[his] reason for signing was because Commandant Nettleton and Major Graves were not on good terms'. This also became evident during Major Graves' own evidence when, under heavy questioning, he became rather incoherent, claiming: 'I don't know that Nettleton was in the Army. He's not in the Army.' (This was perfectly correct, but Nettleton had, in truth, served with some distinction as a civilian volunteer under Lord Chelmsford in the Ninth Frontier War in 1878.[40])

Two other unpleasant incidents also occurred. They both took place at a parade of NCOs of the 2nd Battalion on 7 February after the African troops had left for their homes.[41] During the parade a Sergeant Warren handed a letter to Major Graves 'setting forth the grievances of the non-commissioned officers generally'. Graves continued:

> The salient point of the document was that they wished an enquiry into the march from Etshowe to know what orders or plan was decided upon for the return to the Tugela, and also to inquire for certain comrades of theirs who were supposed to be saved. I informed them in a body of the disposition of the forces, and of what I had done to bring them to the Tugela. I told them after explaining the various points in this document to take it back, consider over it, and if after my explanations they still wished it sent to Lord Chelmsford, I would do so with great pleasure. That document was not brought back to me.

The second incident followed hard on the heels of the first, again described by Major Graves:

During the parade, a drunken non-commissioned officer came on, and on the dismissal of the parade, which followed immediately, the non-commissioned officer called me a coward and threatened to strike those present with his rifle. He was by my orders arrested, disarmed, and placed, I was afterwards informed, in the guard tent of the 99th regiment. I then directed Commandant Nettleton to pay that man up to date on the following morning, and dismiss him from the corps. Commandant Nettleton informed me that he had carried out my orders, and that the non-commissioned officer had expressed contrition for what he had done, and that he was drunk at that time.

A similar version was given by Captain Burnside:

The man who called Major Graves a coward came on parade drunk without his rifle. He was sent back for it, and returned after the men had been dismissed, and going up to Major Graves, he called him a coward. Major Graves took no notice of him, as he was drunk and told him to go away. The same man afterwards came up to witness [Burnside] and insulted him. He had him disarmed and turned out of camp. Subsequently, he heard that Commandant Nettleton had sent to Major Graves for orders to keep him in the guard room all night, and dismissed the next morning. He was one of Nettleton's men and was about the most insubordinate man in the corps during the march down.

Perhaps the most trenchant, and voluble, criticism was offered by a very junior officer of the 2nd Battalion, Lieutenant Hayes.[42] The following exchange occurred during his examination by counsel for the defendant:

Q. What is your opinion as to the manner in which that march was conducted by the officer in command?
A. I do not consider that it was conducted at all.
Q. In what terms would you speak of the march?
A. I have always called it a disgraceful run.
Q. Could the march have been conducted in an orderly manner?
A. I don't see why it should not.
Q. For a disorderly march, who would be responsible?
A. The officer commanding would be directly responsible.

On the last day, after counsel had presented their final addresses and the judge had summed up the case for the jury, the six men retired; a scant eight minutes later they returned with their verdict: 'We find for the plaintiff, £100 damages; and we have to record our conviction that Major Graves has done nothing to forfeit his character as a British officer and a gentleman.'[43] Graves left the court with the cheers of his friends ringing in his ears.

Captain Montgomery's Secret

In late November 1878, a Captain Montgomery was appointed as one of several commandants of the nascent Natal Native Contingent.[44] One week later, his appointment was confirmed as commandant of the 1st Battalion, 1st Regiment, NNC.[45]

There is something of a conundrum about this man because in both announcements of the appointment by the Deputy Adjutant-General, Montgomery was referred to as 'R.P. Montgomery, J.P. Esquire, late 7th Fusiliers . . .' However, in the substantial, and generally very reliable, work on the NNC written by Paul Thompson, the commandant of the 1st Battalion is given the forename 'Alexander'.[46] Since the secret about to be divulged in this paper was that of one Alexander Nixon Montgomery, this is a matter we must first address.

Forenames or their initials seemed to matter little to military officialdom, presumably because the combination of rank, surname and battalion or unit was normally a sufficiently unique identification. In this case, happily, both rank and unit are the same: our man was previously a captain in the 7th (Royal Fusiliers) Regiment. An examination of the officer's record of service reveals that his forenames were indeed Alexander Nixon.[47]

There is also some confusion over Montgomery's birth month, which can be determined as either March or May 1839.[48] In any case, at the time of joining his command in the NNC, he was thirty-nine years of age. Montgomery was the son of Hancock Montgomery, of Bessmont Park, County Monaghan, Ireland and was appointed ensign by purchase in the 7th Regiment of Foot at the age of sixteen years and two months on 1 June 1855.[49] His career with the regiment was unremarkable other than his rapid first promotion: he was made lieutenant in November 1855, still aged sixteen, and then to captain in July 1863 aged twenty-four, his captaincy being also by purchase.[50] After selling his commission in 1872, he migrated to South Africa where he became a military captain grantee of land in Natal.[51] He had a farm near Mid-Ilovo, not far from Pietermaritzburg, which he named 'Ismont'. He was a justice of the peace and involved himself, not very successfully, in local politics. He was, in short, a member of the local gentry.

Montgomery's battalion was one of three assigned to the 1st Regiment under the command of Lieutenant-Colonel Anthony Durnford, whose

Second Column was based at the Middle Drift of the Thukela River. While three companies of Montgomery's battalion had gone off with Durnford to Rorke's Drift and thereafter had taken part in the battle of Isandlwana, the rest of the battalion had remained at its original base at Kranskop. The station was, for the most part, an uninteresting backwater and the officers seem to have spent much of their time in a state of inebriation.[52] Anxious to see action, Montgomery applied for a transfer to a more active unit but was instead transferred out of the NNC in June 1879 to take up a position as commandant of Colonial Defensive District No. 1.[53] This providential posting would offer him protection when some very personal material later became known. As a result, the story of Captain Montgomery's venery was then, and still is, confined to the pages of government correspondence.

On 9 October 1879 the following memorandum was sent to the Colonial Secretary by Mr Marshall, resident magistrate of Pietermaritzburg:[54]

> I enclose these Depositions for the information of His Excellency the Lieut. Governor as Capt. Montgomery holds the appointment of a Justice of the Peace for Pietermaritzburg County and has also acted as Resident Magistrate for the Upper Umkomanzi Div. and was so acting in March 1878.
>
> On Saturday last Capt. Montgomery entered into a Recognizance to Keep the Peace towards Miss Hornby and all Her Majesty's liege subjects for six months, himself in £300 and two Sureties to my satisfaction in £150 each.
>
> I may add that Capt. Montgomery informed me the contents of Miss Hornby's Deposition were not all true. Whether he is going to take any steps in regard thereto I am unable to say at present.

The two depositions were dated 9 September 1879 and had been taken before Mr H.C. Campbell, acting resident magistrate of the City (Pietermaritzburg) Division.

The principal deponent, Miss Jessie Hornby, aged twenty, stated that in March 1877 she had been seduced by Captain Montgomery under threat of his shooting both himself and Miss Hornby during a visit she had made to his home.[55]

Three months later, following the accidental burning of her father's house, she and her mother took temporary refuge in the home of Captain Montgomery, his wife and his daughter Aletha. While out riding with Aletha on 22 June, she was again seduced by Montgomery after having sent Aletha away. The result of this union was the birth of a male child on 29 March 1878. The child was subsequently taken away from her by an African servant of the captain, who took it to his homestead some twenty miles away. There the child lived for a period of four months, after which it died, perhaps of a bronchial infection.

Since that time Miss Hornby had returned to her father's restored house and Captain Montgomery had continued to have intercourse with her on a number of occasions, frequently preceded by violent rages and threats to expose her and thus ruin her reputation. The last occasion occurred in May 1878 after she had recovered from the birth of her child:

> When near New Leeds he became violent but nothing occurred until I reached my father's house, where he again had intercourse with me. I resisted by imploring him not to, but he always overcame my resistance by holding before me the consequences of exposure. A bed was made for him in the sitting room and he forced me to come to him. I was sobbing in the morning and when my mother questioned me, he told her that he had had improper intercourse with me long before that, but upon one occasion only. My mother was greatly agitated upon hearing this, and when he left, I told her all except about the child.

Jessie had written to him, and also told him personally, that she did not wish the relationship to continue and after this event she had no further physical relations with him. He was not to be deterred, however, and persistently pursued her in front of relatives and friends, frequently giving vent to violent bouts of anger.

In April or May of 1879 she saw him in Pietermaritzburg, where he told her that he had come down with the full intention of destroying or disgracing her and that he had purposely left his pistols behind as he feared to trust himself with them.[56] He even offered marriage to her 'when he became free from his present wife'.

> . . . I did not see him again until Sunday the 7th of June [1879], when thinking I had slighted him, he was very violent in his language. He then told my sister Mrs. Robert Woolley, with whom I was walking in the street, of the circumstance of the birth of the child. He said to her in a sneering way when Mrs. Woolley objected to his seeing me alone 'Perhaps you are not aware she has had a child by me.' He appeared to regret having said this to Mrs. Woolley, for he immediately said to her violently and earnestly 'You had better take your solemn oath to God never to mention a word about it.'

Shortly afterwards Montgomery went to her father's house and demanded to see her despite the presence of her two sisters. On being refused, he broke a window with his riding crop to gain entry to the house and subsequently smashed the door of a bedroom in which she had sought refuge. Then, seizing her in his arms, he made her sit on the bed with him. 'This was my last interview with him although he has made an attempt to see me. From first to last, I have yielded to him both from fear of personal violence as well as from fear of exposure. I am in daily fear of him. My fears place me completely in his power.' One must presume that it was on the evidence of his violence and continued harassment that he was compelled to give his 'Recognizance to Keep the Peace' towards Miss Hornby.

The second deposition, by Mr Robert Woolley, Miss Hornby's brother-in-law, was also made on 9 September 1879 and confirmed virtually all of what Jessie had herself deposed, although much of what he said was hearsay. He had been unable to provide any support for either his sister-in-law or his wife at the time, being militarily engaged 'at the front'.[57] He called for a 'warrant for the arrest of Alexander Nixon Montgomery'.

These depositions were of such a serious nature as to require them to be brought to the attention of the lieutenant-governor of the colony, Sir Henry Bulwer, to which his response on 13 October 1879 was as follows:

This is a very sad story.

I think the Attorney General should see these papers in case there should be anything required to be done by the public authorities in the matter. The concealment of both the birth & the death of the child may perhaps under some investigation [be] necessary. As for Captain Montgomery, I do not know what position he holds towards the Government exactly as a Justice of the Peace.

If the enclosed statements are correct, he of course ought no longer to hold the Commission of the Peace. But I perceive that he should have an opportunity of being heard.

On 20 October, M.H. Gallwey, the Attorney-General, presented the results of his enquiries in a memorandum:

I am informed that a singcon [*isangoma*=witch-doctor?] and a nurse were in attendance at the birth of this child and the child lived for some time.

Neither was there any disposing or burying of the child, which is necessary to prove on trial for concealment of birth.

The Act of Registration of Births and Deaths 1867 has been contravened as neither the birth nor the death were registered.

The Registration District where the birth should have been registered was Richmond (Umkomanzi).

The child was born on the 29th March 78.

The Resident Magistrate is the Registrar of Births there.

Capt. Montgomery was acting Resident Magistrate for that District from 9th March to April 22, 1878.

The child was illegitimate; the mother was the person bound to give the information and she omitted to register the birth and is liable to the penalty imposed by the Law £5.0.0.

The Registrar does not appear to have committed any contravention of the Law for which he is criminally responsible.

Instructions have been now issued to institute an enquiry into this alleged death of the child.

In any case, no step to remove Capt. Montgomery from the Commission of the Peace should be taken until he has had afforded to him the opportunity of offering some explanation in this sad case.

Meanwhile, investigations concerning the child proceeded apace; on 21 October the Attorney-General was able to forward a minute, dated 19 September, from the resident magistrate of the City Division to the effect that: 'No registration of either the birth or the death of any child of Miss Jessie Hornby has been registered in the Register books at my office.' He also requested a similar investigation by the resident magistrate of the Umkomanzi District, wherein lay Captain Montgomery's residence:

You will be pleased again to note the contents of the above minute.

There is evidence as to the birth 29/3/78 of the child referred to, but although the infant's said to have died about four months after birth, there is no evidence as to the fact. I have therefore to request that you will institute the necessary enquiries with a view to ascertain whether the child has actually died & if it has, to place on record the circumstances connected therewith.

You will be pleased to communicate to me the result of your investigation. The child is said to have been removed from its mother by Captain Montgomery, of Ismont in your Division.

On 22 October, in response to Mr Gallwey's letter, Sir Henry Bulwer noted:

If there is any truth in this story – and from the Resident Magistrate's minute I am led to infer that Captain Montgomery does not deny the truth, in part, of the story – I do not see how Captain Montgomery's name can be kept on the

Commission of the Peace. If any further proceedings are being taken, and if, pending those proceedings, any action taken by the Government in this matter could appear to prejudge the case, it would perhaps be better to await the result of the proceedings for that reason. But if no proceedings are being taken, then I do not think our action might be delayed.

One might be surprised to note that the principal cause for the governor's concern was Montgomery's occupying the position of justice of the peace rather than the circumstances of any innocent party or the concealment of a child's birth and death. Then, as now, however, any contentious issue first required the elimination of any potential embarrassment for the government of the day. Finally, on 31 October 1879 came a covering letter from Mr Gallwey:

I enclose for His Excellency's information the report of the Res. Magistrate Upper Umkomanzi, together with certain depositions made before him by some natives in reference to the death of a white child handed over to their custody and to its death while at their kraal.

The most important witness in the case, the native who it is said acquired the child from Capt. Montgomery, and his directions concerning the child, is absent, and his return is uncertain. No action can be taken in the interim.

Bobiana, the head of the homestead to which the child was taken, gave his deposition together with two of his wives, Manyoni and Mandowanina. The most important witness, the African servant Uhai, who had taken the child to his homestead, had run away and his statement was not taken until some time later.[58]

Uhai said that he was in the service of Captain Montgomery and that some eighteen months earlier, when Montgomery was at Richmond, he was in the house when the child was born. About a week later he was instructed by Montgomery to take the child to his homestead and have it cared for. 'I told him that none of the women were suckling children and that they were old; he said I was to take it and that he would see that the people of the kraal did not make a fuss about it.'

Montgomery, Jessie and 'another small girl' (perhaps Aletha Montgomery) brought the baby in a wagon. The child had some clothes and a bottle of milk. It was subsequently fed with cow's milk and Uhai reported to Jessie from time to time as to the child's progress. It apparently caught a cold and Jessie gave Uhai some medicine for it. 'The child died shortly afterwards from the cough on its chest. I took it up to Captain Montgomery at Ismont but as he was not at home and not wishing to tell any body about it, I buried it myself. Captain Montgomery was at Richmond when Miss Jessie gave me the child. He was at Richmond.'

On the evidence of Uhai's statement the child's death could not have been the result of inanition since he said it was fed with cow's milk. It is more likely that the death was the result of an infection due to the unhygienic conditions in which the infant found itself.

This account must end without a satisfactory conclusion. We do not know if Captain Montgomery made any statement in his own defence, although he had admitted the substance of the charges. It seems that no criminal or other charges were brought against either Montgomery or Miss Hornby, or any other person. The matter was quietly laid to rest but Montgomery's professional career in the colony was finished.

Jessie Hornby did find a husband: she finally married James Baily Cox in Pietermaritzburg. She died at the age of seventy-eight years at Eshowe on 6 May 1938.[59] The executor of her estate was one Arthur Ray Hornby and one might speculate that this man was her brother. If this were the case, then it establishes a sibling relationship between Jessie, George and Arthur Hornby and links them all closely to Montgomery.

Montgomery died insolvent on 19 January 1911, aged seventy-one years . He had continued to live on his property Ismont but at the time of his death it was owned by his son-in-law:

> The farm 'Ismont' was mortgaged in favour of the late Mr Quentin Hogg under Bond dated 24th September 1884 for £2500.
>
> For many years the Income derived from the farm has been wholly insufficient to meet the Interest, but in view of the settlement which was exacted by Mr Quentin Hogg in favour of the informant . . . the interest has not been exacted but the informant has cultivated in part the farm 'Ismont' and has provided a home for the Deceased.[60]

So Captain Montgomery took his secret to the grave.

The Zulu Use of Drugs

The Zulu warrior has always been renowned for his great courage; it is this, perhaps more than any other quality, that has seemingly set him apart from his fellow Nguni. His often irrational bravery, though, may not be entirely a Zulu characteristic: the later Zulu people were, after all, originally fashioned from many other Nguni people beyond the area now known as

KwaZulu-Natal. But they were not, in truth, any braver than their fellows, a Zulu chief freely admitting after Isandlwana: 'You know what we are, when we once give way and run. There is no stopping us to fight the pursuer.'[61]

It would be reasonable, therefore, to suggest that what eventually developed into the concept of courage was brought about by fear of failure during the formative years of the Zulu army under the tutelage of King Shaka, whose pitiless drive created the Zulu nation. Furthermore, the *esprit de corps* that he, and later rulers, infused into each regiment by constant competition through dancing displays (*ukugiya*) and boasting must have contributed to each individual's store of valour.[62]

There is, however, a less well-known agency that may also have played a vital role in the development of his courage: the pre-battle process of doctoring. This was an extended procedure lasting several days, during which the warriors were subject to various techniques all aimed at the infusion of the extra spirit which was needed to ensure victory. There was, first, the psychological build-up as the communal will was whipped to its greatest intensity through inter-regimental rivalry, as each regiment was singled out to promise the execution of great deeds, accompanied as always by the *giyas* of individual warriors as their promises were sworn.[63]

There were also physical methods by which various medicinal concoctions were administered. Some of these may simply have had an emetic, or even a placebo, effect but others are known to have affected the mind by more direct means. 'One of the ingredients was probably *dagga* (or Indian hemp), for many of those who drank it said that "it made their hearts feel very bad indeed, full of cruelty and daring".'[64]

The use of the drug known as *dagga* was extremely common in much of Africa since well before the arrival of the Europeans.[65] In south-east Africa, the plant *cannabis sativa* had been widely grown and used for hundreds of years and was well known to the Zulu people, to whom it was known as *intsangu*.[66] Allen Gardiner, writing in 1836, said: 'Dacca is indigenous through-out the country . . .'[67]

However, there is little doubt that they also took cannabis in the form of snuff, whether or not it was mixed with tobacco:

Tobacco composed of the dried leaf of the wild hemp, here called Dacca, is in general use, and has a very stupifying effect, frequently intoxicating . . . Though smoking is comparatively confined to few, all, without exception, are passionately fond of snuff, and no greater compliment can be offered than to share the contents of a snuff calabash with your neighbour.[68]

The other, and to them less potent, drug was tobacco, which arrived on the scene some time later: '. . .tobacco is frequently seen growing wild near deserted villages, but it has, I understand, been imported.'[69] Du Toit quotes Andrew Smith as saying: 'Those that can procure both tobacco and dakka [sic] smoke the former and snuff the latter.'[70]

The presence of *dagga* during 1879 is attested by an officer talking about his Natal Pioneers: 'They love snuff dearly; but, instead of sneezing, it makes them yawn. A few of them smoke tobacco, and a native compound called *dagga*; the latter has an exciting effect similar to liquor . . .'[71]

There is also no doubt that, while used as an everyday indulgence, it came into its own during outbreaks of violence. 'It was especially at times of war that men would smoke the herb . . .'[72] This might explain the break taken by the Zulu reserve after Isandlwana which, after crossing the Mzinyathi River, rested for a while on a nearby hill where it sat down and took snuff before going on to attack Rorke's Drift.[73] It has also been assumed that because of the haste with which the battle of Isandlwana was precipitated, the doctoring process was incomplete. This may not necessarily be so since it is clear that such drugs were often taken to war, this process being described by Mpatshana: 'Many who went to fight took the precaution of carrying drugs in their medicine-bags with which to *ncinda*[74] . . . They were not doctored by an *inyanga*.'[75]

Just what were the effects of the drug? These largely turned upon the personalities of the individual user and are reported as varying from 'extraordinary hilarity' to 'moroseness', as well as making them feel physically strong and increasing their confidence.[76] We have already noted above that it had a tendency to increase 'cruelty and daring'. According to Bryant, its effect was more aggressive still: quoting David Livingstone, he says, 'This pernicious weed has a strong narcotic effect, causing even a species of frenzy.' (He also noted that our word 'assassin' is a derivative of the Arabic *hashishin*, as applied to a 'medieval military body in Syria whose members were notorious for their murderous exploits when under the influence of *hashish*'.[77])

There are, however, signs of the use of more sophisticated drugs: hallucinogens. For some little time the writer has been interested in bizarre references in Zulu reports of their war-time activities. These illusions infer peculiar states in individuals often coupled with visions very reminiscent of hallucination. The following is an example from the battle of Isandlwana: 'It appeared to me as though the soldiers were opening the breeches of their rifles with their feet in their haste to reload.'[78] This might, at a stretch, be seen as the men doing the same thing as Colonel Durnford did in the donga to clear jammed rifles: 'Sometimes, as he passed amongst us, one or another of the men brought him his gun with the old cartridge sticking, and he dismounted, and taking the gun between his knees, because of having only one hand with strength in it, he pulled the cartridge out and gave back the gun.'[79]

Alternatively, they may have been kicking the breech lever of a jammed rifle to achieve the same end. The following is, however, quite unequivocal, occurring at Khambula:

> Further the Zulus asked me 'what it meant that at the beginning of a battle so many white birds, such as they had never seen before, came flying over them from the side of the Whites? And why were they attacked also by dogs and apes, clothed and carrying firearms on their shoulders?' One of them even told me that he had seen four lions in the laager. They said, 'The Whites don't fight fairly; they bring animals to draw down destruction upon us.'[80]

Similar illusions were seen at the battle of Ulundi:

> 'Myself and three friends determined to get nearer to your guns than any other Zulu, and we did' – three or four men actually got within thirty yards of one face of the square – 'Then my three friends were killed – pouf – pouf – pouf' – and he imitated the bullets whistling, and his head bobbing – 'so I ran away; but you had put iron palings in front of your men, and hung red coats on them, so that our guns could not kill them. I saw myself the bullets fall off them.' Everyone said this same thing; it was only that which beat them.[81]

What could account for these strange observations? It seems clear that they were the result of at least some warriors having consumed, by some means, more than just cannabis: some form of hallucinogenic substance.

The most common vehicle for such substances is the edible mushroom. These are not the common field variety but rather a different species which contain a specific substance known as *psilocybin*. This substance is known to exist in several varieties of mushroom such as *psilocybin cubensis* and *psilocybin semilanceata*, among others. The oral consumption of these mushrooms, either raw or dried, can bring about prolonged episodes of perceptual distortion. These begin about thirty minutes after ingestion and can last from three to six hours depending upon the amount consumed. It is thought that the intensity of the effect is greater when fresh, rather than dried, fungi are used. It is also known that the use of the mycelium, that is, the underground network of fine white filaments that constitute the vegetitive part of the fungus, is almost as effective as the fungus itself.

An alternative method of preparation is to grind the dried fungus into a fine powder and ingest it through the nose in much the same way as snuff is taken. It may, therefore, be presumed that if these fungi were used, as seems likely, the powder was mixed with the more usual snuff, providing a potent combination of tobacco, cannabis and the hallucinogen. Such a combination is not entirely unknown in modern times, the exposure of American troops in Vietnam to cannabis and cocaine being well documented. While the species of mushroom previously described may not be specifically located in Zululand, mushrooms with a similar effect were almost certainly to be found there.

The Zulu use of drugs, then, is well documented and there is every reason to believe that they were used, not just for recreational purposes, but for the more serious purpose of making war.

Notes

Chapter 1

1 A.R. Skelley, *The Victorian Army at Home*, London: Croom Helm, 1977, Appendix II, p. 310, indicates that in 1877 no less than 76 per cent of recruits *entering* the Army were able to read and write. This should be qualified by his figure of only 42.7 per cent of those *in* the army in 1878 who could read and write (p. 89).

2 Colonel G. Hamilton-Browne, *A Lost Legionary in South Africa*, London: T. Werner Laurie, 1912, p. 247.

3 Frederic Augustus Thesiger (1827–1905) began his military career in 1844 when he obtained a commission by purchase in the Rifle Brigade. He bought a transfer into the more acceptable Grenadier Guards in 1845 and found regular promotion thereafter. By 1868 he was a major-general, having served in the Crimea, Sardinia, Turkey and India. It is fair to note that much of his service life was spent in administration, acting as Deputy Adjutant-General and Quartermaster-General in most of his postings. On the death of his father on 5 October 1878 Thesiger succeeded to the title as the second Baron Chelmsford. This latter name has been used throughout to avoid confusion.

4 Hamilton-Browne, p. 99.

5 Hamilton-Browne, p. 100.

6 General Order No. 213, dated 3 December 1878, *Times of Natal*, 6 December 1878; see Keith Smith, *Local General Orders Relating to the Anglo–Zulu War 1879*, Banora Point, NSW: privately published, 2005.

7 General Order No. 9, dated 12 January 1879, *Times of Natal*, 15 January 1879.

8 It is only fair to point out that another observer also gives Hamilton-Browne the role of commandant at Sihayo's homestead: Charles Norris-Newman, *In Zululand with the British Throughout the War of 1879*, London: W.H. Allen, 1880, re-published London: Greenhill, 1988, p. 39.

9 General Order No. 203, dated 21 November 1878, and No. 209, dated 28 November 1878. The same situation obtained with Commandant Graves of the 2nd Regiment.

10 'Distribution of Troops in the Field', *Times of Natal*, 20 January 1879.

11 Hamilton-Browne, p 109. There is some support for the sunstroke incident: it was reported in the *Natal Witness*, 16 January 1879.

12 Daphne Child (ed.), *The Zulu War Journal of Colonel Henry Harford*, Pietermaritzburg: Shuter and Shooter, 1978, p. 14.

13 Child, pp. 14–15.

14   Hamilton-Browne, p. 128. See also Norris-Newman, p. 49 and Child, p. 23.

15   Hamilton-Browne, p. 107. Note that unlike the Amabhele, the Izigqoza was not a clan but a Zulu faction associated with Cetshwayo's half-brother Mbuyazi kaMpande. The latter was killed in the battle of Ndondakuzuka in December 1856 fighting Cetshwayo's Usuthu faction.

16   Hamilton-Browne, pp. 106–7.

17   No. 9 Company, under Captain James Lonsdale, was on piquet duty near the 'Conical Koppie' (Amatutshane) about 2,500 metres to the left front of the camp.

18   Hamilton-Browne, p. 106.

19   His appointment was announced in General Order No. 213, dated 3 December 1878.

20   Hamilton-Browne, p. 115.

21   Hamilton-Browne, p. 118.

22   Hamilton-Browne, p. 119.

23   Hamilton-Browne, p. 119.

24   Child, p. 24.

25   Norris-Newman, pp. 49–50.

26   John Maxwell, *Reminiscences of the Zulu War*, ed. L.T. Jones, Cape Town: Universities of Cape Town Libraries, 1979, p. 1. Jones suggests that the document was written for publication because a similar account by Maxwell appeared in the *Natal Witness*, Christmas edition, 1884, p. ix.

27   Hamilton-Browne, pp. 119–20. Note, however, that he says he did not emerge from the valley until late afternoon.

28   Maxwell, p. 1.

29   F.W.D. Jackson, *Hill of the Sphinx: The Battle of Isandlwana*, London: Westerners Publications Ltd, 2002, p. 60.

30   TNA, WO33/34, p. 273: Enclosure 1 in No. 96, dated 2 February 1879.

31   Times noted with '?' reflect my own speculation.

32   Hamilton-Browne spells his name 'Hays' but see General Order No. 213, dated 3 December 1878, *Times of Natal*, 6 December 1878, in which 'P. W. Hayes' is appointed captain in the 1st Battalion, 3rd Regiment, NNC. There was no officer named 'Hays' in the 3rd Regiment, although there was a Captain Hay in the 1st Battalion, 1st Regiment, NNC.

33   Hamilton-Browne, pp. 127–36, *passim*.

34   Stafford wrote two other narratives in 1938 and 1939, the first of which was notarised by a solicitor, but they are very muddled accounts. Copies may be found in KCAL and the Talana Museum, Dundee, South Africa.

35   At least Davies had the good sense also to write an official report shortly after the battle; see TNA, WO 33/34, Enclosure 2 in No. 96.

36   Julian Whybra, Essex Curriculum Extension Project No. 4: The Battle of Isandhlwana, Essex County Council, 1984.

37   Oliver Ransford, 'The Gaudy Cloth', *Blackwood's Magazine*, No. 34, 1954, pp. 10–12.

38   See Julian Whybra, 'Zabange – Pure Fiction', *Soldiers of the Queen*, No. 58, 1989, pp. 23–7.

39   Donald R. Morris, *The Washing of the Spears: The Rise and Fall of the Zulu Nation*, London: Jonathan Cape, 1965, revised edition London: Pimlico, 1994, p. 617.

40 Both incidents are described in TNA, WO 33/34, Enclosure 1 in No. 101.

41 The emphasis is mine.

42 War Office (Intelligence Branch), *Narrative of the Field Operations Connected with the Zulu War of 1879*, comp. Captain J.S. Rothwell, first published London: H.M.S.O., 1881, re-published London: Greenhill, 1989, p. 32.

43 General Sir Horace Smith-Dorrien, *Memories of Forty-Eight Years Service*, London: John Murray, 1925, p. 10.

44 Stafford, *Natal Mercury*, 22 January 1929: 'Survivor's Desperate Ride for Life'.

45 Captain Henry Hallam Parr, *A Sketch of the Kafir and Zulu Wars: Guadana to Isandhlwana*, London: Keegan Paul, 1880, p. 202.

46 TNA, WO 33/34, Enclosure 3 in No. 96.

47 TNA, WO 33/34, Enclosure in No. 69: Court of Enquiry; see also BPP, C. 2260: Evidence to Court of Enquiry, item B, Enclosure 2 in No. 13.

48 BPP, C. 2260: Evidence to Court of Enquiry, item A, Enclosure 2 in No. 13.

49 TNA, WO 33/34, Enclosure 4 in No. 96.

50 Davies says that they left Rorke's Drift at 7.30 am and arrived at the camp two and a half hours later: TNA, WO 33/34, Enclosure 2 in No. 96.

51 TNA, WO 33/34, Supplementary Report, Enclosure 10 in No. 96.

52 TNA, WO 33/34, Enclosure 4 in No. 96.

53 TNA, WO 33/34, Enclosure 4 in No. 96. The name is misprinted as Private E. Dillon; see Norman Holme, *The Noble 24th: Biographical Records of the 24th Regiment in the Zulu War and the South African Campaign 1877–1879*, London: Savannah, 1999, p. 196.

54 Peter Hathorn and Amy Young, *Henderson Heritage*, Pietermaritzburg: privately published, 1972, p. 229: letter dated 26 January 1879.

55 TNA, WO 33/34, Enclosure 4 in No. 96.

56 Regimental Museum of the Royal Welsh: W. Penn Symons, *The Battle of Isandlwana and the Defence of Rorke's Drift 1879*, manuscript account.

57 Letter to Colonel Home, Intelligence Branch, War Office, quoted in Sonia Clarke, *Zululand at War*, Houghton: Brenthurst Press, 1984, p. 148. This section of the letter was dated 28 March.

58 TNA, WO 32/7750: Entry for 6 May, Quartermaster General's Department, 1st Division Diary, 27 Apr–21 May.

59 Dava Sobell, *Longitude The True Story of a Lone Genius Who Solved the Greatest Scientific Problem of His Time*, London: Fourth Estate Ltd, 1998, pp. 167–8. Even then France insisted on using its own Paris meridian until 1911.

60 *Natal Almanac, Directory and Yearly Register, 1879*, Pietermaritzburg: P. Davis & Sons, 1878, p. 4.

61 The most famous of these is now used to mark midnight on New Year's Eve in Times Square, New York but noon is still reported daily in Sydney, Australia, by lowering a ball on a mast on Observatory Hill, which overlooks the harbour.

62 *Natal Almanac*, p. 4.

63 One must assume that the time of the gun changed between 1875 and 1879.

64 Frances E. Colenso, assisted by Lieutenant-Colonel E. Durnford, *History of the Zulu War and Its Origin*, London: Chapman & Hall Ltd, 1880, pp. 81–2.

65 *Natal Almanac*, p. 5.

66 Evan S. Connell, *Son of the Morning Star*, San Francisco: North Point Press, 1984, p. 304.

67 Wrist watches, of course, had not yet been developed.

68 Lord Chelmsford would have described himself as having only moderate means and was certainly not regarded as being wealthy. See for example, his handwritten record of his military service in the National Army Museum (NAM), 6807/386-18-34: 'Asked permission to decline [a home command] on account of limited private income . . .'

69 The writer is indebted to Dr Matthew Read, Assistant Curator of Horology, National Maritime Museum, Greenwich, UK, for advice regarding the state of time measurement in 1879.

70 A. Taylerson, 'Watches Issued to British Armed Forces 1870–1970', Part 1, in *Horological Journal*, September 1995, pp. 293–6.

71 Taylerson, pp. 293–6.

72 Major-General W.C.F. Molyneux, *Campaigning in South Africa and Egypt*, London: MacMillan, 1896, p. 154.

73 See F.W.D Jackson, 'Isandlwana 1879: The Sources Re-Examined', first published in the *Journal for Army Historical Research* Vol. 43, Nos 173, 175 and 176, 1965, re-published in pamphlet form RRW Museum, p. 16.

74 Lieutenant W. Vause: Vause diary, KCAL, KCM 16020; Lieutenant H.D. Davies: WO 33/34, Enclosure 2 in No. 96.

75 Lieutenant Cochrane, TNA, WO 33/34, Enclosure 1 in No. 80.

76 Also confirmed in the report of Lieutenant H.D. Davies, TNA, WO 33/34, Enclosure 2 in No. 96.

77 I have omitted the brief stop to talk to Lieutenant Chard, RE, on the way, but this would have been for only a few minutes.

78 Wolseley, p. 34.

79 One might assume that they arrived about 11.15, since Grant, Johnson and Trainer all say that they left with Durnford about fifteen minutes or so after arriving (TNA, WO 33/34, Enclosure 4 in No. 96).

80 KCAL, KCM 16020: Vause diary.

81 Morris, p. 246.

82 Cornelius W. de Kiewiet, *The Imperial Factor in South Africa: A Study in Politics and Economics*, London: Frank Cass, 1965, p. 129.

83 The issue of Boer land claims, and temporising by the British and colonial governments in resolving the issue following many Zulu complaints, is dealt with at length in Colenso, chapter IX.

84 BPP, C. 2220, Appendix II, Enclosure 1 in No. 1: Report of the boundary commissioners.

85 Richard Cope, *Ploughshare of War: The Origins of the Anglo-Zulu War of 1879*, Pietermaritzburg: University of Natal Press, 1999, p. 214.

86 Shepstone did not respond with his comments on the findings until 17 October 1878 (BPP, C. 2222, Enclosure 10 in No. 19). The response of Attorney-General M.N. Gallwey was not much earlier, being dated 27th September 1878 (BPP, C. 2222, Enclosure 7 in No. 19).

87 See the examples cited in E.H. Brookes and C. de B. Webb, *A History of Natal*, Pietermaritzburg: University of Natal Press, 1965, p. 129.
88 BPP C. 2222, No. 119: Hicks Beach to Frere, 21 November 1878.
89 Colenso, p. 196.
90 BPP, C. 2222, No. 111, p. 305: Frere to Hicks Beach, 6 October 1878.
91 BPP, C. 2220, No. 40, p. 124: Bulwer to Hicks Beach, 9 August 1878.
92 BPP, C. 2220, No. 40, p. 124: Bulwer to Hicks Beach, 9 August 1878.
93 BPP, C. 2220, Enclosure in No. 89, p. 266: Cetshwayo to Bulwer, 24 August 1879.
94 BPP, C. 2220, No. 105:p. 280 Frere to Hicks Beach, 30 September 1878.
95 See, for example, BPP, C. 2222, Enclosure 13 in No. 19 and Enclosure 1 in No. 43.
96 Very compelling arguments against the cynical terms of the ultimatum are set out in Colenso, chapter XI.
97 BPP, C. 1137 p. 9: Report of the expedition sent by the government of Natal to install Cetywayo as King of the Zulus, para. 35.
98 BPP, C. 1137 p. 14: Report of the expedition, para. 60.
99 BPP, C. 1137 p. 16: Report of the expedition, para. 67.
100 BPP, C. 1137 p. 16: Report of the expedition, para. 68.
101 Colenso, p. 239.
102 Colenso, p. 239.
103 BPP, C. 2260, Enclosure 2 in No. 6, p.46: Memorandum dated 16 January 1879.
104 C. de B. Webb, 'Lines of Power: The High Commissioner, the Telegraph and the War of 1879', *Natalia*, Vol. 8. December 1993, pp. 31–7.
105 Webb, 'Lines of Power', pp. 34–5.
106 BPP, C. 2222, No. 11, p. 17: Frere to Hicks Beach, 11 November 1878.
107 BPP, C. 2222, No. 19, p. 23: Frere to Hicks Beach, 16 November 1878 and received 19 December 1878.
108 TNA, CO 879/14, No. 164: 'Memorandum on the Zulu Question', dated 19 March 1879, from Sir Michael Hicks Beach to Sir Bartle Frere, p. 21.
109 Hicks Beach to Lord Beaconsfield, 3 November 1878, quoted in Jeff Guy, *The Destruction of the Zulu Kingdom: The Civil War in Zululand, 1879–1884*, Pietermaritzburg: University of Natal Press, 1994, p. 49.
110 Based upon those listed in Colenso, pp. 237–8.

Chapter 2

1 Morris, p. 323.
2 Knight, *The Sun Turned Black*, pp. 50 and 53. Cf. John Young, *They Fell Like Stones: Battles and Casualties of the Zulu War, 1879*, London: Greenhill, 1991, p. 25: 'Having taken up positions before the main kraal of Sihayo, at about 7.15 a.m., the British were challenged by a Zulu'; p. 27: 'A reserve force comprised of the 2nd Battalion of the 24th (2nd Warwickshire) Regiment of Foot took possession of a secondary kraal, only to find it deserted.'
3 *Narrative of the Field Operations*, p. 26.
4 *Narrative of the Field Operations*, p. 27.
5 Child, p. 21.
6 Norris-Newman, p. 38.

7 Patrick Coghill (comp.), *Whom the Gods Love*, Halesowen: privately published, 1968, p. 103. Also quoted in Frank Emery (ed.), *The Red Soldier: Letters from the Zulu War, 1879*, London: Hodder and Stoughton: 1977, p. 73. Lieutenant Coghill also seems to have confused the two battalions of the NNC.

8 Laband, *Lord Chelmsford's Zululand Campaign*, p. 60: Lord Chelmsford to Sir Bartle Frere, 12 January 1879.

9 Norris-Newman, pp. 40–1.

10 RMRW, File 2002-25: Letter from Colour-Sergeant William Edwards, 1/24th Regiment, to his wife.

11 Norris-Newman, p. 41.

12 G. Paton, F. Glennie, and W. Penn Symons, *Historical Records of the 24th Regiment from its Formation in 1689*, London: Simkin, Marshall, Hamilton, Kent & Co., 1892, p. 228.

13 Hamilton-Browne, p. 105.

14 Hamilton-Browne, p. 105.

15 Child, p. 19.

16 Map 2830BC: Rorke's Drift in the topographic 1:50000 series published by Chief Directorate: Surveys and Mapping, Mowbray, South Africa, 1981.

17 Child, p. 21.

18 Bertram Mitford, *Through the Zulu Country: Its Battlefields and People*, first published London: Keegan Paul, Tench, 1883, re-published London: Greenhill, 1992, pp. 48–9.

19 Coghill, p. 104 and Emery, p. 73.

20 RMRW: Penn Symons, The Battle of Isandlwana MS.

21 RMRW, Letter of Colour-Sergeant Edwards.

22 TNA, WO 33/34, No. 55: Report from Lord Chelmsford to the Secretary of State for War, 14 January 1879.

23 Coghill, p. 104.

24 Thomas B. Jenkinson, *Amazulu: The Zulus, Their Past History, Manners, Customs and Language*, London: W.H. Allen, 1882, re-printed New York: Negro Universities Press, 1969, p. 95. They thus had a close relationship to the Hlubi.

25 Jenkinson, p. 146 and note.

26 BPP, C. 2242, No. 20: Memorandum by Lord Chelmsford, 16 January 1879. The 'swamps' would have been at the crossings of the Batshe and Manzimnyama streams.

27 Named for Major Wilsone Black, 2/24th Regiment, who commanded the party which 'took' the hill on the return of Chelmsford's force to the devastated camp on the evening of 22 January.

28 The Zulu name is given in C. de B. Webb, 'A Zulu Boy's Recollections of the Zulu War', *Natalia*, No. 8, December, 1978, p. 6.

29 This was the area designated by the British as 'Matshana's Stronghold'.

30 A feature noted in their work: Ron Lock and Peter Quantrill, *Zulu Victory: The Epic of Isandlwana and the Cover-up*, London: Greenhill Books, 2002, p. 99.

31 *Regulations: Field Forces in South Africa*, Pietermaritzburg: HMSO, 1878, para. 75.

32 For example, *Narrative of the Field Operations*, p. 48. Cf. John Laband, *Kingdom in Crisis: The Zulu Response to the British Invasion of 1879*, Manchester: Manchester University Press, 1992, p. 74, and Jackson, *Hill of the Sphinx*, pp. 65–6.

33 Julian Whybra, 'Contemporary Sources and the Composition of the Main Zulu Impi, January 1879', *Soldiers of the Queen*, No. 53, June 1988.

34 For example, Nzuzi (*Natal Mercury*, 22 January 1929) refers only to Koza and Ntuli, which really represents [Ntshingwayo kaMahole] K[h]oza and [Mavumengwana kaNdlela] Ntuli.

35 The particle 'ka' has the same function in Zulu as 'son' in English names and therefore tells us that Ntshingwayo's father was named Mahole.

36 Mbonambi warrior, quoted in Mitford, pp. 25–6.

37 Statement of Sidungi, quoted by Ucadjana, BPP, C. 2260, p. 63.

38 C. de B. Webb and J.B. Wright (eds), *The James Stuart Archive of Recorded Oral Evidence Relating to the History of the Zulu and Neighbouring Peoples*, Pietermaritzburg: Killie Campbell Africana Library and University of Natal Press, Vol. III, 1982, p. 307: Mpatshana kaSodondo. (Hereafter *JSA*.)

39 Zulu deserter from the Nokhenkhe regiment, in TNA, WO 33/34, Enclosure 2 in No. 80.

40 Mbonambi Warrior.

41 Account of Mehlokazulu kaSihayo, *Natal Witness*, 2 October 1879.

42 Mehlokazulu.

43 Zulu deserter.

44 Shilahla, in BPP, C. 2454: Sub-enclosure 1 in No. 34, p. 100.

45 Uguku, quoted in Colenso, pp. 410–13. He also implies that the Umkhulutshane were there, based on the occupation of the Nodwengu *ikhanda*, but this is unlikely as they would have been too old.

46 Mbonambi warrior.

47 Umtegalalo, in BPP, C. 2260, Enclosure 2 in No. 12. See also Umtyololo in TNA, WO 33/34, Enclosure 3 in No. 72, which is the same evidence.

48 Nzuzi, *Natal Mercury*, 22 January 1929.

49 Webb and Wright, *A Zulu King Speaks*, p. 35.

50 Sidungi of the Nokhenkhe, as told to Ucadjana, BPP, C. 2260, p. 63.

51 Gumpega Gwabe: *Natal Mercury*, 22 January 1929. He also mentions the 'Ingwengwe', which is probably the Indluyengwe.

52 Otherwise known as the iMpunga, *JSA*, Vol. IV, p. 72 – Mtshapi kaNoradu: 'The Umpunga regiment is the same age as the Mxapo; they were incorporated into one another.' There was probably only a small number of this regiment present because most of them fought at Nyezane on the same day: Zimema, *Natal Mercury*, 22 January 1929. Cf. Ian Knight, 'A Note on the umPunga', *Soldiers Of The Queen*, No. 33, July 1983.

53 This was the *isithakazela*, or nickname, for the Ukhandempemvu Regiment. Mcijo will be used throughout unless specifically used in a quotation.

54 The Mbonambi warrior said that the Uve formed a part of the Ngobamakhosi. See also the evidence of JSA, Vol. III, p. 296: Mpatshana, who says the same thing.

55 This regiment was also known as Amashishi, or Amatishe as it was referred to by Nzuzi (*Natal Mercury*, 22 January 1929.) See also Eileen Jensen Krige, *The Social System of the Zulus*, Pietermaritzburg: Shuter and Shooter, 1977, p. 406.

56 This regiment is identified by Krige as stationed at Nodwengu with the Mbube and as being the same age: p. 406, n. 2.

57 See Appendix I.

58 *JSA*, Vol. III, p. 315: Mpatshana.

59 A.T. Bryant, *Olden Times in Zululand and Natal*, London: Longmans, Green, 1929, p. 645.

60 Krige, p. 405, n. 4

61 H.B. Fynney, *The Zulu Army and Zulu Headmen*, Pietermaritizburg: published by Direction of the Lieutenant-General Commanding, 1879, p.9.

62 *JSA*, Vol. V, p. 82: Mtshapi. See also Krige, p. 405.

63 Krige, p. 406, shows them as part of the Amaphela, born 1826–31. In this she was following R.C.A. Samuelson, *Long, Long Ago*, Durban: Knox Print & Publishing, 1929, pp. 239–45 and Bryant, *Olden Times*, pp. 645–6.

64 C.M. Doke and B.W. Vilikazi, *Zulu–English Dictionary*, Johannesburg: Witwatersrand University Press, 1958, p. 754: umSikaba.

65 *JSA*, Vol. IV, p. 84: Mtshapi. There were a number of *izigaba* in a regiment.

66 *JSA*, Vol. IV, p. 85: Mtshapi; the illustration shows there were two *izinhlangothi* in a regiment, representing the 'side', left or right, in the *ikhanda* where they were based.

67 Fynney, p. 8.

68 Samuelson, p. 236.

69 Nor is the Umhlanga mentioned by Ian Knight in his comprehensive list in *The Anatomy of the Zulu Army: From Shaka to Cetshwayo, 1818–1879*, London: Greenhill, 1995, pp. 261–8.

70 Krige, pp. 404–7.

71 *JSA*, Vol. III, p. 301: Mpatshana kaSodondo.

72 This term was used to describe the 'side', left or right, of the *ikhanda* where they were accommodated.

73 *JSA*, Vol. III, p. 165: Mkando ka Dhlova.

74 *JSA*, Vol. IV, p. 85: Mtshapi, illustration. See also Fynney, p. 4.

75 *JSA*, Vol. IV, p. 84: Mtshapi.

76 *JSA*, Vol. III, pp. 315–16.

77 *JSA*, Vol. III, pp. 315–16.

78 Fynney, p. 4. Cf. Norris-Newman, p. 254.

79 Shilahla.

80 Fynney, p. 4.

81 Shilahla says that he fought at Nyezane with the Mxapho. See also Zimema, *Natal Mercury*, 22 January 1929.

82 Cetshwayo kaMpande, quoted in Webb and Wright, *A Zulu King Speaks*, p. 36.

83 John Laband, and Paul Thompson, *Kingdom and Colony at War*, Cape Town/Pietermaritzburg: North & South Press, 1990, p. 37. See also Webb and Wright, *A Zulu King Speaks*, pp. 35–6.

84 Mehlokazulu says that there were fifteen *amaviyo* of the Mxapho at Isandlwana. Shilahla, a member of the regiment, does not mention it.

85 Using seventy men per *iviyo*.

86 JSA, Vol. III, p. 165: Mkando gives twenty *amaviyo* in this regiment.

87 This includes the Mbube.

88 Mbonambi warrior, Nokhenkhe deserter and Uguku. Fynney places the Nokhenkhe in the right centre but this is unlikely.

89 Mbonambi warrior.

90 Uguku, a member of the Mcijo.

91 KCAL, Symons Papers, MS 1072: Statement of Mhoti.

92 Mehlokazulu.

93 Nzuzi, *Natal Mercury*, 22 January 1929. We have already noted that this regiment was treated as part of the Ngobamakhosi.

94 Mbonambi warrior and Zulu deserter. Fynney said that they formed 'the right of the Zulu left wing'.

95 Umtegalalo, Nokhenkhe deserter and Uguku.

96 Mbonambi warrior, Fynney says that they 'formed the extreme left'.

97 Uguku.

98 Umtegolalo.

99 Uguku.

100 Mehlokazulu.

101 TNA, WO 33/34, Enclosure 1 in No. 96: Report of Commandant Hamilton-Browne.

102 TNA, WO 33/34, Enclosure 2 in No. 96: Report of Lieutenant H.D. Davies, Edendale Troop, NNMC.

103 Norris-Newman, p. 254, based on a record of conversations with Cetshwayo on board SS *Natal*. Morris, p. 363, states that part of the Undi brigade and the Dloko were late and bivouacked in a second ravine a mile behind the large one. I have thus far seen no primary evidence to support this assertion.

104 F.W.D. Jackson and Julian Whybra, 'Isandhlwana and the Durnford Papers', *Soldiers of the Queen*, No. 60, March 1990.

105 Jackson and Whybra.

106 Sir Reginald Coupland, *Isandhlwana: Zulu Battle Piece*, first published London: William Collins, 1948, re-published London: Tom Donovan, 1991, p. 79.

107 R.W.F. Droogleaver, *The Road to Isandlwana: Colonel Anthony Durnford in Natal and Zululand*, London: Greenhill, 1992, p. 196. Droogleaver dates the Zulu movement to the Ngwebeni one day earlier than it actually took place. They spent the night of 20/21st north of iSiphezi Hill and moved to their Ngwebeni valley bivouac on the afternoon and evening of the 21st.

108 Laband, *Kingdom in Crisis*, p. 75. See also the same author, *The Rise and Fall of the Zulu Nation*, London: Arms and Armour, 1997, p. 219 and Knight, *The Sun Turned Black*, p. 103.

109 Jackson, 'Isandlwana: The Sources Re-Examined', p. 22. Jackson is surely here referring to the upper Ngwebeni Valley?

110 KCAL, Wood Papers, KCM 89/9/32/1: Letter from Inspector George Mansel of the Natal Mounted Police to Edward Durnford, Colonel Anthony Durnford's brother, dated 1 November 1879.

111 Ron Lock, *Blood on the Painted Mountain: Zulu Victory and Defeat, Hlobane and Kambula, 1879*, London: Greenhill, 1995, p. 48. Lock is in error in identifying Colonel Edward Durnford as Anthony's father. Although they shared the same forename, the Edward in question was Anthony's brother, as the Mansel letters make clear.

112 TNA, WO 33/34, Enclosure 2 in No. 80: Evidence of a Zulu deserter of the Nokhenke Regiment.

113 Mehlokazulu kaSihayo, *Natal Witness*, 2 October 1879.

114 These dispositions are shown quite precisely on the map in Laband, *Kingdom in Crisis*, p. 77.

115 Lock and Quantrill, *Zulu Victory*, p. 151.

116 Jackson, *Hill of the Sphinx*, p. 1.

117 Jackson, *Hill of the Sphinx*, p. 25. The map on p. 30 is rather more ambiguous.

118 These have been edited and annotated by Jackson and Whybra in 'Isandhlwana and the Durnford Papers'.

119 The maps were drawn by Captain T.H. Anstey and Lieutenant C. Penrose, Royal Engineers, in November 1879 and were published in the original *Narrative of the Field Operations*.

120 This was one of the most advanced vedettes: *Narrative of the Field Operations*, p. 30 and note.

121 KCAL, Wood Papers, file 32, KCM 89/9/32/1: Inspector George Mansel, Natal Mounted Police, to Colonel Edward Durnford, 1 November [1879].

122 Trooper Barker in Reverend John Stalker, *The Natal Carbineers*, Pietermaritzburg: P. Davies & Sons, 1912, p. 99.

123 Lock and Quantrill, *Zulu Victory*, p. 133.

124 Barker in Stalker, p. 99.

125 There is ample evidence that many groups of warriors were observed wandering around on the plateau on the morning of the 22nd.

126 This vedette may well have been replaced by Captain Barry's No. 5 Company, 2/3rd Regiment, NNC, which acted as a piquet there on that day.

127 Mehlokazulu and Zulu deserter. See also: Umtegalalo (BPP C. 2260, Enclosure 2 in No. 12), Mbonambi warrior (Mitford, pp. 25–6.), Nzuzi.

128 As expounded by Droogleever, p. 196; the Zulu, and perhaps even the British, were quite ignorant of the forthcoming phenomenon.

129 Mehlokazulu.

130 TNA, WO 33/34, Enclosure 1 in No. 80: Lieutenant W.F.D. Cochrane, transport officer to Colonel A. Durnford, supplementary report. Cochrane is clear that the advancing Zulu were both to their front and to their left. This is confirmed by a warrior of the Uve regiment, who describes how his regiment left the bivouac to confront Durnford's force. See the account of Nzuzi and also TNA, WO 33/34, Enclosure 2 in No. 96: Lieutenant H.D. Davies: 'We looked up to the ridge on our front.'

131 This map is not reproduced in the recent reprint of the *Narrative of the Field Operations*. A copy is to be found in the Talana Museum, Dundee, KwaZulu-Natal.

Chapter 3

1 The proposition was originally conveyed to me by Ron Lock at a discussion at the home of Nikki van der Heyde in Durban in 2001.

2 Lock and Quantrill, *Zulu Victory*.

3 This matter is argued in the earlier paper.

4 Morris, p. 360.

5 See, for example, Laband, *Kingdom in Crisis*, p. 80; Knight, *The Sun Turned Black*, p. 209.

6 Jackson, 'Isandlwana 1879'. In the thirty-seven years since this admirable article was written, Jackson has 'seen nothing that has significantly altered [his] previous interpretation', and continues to hold the same view on this matter. Jackson, *Hill of the Sphinx*, p. 1.

7 TNA, WO 32/7387: Barton's own description of his function, given in his report supporting the award of the Victoria Cross to Private Wassall.

8 Most writers describe Hamer as a 'civilian commissariat officer', which is probably attributable to the words 'Engaged in the commissariat by Colonel Durnford' introducing his letter to his father (NAM, reference 6807-386-8-14). An announcement in General Order No 20, dated 29 January 1879, states 'Mr. Hamer, storekeeper, pay increased to 10s per diem, from 6th December, 1878.' (*Times of Natal*, 31 January 1879.)

9 *Narrative of the Field Operations*, p. 33.

10 TNA, WO 33/34, Enclosure 1 in No. 91: Lieutenant C.H. Raw, Native Mounted Contingent.

11 NAM, reference 6807-386-8-14: Hamer. The underscore of the word 'Ants' is in the original.

12 TNA, WO 33/34, Enclosure 2 in No. 91: Nyanda, Native Mounted Contingent.

13 TNA, WO 33/34, Enclosure 2 in No. 80: Zulu deserter.

14 Suggested by Fynn, in 'My Recollections of a Famous Campaign and a Great Disaster', KCAL, KCM 98/69/13/5.

15 Cornelius Vijn, *Cetshwayo's Dutchman* (tr. and ed. J.W. Colenso) first published London: Longmans, Green, 1880, re-published London: Greenhill, 1988, pp. 30-31. This is implicitly confirmed by Cetshwayo himself: see Webb and Wright, *A Zulu King Speaks*, p. 34.

16 See, for example, the evidence of Mpitimpiti, who says, 'We had come by way of Nqutu and at the spot called Matsheni, where the cliffs and huge boulders hid us, we gathered in the dark of the night on Jan. 21, 1879.' (KCAL, Newspaper Cuttings No. 32, Page 1F.)

17 TNA, WO 30/129: Lord Chelmsford to General Ellice, 11 April 1879: 'My orders to that officer were distinct, that he was to return to camp after completing his reconnaissance, and I was much vexed at my orders not being attended to.'

18 TNA, WO 33/34, Enclosure 1 in No. 101: Report of Major C.F. Clery, staff officer to Colonel Glyn.

19 BPP, C. 2260, Enclosure 2 in No. 12, p. 102: Umtegelalo; Mbonambi Warrior: Mitford, p. 25; Nzuzi: *Natal Mercury*, 22 January 1929; Zulu deserter.

20 For details of doctoring, see the paper The Zulu Use of Drugs in chapter 8.

21　Quoted in Alan F. Hattersley (ed.), *The Later Annals of Natal*, London: Longmans, Green, 1958, p. 161.

22　TNA, WO 33/34, Enclosure 1 in No. 72: Statement of Lieutenant-Colonel J.N. Crealock, assistant military secretary to Lord Chelmsford.

23　Lock and Quantrill, *Zulu Victory*, pp. 168–9. This is based on Barker's account in Stalker, p. 99.

24　I agree that Barker was on Qwabe. Lock and Quantrill argue that Whitelaw was on Nyezi Hill rather than Ithusi, the former being still further east across the plain than Qwabe (*Zulu Victory*, p. 165), but see Stalker, p. 99: '. . . before we had gone far we saw Zulus on the hill we had just left, and others advancing from the left flank where two other videttes, Whitelaw and another, had been obliged to retire from.'

25　This was the catalyst for the Lock and Quantrill response in the form of their paper known as 'The Missing Five Hours'.

26　Lieutenant-Colonel Mike Snook, *How Can Man Die Better: The Secrets of Isandlwana Revealed*, London: Greenhill, 2005, pp. 149–50.

27　Snook, p. 150.

28　Snook, p. 156.

29　Stalker, p. 99. Snook does not quote this extract, or any other; nor does he offer notes as to the sources for his statements.

30　Mehlakazulu: *Royal Engineer Journal*, 2 February 1880, pp. 23–4.

31　Circling their horses to signal sighting the enemy.

32　Barker notes that, by this time, their attempts to retrieve their vedette posts had failed.

33　Stalker, pp. 99–100.

34　TNA, WO 33/34, Enclosure 3 in No. 96: Higginson. See also *Narrative of the Field Operations*, p. 31.

35　KCAL, KCM 16020: Vause diary.

36　Higginson.

37　Jackson, *Hill of the Sphinx*, p. 28.

38　Wolseley, p. 72.

39　A good horse can, of course, gallop at a faster rate but here we are talking about African Basotho ponies, which were known for their endurance rather than speed.

40　KCAL, KCM 98/69/13/5: Fynn Papers: My Recollections of a Famous Campaign.

41　The identification of Fynn's 'cock's comb' feature with Ithusi Hill was made by Lock and Quantrill, *Zulu Victory*, in the photograph on p. 99.

42　KCAL, KCM 89/9/81/23 and 24. The maps were the subject of an article by the writer: see Keith Smith, 'The Annotated Maps of Isandlwana', in *Soldiers of the Queen*, No. 130, September 2007, reproduced in the next chapter.

43　Royal Engineers Museum, ref. 4901.44.12: Durnford Papers.

44　Jackson and Whybra, 'Isandhlwana and the Durnford Papers'.

45　Personal correspondence with authors Lock and Quantrill.

46　The underscore is in the original.

47　Inserted in pencil above 'Undi Corps' are the words 'and Qikazi battalion' (Ugqikazi was an alternative name for the Dloko: see Krige, p. 406).

48　This is clearly the origin of Jackson's notion of the Zulu bivouac.

49 Nokhenke deserter: TNA, WO 32/7713; Mhoti: Symons Papers, KCAL; Mbonambi warrior: Mitford, pp. 25–9; Nzuzi: *Natal Mercury*, 22 January 1929; Uguku: Colenso, p. 410; Mehlakazulu: *Royal Engineer Journal*, 2 February 1880, pp. 23–4.

50 Stalker, p. 99, account of TroopeBarker.

51 Lock and Quantrill, *Zulu Victory*, pp. 168–9.

52 Gumpega Gwabe of the Mcijo regiment: *Natal Mercury*, 22 January 1929.

53 *JSA*, Vol. III, p. 301: Mpatshana, 'We had no Sundays in Zululand; what we went by was the waning of the moon'.

54 Mbonambi warrior.

55 Uguku: Colenso, p. 410.

56 KCAL, MS 1072, Symons papers: Mhoti of the Ngobamakhosi regiment.

57 Mehlokazulu: *Natal Witness*, 2 October 1879.

58 Captain Essex, WO 33/34, p. 237; BPP C. 2260, p. 82: Court of enquiry.

59 Nzuzi.

60 Lieutenant-Colonel Edward Durnford, *Isandhlwana: Lord Chelmsford's Statements Compared with the Evidence*, a pamphlet published in London, 1880. The officer was probably Colonel Evelyn Wood.

61 Coupland, p. 83.

62 C.T. Binns, *The Last Zulu King: The Life and Death of Cetshwayo*, London: Longmans, 1963, pp. 127–8.

63 RMRW: Penn Symons, *Battle of Isandlwana*.

64 *Natal Almanac*, p. 13. Data for first and last light provided on internet site www. fliteguide.co.za/Forum.Useful_Information/, accessed 5 June 2002.

65 I am indebted to Dr Steve Bell of HM Nautical Almanac Office, Didcot, UK, for information about the eclipse. See also *Natal Almanac*, p. 5, which gives the time of the eclipse at Pietermaritzburg as 2.29 p.m.

66 BPP, C. 2260, Enclosure 2 in No. 13: Evidence of Major Clery to court of enquiry.

67 *Oldham Weekly Chronicle*, 26 April 1879: Account of 1939 Drummer William Sweeney, 2nd Battalion, 24th Regiment.

68 See the earlier paper 'A Question of Time', in which the accounts are identified.

69 Davies says that they left at 7.30 am. I have used a fast walk for Durnford's speed, based on Wolseley's rate 'not to exceed than 4 miles per hour' (Wolseley, p. 72).

70 A time used by the *Narrative of the Field Operations*, p. 32 and Jackson, *Hill of the Sphinx*, p. 20. See also a discussion of the time taken to travel from Rorke's Drift to Isandlwana, and the return, in the paper 'A Question of Time' in chapter 1.

71 Erskine: *Times of Natal*, 26 February 1879.

72 TNA, WO 33/34, Enclosure 3 in No. 101: Statement of Captain C. Nourse. See also BPP, C. 2260, Enclosure 2 in No. 13.

73 TNA, WO 33/34, Enclosure 2 in No. 96: Davies.

74 KCAL, KCM 16020: Vause diary.

75 The times for this event vary widely, even as impossibly early as 9 a.m. (Private Bickley, TNA, WO 33/34, Enclosure 4 in No. 96). Brickhill, quoted in Hattersley, p. 151, taken from the *Natal Magazine*, September 1879, says 11 (although one might argue that he confused this with Lieutenant Vause's departure). Cf. Davies

(TNA, WO 33/34, Enclosure 2 in No. 96), who says they left half an hour before Durnford.

76 NAM, 6807-386-8-14: Account of James Hamer.

77 TNA, WO 33/34, Enclosure 1 in No. 91: Raw.

78 TNA, WO 33/34, Enclosure 2 in No. 96: Davies.

79 Who ordered Cavaye out has been argued by a number of writers, e.g. French, p. 148: '[Cavaye's deployment] was done at Col Durnford's order.' This merely echoes Lord Chelmsford's own words in his undated notes on the findings of the court of enquiry, quoted in Laband, *Lord Chelmsford's Zululand Campaigns, 1878–1879*, Stroud: Army Records Society/Alan Sutton Publishing, 1994, p. 96. The contrary view may be given by Captain Alan Gardner, evidence to the court of enquiry (TNA, WO 33/34, Enclosure in No. 69; also BPP, C. 2260, Enclosure 2 in No. 13). See also Gardner's supplementary report: (TNA, WO 33/34, Enclosure 2 in No. 7; BPP, C. 2260, Enclosure 2 in No. 12). These both state that Pulleine sent Cavaye, but it might still have been at Durnford's behest.

80 TNA, WO 33/34, Enclosure 4 in No. 96: Statement of Private E. Wilson (incorrectly named as Dillon).

81 Philip Gon, *The Road to Isandlwana: The Years of an Imperial Battalion*, London: A.D. Donker, 1979, p. 227, says it was 'an easy climb', and estimates fifteen minutes, but this seems too fast for a steep uphill march of nearly a mile.

82 Times of 10.30 a.m. (Private Trainer) to 11.00 am (Privates Grant and Johnson) are given (TNA, WO 33/34, Enclosure 4 in No. 96).

83 TNA, WO 33/34, Enclosure 1 in No. 80: Cochrane, supplementary report. The troops were the Edendale troop under Lieutenant H.D. (Harry) Davies and Hlubi's baSotho under Lieutenant Alfred F. Henderson.

84 Times for the departure are given as 11: *Narrative of the Field Operations*, p. 33 and 11.15: Grant and Johnson. Davies says: 'About half an hour after Raw and Barton [left], Colonel Durnford rode up, telling us to mount our men and follow him . . .'

85 TNA, WO 33/34, Enclosure 1 in No. 80: Cochrane.

86 Young, p. 49.

87 Nourse said that he had 248 men, but this was almost certainly an error (TNA, WO 33/34, Enclosure 3 in No. 101). Davies gives a figure of 120 men; Young estimates 240 men for both of the companies of NNC in Durnford's command.

88 Stalker, p. 99: account of Trooper Barker.

89 TNA, WO 33/34, Enclosure 4 in No. 96: Johnson.

90 TNA, WO 33/34, Enclosure 4 in No. 96: Johnson and Trainer.

91 TNA, WO 33/34, Enclosure 4 in No. 96: Grant says six kilometres (or four miles).

92 To maintain a cohesive narrative, details of calculations have been placed in an appendix, 'Notes on Time Calculations', later in the section; see item 1 therein.

93 TNA, WO 33/34, Enclosure 2 in No. 96: Davies.

94 TNA, WO 33/34, Enclosure 1 in No. 80: Cochrane, supplementary report.

95 TNA, WO 33/34, Enclosure 2 in No. 96: Davies.

96 See 'Notes on Time Calculations', item 2.

97 See 'Notes on Time Calculations', item 3.

98 TNA, WO 33/34, Enclosure 2 in No. 96: Davies.

99 TNA, WO 33/34, Enclosure 1 in No. 80: Cochrane, supplementary report.

100 Barker in Stalker, p. 100.
101 Barker in Stalker, p. 99.
102 *Narrative of the Field Operations*, p. 33.
103 Mitford, p. 26: Mbonambi warrior.
104 Lieutenant H.L. Smith-Dorrien, letter to his father dated 25 January 1879 in French, pp. 98–101.
105 See 'Notes on Time Calculations', item 4.
106 TNA, WO 33/34, Enclosure 2 in No. 96: Davies.
107 TNA, WO 33/34, Enclosure 1 in No. 80: Cochrane, supplementary report.
108 TNA, WO 33/34, Enclosure 1 in No. 80: Cochrane, supplementary report.
109 Colenso, p. 410: account of Uguku.
110 TNA, WO 33/34, Enclosure 2 in No. 96: Davies.
111 TNA, WO 33/34, Enclosure in No. 69: Lieutenant Curling, RA: evidence to the court of enquiry.
112 TNA, WO 33/34, Enclosure 1 in No. 80: Cochrane, supplementary report.
113 TNA, WO 33/34, Enclosure 1 in No. 80: Cochrane, supplementary report.
114 TNA, WO 33/34, Enclosure 2 in No. 96: Davies.
115 *Natal Colonist*, 28 February 1879: account of Jabez Molife. See also the Royal Engineers Museum, Durnford Papers, reference 4901.44.2.
116 TNA, WO 33/34, Enclosure 2 in No. 72: Gardner, supplementary report.
117 TNA, WO 33/34, Enclosure 2 in No. 96: Davies. See also TNA, WO 33/34, Enclosure 1 in No. 80: Cochrane, supplementary report.
118 TNA, WO 33/34, Enclosure 3 in No. 96: Higginson.
119 TNA, WO 33/34, Enclosure 3 in No. 96: Higginson.
120 TNA, WO 33/34, Enclosure 3 in No. 96: Higginson.
121 Jackson, *Hill of the Sphinx*, p. 28.
122 TNA, WO 33/34, Enclosure 1 in No. 91: Raw.
123 NAM, 6807/386-8-14: Hamer.
124 TNA, WO 33/34, Enclosure 2 in No. 72: Gardner, report, in which he gives the time as between 1 and 2 p.m.
125 *Narrative of the Field Operations*, p. 33.
126 TNA, WO 33/34, Enclosure in No. 69, attachment A: Essex.
127 TNA, WO 33/34, Enclosure 4 in No. 96: Private Bickley witnessed both incidents.
128 KCAL, KCM 16020: Vause diary.
129 Essex says five minutes but it may have been longer.
130 TNA, WO 33/34, Enclosure in No. 69, attachment A: Essex.
131 TNA, WO 33/34, Enclosure in No. 69, attachment A: Essex.
132 TNA, WO 33/34, Enclosure in No. 69, attachment B: Curling.
133 *Natal Mercury*, 22 January 1929: Captain W.H. Stafford.
134 Hamilton-Browne, p. 131.
135 TNA, WO 33/34, Enclosure in No. 69, attachment B: Curling.
136 TNA, WO 33/34, Enclosure 1 in No. 96: report of Hamilton-Browne.
137 TNA, WO 33/34, Enclosure in No. 69, attachment B: Curling.
138 RMRW: Penn Symons, The Battle of Isandlwana.
139 BPP, C. 2454, Sub-enclosure p. 182: Statement of Lieutenant A. Milne, RN.
140 BPP, C. 2260, Enclosure 2 in No. 12: Colonel J.N. Crealock.

141 BPP, C. 2260, Enclosure 2 in No. 12: Colonel J.N. Crealock.

142 Hattersley, p. 153: Brickhill.

143 TNA, WO 33/34, Enclosure 4 in No. 96: Wilson (erroneously named Dillon).

144 TNA, WO 33/34, Enclosure 2 in No. 96: Davies.

145 Hattersley, p. 154: Brickhill.

146 Hamilton-Browne, p. 131. Hamilton-Browne should have said 'left of the camp' from his viewpoint. The use of cattle by the Zulu, presumably the column's own oxen, to screen their advance is not mentioned in any other account and may be the result of Hamilton-Browne's propensity to add 'local colour'.

147 TNA, WO 33/34, Enclosure 2 in No. 72: Gardner, report.

148 KCAL, MS 1072, Symons papers: Mhoti.

149 TNA, WO 33/34, Enclosure in No. 70: report of Lieutenant Chard.

150 Morris, p. 392.

151 TNA, WO 33/34, Enclosure in No. 70: Chard.

152 Binns, p. 137.

153 TNA, WO 32/7387: Account of Private Westwood, 80th Regiment, serving with the Mounted Infantry.

154 TNA, WO 33/34, Enclosure in No. 69, attachment A: Essex.

155 Times of Natal, 3 February 1879: Account of Conductor Foley.

156 Narrative of the Field Operations, p. 38.

157 Narrative of the Field Operations, note on p. 43.

158 As related to Norris-Newman, p. 59.

159 Statement of Commandant Lonsdale, in an account by H.G. Mainwaring, written 22 January 1895 in Cairo and quoted in Holme, p. 199.

160 TNA, WO 33/34, Enclosure 1 in No. 96: Hamilton-Browne.

161 Snook, p. 285.

162 The word 'idler' does not imply indolence. It was originally a Royal Navy expression used to identify the men who worked normal 'daylight' hours, as opposed to the majority of the crew who worked four-hour watches. In this context, it meant non-military men such as wagon-drivers, conductors, etc.

163 Higginson (TNA, WO 33/34, Enclosure 3 in No. 96) gives a distance of 6.4 kilometres (four miles), Cochrane (TNA, WO 33/34, Enclosure 1 in No. 80) says eight kilometres (five miles), and also that the Zulu attacking the horsemen were easily able to keep up with them, suggesting quite a low speed over very difficult ground.

164 Davies (TNA, WO 33/34, Enclosure 2 in No. 96) says twenty-four kilometres (fifteen miles).

165 Jackson, Hill of the Sphinx, p. 47.

166 Times of Natal, 26 February 1879: Erskine.

167 This distance would have been completed mostly at a walk, since the horses would have had hard use by this time.

168 Gardner, Hamer, Erskine, Higginson and Wilson respectively. Higginson apparently spent some time in the river assisting Melvill; Wilson spent at least part of his journey on foot and so would have travelled more slowly.

169 Narrative of the Field Operations, p. 48, footnote. As adjutant, one might expect Melvill's watch to be reliable and accurate.

170 Durnford, Isandhlwana.

171 A warrior of the Uve, quoted in Colenso, p. 344.
172 Jackson, *Hill of the Sphinx*, p. 47.
173 Estimate for a mix of canter and a slower gait. Wolseley, p. 72, said that a horse could trot easily at about 13.5 kilometres (8.5 miles) an hour.
174 Estimated speed of Zulu advance with which Durnford's men would have kept pace.
175 TNA, WO 33/34, Enclosure 1 in No. 80: Cochrane: 'between 5 and 6 miles'; TNA, WO 33/34, Enclosure 2 in No. 96: Davies: 'about 3½ miles'.
176 Morris, p. 329.
177 A brisk walking pace is nearly five kilometres (three miles) an hour.
178 See, for example, the quotations in Knight, *The Sun Turned Black*, pp. 137–8.
179 Laband, *The Rise and Fall of the Zulu Nation*, p. 226. See also Knight, *The Sun Turned Black*, p. 137 and Droogleever, p. 230. Strangely, Mitford, p. 28, n. 1, had it right.
180 *Natal Almanac*, p. 5.
181 *Natal Almanac*, p. 5.
182 I am indebted to Dr Steve Bell of HM Nautical Almanac Office, Didcot, UK, for this information.
183 Mitford, p. 28: Mbonambi warrior.
184 Mitford, p. 28, n. 1.
185 Mitford, p. 31: Nokhenke warrior.
186 C. de B. Webb, 'A Zulu Boy's Recollections', p. 10.
187 KCAL, KCM 89/9/32/10: letter from Inspector George Mansel, to Lieutenant-Colonel Edward Durnford.
188 KCAL, MS 1072, Symons Papers.
189 Gon, p. 228.
190 Email to the author from Major Martin Everett, Curator, RMRW, 2 May 2003. The emphasis is mine. I have subsequently seen the diary for myself and can confirm these details.
191 TNA, WO 33/34, Enclosure 5 in No. 72: Commandant Schermbrucker to Colonel E. Wood, 23 January 1879.
192 Interview with Sergeant Booth, *County Express*, 9 April 1898.
193 George Mossop, *Running the Gauntlet*, first published London: Thomas Nelson, 1937, re-published Pietermaritzburg: G.C. Button, 2nd edition, 1990, p. 71.
194 Holme, pp. 377–8. Some of the units cited by Holme would not have been in the firing line, being bandsmen or other specialists.
195 Droogleever, p. 214, says that it was about three hundred yards. P.S. Thompson, *The Natal Native Contingent in the Anglo-Zulu War 1879*, Pietermaritzburg: privately published, 1997, p. 55, thinks it was six hundred yards.

Chapter 4

1 Jackson and Whybra, 'Isandhlwana and the Durnford Papers'.
2 The statement is from the *Natal Magazine* of September 1879, Vol. IV, No. 17, and is annotated by Lieutenant Alfred F. Henderson, who commanded the Hlubi troop of the Natal Native Horse as part of Durnford's force. Royal Engineers Museum reference 4901.44.11.

3   The Zulu were Gamdana kaXongo, brother of Sihayo, and his men. Their surrender had actually occurred on 21 January (TNA, WO 32/7725 and BPP, C. 2454, p. 182: Statement of Lieutenant A. Milne, RN).

4   Copyright issues prevent the reproduction of the maps in this paper.

5   The museum catalogue entry for the maps reads: 'Two lithographed cloth maps of Isandlwana area . . . with MS notes on progress of the battle, possibly by A.F. Henderson'.

6   I am indebted to Julian Whybra for permission to publish a copy of the conflated map here.

7   KCAL, KCM 89/9/81/23 and 24.

8   The underline is in the original.

9   Inserted in pencil above 'Undi Corps' are the words 'and Qikazi battalion' (Ugqikazi was an alternative name for the Dloko: see Krige, p. 406).

10 Colenso, *History of the Zulu War and Its Origin*.

11 Quoted in Peter Hathorn and Amy Young, *Henderson Heritage*, Pietermaritzburg: privately published, 1972, p. 232. I am indebted to the late Huw Jones for bringing this passage to my attention.

12 See Child, p. 2.

13 Nokhenke deserter: WO 32/7713; Mhoti: Symons Papers, KCAL; Mbonambi warrior: Mitford, p. 25–9; Nzuzi: *Natal Mercury*, 22 January 1929; Uguku: Colenso, p. 410; Mehlokazulu: *Royal Engineer Journal*, 2nd February 1880, pp. 23–4.

14 Stalker, p. 99, account of Trooper Barker.

15 'The Discovery of the Zulu Army': this paper is to be found in chapter 3.

16 Lock and Quantrill, *Zulu Victory*, pp. 168–9.

17 This question has been answered by an unpublished paper by Ron Lock and Peter Quantrill entitled 'The Missing Five Hours'. This paper may be found at http://rorkesdriftvc.com/pdf/TheMissingFiveHours.pdf.

18 TNA, WO 33/34, Enclosure 2 in No. 91, p. 271: Statement of Nyanda.

19 Morris, p. 360.

20 TNA, WO 33/34, Enclosure 2 in No. 96: Davies.

21 BPP, C. 2252, Enclosure 5 in No. 2: Statement of Mr Brickhill.

22 See 'The Discovery of the Zulu Army' in chapter 3.

23 KCAL, KCM 89/9/34/13: Letter from Edward Durnford to Evelyn Wood, 4 October 1880.

24 Lock and Quantrill, 'The Missing Five Hours'.

25 The reference is quite inadequate, merely stating that the source was Trooper W.J. Clarke of the Natal Mounted Police, with a reference to 'Killie Campbell Africana Library for Research Purposes'. The correct citation should be Clarke Papers, Killie Campbell Africana Library (KCAL), KCM 65584. Not having the whole document, but merely pages 1–39, I would guess that the quotation comes from a section identified as 'In escort accompanying Empress Eugenie to scene of Prince Imperial's death', pp. 46–53.

26 Sir Evelyn Wood, *Winnowed Memories*, London: Cassell & Co., 1917, pp. 75–6.

27 TNA, WO 30/129: General Ellice to Lord Chelmsford, 6 March 1879.

28 TNA, WO 30/129: Lord Chelmsford to General Ellice, 11 April 1879.

29 Keith Smith, *The Wedding Feast War: The Final Tragedy of the Xhosa People*, London: Frontline Books, 2012, passim.

30 Matshana kaMondise's people lived in the Mangeni Valley on the far side of the Malakatha hills.

31 TNA, WO 34/34, Enclosure 1 in No. 101: Report of Major Clery, dated 7 February 1879.

32 Talana Museum, Dundee: Report from Colonel R.J. Glyn to Colonel W. Bellairs, deputy adjutant general, dated 6 February 1879.

33 BPP, C. 2454, pp. 182–3: Statement of Lieutenant A. Milne, RN. Cf. TNA, WO 33/34, Enclosure 1 in No. 101: Major Clery.

34 TNA, WO 33/34, No. 58: Lord Chelmsford to Secretary of State for War, 27 January 1879.

35 TNA, WO 30/129: Lord Chelmsford to General Ellice, 11 April 1879.

36 TNA, WO 33/34, Enclosure 1 in No. 101, 7 February 1879: Major Clery.

37 TNA, WO 33/34, Enclosure in No. 69: Evidence of Major Clery to the Isandlwana court of enquiry. Clery describes this interview with Chelmsford in considerable detail in a letter reproduced in Clarke, *Zululand at War*, p. 83.

38 Lieutenant Pope's G Company was left behind because it had been on piquet duty all night. See the last entry in the diary of Lieutenant C. Pope, quoted in Norris-Newman, p. 180.

39 TNA, WO 33/34, Enclosure 6 in No. 96: Bellairs to Glyn, 18 February 1879.

40 TNA, WO 33/34, Enclosure 1 in No. 101, 7 February 1879: Major Clery. Lord Chelmsford later challenged this statement.

41 TNA, WO 33/34, Enclosure in No. 69: Evidence of Captain Gardner to the Isandlwana court of enquiry. See also BPP, C. 2260, Enclosure 2 in No. 12 for the same report.

42 TNA, WO 33/34, Enclosure in No. 69: Evidence of Captain Gardner.

43 TNA, WO 33/34, Enclosure 2 in No. 72: Supplementary statement of Captain Gardner, 26 January 1879. See also TNA, WO 33/34, No. 69: Gardner's evidence to the court of enquiry.

44 TNA, WO 33/34, Enclosure 9 in No. 96: Copies of both messages were enclosed with a note from Assistant Military Secretary Crealock in a memorandum of 24 February 1879 to Colonel Bellairs, deputy adjutant-general.

45 Noted in parentheses after the text of the message.

46 Indicated in one line above, and a second below, the message.

47 TNA, WO 33/34, Enclosure 9 in No. 96: Crealock to Bellairs, 24 February 1879.

48 TNA, WO 33/34, Enclosure 2 in No. 101: Minute on Major Clery's evidence, 19 March 1879.

49 TNA, WO 33/34, Enclosure 2 in No. 101: Minute on Major Clery's evidence, 19 March 1879.

50 Hamilton-Browne, pp. 127–36. See also my commentary on them in my earlier paper 'The Hazards of Primary Sources'.

51 TNA, WO 33/34, Enclosure 1 in No. 96: Hamilton-Browne report, 2 February 1879.

52 TNA, WO 33/34, Enclosure 2 in No. 101: Lord Chelmsford's minute on Major Clery's statement, 19 March 1879.

53 TNA, WO 33/34, Enclosure 1 in No. 72: Statement of Lieutenant-Colonel Crealock. See also BPP, C. 2260, Enclosure 2 in No. 12 for the same report.
54 TNA, WO 33/34, Enclosure in No. 143: Report of Lieutenant-Colonel Russell, 1 April 1879.
55 Neither Walsh nor Davy [Davies?] are identified in any other document.
56 BPP, C. 2454, pp. 182–3. Statement of Lieutenant A. Milne, RN.
57 Norris-Newman, p. 58.
58 Major Gossett, quoted in French, pp. 103–5.
59 Durnford, *Isandhlwana*: a narrative compiled from official and reliable sources, p. 23.
60 Statement by Major General M. Gosset, in French, p. 104.
61 Sonia Clarke, *Invasion of Zululand*, Houghton: Brenthurst Press, 1979, p. 70: Private letter from Harness, dated 25 January 1879.
62 BPP, C. 2454, p. 184: Report of Lieutenant A. Milne.
63 Child, p. 14. Harford dates the incident because it took place 'nearing the 11th January' (p. 12).
64 Child, p. 22.
65 Statement of Commandant Lonsdale in an account of Isandlwana by H.G. Mainwaring written 22 January 1895 in Cairo and quoted in Holme, p. 199.
66 This should read 'Commandant'. There was also a Captain James Lonsdale who commanded one of the Izigqoza companies of the 1st Battalion, NNC, still at the camp.
67 Gosset, in French, p. 104.
68 As related to Norris-Newman, p. 59.
69 Statement of Commandant Lonsdale in an account by H.G. Mainwaring, quoted in Holme, p. 199.
70 TNA, WO 33/34, No. 58: Lord Chelmsford's report to the Secretary of State for War, 27 January 1879. Cf. Crealock, TNA, WO 33/34, Enclosure 1 in No. 72, undated statement.
71 TNA, WO 33/34, Enclosure 1 in No. 96: Hamilton-Browne report.
72 TNA, WO 32/7731: Bellairs to Wood, 20 March 1879.
73 TNA, WO 32/7731: Bellairs to Wood, 20 March 1879.
74 A marginal note is written here by Lieutenant-Colonel Crealock: 'If this was given to the General or his staff it could not have been 2.30 pm but for the fact that no one with the Gen'l up to 4 o'clock had any reason to doubt for the safety of the camp. It is probable it was not given then. JNC.'
75 TNA, WO 33/34, Enclosure in No. 143: Report of Lieutenant-Colonel Russell. Another marginal note is written here, again by Crealock: 'He owns it was lost. JNC.'
76 Examples of this are to be found throughout General Orders.
77 Morris, *passim*, refers to two of these officers as though they were one. This may have been the result of following D.C.F. Moodie's work, which managed to confuse all three: see D.C.F. Moodie, *Moodie's Zulu War*, ed. John Laband, Cape Town: North and South Press, 1988.
78 Mackinnon and Shadbolt, *The South African Campaign of 1879*, London: Sampson, Low, Marston, Searle and Rivington, 1880, re-published London: Greenhill, 1995, pp. 89–90.

79 TNA, WO 132/1: Personal letter, dated 5 April 1879.
80 The unusual spelling of Barton's first name is correct.
81 MacKinnon and Shadbolt, p. 308.
82 Laband, *Lord Chelmsford's Zululand Campaign*, p. 272.
83 Laband, *Lord Chelmsford's Zululand Campaign*, p. 4. See also General Order No. 218, dated 9 December 1878, *Times of Natal*, 11 December 1878.
84 *Narrative of the Field Operations*, p. 142.
85 *Narrative of the Field Operations*, pp. 147 and 153.
86 Mackinnon and Shadbolt, p. 11.
87 Morris, pp. 357, 360.
88 Laband also confuses other individuals: in his *The Rise and Fall of the Zulu Nation*, p. 222, he says that Colonel Durnford 'ordered Captain Theophilus Shepstone, Jnr. out with a patrol of Natal Mounted Contingent along the Nyoni Heights . . .' In fact, this officer was Captain George Shepstone – his brother Theophilus was in command of the Natal Carbineers, who were serving with Lord Chelmsford some miles to the east of the camp at that time.
89 Jackson, 'Isandlwana, 1879', p. 55. See also Holme, p.377 and Young, p. 49.
90 Jackson, 'Isandlwana, 1879', p. 55, n. 257.
91 *Times Weekly Edition*, 30 May 1879, cited in the *Journal of the Anglo-Zulu War Research Society*, Vol. 2, No. 1, p. 20. I am indebted to author John Young for bringing this to my notice.
92 PAR, CSO 668/4338, dated 21 November 1878.
93 *Times of Natal*, 25 November 1878.
94 *Times of Natal*, 28 November 1878.
95 *Times of Natal*, 25 December 1878. There was no other Lieutenant Barton in the contingent.
96 *Times of Natal*, 11 December 1878.
97 Lieutenant-Colonel E.C.L. Durnford, *A Soldier's Life and Work in South Africa*, London: Sampson, Low, Marston, Searle and Rivington, 1882, p. 201.
98 Both Westwood and Wassall were serving on detachment with the Imperial Mounted Infantry.
99 TNA, WO 32/7387. I am indebted to author Ron Lock for bringing this reference to my attention.
100 Jantze's troop of horse had been left behind at Kranskop. The two other troops were Hlubi's Basotho, led by Lieutenant Alfred Henderson and men from the Edendale district commanded by Lieutenant Harry Davies.
101 NAM, 6807-386-8-14: Hamer account of Isandlwana.
102 NAM, 6807-386-8-14: Hamer account of Isandlwana.
103 NAM, 6807-386-8-14: Hamer account of Isandlwana.
104 See Droogleever, p. 178, who offered this suggestion, perhaps in an effort to resolve this very problem.
105 KCAL, KCM 16020: Vause diary.
106 PAR, 1/BGV/4, No. 97/1879, pp. 326–7.
107 PAR, 1/BGV/4, No. 100/1879, p. 328.
108 General Order 205, dated 23 November 1878: 'to serve for six months from date of enrolment'.

109 KCAL, KCM 16020: Vause diary, entry for 14 May 1879.

110 Norris-Newman, p. 63.

111 TNA, WO 100/49.

112 Droogleever, p. 193; Knight, *The Sun Turned Black*, p. 88.

113 Durnford, *A Soldier's Life*, p. 213.

114 I am indebted to Simon Moody of the National Army Museum for drawing my attention to this new acquisition, which turned out to be gold-plated.

115 NAM, Pearson Papers, 2004-05-73-5-16: Captain Geoffry Barton to Colonel Pearson, 11 January 1879.

116 *Natal Mercury*, 22 January 1879: 'From Kranz Kop'. This writer has inserted the initials. See also the *Natal Witness*, 21 January 1879.

117 TNA, WO 33/34 p. 230.

118 John Laband and P.S. Thompson, *War Comes to Umvoti*, Pietermaritzburg: University of Natal Press, 1980, p. 109.

119 *Times of Natal*, 24 February 1879.

120 General Order No. 43, dated 26 February 1879, *Times of Natal*, 3 March 1879.

121 D.W. Kruger and C.J. Beyers (eds), *Dictionary of South African Biography*, Cape Town: Human Sciences Research Council, 1977, Vol. III, p. 52.

122 *Natal Mercury*, 26 February 1879, from an account in the *Watchman*.

123 Adrian Preston, *The South African Journal of Sir Garnet Wolseley 1879–1880*, Cape Town: A.A. Balkema, 1973, p. 70, entry dated 3 August 1879. Wolseley had that day presented Henry Hook with his Victoria Cross at Rorke's Drift and then went on to visit Fugitive's Drift and the grave site of Melvill and Coghill.

124 Coghill, p. 97.

125 TNA, WO 33/34, Enclosure in No. 89: Colonel Richard Glyn to deputy adjutant-general (Colonel Bellairs).

126 Child, p. 48. Harford was staff officer to Commandant Lonsdale, commanding officer of the 3rd Regiment, NNC.

127 Child, p. 49.

128 Child, pp. 49–50.

129 Child, pp. 50–1.

130 NorrisNewman, p. 116.

131 *Times of Natal*, 11 February 1879.

132 *Natal Mercury*, 11 February 1879, and in Moodie, pp. 50–1.

133 Hamilton-Browne, p. 158.

134 It should be remembered that by this date, the 3rd Regiment, NNC had been disbanded, leaving behind only the officers and NCOs.

135 RMRW, R1950.41: Records of the 1st Battalion, 24th Regiment 1689-1905; I am indebted to Major Martin Everett, curator of the museum, for sending me this extract.

136 All of these officers, except one, were drawn from the defunct 3rd Regiment, NNC. Raw was from Durnford's Natal Native Mounted Contingent. Since they were under a six-month contract, they could not be demobilised. They were eventually distributed to other African infantry or mounted units.

137 Roger Hudson, *William Russell, Special Correspondent of* The Times, London: Folio Society, 1995, p. 370.

Chapter 5

1 Holme, p. 337.
2 Coupland, pp. 103–11.
3 Laband, *Kingdom in Crisis*, chapter 5.
4 Preston, p. 57: entry for 15 July 1879.
5 Preston, p. 57.
6 Preston, p. 112: entry for 11 September 1879.
7 Perhaps this was a symptom of what today might be called post-traumatic stress disorder.
8 Clarke, *Zululand at War*, p. 131: Letter from Major Clery to Lady Alison, 16 May 1879.
9 Clarke, *Zululand at War*, p. 131; see also p. 100: Letter to Sir Archibald Alison.
10 Preston, p. 57.
11 Emery, p. 241: Letter from Captain Walter Parke Jones, RE, 2 August 1879.
12 In 1878, 43 per cent of men in the British Army were less than five feet seven inches in height: Skelley, table on p. 307.
13 Quoted in Adrian Greaves and Brian Best (eds), *The Curling Letters of the Zulu War*, Barnsley: Leo Cooper, 2001, p. 122. Curling was born in July 1847 and was thus only two years younger than Bromhead, hardly qualifying the latter to be referred to as an 'old fellow'!
14 This was probably Sergeant F. Millne, 2nd Battalion, 3rd (East Kent) Regiment of Foot (the 'Buffs'). He was not decorated for any part he took in the action. See also Morris, pp. 391, 395.
15 KCAL, MS 1072: Symons Papers.
16 Clarke, *Zululand at War*, p. 131.
17 Purchase of commissions was abolished in 1872.
18 Lieutenant-General H.G Hart, *New Annual Army List for 1879*, London: John Murray, 1879.
19 Major Spalding used an Army List to determine the senior of Bromhead and Chard when he left for Helpmekaar on the afternoon of 22 January; see Chard's letter to Queen Victoria in Holme, p. 272. (The letter is in the Royal Archives, RA/VIC/O 46/4.)
20 He was also therefore slightly younger than Curling.
21 Coupland, p. 104.
22 Promotion by purchase was never an option in the Royal Engineers.
23 Holme gives his date of birth as 27 April 1853, see p. 324.
24 Letter from Sir Henry Ponsonby to his wife, quoted in Preston, p. 319, note 35.
25 *Narrative of the Field Operations*, p. 45. This is clearly based on Chard's official report, found in TNA, WO 32/7737: Reports on defence of Rorke's Drift, with plan, and TNA, WO 33/34, Enclosure in No. 70.
26 Chard's account sent to Queen Victoria in Holme, p. 273.
27 Walter Wood (ed.), 'How they Held Rorke's Drift; from the Narrative of Sergeant Henry Hook V.C.', *Royal Magazine*, February 1905.
28 BPP, C. 2434, Army Medical Department report for the year 1878, Vol. XX (1880): Statistical, sanitary and medical reports of the Army Medical Department,

Appendix V, pp. 261–3: Surgeon-Major James Henry Reynolds, M.B., V.C., Report of the defence of Rorke's Drift.

29 Preston, p. 57. One might also apply this same remark to Assistant Commissary W.A. Dunne, Dalton's superior officer at Rorke's Drift, who went unrewarded, despite his great efforts during the defence. Lord Chelmsford made a recommendation that both Dunne and Dalton be awarded the Victoria Cross (TNA, WO 32/7386).

30 Molyneux, p. 207.

31 Ian Knight, *Nothing Remains But To Fight: The Defence of Rorke's Drift, 1879*, London: Greenhill, 1993.

32 Knight, *Nothing Remains But To Fight*, p. 44.

33 Child, p. 23: 'I am here discounting the return of Murray's company to the camp.'

34 Quoted in the account of Rorke's Drift by Lieutenant J.R.M. Chard, RE, written for Queen Victoria (Holme, pp. 270–8).

35 BPP, C. 2234, pp. 39–40. See also General Order No. 205, dated 17 November 1878, *Times of Natal*, 23 November 1878.

36 General Order No. 213, dated 3 December 1878, *Times of Natal*, 6 December 1878.

37 Jackson, *Hill of the Sphinx*, p. 68.

38 General Order No. 213, dated 3 December 1878, *Times of Natal*, 6 December 1878.

39 Lieutenant-Colonel Frank Bourne, transcript of a BBC broadcast, *The Listener*, 30 December 1936 and quoted in Holme, pp. 279–82.

40 Reverend George Smith, quoted in Paton, Glennie and Penn Symons, pp. 251–5.

41 H.C. Lugg, *A Natal Family Looks Back*, Durban: Griggs & Co., 1970, p. 20.

42 After the NNC departure, Chard ordered that another wall be built, excluding the hospital building, so forming a smaller perimeter.

43 Child, p. 12.

44 Thompson, p. 32.

45 PAR, CSO 1925, No. 494: Harford to Moodie.

46 PAR, CSO 1925, No. 494: Harford to Moodie.

47 TNA, WO 32/7737: Chard's official report.

48 Account by Private Henry Hook, in *Royal Magazine*, February 1905.

49 Reverend George Smith, in Paton, Glennie and Penn Symons, pp. 251–5.

50 Account of Jabez Molife, Natal Native Mounted Contingent, in REM, Durnford Papers, 4901.44.2. See also Chard's account for Queen Victoria (Holme, pp. 270–8) for Henderson's reasons for leaving.

51 TNA, WO 33/34, Enclosure 3 in No. 96: Statement of Lieutenant Higginson, adjutant of 1/3rd NNC.

52 Lieutenant Purvis, 1/3rd NNC, had been wounded in the arm at the skirmish at Sihayo's homestead on 12 January.

53 Captain James Lonsdale is not to be confused with Commandant Rupert Lonsdale, nor Captain C.A. Erskine with Lieutenant W. Erskine, who survived.

54 Lieutenants Adendorff, Vaines and Higginson.

55 General Order No. 37, dated 19 February 1879, *Times of Natal*, 21 February 1879.

56 Lock and Quantrill, *Zulu Victory*.

57 Clarke, *Zululand at War*, p. 100: Clery to General Alison, 11 March 1879.

58 This paper quotes extensively from a number of documents but to truncate or summarise them would minimise their impact.

59 See TNA, WO 32/7738: Correspondence regarding the absence of Major Spalding from Rorke's Drift.

60 TNA, WO 32/7738: Lord Chelmsford to General Ellice, DAG, 19 May 1879.

61 Lieutenant-General H.G. Hart, *New Annual Army List for 1885*, London: John Murray, 1885, pp. 28 and 15, n. 100.

62 TNA, WO 33/34 No. 55.

63 Clarke, *Zululand at War*, p. 82: Clery to Colonel Harman, 17 February 1879.

64 Clarke, *Zululand at War*, p. 100; Clery to General Alison, 11 March 1879. The emphasis is indicated by underlining in Clery's original.

65 TNA, WO 33/34, paper 766 (Correspondence relative to military affairs in South Africa).

66 Talana Museum, Dundee: Copy of handwritten MS, Glyn to Bellairs, 6 February 1879.

67 TNA, WO 33/34, Enclosure 5 in No. 96: Bellairs to Glyn, 7 February 1879.

68 TNA, WO 33/34, Enclosure 5 in No. 96: Glyn to Bellairs, 14 February 1879.

69 TNA, WO 33/34, Enclosure 6 in No. 96: Bellairs to Glyn, 18 February 1879.

70 TNA, WO 33/34, Enclosure 8 in No. 96: Crealock to Lord Chelmsford, 20 February 1879.

71 TNA, WO 33/34, Enclosure 5 in No. 96: Lord Chelmsford to Bellairs, 20 February 1879.

72 Clarke, *Zululand at War*, p. 102: Letter from Clery to Sir Archibald Alison, 11 March 1879.

73 TNA, WO 33/34, Enclosure 8 in No. 96: Glyn to Bellairs, 26 February 1879.

74 TNA, WO 33/34, Enclosure 8 in No. 96: Lord Chelmsford to Bellairs, 4 March 1879.

75 While the map is not attached, the same information is provided on the map prepared by Captain T.A. Anstey, RE, and Lieutenant Penrose, RE, in November 1879 entitled 'Military Survey of the Battle-Field of Isandhlwana', to be found in *Narrative of the Field Operations*.

76 TNA, WO 33/34, Enclosure 6 in No. 96: Glyn to Bellairs, 26 February 1879.

77 TNA, WO 33/34, Enclosure 6 in No. 96: Glyn to Bellairs, 26 February 1879.

78 TNA, WO 33/34, Enclosure 6 in No. 96: Lord Chelmsford to Bellairs, 4 March 1879.

79 TNA, WO 33/34, Enclosure 1 in No. 101: Clery statement, 7 February 1879.

80 Clarke, *Zululand at War*, p. 129: Clery to Allison, 28 April 1879.

81 TNA, WO 33/34, Enclosure 1 in No. 101: Lord Chelmsford minute on Clery's statement, 19 March 1879.

Chapter 6

1 Hart, *Army List for 1885*, p. 43.

2 General Order No. 209, dated 28 November 1878, *Times of Natal*, 2 December 1878.

3 'Distribution of Troops in the Field', *Times of Natal*, 20 January 1879.

4   General Order No. 228, dated 18 December 1878, *Times of Natal*, 20 December 1878

5   BPP, C. 2260, Item A in Enclosure in No. 3. This item states the time of receipt by Pearson as 11 a.m. In BPP, C. 2367, Item A, Enclosure in No. 19, Pearson gives the times as 9 a.m., as does the *Narrative of the Field Operations*, p. 53.

6   TNA, WO 33/34, Enclosure 1 in No. 141. See also *Times of Natal*, 28 February 1879.

7   *Natal Mercury*, 1 February, 1879, 'Major Graves and the Native Contingent'.

8   *Natal Mercury*, 1 February, 1879, 'Return of Major Barrow's Horse'. See also Norris-Newman, pp. 91–2.

9   *Natal Mercury*, 3 February 1879, 'The Native Contingent'.

10 *Natal Colonist*, 18 February 1879: a correspondent quoted in the leader article.

11 General Order No. 43, dated 26 February 1879, *Times of Natal*, 3 March 1879.

12 In mid-March, the contingent was reorganised into five discrete battalions; see General Order No. 59, dated 18 March 1879, *Natal Mercury*, 20 March 1879.

13 *Natal Colonist*, 13 March 1879.

14 *Natal Colonist*, 22 March 1879; *Natal Mercury*, 29 March, 1879.

15 General Order No. 38, dated 20 February, 1879, *Times of Natal*, 24 February 1879.

16 General Order No. 43, dated 26 February, 1879, *Times of Natal*, 3 March 1879.

17 General Order No. 43, dated 26 February, 1879, *Times of Natal*, 3 March 1879.

18 PAR, CSO 2554, No. C42: Colonial Secretary Mitchell to Sir Henry Bulwer, 20 February 1879.

19 PAR, CSO 2554, No. C42: Lord Chelmsford to Colonial Secretary, 19 February 1879.

20 *Natal Government Gazette*, 18 March 1879: Government Notice No. 70, 1879.

21 PAR, CSO 2554, No. C42. Emphases are in the original.

22 The text of this paper is entirely unchanged; the endnotes have been modified to conform to the appropriate style guide.

23 Evelyn Wood, *From Midshipman to Field Marshal*, Vol. II, pp. 48–56.

24 TNA, WO 32/7726: From Colonel Evelyn Wood commanding No.4 Column, to the deputy adjutant-general, Camp Kambula, Zululand, 30 March 1879. This despatch was printed in the supplement to the *London Gazette* of Tuesday 6 May 1879, No. 24719, published on 7 May 1879. There are also three copies in the NAM, Chelmsford Papers, 6807-386-14-13, two of which carry the notation 'A, correct copy but not verified E.W.'

25 Norris-Newman, pp. 156–9.

26 Charles Williams, *The Life of Lieutenant-General Sir Henry Evelyn Wood*, London: Sampson, Low, Marston and Co., 1892, pp. 87ff.

27 NAM, 8412-46-1 and 2, Dr P.H. Butterfield, 'The Minor Writings of Sir Evelyn Wood', a typescript of two articles by Wood published in *Pearson's Magazine*, 1896.

28 Sir Evelyn Wood (ed.), *British Battles on Land and Sea*, London: Cassell & Co., 1915, pp. 754ff. I am grateful to M.J. Everett, curator of RMRW, for bringing this work to my attention.

29 NAM 6807-386-14, Chelmsford Papers, an editorial annotation; Gossett served on Lord Chelmsford's staff in 1878–9.

30 NAM 6807-386-14-10, memorandum dated 29 March 1879, 7 pm, to Lord
    Chelmsford and others; NAM 6807-386-14-23, Lord Chelmsford to the
    Secretary of State for War, Durban, 14 April 1879.
31 NAM 6807-386-14-20, Wood to Frere, Kambula Hill, Zululand, 29 March 1879.
32 PAR, II/2/4, Evelyn Wood Papers, Frere to Wood, Newcastle, 30 March 1879.
33 Transvaal Archives, Pretoria: *Transvaal Government Gazette Extraordinary*, Vol.
    III, No. 111, Pretoria, Transvaal, Thursday, 3 April 1879; Government Notice No.
    38, 1879. The letter and the abbreviated Hlobane despatch were published in the
    Cape Times on Thursday 17 April 1879.
34 *Cape Mercury*, King William's Town, Wednesday 2 April 1879.
35 *Cape Times*, Cape Town, 10 April 1879.
36 *Daily Chronicle*, Newcastle-upon-Tyne, 3 May 1879.
37 *Cape Times*, 18 April 1879.
38 TNA, WO 32/7724, telegram via St. Vincent [Sao Vicente] from Colonel W.
    Bellairs to the Secretary of State for War, Durban, 5 April 1879.
39 *The Times*, Tuesday 22 April 1879.
40 *The Times*, Monday 5 May 1879.
41 The correspondent was Lieutenant A.J. Bigge, RA, who commanded a mounted
    rocket detachment in Russell's column at Hlobane. Clarke, *Invasion of Zululand*,
    p. 109: letter from Brevet Lieutenant-Colonel A. Harness to his sister Caroline,
    Helpmekaar, 9 April 1879.
42 Supplement to the *London Gazette* of Tuesday 6 May, No. 24719, published
    Wednesday 7 May 1879. The text is complete with the exception of one
    sentence in Buller's report on Hlobane, dated 29 March 1879. In the copy in
    TNA, WO32/7726, the order 'Omit this from Gazette' is side-lined against the
    sentence: 'By right I meant the north side of the mountain but Capt. Barton
    must have understood me to mean the south side and to my careless expression
    must I fear be attributed the greater part of our heavy loss that day.'
43 NAM 6807-386-14-23, Lord Chelmsford to the Secretary of State for War,
    Durban, 14 April 1879.
44 Transvaal Archives, Pretoria: ATC, AI/45 Despatches administrator Transvaal
    to high commissioner, January 1878–February 1879; SS1278/79, Wood to acting
    Colonial Secretary Transvaal, Kambula Hill, 12 April 1879 and Lanyon's minute
    to secretary to Government of 17 April.
45 *Transvaal Argus and Commercial Gazette*, supplement, April 1879; report from
    Camp Kambula dated 17 April; the correspondent was probably an officer in the
    13th Light Infantry.
46 *Times of Natal*, Pietermaritzburg, 28 April 1879.
47 Clarke, *Zululand At War*, p. 205: letter from Lieutenant-Colonel J.N. Crealock to
    General Sir Archibald Alison, Camp Upoko River, 10 June 1879.
48 Huw M. Jones, 'Blood on the Painted Mountain; Zulu Victory and Defeat,
    Hlobane and Kambula, 1879: A Review Article', *Soldiers of the Queen*, No. 84,
    March 1996, pp. 20–9.
49 Transvaal Archives, Pretoria: A1889, Memoirs of C.G. Dennison MS, chapter 5.
    I am grateful to Lionel Wulfsohn of Rustenburg for first drawing my attention
    to this manuscript and to the archives staff for their help in locating and copying

the chapter on Hlobane. There is no information as to when it was written, but it was probably completed in 1903.

50   Major C.G. Dennison, DSO, *A Fight to a Finish*, London: Longman, Green, 1904.
51   There are, unfortunately, no records in the Langmans collection in the University of Reading library which shed any light on how Dennison's manuscript was handled for publication. I am grateful to Frances Miller for her assistance.
52   *Independent*, South African Diamond Fields, Thursday 17 April 1879, and TAP, A1889, Dennison memoirs.
53   Dennison, Vol. V, p.324.
54   Lionel Wulfsohn, *Rustenburg At War*, Rustenburg: self-published, second revised edition, 1992, p. 9; Fred Jeppe, *Transvaal Book Almanac and Directory*, Pietermaritzburg: n.p., 1877, p. 62.
55   TAP, A1889, Dennison memoirs, p. 67.
56   Or Makateeskop, Eloya or Ronde Kop. It probably takes its name from Makhatha Shabalala, a Hlubi induna of the iziYandane regiment posted in this area.
57   TNA, CO 291/2, Enclosure 5 in Transvaal, No. 3 to the high commissioner, Pietermaritzburg; N. Osborn, secretary to government, Pretoria, to Shepstone, 29 January 1879.
58   NAM 6807-386-9-112, Wood to Crealock, Kambula Hill, 18 March 1879.
59   *Cape Times*, Cape Town, 17 April 1879.
60   TNA, WO 31/1077: F.A. Weatherley to Major-General Sir Charles Yorke, military secretary, Horse Guards, s.d., but received 12 March 1855; *Graphic*, 24 May 1879, p. 502 was incorrect.
61   Weatherley's uncle, Captain J.D. Weatherley, 60th Rifles, was a Peninsular veteran, whilst another relative of that generation, H.O. Weatherley, had been private secretary to Prince Esterhazy, the Austrian ambassador in London: Richard Welford, *Men of Mark Twixt Tyne and Tweed*, Vol. III, London: Walter Scott Ltd, 1895, pp. 589–95. I am grateful for this reference to Barbara Heathcote, local studies librarian of the central library, Newcastle-upon-Tyne.
62   *Transvaal Argus and Commercial Gazette*, Pretoria, 8 December 1877.
63   TNA, WO 31/1077, Commander-in-Chief's Memoranda.
64   TNA, WO 31/1087, Commander-in-Chief's Memoranda.
65   *Transvaal Argus and Commercial Gazette*, Pretoria, Wednesday 27 November 1878. I am grateful to the State Library, Pretoria, for providing a copy of this edition.
66   TNA, WO 31/1142, Commander-in Chiefs Memoranda.
67   TNA, WO 31/1087, Commander-in Chiefs Memoranda: Lord Raglan to HRH the general, commander-in-chief, from Madresfield Court, Great Malvern, 22 and 23 October 1861; Hart's Army List 1868.
68   TNA, CO 291/1: F.A. Weatherley to Sir Theophilus Shepstone, Pretoria, 29 October 1878; Hart's Army List 1875.
69   Thomas Baines, *The Gold Regions of South Eastern Africa*, London: Edward Stanford, 1877, p.96.
70   Roche, Harriet A., *On Trek in the Transvaal*, London: Sampson Low, Marston, Searle & Rivington, 1878. A.R. Roche, her husband, was also one of the initial subscribers to the Eersteling project: Baines, p. 96.

71 *Transvaal Argus and Commercial Gazette*, Pretoria, Wednesday 27 November 1878.

72 S.P. Engelbrecht, *Thomas Francois Burgers: A Biography*, Pretoria and Cape Town: J.H. de H. Bussy, 1946, p. 274.

73 E.D. McToy, *A Brief History of the 13th Regiment (P.A.L.I.) in South Africa during the Transvaal and Zulu Difficulties*, Devonport: A.H. Swiss, 1880, p. 5.

74 Newnham-Davis, N., *The Transvaal Under The Queen*, London: Sands & Co., 1900, p.30.

75 TNA, CO 291/1: Sir Theophilus Shepstone to Lord Carnarvon, Government House, Pretoria, No. 38, dated 1 August 1877, enclosing a copy of a memorial from the officers and men of the Pretoria Mutual Protection Association.

76 TNA, CO 292/1: F.A. Weatherley to Sir Theophilus Shepstone, Pretoria, 30 October 1878, enclosing District Order, Dover, 1 August 1877 announcing Weatherley's resignation because he 'has a military command in South Africa'.

77 TNA, CO 291/1: Barlow to Brooke from Eersteling, 8 December 1877.

78 Transvaal Argus and Commercial Gazette, Pretoria, 8 December 1877.

79 TNA, CO 291/1: Sir Theophilus Shepstone to the Secretary of State for the Colonies, Government House, Pretoria, No.50, dated 15 May 1878.

80 *Die Volksstem*, Pretoria, Tuesday 29 January 1878.

81 Although Weatherley has been ridiculed for being taken in by Stewart, Stewart was a plausible rogue. During his trial, the *Cape Times* wrote of him that: 'Most persons who know Gunn, have a kindly feeling for him, and the essential harmlessness of his character appears in his signature "Gunn of Gunn" to his letter addressed to the Governor of the colony.' *Cape Times*, Monday 29 July 1878.

82 TNA, CO 291/1: Sir Theophilus Shepstone to the Secretary of State for the Colonies, Government House, Pretoria, No. 50 dated 15 May 1878.

83 Transvaal Archives, Pretoria, A1/45, General Letter Book HM Special Commissioner to Transvaal: 2/11 1876–9/12 1878, p. 472, Shepstone to Frere, No. 49, Government House, Pretoria, 20 August 1878.

84 *Cape Times*, Monday 5 August 1878.

85 TNA, CO 291/1: F.A. Weatherley to Sir Theophilus Shepstone, Pretoria, 26 and 29 October 1878.

86 Kenneth Wyndham Smith, 'The Campaigns against the Bapedi of Sekhukhune, 1877–1879', *Archives Year Book for South African History*, 1967, Vol. II, p. 36.

87 Not 'Lancers', as used, for example, in Weatherley's obituary in the *Graphic*, 24 May 1879, p. 502, and perpetuated by others, most recently Lock, p. 116.

88 NAM 6807-386-18-9 and 11, F.A. Weatherley to Lord Chelmsford, Pretoria, 2 and 15 November 1878.

89 TNA, CO 291/2: Annual return of armed land forces – Transvaal, year ending 31 December 1878.

90 Lys, the brother of J.R. Lys, a well-known Pretoria merchant and member of the Volksraad, had seniority as second master of HMS *Rifleman* from 27 August 1862 and retired in 1871 as navigating lieutenant on HMS *Seringapatam*, a hulk used as a receiving ship at the Cape of Good Hope; various Navy Lists. He was an accomplished surveyor: *Independent*, South African Diamond Fields, 17 April 1879.

91 TNA, WO 32/7726, Capt C.G. Dennison to Colonel Buller, Kambula, 29 March 1879, written on Buller's orders on 'the disaster at Ihlabana [*sic*]'.

92 TNA, WO 32/7726, Buller's report, Camp Kambula, 29 March 1879.

93 Selby, John, *Shaka's Heirs*, London: Allen & Unwin, 1971, p. 106; it has been further elaborated in the latest description of Hlobane by Lock, p. 134, where the Border Horse is described as 'not prepared to risk their lives in a frontal attack on a strongly held natural fortress'.

94 Williams, p. 92.

95 Wood, *British Battles on Land and Sea*, p. 757.

96 Wood, *From Midshipman to Field Marshal*, Vol. II, pp. 52–3.

97 KCAL, KCM 65234, letter from Charles Hewitt to his sister Annie dated 3 January 1920, pp. 21 and 22 (I am grateful to Mrs J.M. Simpson, librarian, for drawing my attention to this manuscript.); Mossop, p. 74.

98 Laband, John, 'The Battle of Khambula, 29 March 1879: A Re-examination from the Zulu Perspective', in *There Will be An Awful Row At Home About This*, Shoreham-by-sea: Victorian Military Society, 1987, p. 21.

99 BPP, C. 3182, 1882, Correspondence re affairs of Natal and Zululand, p. 49.

100 Wood's Hlobane dispatch, dated 30 March 1879; cf. note 2 above.

101 PAR, Shepstone Papers, Vol. 39, addendum to statement made by Piet Uys, junior to H.C. Shepstone, at Utrecht, 29 March 1879.

102 *The Times*, Monday 5 May 1879. The account by *The Times*' own correspondent written on 30 March and published on 17 May follows Wood's account, but notes only that before daybreak he met Weatherley who was ordered to follow Wood.

103 TNA, WO 32/7834: Major-General Sir Evelyn Wood to the military secretary, Horse Guards, from Government House, Pietermaritzburg, 15 October 1881; also published in Emery, p. 177.

104 *Pearson's Magazine*, February 1896, Vol. 1, No. 9, p. 129.

105 NAM, 6307-386-9-103, Wood to Crealock, Kambula Hill, Sunday 16 February 1879.

106 Butterfield, 'The Minor Writings of Sir Evelyn Wood'.

107 Sir Evelyn Wood, *British Battles on Land and Sea*, p. 756.

108 In a previous paper, I have suggested that the primary reason for the assault on Hlobane was to collect cattle. In addition to the evidence presented there, and Dennison's comment, it is interesting to note that the correspondent of the *Cape Argus* wrote that 'Colonel Wood had already descended with his escort and returned to camp, thinking, no doubt, all was well, and that an immense take of cattle would be the day's result'; Jones, 'Blood on the Painted Mountain' and Moodie, p. 122.

109 Sir Evelyn Wood, *From Midshipman to Field-Marshal*, Vol. II, pp. 48 and 50.

110 Moodie, p. 122.

111 Major W. Ashe, and Captain E.V. Wyatt-Edgell, *The Story of the Zulu Campaign*, London: Sampson Low, Marston, Searle and Rivington, 1880, re-published Cape Town: N and S Press: 1989, p.124.

112 Moodie, pp. 122 and 123.

113 Lock, p. 179. Poulet Weatherley arrived at Khambula after the action at Hlobane and returned to Pretoria on Tuesday 7 April; *Die Volksstem*, Friday 11 April 1879.

114 TNA, WO 32/7726, Lieutenant-Colonel R.H. Buller's report, Camp Kambula, 29 March 1879.

115 TAP, A1889, Dennison memoirs, p. 88.

116 Dennison, p. 8.

117 TAP, A1889, Dennison memoirs, p. 94.

118 William Macdonald, *Romance of the Golden Rand*, London: Cassell & Co., 1933, p. 230.

119 It should be added that he was later commissioned as a lieutenant in the 80th (South Staffordshire) Regiment and saw service in the Sudan and Upper Nile campaigns; TNA, WO 76/97, f. 77 and WO 76/99, f. 20.

120 *Cape Times*, 5 May 1879.

121 NAM 6302-48, W.F. Fairlie's diary.

122 Among other sources: BPP, C. 2318, p. 160, Wood to military secretary, 22 April 1879; the entry for 17 April 1879 in Captain E.R.P. Woodgate's diary (I am grateful to Dr G. Kemble Woodgate for sight of the diaries covering this period); and *Cape Times*, 5 May 1879.

123 Or Ngogo or Pypklipberg.

124 NAM, 7411-8, Diary of the Zululand Boundary Commission.

Chapter 7

1 Much of the detail of the route can be found in the *Narrative of the Field Operations*. This has been supplemented, and sometimes contradicted, by the diaries of the 2nd Division in TNA, WO 32/7761 and WO 32/7767.

2 PAR, Wood Papers, II/2/2, Chelmsford to Wood, 15 [?] April 1879.

3 NAM, CP 6807/386-24-5: Draft response to the critical article by Archibald Forbes, 'Lord Chelmsford and the Zulu War', *Nineteenth Century Magazine*, Vol. VII, February 1880, pp. 216–34.

4 PAR, Wood Papers, II/2/2: Chelmsford to Wood, 25 April 1879.

5 Prescient words indeed. GRO, Commeline Letters, D1233/45/7, letter to his father dated 16 March 1879.

6 NAM, CP 6807/386-24-5: Draft response to the critical article by Archibald Forbes.

7 PAR, Wood Papers, II/2/2: Chelmsford to Wood, 11 May 1879.

8 TNA, WO 33/34, Enclosure in No. 175, 31 May 1879. It is not generally appreciated that Prince Louis Bonaparte, Prince Imperial of France, reconnoitred a part of the route and his handwritten report still exists (TNA, WO 32/7735, Prince Imperial's reconnaissance report, 23 May 1879).

9 A strongpoint was built here in May called Fort Whitehead, which is about three kilometres due south of the knoll still known as Koppie Alleen.

10 Captain W.E. Montague, *Campaigning in South Africa: Reminiscences of an Officer in 1879*, London: Blackwood & Sons, 1880, p. 151.

11 *Narrative of the Field Operations*, p. 100.

12 TNA, CO700/ZULULANDII: Zululand, compiled by the Intelligence Department of the War Office and dated 1879, revised in March 1880.

13 TNA, MPHH 1/525: 'Map of Zululand compiled from the most recent information', Intelligence Branch, Quarter-Master General's Department, July 1879.

14 PAR, Wood Papers, A598, WC II/2/2: Wood to Lord Chelmsford, 10 May 1879.

15 John Laband, and P.S. Thompson, *Field Guide to the War in Zululand and the Defence of Natal 1879*, Pietermaritzburg: University of Natal Press, 1983, p. 100.

16 Laband and Thompson, *Field Guide*, p. 100.

17 *Narrative of the Field Operations*, p. 101.

18 It was on this day that the Prince Imperial was killed near the Ityotyosi River, and Wood and Buller actually intercepted Lieutenant Carey during his flight back to the 2nd Division camp.

19 Wood, From Midshipman to Field Marshal, Vol. II, p. 74.

20 Lieutenant-Colonel J.T.B. Brown, 'An Account of the March of Lord Chelmsford's Column to Ulundi, in June and July 1879', in *Minutes of the Proceedings of the Royal Artillery Institution*, Woolwich: Royal Artillery Institution, 1891, vol. XI, p. 147.

21 Montague, pp. 152–3.

22 Molyneux, p. 160.

23 There is a magnificent painting by Lieutenant W.W. Lloyd called 'Isepezi Hill' that illustrates just such a scene. It is to be found in David Rattray, *A Soldier-Artist in Zululand: William Whitelocke Lloyd and the Anglo-Zulu War of 1879*, Rorke's Drift: Rattray Publications, 2007, p. 136.

24 Brown, p. 147. Coincidentally, the work also includes a copy of the western part of the map of Zululand to which reference has already been made.

25 *Narrative of the Field Operations*, p. 96.

26 Ron Lock and Peter Quantrill (comp.), *The 1879 Zulu War Through the Eyes of the Illustrated London News*, Kloof: Q-Lock Publications, 2003, pp. 186–7.

27 TNA, WO 32/7754.

28 Brown, p. 148.

29 Lieutenant Commeline called this river the 'Whitestone', which does not help our investigation. (GRO, D1233/45/15: letter dated 6 June 1879.)

30 A footnote in the *Narrative of the Field Operations*, p. 96, also refers to this river as the 'Teneni', closer to its modern name of Ntinini.

31 *Narrative of the Field Operations*, p. 96.

32 Another of Lloyd's paintings shows this tragic event with great solemnity. See Rattray, p. 124.

33 Thompson, p. 131.

34 'With General Wood's Column', *Times of Natal*, 20 June 1879, dated 10 June.

35 I note that John Laband shares my view of the identity of this hill. In his paper 'Chopping Wood with a Razor: The Skirmish at eZungeni Mountain and the Unnecessary Death of Lieutenant Frith, 5 June 1879', *Soldiers of the Queen*, No. 74, September 1992, he illustrates the features of the engagement in a map on p. 7 on which the hill is clearly marked.

36 PAR, Wood Papers, A598, WC II/2/2: Chelmsford to Wood, 19 May 1879.

37 PAR, Wood Papers, A598, WC II/2/2: Chelmsford to Wood, 30 May 1879.

38 *Narrative of the Field Operations*, p. 97.

39 GRO, Commeline Letters, D1233/45/15, dated 9 June 1879.

40 Brown, p. 149.

41 TNA, WO 32/7754.

42 GRO, Commeline Letters, D1233/45/16a, dated 23 June 1879.

43 Brown, p. 149.

44 Rattray, p. 134.

45 Montague, p. 210.
46 TNA, WO 32/7767.
47 Montague, pp. 221–2.
48 Brown, p. 150.
49 Montague, p. 222.
50 TNA, WO 32/7767.
51 Brown, p. 150.
52 Unlike Forts Newdigate and Marshall, Fort Evelyn is not marked by any modern signposts. It is also interesting to note that the official map of this area shows Fort Evelyn wrongly placed about a kilometre west of Babanango township, whereas it is actually about twelve kilometers (7.5 miles) slightly east of south from there on the modern R88, at a point two kilometres from its junction with the Nkandla road. The site can be clearly seen using Google Earth, its co-ordinates being 28 29 05.38S, 31 06 51E.
53 TNA, WO 32/7767.
54 For those wishing to visit, and who possess a GPS, the co-ordinates are: 28 29 06S 31 06 51E.
55 TNA, WO 32/7761.
56 The feature is given this name in the *Narrative of the Field Operations*, p. 110.
57 Brown, p. 151.
58 Brown, p. 151.
59 *JSA*, Vol. IV, p. 280, Ndukwana: 'The inkata [was a large ring] used by the king when he stirred up medicines and washed, and which was made of grass stolen from the archways, the doors of other kinglets' huts.'
60 Brown.
61 In a recent book, Ron Lock and Peter Quantrill wrongly assert that this area was the site of Fort Victoria (*Zulu Vanquished: The Destruction of the Zulu Kingdom*, London: Greenhill, 2005, p. 230). This error is not uncommon (but see Laband and Thompson, *Field Guide*, p. 93). The fort was not built until August 1879 and was near the next camp site.
62 TNA, WO 32/7762, Chelmsford to King Cetshwayo, 27 June 1879.
63 John Laband, *The Battle of Ulundi*, Pietermaritzburg: KwaZulu Monuments Council and Shuter and Shooter, 1988, map 1 on p. 12.
64 TNA, WO 32/7767: Entry in 2nd Division operations diary for 30 June.
65 Molyneux, p. 180. This entry might explain the three distances we have been given from Mthonjaneni of four, five and six miles.
66 *Narrative of the Field Operations*, p. 112.
67 Laband and Thompson, *Field Guide*, p. 93.
68 TNA, WO 33/34, No. 219: Sir Garnet Wolseley to the Secretary of State for War, 13 August 1879.
69 Molyneux, p. 182.
70 See, for example, the account of Bandsman Joseph Banks, 90th Regiment, in Emery, pp. 233–5.
71 H.M. Bengough, *Memories of a Soldiers Life*, London: Edward Arnold, 1913, pp. 135–6.
72 TNA, WO 32/7382.

73 David Clammer (ed.), 'The Recollections Of Miles Gissop', *Journal of the Society for Army Historical Research*, Vol. 58, 1980, pp. 85–6.
74 GRO, Commeline letters, D1233/45/15, 9 June 1879. See also Guy C. Dawnay, *Campaigns: Zulu 1879, Egypt 1882, Suakim 1885: Being the Private Journal of Guy C. Dawnay*, privately published c.1886; re-published, Cambridge: Ken Trotman, 1989, pp. 46-47.
75 Brevet Major J.V. Hesse, 58th Regiment.
76 TNA, WO 32/7754.
77 Sir Henry Ernest Gascoyne Bulwer (1836–1914) was appointed lieutenant-governor of the colony of Natal in 1875, following the first brief administration of Sir Garnet Wolseley. He had enjoyed a diplomatic career, beginning as secretary to the lieutenant-governor of Prince Edward Island, Canada in 1859 after graduating from Cambridge University. From there, he was appointed resident to Paxo, in the Ionian Islands, in 1860, and Cerigo in 1862. From 1865 to 1870 he was receiver-general in Trinidad and administered Dominica concurrently in 1867–8. He was appointed governor of Lebuan in 1870.
78 Letter from Bulwer to his brother Edward, 8 December 1878, quoted in Clarke, *Invasion of Zululand 1879*, pp. 213–14.
79 Lord Chelmsford to Sir Bartle Frere, dated only to July, presumably 1878: quoted in French, p. 41.
80 'The Watchman', *Times of Natal*, 4 October 1878.
81 Thompson, p. 1.
82 PAR, GH 1411, pp. 81–105; for the results of the delay, see Parr, p. 153.
83 French, p. 47: Chelmsford to Frere, 11 September 1878.
84 French, p. 47: Chelmsford to Frere, 11 September 1878.
85 PAR, GH 1421, No. 1053: Bulwer to Chelmsford, 7 February 1879.
86 PAR, GH 1421, unnumbered, p. 113: Chelmsford to Bulwer, 7 March 1879.
87 PAR, GH 1421, No. 20: Bulwer to Frere, 7 March 1879.
88 PAR, Wood Papers, II/2/2: Lord Chelmsford to Colonel Evelyn Wood, 3 March 1879.
89 PAR, GH 1421, No. 21: Frere's handwritten note on a memorandum from Sir Henry Bulwer, dated 11 March 1879, establishes the date of the meeting, 'As the Lt.-Gov'r & Lt.-Gen'l were to meet today at Pinetown to discuss this subject I think it will not be necessary to continue the discussion further by Minute.'
90 BPP, C. 2367, Enclosure 1 in No. 22: Wheelwright to Cherry, 21 March 1879.
91 PAR, Wood Papers, II/2/2: Lord Chelmsford to Wood, 17 March 1879.
92 In his report on the Hlobane incident Wood explicitly claims that the raid was a part of the diversion in aid of the Eshowe relief column. For his report see supplement to the *London Gazette*, 7 May 1879.
93 Laband, 'Bulwer, Chelmsford and the Border Levies', in Laband and Thompson, *Kingdom and Colony at War*, p. 156.
94 BPP, C. 2367, Enclosure 1 in No. 22: Major Twentyman to deputy adjutant-general, 29 March 1879.
95 BPP, C. 2367, Enclosure 1 in No. 22: Major Twentyman to deputy adjutant-general, 2 April 1879.

96 BPP, C. 2367, Sub-enclosure 2 in Enclosure 1 in No. 37: Special Border Agent Fannin to Colonial Secretary, 4 April 1879.

97 BPP, C. 2367, Sub-enclosure 3 in Enclosure 1 in No. 37: Fannin to Colonial Secretary, 5 April 1879.

98 BPP, C. 2367, Enclosure 1 in No. 22: Natal secretary for native affairs, 19 March 1879.

99 PAR, CSO 1926, No. 1083/1879: Montgomery to secretary for native affairs, 24 March 1879.

100 PAR, SNA 1/1/33, No. 1883: Bulwer to John Shepstone, 29 March 1879.

101 PAR, SNA 1/1/33, No. 1883: John Shepstone to Bulwer, 29 March 1879.

102 BPP, C. 2367, Enclosure 1 in No. 37: Bulwer to Frere, 9 April 1879. The Zulu eventually responded exactly as Bulwer and Fannin had predicted, making reprisal raids across the river near the Middle Drift leading to deaths and loss of cattle. (BPP, C. 2454, Enclosure 6 in No. 60: Fannin to Colonial Secretary, 25 June 1879.)

103 BPP, C. 2318, Enclosure 1 in No. 13: Bulwer to Chelmsford, 9 April 1879.

104 BPP, C. 2318, Enclosure 2 in No. 13: Chelmsford to Secretary of State for War, 11 April 1879.

105 BPP, C. 2318, Enclosure 2 in No. 13: Chelmsford to Secretary of State for War, 11 April 1879.

106 NAM, Chelmsford Papers, 6807/386-26-28: Chelmsford to Duke of Cambridge, 11 April 1879.

107 BPP, C. 2318, Enclosure 2 in No. 13: Chelmsford to Bulwer, 12 April 1879.

108 BPP, C. 2318, Enclosure 3 in No. 13: Bulwer to Chelmsford, 15 April 1879.

109 BPP, C. 2318, No. 13: Bulwer to Hicks Beach, 16 April 1879.

110 BPP, C. 2318, No. 13: Bulwer to Hicks Beach, 16 April 1879.

111 BPP, C. 2318, No. 18: Chelmsford to Bulwer, 18 April 1879.

112 BPP, C. 2367, Enclosure 2 in No. 44: Bulwer to Chelmsford, 22 April 1879.

113 BPP, C. 2367, Enclosure 4 in No. 44: Bulwer to Chelmsford, 25 April 1879.

114 BPP, C. 2367, Enclosure 3 in No. 44: Executive Council minute, 23 April 1879.

115 BPP, C. 2367, Sub-enclosure in Enclosure 1 in No. 54: Fynney to Secretary of Native Affairs, 19 April 1879.

116 BPP, C. 2374, Enclosure in No. 25: Lord Chelmsford to Sir Henry Bulwer, 7 May 1879.

117 BPP, C. 2318, No. 11: Hicks Beach to Bulwer, 19 May 1879.

118 TNA, WO 33/34, No. 149: Secretary of State for War to Lord Chelmsford, 28 May 1879.

119 TNA, WO 33/34, No. 150: Secretary of State for War to Chelmsford, 29 May 1879.

120 Colonel William Owen Lanyon was the administrator of the Transvaal, replacing Sir Theophilus Shepstone in March 1879.

121 W. Basil Worsfold, *Sir Bartle Frere: A Footnote to the History of the British Empire*, London: Thornton Butterworth, 1923, p. 258: Hicks Beach to Frere, 29 May 1879.

122 The reference was to Greytown Correspondence 21/3, No. 168/79 and was cited in Laband's paper 'Bulwer, Chelmsford and the Border Levies' in Laband and Thompson, *Kingdom and Colony at War*, p. 164, n. 28.

123 PAR, 1/GTN, No. 1552: Minute by Sir Henry Bulwer to the Natal Colonial Secretary, 15 March 1879.

124 PAR, 1/GTN, No. 1552: Circular addressed to W.D. Wheelwright, 11 March 1879.

Chapter 8

1 See, for example, Durnford's letters in NAM, 6807/386-22-5 to 7; examples of Durnford's pamphlets can be found in his *Isandhlwana, 22nd January, 1878*; a circular written as late as 1884 is to be found in REM, 4901.44.15.

2 The offending publication was BPP, C. 2482.

3 Unless otherwise indicated, the source for what follows is drawn from TNA, WO 32/7795.

4 In the original holograph the words 'mutilation' and 'mutilated' are followed by the words 'and garbling' and 'and garbled' respectively but are crossed through.

5 The attached documents were each identified by a capital letter but there were errors in their application in Chelmsford's covering letter where documents C and D are confused. Lord Chelmsford's original lettering is shown here.

6 Major-General Henry Hope Crealock was in command of the 1st Division which had made little headway in its march to Ulundi. Crealock was an older brother of Lieutenant-Colonel John North Crealock, military secretary to Lord Chelmsford.

7 Major-General the Honourable Henry Hugh Clifford was inspector-general of lines of communications and base located at Pietermaritzburg.

8 Lord Chelmsford notes that the telegram appears in its correct form on p. 103, but in its corrupt form on p. 45 of the offending Blue Book.

9 The emphasis by underlining is in the original.

10 Forbes, pp. 216–34.

11 NAM, 6807/386-28: Lord Chelmsford to Colonel Stanley, 10 June 1879.

12 The date is omitted from Lord Chelmsford's attachment but he gives it in his covering letter; a dated copy is also to be found in NAM, 6807/386-21-1.

13 The 2nd Division, under its commander Major-General Edward Newdigate, retired to Mthonajaneni by the way it had come while Lord Chelmsford accompanied Brigadier Evelyn Wood's flying column to kwaMagwasa.

14 BPP, C. 2584, No. 55.

15 King Cetshwayo was finally captured on 28 September 1879, following which he was sent into exile in Cape Town.

16 The 'letter enclosed' is no longer in this file.

17 NAM, Chelmsford Papers, 6807/386-18-34: Lord Chelmsford's own record of service.

18 NAM, Chelmsford Papers, 6807/386-18-34.

19 See The NNC Withdrawal from Eshowe in chapter 6.

20 This was Captain R. Bovey of Nettleton's battalion; he was a lieutenant at the time of the withdrawal.

21 PAR, CSO 721, No. 4458: Subpoena in *Graves v Sanderson*.

22 'Major Graves and the Press', *Natal Mercury*, 10 October 1879. The case had begun the previous day.

23 The details of the case given in this paper are drawn from the court reports of the *Natal Mercury* for 10, 11, 13 and 14 October 1879.

24 Long after writing this paper, I found that Shervington's name was actually spelled 'Shervinton', as evidenced in Kathleen Shervinton, *The Shervintons, Soldiers of Fortune*, London: T. Unwin, 1899.

25 *Natal Mercury*, 9 April 1879: 'Major Graves and the Press'.
26 PAR, CSO 2554, No. C42: Lord Chelmsford to Colonial Secretary, 19 February 1879. This matter is fully described in the earlier paper.
27 Evidence of Major Graves.
28 Evidence of Lieutenant Hayes, 2nd Battalion, for the defendant.
29 Evidence of Major Barrow, given by commission.
30 Evidence of Major Graves.
31 Evidence of Lieutenant Hayes, 2nd Battalion, for the defendant.
32 Evidence of Major Barrow.
33 Evidence of Captain Shervington.
34 Evidence of Captain Burnside, 2nd Battalion, for the plaintiff. This was confirmed by a number of other witnesses including Captain Hart and Commandant Nettleton.
35 Evidence of Lieutenant Hayes.
36 Evidence of Corporal James.
37 Evidence of Captain Fitzroy Hart.
38 B.M. Hart-Synnot, *Letters of Major-General Fitzroy Hart-Synnot*, London: Edward Arnold, 1812, pp. 118–19.
39 Evidence of Lieutenant Hayes, 2nd Battalion, for the defendant.
40 Nettleton commanded the sixty-strong Port Elizabeth Volunteer Horse during that campaign. (Major G. Tylden, *The Armed Forces of South Africa 1659–1954*, Johannesburg: Frank Connock Publications, 1954, p. 138.)
41 Lieutenant Hayes declared that these incidents occurred at two different parades, presumably on the same day.
42 Lieutenant Hayes is not mentioned in any extant general order and was certainly not appointed at the same time as the other lieutenants of the battalion were announced.
43 *Natal Mercury*, 14 October 1879.
44 General Order No. 203, dated 21 November 1878, *Times of Natal*, 25 November 1878.
45 General Order No. 209, dated 28 November 1878, *Times of Natal*, 2 December 1878.
46 Thompson, p. 23.
47 TNA, WO 31/1084: Record of commission, dated 9 June 1855.
48 His age as shown in his record of service and in his death notice, in PAR, MSCE 40/166, give different results when his birth month is calculated from these two documents.
49 TNA, WO 31/1084: Record of commission, dated 9 June 1855.
50 Colonel H.G. Hart, *New Annual Army List for 1870*, London: John Murray, 1870.
51 He was presumably granted land by the Natal government on the basis of his previous military service.
52 PAR, A863J, Fannin Letters: J. Eustace Fannin to his wife, 13 June 1879.
53 PAR, A863J, Fannin Letters: Fannin to his wife, undated; unnumbered general order, the *Natal Witness*, 3 July 1879.
54 PAR, CSO 2554 C114. The details which follow are also drawn from this same file unless otherwise stated.

55 The name Hornby is noteworthy because two Hornby brothers served in Montgomery's battalion. While not able to be proven at this point in time it is extremely likely that Miss Hornby and the two brothers were siblings.

56 Montgomery was at that time stationed at Kranskop near the Middle Drift of the Thukela River.

57 Woolley was a lieutenant in the 20th (East Devonshire) Regiment but was no longer serving in HM forces in 1879 (Colonel H.G. Hart, *New Annual Army List for 1872*, London: John Murray, 1872). He may have been a member of a volunteer unit at that time. His unit is identified in his marriage certificate, dated 7 May 1870 (PAR, CSO 2285, p. 57). His wife is named as Ellen Charlotte Hornby.

58 PAR, CSO 2554 C127.

59 PAR, MSCE 27207/1938.

60 PAR, MSCE, 40/166.

61 A Zulu chief, quoted in Hattersley, p. 161.

62 Edgerton, p. 36.

63 *JSA*, Vol. III, pp. 306–7: Mpatshana. *Ukugiya* was to dance individually in front of one's peers, to show off.

64 Binns, p. 217.

65 Brian M. Du Toit, 'Dagga: The History and Ethnographic Setting of Cannabis Sativa in Southern Africa', in Vera Rubin (ed.), *Cannabis and Culture*, The Hague and Paris: Mouton Publishers, 1976, p. 81.

66 A.T. Bryant, *The Zulu People As They Were Before the White Man Came*, Pietermaritzburg: Shuter and Shooter, 1949, pp. 221–2, describes the methods by which cannabis was administered.

67 Allen F. Gardiner, Narrative of a Journey to the Zoolu Country in South Africa, Cape Town: C. Struik, 1966, p. 106.

68 Gardiner, p. 106.

69 Gardiner, p. 106.

70 Du Toit, 'Dagga', p. 90, quoting Percival Kerby (ed.), *The Diary of Andrew Smith (1834–1836)*, Cape Town: Van Riebeeck Society, 1939, Vol. I, p. 312.

71 'An officer of the Natal Native Pioneers', *North Devon Herald*, 22 May 1879, quoted in Emery, p. 53.

72 Du Toit, 'Dagga', p. 91.

73 *Natal Mercury*, 7 April 1879: 'Defence of Rorke's Drift' by an eye-witness, thought to be Reverend George Smith. See also Laband, *Kingdom in Crisis*, p. 98, who explicitly mentions *cannabis sativa* in relation to this incident.

74 The doctoring process.

75 *JSA*, Vol. III, p. 304: Mpatshana.

76 *JSA*, Vol. III, p. 304: Mpatshana.

77 Bryant, *The Zulu People*, p. 223.

78 KCAL, MS 1072: Letters and diary of J.P. and F. Symons, statement of Mhoti.

79 REM, 49014412: Jabez Molife, Natal Native Mounted Contingent.

80 Vijn, p. 38.

81 Quoted in Montague, pp. 310–11.

Bibliography

I. Manuscripts

United Kingdom
A. The National Archives, London
1. WAR OFFICE RECORDS (WO)

WO 30/129 Copies of correspondence principally between the Adjutant-General (General C.H. Ellice) and the General Officer Commanding, Cape of Good Hope, (Lt.-General Lord Chelmsford) and memoranda relating to the Isandlwana disaster of 21 and 22 January 1879.

WO 31/1077 Gazette, 30 March 1855.

WO 31/1084 Army Commission of Alexander Nixon Montgomery.

WO 31/1087 Gazette, 22 June, No. 1, 1855.

WO 31/1142 Gazette, June 1857.

WO 32/7382 Victoria Cross: Award to Capt. Lord W. Beresford, 9th Lancers for action in Zulu War.

WO 32/7386 Victoria Cross: Award to Acting Assistant (now Sub-Assistant) Commissary J. Dalton for action against Zulus.

WO 32/7387 Victoria Cross: Recommendations and awards concerning Major E. Leet, 13th Regt, Surgeon Major J. Reynolds, Army Medical Dept, Capt and Brevet Lieut. Colonel Redvers Buller, 60th Rifles, Lieut. E. Browne 24th Regt and Pte. Wassall, 80th Regt, for action in Zulu War.

WO 32/7700 Zulu War: Reports and memorandum by General Thesiger and local commander of operations against Chiefs Sekukuni and (C) Ketchwayo, King of Zulus, North East Transvaal; disposition of forces, returns of casualties in Cape Frontier War (Kaffir) with map.

WO 32/7713 Dispatch from General Chelmsford on military situation forwarding account and statements relating to battle at Islandana (Isandhlwana (Rorke's Drift)).

WO 32/7724 Dispatches relating to victories at Kambula and Ginghilovo.

WO 32/7725 Report by General Chelmsford on events leading up to disaster at Insalwana (Isandhlwana), Rorke's Drift and of action there.

WO 32/7726 Reports, statements and proceedings of Court of Enquiry into battle at Isandhlwana, Rorke's Drift. Actions at Izoblane [Hlobane] Mountain and Kambula.

WO 32/7731 Report by Lt Colonel J Russell, 12th Lancers, Special Service, on action at Isandhlwana.

WO 32/7735 Diary of operations by 2nd Division under Major General E. Newdigate 26 April to 24 May, with reconnaissance reports, including one by Prince Imperial L. Napoleon.

WO 32/7737 Reports on defence of Rorke's Drift, with plan.

WO 32/7738 Lord Chelmsford on absence of Major Spalding from action at Rorke's Drift. Statements by Major Spalding and Colonel Glyn.

WO 32/7750 (1) Journals of Officer Commanding, 2nd Brigade, 7 Apr–18 May and (2) Quartermaster General's Department, 1st Division, 27 Apr–21 May.

WO 32/7753 Telegraphic report on battle at Ulundi from General Clifford. General Wolseley on possibility of war ending.

WO 32/7754 Diaries and journals of 2nd Division, 2nd Brigade and Quarter Master General's Department 19 May–28 June.

WO 32/7761 Diary of 2nd Division under Major-General Newdigate 23–29 June.

WO 32/7762 Dispatch from Lord Chelmsford on operations with medical and veterinary reports. Copies of letters to and from King Cetywayo (Ketchwayo).

WO 32/7767 Diary of 2nd Division 16 June–7 July and précis of diaries of officers commanding forts on frontier and lines of communication, 19 June–9 July.

WO 32/7770 Correspondence relative to resignation of Lord Chelmsford from present command of forces in South Africa.

WO 32/7771 General Wolseley on interpretation of his instructions to Lord Chelmsford following battle of Ulundi enclosing memorandum on communications.

WO 32/7795 Correspondence with Lord Chelmsford over conduct of operations during Zulu War and publication of letters and dispatches; copies of dispatches, 1879.

WO 32/7834 Victoria Cross: Awards to Lysons and Fowler.

WO 33/29 Report of Committee on Boy Enlistment, 1876.

WO 33/34, Paper 766: Correspondence relative to military affairs in South Africa.

WO 76/97: Officers' records of service: South Staffordshire Regt (38th and 80th Foot): 80th Foot.

WO 76/99: Officers' records of service: South Staffordshire Regt (38th and 80th Foot): 38th Foot.

WO 100/49 Award of South African Medal to Captain W. Barton.

WO 132/1 Papers relating to the Zulu War, including an account of the fighting by Lt Col Buller, 1878–1879.

2. COLONIAL OFFICE RECORDS (CO)

CO 291/1: Colonial Office: Transvaal Original Correspondence; Correspondence, Original – Secretary of State, 1877–78.

CO 291/2: Colonial Office: Transvaal Original Correspondence; Correspondence, Original – Secretary of State, 1879.

3. MAPS

CO700/ZULULAND11: Map of Zululand, compiled at the Intelligence Dept., Horse Guards, from the Military Trigonometrical Surveys and the various Topographical Sketches made by Officers during the Campaign of 1879.

B. *Gloucestershire Record Office*
Commeline Letters D1233, File 45.

C. *The National Army Museum, London*
1. CHELMSFORD PAPERS 6807/386
Files 8, 9, 14, 18, 21, 22, 24, 26, 28.

2. PEARSON PAPERS 2004-03-73-5
File 5.

3. OTHER
6302-48, W.F. Fairlie diary.
7411-8, Diary of the Zululand Boundary Commission.
8412-46-1 and 2.

D. *Royal Engineers Museum, Chatham*
Durnford Papers 4901.44.

E. *Regimental Museum of the Royal Welsh, Brecon*
File 2002-25: Letter of Colour Sergeant William Edwards, 1/24th Regiment.
File R1950.41: Records of the 1st Battalion, 24th Regiment 1689–1905.
File ZB 1/9: Lieutenant H.L. Smith-Dorrien, account of Isandlwana 'written specially at the request of the Officers of the South Wales Borderers in 1907'.
Symons, W. Penn, The Battle of Isandlwana and the Defence of Rorke's Drift 1879, manuscript account.

South Africa
A. *Pietermaritzburg Archives Repository*
1/BGV/4.
1/GTN
AGO 1/4/21.
CSO 44(2), 668, 696, 698, 721, 1925, 1926, 2285, 2554.
GH 1411, 1421, 1423.
MSCE 40/166.
RSC 1/5/91.
SNA 1/1/1. 1/1/33.
A863J, Fannin Papers.
Shepstone Papers: Volume 39.
II/2/2, II/2/4, Wood Papers.

B. *Killie Campbell Africana Library, Durban*
KCM 16020: Diary of Lieutenant Richard Wyatt Vause.
KCM 42310: Stafford Account of Isandlwana.

KCM 55067: Letter from Private Charles [Fred] Mason to his brother Cary.

KCM 65234: Reminiscences of Trooper C. Hewitt, Frontier Light Horse, in the form of a letter.

KCM 89/9/32/1: Insp. George Mansel, Natal Mounted Police, letter to Colonel Edward Durnford dated 1 November [1879?].

KCM 89/9/32/10: Insp. George Mansel, Natal Mounted Police: letter to Colonel Edward Durnford dated 23 November, 1879.

KCM 89/9/81/23: Henderson Map, No. 2.

KCM 89/9/81/24: Henderson Map, No. 3a.

KCM 98/69/13/5: Fynn Papers: My Recollections of a Famous Campaign and a Great Disaster.

MS 1072: Symons Papers (includes statement of Mhoti).

C. Talana Museum, Dundee
Report of Col. R.T. Glyn to Col. W. Bellairs, 6 February 1879.

D. Transvaal Archives, Pretoria
Transvaal Government Gazette Extraordinary, Vol. III, No. 111, Pretoria, Transvaal, Thursday, 3 April 1879

A1889, Memoirs of C.G. Dennison MS, chapter 5.

A1/45, General Letter Book H.M. Special Commissioner to Transvaal.

II. *Official Publications*

A. British Parliamentary Papers (Command Series)

C. 1137: Report of the Expedition Sent by the Government of Natal to instal Cetywayo as King of the Zulus, February 1875.

C. 2220: Further Correspondence respecting the Affairs of South Africa, December, 1878.

C. 2222: Further Correspondence respecting the Affairs of South Africa, February 1879.

C. 2234: Correspondence Relative to Military Affairs in Natal and the Transvaal, February 1879.

C. 2242: Further Corresponding respecting the Affairs of South Africa, in continuation of C. 2222 of February 1879; February 1879.

C. 2260: Further Correspondence respecting the Affairs of South Africa, March 1879.

C. 2308, Further Correspondence respecting the Affairs of South Africa, March 1879.

C. 2318: Further Correspondence respecting the Affairs of South Africa, May 1879.

C. 2367: Further Correspondence respecting the Affairs of South Africa, July 1879.

C. 2374: Further Correspondence respecting the Affairs of South Africa, July 1879.

C. 2434: Army Medical Department report for the year 1878. Volume XX (1880): Statistical, Sanitary and Medical reports of the Army Medical Department, Appendix V, pp. 261–263: Surgeon-Major James Henry Reynolds, M.B., V.C., Report of the Defence of Rorke's Drift.

C. 2454: Further Correspondence respecting the Affairs of South Africa, August 1879.

C. 2482: Further Correspondence respecting the Affairs of South Africa, February 1880.
C. 2584: Further Correspondence respecting the Affairs of South Africa, June 1880.
C. 3182: Correspondence respecting the Affairs of Natal and Zululand, 1882.

B. Natal Colonial Publications, KwaZulu-Natal.
Natal Government Gazette, 1849, 1879.

III. Newspapers

Cape Mercury, 1879.
Cape Times, 1879.
County Express, 1898.
Daily Chronicle, Newcastle-upon-Tyne, 1879.
Die Volksstem, Pretoria, 1878.
Independent, South African Diamond Fields, 1879.
Illustrated London News, 1879.
London Gazette, 1879.
Natal Advertiser, 1879.
Natal Colonist, 1879.
Natal Mercury, 1879.
Natal Witness, 1879.
Oldham Weekly Chronicle, 1879.
South Wales Daily Telegram, 1879.
Graphic, 1879.
The Times, 1879.
Times of Natal, 1878, 1879.
Times Weekly Edition, 1879.
Transvaal Argus and Commercial Gazette, 1879.

IV. Books and Compilations

Ashe, Major W. and Wyatt-Edgell, Captain E.V., *The Story of the Zulu Campaign*, London: Sampson Low, Marston, Searle and Rivington, 1880; republished Cape Town: North and South Press: 1989.
Baines, Thomas, *The Gold Regions of South Eastern Africa*, London: Books of Rhodesia, 1877.
Bengough, H.M., *Memories of a Soldiers Life*, London: Edward Arnold, 1913.
Binns, C.T., *The Last Zulu King: The Life and Death of Cetshwayo*, London: Longmans, 1963.
Bond, Brian, *The Victorian Army and the Staff College, 1854–1914*, Eyre, London: Methuen, 1972.
Brookes, E.H. and Webb, C. de B., *A History of Natal*, Pietermaritzburg: University of Natal Press, 1965.
Bryant, A.T., *Olden Times in Zululand and Natal*, London: Longmans, Green, 1929.

— *The Zulu People as They Were Before the White Man Came*, Pietermaritzburg: Shuter and Shooter, 1949.

Child, Daphne (ed.), *The Zulu War Journal of Colonel Henry Harford*, Pietermaritzburg: Shuter and Shooter, 1978.

Clarke, Sonia (ed.), *Invasion of Zululand 1879*, Houghton: Brenthurst Press, 1979.

— *Zululand at War 1879*, Houghton: Brenthurst Press, 1984.

Coghill, Patrick (compiler), *Whom the Gods Love*, Halesowen: privately published, 1968.

Colenso, Frances E., assisted by Lt-Col. E. Durnford, *History of the Zulu War and Its Origin*, London: Chapman and Hall Ltd, 1880.

Connell, Evan S., *Son of the Morning Star*, San Francisco: North Point Press, 1984.

Cope, Richard, *Ploughshare of War: The Origins of the Anglo-Zulu War of 1879*, Pietermaritzburg: University of Natal Press, 1999.

Coupland, Sir Reginald, *Isandhlwana: Zulu Battle Piece*, London: William Collins, 1948.

Dawnay, Guy C., *Campaigns: Zulu 1879, Egypt 1882, Suakim 1885: Being the Private Journal of Guy C. Dawnay*, privately published c.1886; re-published, Cambridge: Ken Trotman, 1989.

Dennison, Major C.G., DSO, *A Fight to a Finish*, London: Longmans, Green, 1904.

Doke, C.M. and Vilikazi, B.W., *Zulu–English Dictionary*, Johannesburg: Witwatersrand University Press, 1958.

Drooglever, R.W.F., *The Road to Isandlwana: Colonel Anthony Durnford in Natal and Zululand*, London: Greenhill, 1992.

Durnford, E., *A Soldier's Life and Work in South Africa*, London: Sampson, Low, Marston, Searle and Rivington, 1882.

Edgerton, Robert B., *Like Lions They Fought: The Zulu War and the Last Black Empire in South Africa*, The Free Press: New York, 1988.

Emery, Frank (ed.), *The Red Soldier: Letters from the Zulu War, 1879*, London: Hodder and Stoughton, 1977.

Engelbrecht, S.P., *Thomas Francois Burgers: A Biography*, Pretoria and Cape Town: J.H. de H. Bussy, 1946.

Fannin, Natalie (ed.), *The Fannin Papers: A Pioneer's Story in South Africa*, Durban: Robinson, 1932.

Farwell, Byron, *Queen Victoria's Little Wars*, London: Allen, Lane, 1972.

Fergusson, Thomas G., *British Military Intelligence 1870–1914*, London: Arms and Armour Press, 1984.

French, Major The Hon. Gerald, *Lord Chelmsford and the Zulu War*, London: Bodley Head, 1939.

Fynney, H.B., *The Zulu Army and Zulu Headmen*, Pietermaritizburg: published by Direction of the Lieutenant-General Commanding, 1879.

Gardiner, Allen F., *Narrative of a Journey to the Zoolu Country in South Africa*, London: William Crofts, 1836.

Gon, Philip, *The Road to Isandlwana: The Years of an Imperial Battalion*, London: A.D. Donker, 1979.

Greaves, Adrian and Best, Brian (eds), *The Curling Letters of the Zulu War: 'There Was Awful Slaughter'*, Barnsley: Leo Cooper, 2001.

Guy, Jeff, *The Destruction of the Zulu Kingdom: The Civil War in Zululand, 1879–1884*, Pietermaritzburg: University of Natal Press, 1994.

Hamilton-Browne, Colonel G., *A Lost Legionary in South Africa*, London: T. Werner Laurie, 1912.

Hart, Col. H.G., *New Annual Army List for 1870*, London: John Murray, 1870.

— *New Annual Army List for 1872*, London: John Murray, 1872.

— *New Annual Army List for 1879*, London: John Murray, 1879.

— *New Annual Army List for 1885*, London: John Murray, 1885.

Hathorn, Peter and Young, Amy, *Henderson Heritage*, Pietermaritzburg: privately published, 1972.

Hattersley, Alan F. (ed.), *The Later Annals of Natal*, London: Longmans, Green, 1958.

Herd, Norman, *The Bent Pine: The Trial of Chief Langalibalele*, Johannesburg: Ravan Press, 1976.

Holme, Norman, *The Noble 24th: Biographical Records of the 24th Regiment in the Zulu War and the South African Campaign 1877–1879*, London: Savannah, 1999.

Hudson, Roger, *William Russell, Special Correspondent of* The Times, London: Folio Society, 1995.

Jackson, F.W.D., *Hill of the Sphinx: The Battle of Isandlwana*, London: Westerners Publications Ltd, 2002.

Jenkinson, Thomas B., *Amazulu: The Zulus, Their Past History, Manners, Customs and Language*, London: W.H. Allen, 1882; reprinted New York: Negro Universities Press, 1969.

Jeppe, Friedrich Heidrich, *Transvaal Book, Almanac and Directory for 1877*, Pietermaritzburg: P. Davis & Sons, 1877

Jones, Huw M., *The Boiling Cauldron: Utrecht District and the Anglo-Zulu War 1879*, Bisley: Shermershill Press, 2006.

Kerby, Percival (ed.), *The Diary of Andrew Smith (1834–1836)*, Cape Town: Van Riebeeck Society, 1939.

de Kiewiet, Cornelius W., *The Imperial Factor in South Africa: A Study in Politics and Economics*, London: Frank Cass, 1965.

Knight, Ian, *Nothing Remains but to Fight: The Defence of Rorke's Drift*, London: Greenhill Books, 1993.

— *The Anatomy of the Zulu Army: From Shaka to Cetshwayo, 1818–1879*, London: Greenhill Books, 1995.

— *The Sun Turned Black: Isandlwana and Rorke's Drift 1879*, Rivonia: William Waterman, 1995.

— (ed.), *There Will be An Awful Row at Home About This*, Shoreham-by-Sea: Victorian Military Society, 1979; second edn, 1987.

Krige, Eileen Jensen, *The Social System of the Zulus*, Pietermaritzburg: Shuter and Shooter, 1977.

Kruger, D.W., and Beyers, C.J. (eds), *Dictionary of South African Biography*, Cape Town: Human Sciences Research Council, 1977, vol. III.

Laband, John, *The Battle of Ulundi*, KwaZulu Monuments Council and Pietermaritzburg: Shuter and Shooter, 1988.

— *Kingdom in Crisis: The Zulu Response to the British Invasion of 1879*, Manchester: Manchester University Press, 1992.

— *The Rise and Fall of the Zulu Nation*, first published as *Rope of Sand*, Jeppestown: Jonathon Ball, 1995; re-published London: Arms and Armour, 1997.

— (ed.), *Lord Chelmsford's Zululand Campaign, 1878–1879*, Stroud: Army Records Society/Alan Sutton Publishing, 1994.

— and Thompson, P.S., *War Comes to Umvoti*, Pietermaritzburg: University of Natal Press, 1980.

— and — *Field Guide to the War in Zululand and the Defence of Natal 1879*, Pietermaritzburg: University of Natal Press, 1983.

— and — *Kingdom and Colony at War*, Cape Town: North and South Press/ Pietermaritzburg: University of Natal Press, 1990.

Lambert, John, *Betrayed Trust: Africans and the State in Colonial Natal*, Pietermaritzburg: University of Natal Press, 1995.

Lock, Ron, *Blood on the Painted Mountain: Zulu Victory and Defeat, Hlobane and Kambula, 1879*, London: Greenhill, 1995.

— and Quantrill, Peter, *Zulu Victory: The Epic of Isandlwana and the Cover-up*, London: Greenhill, 2002.

— and — *Zulu Vanquished: The Destruction of the Zulu Kingdom*, London: Greenhill, 2005.

Lugg, H.C., *A Natal Family Looks Back*, Durban: Griggs & Co., 1970.

Macdonald, William, *Romance of the Golden Rand*, London: Cassel & Co., 1933.

Machin, Ingrid, *Antbears and Targets for Assegais*, Howick: Brevitas, 2002.

Mackinnon, J.P. and Shadbolt, S.H., *The South African Campaign of 1879*, London: Sampson, Low, Marston, Searle and Rivington, 1880; republished London: Greenhill, 1995.

McToy, E.D., *A Brief History of the 13th Regiment (P.A.L.I.) in South Africa during the Transvaal and Zulu Difficulties*, Devonport: A.H. Swiss, 1880.

Marks, Shula, *Reluctant Rebellion: The 1906–8 Disturbances in Natal*, Oxford: Clarendon Press, 1970.

Maxwell, John, *Reminiscences of the Zulu War*, ed. L.T. Jones, Cape Town: University of Cape Town Libraries, 1979.

Meintjes, Johannes, *Sandile: The Fall of the Xhosa Nation*, Cape Town: T.V. Bulpin, 1971.

Mitford, Bertram, *Through the Zulu Country: Its Battlefields and People*, London: Keegan Paul, Tench, 1883; republished London: Greenhill, 1992.

Molyneux, Major-General W.C.F, *Campaigning in South Africa and Egypt*, London: MacMillan, 1896.

Montague, Captain W.E., *Campaigning in South Africa: Reminiscences of an Officer in 1879*, London: Blackwood & Sons, 1880 (reprint).

Moodie, D.C.F., *Moodie's Zulu War*, ed. John Laband, Cape Town: North and South Press, 1988; first published as *The History of the Battles and Adventures of the British, the Boers and the Zulus*, Adelaide: George Robertson, 1879.

Morris, Donald R., *The Washing of the Spears: The Rise and Fall of the Zulu Nation*, London: Jonathan Cape, 1965; revised edition London: Pimlico, 1994.

Mossop, George, *Running the Gauntlet*, London: Nelson, 1937; republished Pietermaritzburg: G.C. Button, 1990.

Natal Almanac and Yearly Register, 1879, Pietermaritzburg: P. Davis & Sons, 1878.

Newnham-Davis, N., *The Transvaal Under The Queen*, London: Sands, 1900.

Norris-Newman, Charles L., *In Zululand with the British Throughout the War of 1879*, London: W.H. Allen, 1880; re-published London: Greenhill, 1988.

Parr, Captain Henry Hallam, *A Sketch of the Kafir and Zulu Wars: Guadana to Isandhlwana*, London: Kegan Paul, 1880.

Paton, G., Glennie, F. and Penn Symons, W., *Historical Records of the 24th Regiment from its Formation in 1689*, London: Simkin, Marshall, Hamilton, Kent & Co., 1892.

Preston, Adrian, *The South African Journal of Sir Garnet Wolseley 1879–1880*, Cape Town: A.A. Balkema, 1973.

Rattray, David, *A Soldier-Artist in Zululand: William Whitelocke Lloyd and the Anglo-Zulu War of 1879*, Rorke's Drift: Rattray Publications, 2007.

Regulations: Field Forces in South Africa, Pietermaritzburg: HMSO, 1878.

Roche, Harriet A., *On Trek in the Transvaal*, London: Sampson Low, Marston, Searle and Rivington, 1878.

Samuelson, R.C.A., *Long, Long Ago*, Durban: Knox, 1929.

Selby, John, *Shaka's Heirs*, London: Allen & Unwin, 1971.

Shervinton, Kathleen, *The Shervintons, Soldiers of Fortune*, London: T. Unwin, 1899.

Skelley, Alan Ramsay, *The Victorian Army at Home: The Recruitment and Terms and Conditions of the British Regular, 1859–1899*, London: Croom Helm, 1977.

Smith, Keith, *The Wedding Feast War: the Final Tragedy of the Xhosa People*, London: Frontline Books, 2012.

Smith, Keith (ed.), *Local General Orders Relating to the Anglo-Zulu War 1879*, Banora Point, NSW: privately published, 2005.

Smith-Dorrien, General Sir Horace, *Memories of Forty-Eight Years Service*, London: John Murray, 1925.

Snook, Lieutenant-Colonel Mike, *How Can Man Die Better: The Secrets of Isandlwana Revealed*, London: Greenhill, 2005.

Sobel, Dava, Longitude: *The True Story of a Lone Genius Who Solved the Greatest Scientific Problem of His Time*, London: Fourth Estate, 1996; reprinted 1998.

Stalker, Reverend John, *The Natal Carbineers*, Pietermaritzburg: P. Davies & Sons, 1912.

Thompson, P.S., *The Natal Native Contingent in the Anglo-Zulu War 1879*, Pietermaritzburg: privately published, 1997, 2003.

Tylden, Major G., *The Armed Forces of South Africa 1659–1954*, Johannesburg: Frank Connock Publications, 1954.

Vijn, Cornelius, *Cetshwayo's Dutchman*, tr. and ed. J.W. Colenso, London: Longmans, Green, 1880; republished London: Greenhill, 1988.

War Office (Intelligence Branch), *Narrative of the Field Operations Connected with the Zulu War of 1879*, comp. Captain J.S. Rothwell, London: HMSO, 1881; republished London: Greenhill, 1989.

van Warmelo, N.J. (ed.), *History of Matiwane and the Amangwane Tribe: As Told by Msebenzi to his Kinsman Albert Hlongwane*, Pretoria: Government Printer, 1938.

Webb, C. de B. and Wright, J.B. (eds), *A Zulu King Speaks*, Pietermaritzburg: University of Natal Press, 1978; reprinted 1987.

— and — (eds), *The James Stuart Archive of Recorded Oral Evidence Relating to the History of the Zulu and Neighbouring Peoples*, in 5 volumes, Pietermaritzburg: Killie Campbell Africana Library and University of Natal Press, 1976–2001.

Welford, Richard, *Men of Mark Twixt Tyne and Tweed*, Vol. III, London: Walter Scott Ltd, 1895.

Williams, Charles, *The Life of Lieutenant-General Sir Henry Evelyn Wood*, London: Sampson, Low, Marston, 1892.

Wolseley, General Viscount, *The Soldier's Pocket Book for Field Service*, London, Macmillan & Co., 1886.

Wood, Sir Evelyn, *From Midshipman to Field Marshal*, in two volumes, London: Methuen, 1906.

— (ed.), *British Battles on Land and Sea*, London: Cassell & Co., 1915.

Worsfold, Basil, *Sir Bartle Frere: A Footnote to the History of the British Empire*, London: Thornton Butterworth, 1923.

Wulfsohn, Lionel, *Rustenburg At War*, second revised edition, Rustenburg: L. Wulfsohn, 1992.

Wylie, Dan, *Myth of Iron: Shaka in History*, Scottsville: University of KwaZulu-Natal, 2006.

Wyndham Smith, Kenneth, 'The Campaigns against the Bapedi of Sekhukhune, 1877–1879', *Archives Year Book for South African History*, 1967.

Young, John, *They Fell Like Stones: Battles and Casualties of the Zulu War, 1879*, London: Greenhill, 1991.

V. Pamphlets, Theses, Articles and Other Papers

Brown, Lieutenant-Colonel J.T.B., 'An Account of the March of Lord Chelmsford's Column to Ulundi, in June and July 1879', in *Minutes of the Proceedings of the Royal Artillery Institution*, Woolwich: Royal Artillery Institution, 1891, Vol. XI, p. 147.

Butterfield, P.H., 'The Minor Writings of Sir Evelyn Wood', *Pearson's Magazine*, 1896.

Clammer, David (ed.), 'Recollections of Miles Gissop', *Journal of the Society for Army Historical Research*, Vol. 58, 1980, pp. 85–6.

Du Toit, Brian M., 'Dagga: The History and Ethnographic Setting of Cannabis Sativa in Southern Africa', in Vera Rubin (ed.), *Cannabis and Culture*, The Hague and Paris: Mouton Publishers, 1976.

Durnford, Lieutenant-Colonel E., *Isandhlwana, 22nd January, 1878: A Narrative Compiled from Official and Reliable Sources*, April 1879, privately published.

— *Isandhlwana: Lord Chelmsford's Statements Compared with the Evidence*, November 1880, privately published.

Forbes, Archibald, 'Lord Chelmsford and the Zulu War', *The Nineteenth Century*, Vol. 7, February 1880.

Hook, Henry, 'Account of Rorke's Drift Defence', *Blackwood's Magazine*, vol. 308, July–December 1970.

Hulme, Major J.J., 'Irregular Units of the 7th Kaffir War, 1846–7', *Journal of the South African Military History Society*, Vol. 1, No. 3, December 1968.

Jackson, F.W.D., 'Isandlwana 1879: The Sources Re-Examined', *Journal for Army Historical Research* Vol. 43, Nos 173, 175 and 176, 1965; republished in pamphlet form, Brecon: South Wales Borderers Museum, 1999.

— and Whybra, Julian, 'Isandhlwana and the Durnford Papers', *Soldiers of the Queen*, No. 60, March 1990.

Jones, Huw M., 'Blood on the Painted Mountain; Zulu Victory and Defeat, Hlobane and Kambula, 1879: A Review Article', *Soldiers of the Queen*, No. 84, March 1996, pp. 20–9.

— 'Hlobane: A New Perspective', *Natalia*, No. 27, 1997.

Knight, Ian, 'A Note of the umPunga', *Soldiers of the Queen*, No. 33, July 1983.

— 'Captain Stephenson's Detachment . . . Left Us', *Journal of the Anglo-Zulu War Historical Society*, Vol. 4, December 1999.

Laband, John, 'The Battle of Khambula, 29 March 1879: A Re-examination from the Zulu Perspective', *There Will be An Awful Row At Home About This*, Shoreham-by-sea: Victorian Military Society, 1987.

Laband, John, 'Chopping Wood with a Razor: The Skirmish at eZungeni Mountain and the Unnecessary Death of Lieutenant Frith, 5 June 1879', *Soldiers of the Queen*, No. 74, September 1992.

Ransford, Oliver, 'The Gaudy Cloth', *Blackwood's Magazine*, vol. 308, July–December 1970.

Taylerson, A., 'Watches Issued to British Armed Forces 1870–1970', Part 1, *Horological Journal*, September 1995.

War Office (Intelligence Branch), *Précis of Information Concerning Zululand*, London: HMSO, 1895.

Webb, C. de B., 'A Zulu Boy's Recollections of the Zulu War', *Natalia*, No. 8, December 1978, p. 6 (an annotated reprint of George H. Swinny's recorded testimony of the same name, originally published in 1884).

— 'Lines of Power: The High Commissioner, the Telegraph and the War of 1879', *Natalia*, Vol. 8, December 1993.

Whybra, Julian, *Essex Curriculum Extension Project No. 4: The Battle of Isandhlwana*, Essex County Council, 1984(?).

— 'Contemporary Sources and the Composition of the Zulu Impi, *Soldiers of the Queen*, No. 53, June 1988.

— 'Zabange – Pure Fiction', *Soldiers of the Queen*, No. 61, June 1990.

Wood, Walter (ed.), 'How They Held Rorke's Drift: From the Narrative of Sergeant Henry Hook V.C.', *Royal Magazine*, February 1905.

Index